ACTS
&PAUL'S
LETTERS

St. Michael's Episcopal Church
Little Rock, Arkansas

080048

THE SERIES

INTERPRETER'S CONCISE COMMENTARY

ACTS & PAUL'S LETTERS

A COMMENTARY ON
ACTS, ROMANS, I & II CORINTHIANS, GALATIANS, EPHESIANS,
PHILIPPIANS, COLOSSIANS, I & II THESSALONIANS,
I & II TIMOTHY, TITUS, PHILEMON

By
William Baird,
Cyril E. Blackman,
James L. Price,
Victor Paul Furnish,
Leander E. Keck,
Eric Lane Titus

Edited by Charles M. Laymon

Abingdon Press
Nashville

Interpreter's Concise Commentary
Volume VII: ACTS AND PAUL'S LETTERS

Copyright © 1971 and 1983 by Abingdon Press

Library of Congress Cataloging in Publication Data

Main entry under title:
Acts and Paul's letters.

   (Interpreter's concise commentary; v. 7)
   "Previously published . . . as part of the Interpreter's
one-volume commentary on the Bible"—Verso t.p.
   Bibliography: p.
   1. Bible. N.T. Acts—Commentaries. 2. Bible. N.T. Epistles of Paul—Commentaries. I. Baird, William, 1924–
II. Laymon, Charles M. III. Series.
BS491.2.I57 1983 vol. 7   [BS2625.3]   220.7s
[227'.07]   83-3767

ISBN 0-687-19238-2 (pbk.)

(Previously published by Abingdon Press in cloth as part of
The Interpreter's One-Volume Commentary on the Bible, regular ed.
ISBN 0-687-19299-4, thumb-indexed ed. ISBN 0-687-19300-1.)

MANUFACTURED BY THE PARTHENON PRESS AT
NASHVILLE, TENNESSEE, UNITED STATES OF AMERICA

EDITOR'S PREFACE

to the original edition

A significant commentary on the Bible is both timely and timeless. It is timely in that it takes into consideration newly discovered data from many sources that are pertinent in interpreting the Scriptures, new approaches and perspectives in discerning the meaning of biblical passages, and new insights into the relevancy of the Bible for the times in which we live. It is timeless since it deals with the eternal truths of God's revelation, truths of yesterday, today, and of all the tomorrows that shall be.

This commentary has been written within this perspective. Its authors were selected because of their scholarship, their religious insight, and their ability to communicate with others. Technical discussions do not protrude, yet the most valid and sensitive use of contemporary knowledge underlies the interpretations of the several writings. It has been written for ministers, lay and nonprofessional persons engaged in studying or teaching in the church school, college students and those who are unequipped to follow the more specialized discussions of biblical matters, but who desire a thoroughly valid and perceptive guide in interpreting the Bible.

The authorship of this volume is varied in that scholars were chosen from many groups to contribute to the task. In this sense it is an ecumenical writing. Protestants from numerous denominations, Jews, and also Roman Catholics are represented in the book. Truth cannot be categorized according to its ecclesiastical sources. It is above and beyond such distinctions.

It will be noted that the books of the Apocrypha have been included and interpreted in the same manner as the canonical writings. The value of a knowledge of this body of literature for understanding the historical background and character of the Judaic-Christian tradition has been widely recognized in our time, but commentary treatments of it have not been readily accessible. In addition, the existence of the Revised Standard Version and the New English Bible translations of these documents makes such a commentary upon them as is included here both necessary and significant.

The commentary as a whole avoids taking dogmatic positions or representing any one particular point of view. Its authors were chosen throughout the English-speaking field of informed and recognized biblical scholars. Each author was urged to present freely his own interpretation and, on questions where there was sometimes a diversity of conclusions, each was also asked to define objectively the viewpoints of others while he was offering and defending his own.

Many persons have contributed to the writing and production of this volume. One of the most rewarding of my personal experiences as editor was corresponding with the authors. On every hand there was enthusiasm for the project and warmth of spirit. The authors' commitment to the task and their scholarly sensitivity were evident in all of my relationships with them. The considerate judgments of the manuscript consultants, Morton S. Enslin, Dwight M. Beck, W. F. Stinespring, Virgil M. Rogers, and William L. Reed, were invaluable in the making of the character of the commentary. The copy editors who have worked under the careful and responsible guidance of Mr. Gordon Duncan of Abingdon Press have contributed greatly to the accuracy and readability of the commentary.

—Charles M. Laymon, Editor

PUBLISHER'S PREFACE

The intent of the *Interpreter's Concise Commentary* is to make available to a wider audience the commentary section of *The Interpreter's One-Volume Commentary on the Bible*. In order to do this, the Publisher is presenting the commentary section of the original hardback in this eight-volume paperback set. At the same time, and in conjunction with our wish to make *The Interpreter's One-Volume Commentary* more useful, we have edited the hardback text for the general reader: we have defined most of the technical terms used in the original hardback text; we have tried to divide some of the longer sentences and paragraphs into shorter ones; we have tried to make the sexually stereotyped language used in the original commentary inclusive where it referred to God or to both sexes; and we have explained abbreviations, all in an attempt to make the text more easily read.

The intention behind this paperback arrangement is to provide a handy and compact commentary on those individual sections of the Bible that are of interest to readers. In this paperback format we have not altered the substance of any of the text of the original hardback, which is still available. Rather, our intention is to smooth out some of the scholarly language in order to make the text easier to read. We hope this arrangement will make this widely accepted commentary on the Bible even more profitable for all students of God's Word.

WRITERS

William Baird
Professor of New Testament, Brite Divinity School, Texas Christian University, Ft. Worth, Texas

Cyril E. Blackman
Professor of New Testament Exegesis, Emmanuel College, Toronto, Canada

James L. Price
Professor of Religion, Department of Religion, Duke University, Durham, North Carolina

Victor Paul Furnish
Associate Professor of New Testament, Perkins School of Theology, Southern Methodist University, Dallas, Texas

Leander E. Keck
Professor of New Testament, Vanderbilt Divinity School, Vanderbilt University, Nashville, Tennessee

Eric Lane Titus
Professor of New Testament, School of Theology at Claremont, Claremont California

CONTENTS

THE ACTS OF THE APOSTLES

William Baird

INTRODUCTION

Nature and Purpose

Acts is the second volume of the historical work Luke-Acts. The Gospel of Luke was a distinctively Christian type of writing. Acts, on the other hand, follows the pattern of Hellenistic historical works. The author is interested in the details of contemporary history (cf. 12:20-23 and 18:2, 12). He describes matters of geography and government with accuracy.

Like the historians of his day this author attributes speeches to his characters. These speeches constitute about a fifth of the total narrative, but are relatively short in comparison with contemporary models. Thus at best they could only approximate what was said. They are mainly compositions of the author, sometimes including authentic material (cf. 13:38-39). He uses these discourses to present his understanding of the Christian message. Throughout his work the author writes history with a religious purpose.

The precise purpose of Acts is debatable. For example, it has been argued that the author is preparing a dossier for use at the trial of Paul, or that he is anxious to harmonize the controversy between Jewish and Gentile factions of the church. Most likely the purpose is twofold:

1

(1) to prove that the church is not in conflict with Rome (25:8);

(2) to describe the spread of Christianity under the guidance of the Spirit (1:8).

The first is directed to Gentiles while the second is instruction for the Christians. In essence the author is champion of the Gentile mission of the church.

Authorship

According to tradition Acts was written by Luke. This tradition is more important for Acts than for the gospel, since authorship by a companion of Paul would mean that the narrative was written by an eyewitness of some of the events. The discussion of this question usually is based on the "we sections," where the narrative switches to the first person plural (16:10-17; 20:5-15; 21:1-18; 27:1–28:16). It is easiest to suppose that these sections were written by the author himself and that in them he envisaged himself as a participant in the events. This could explain the origin of the Lukan tradition. The matter is open to two other interpretations:

(1) The "we sections" are a stylistic device whereby the author changes persons to give his narrative vitality.

(2) The "we sections" represent a source—perhaps a diary or travel itinerary—used by the author.

To solve this problem it is necessary to compare the material in Acts with parallel material from Paul's letters. If Acts was written by a travel companion of Paul the two ought to be consistent. Although the problem is complex, a few illustrations may serve to show that there are discrepancies.

In Acts Paul's attendance at the Jerusalem conference (15:6-29) occurs on his third trip to that city after his conversion. As described in Galatians 2:1-10 the conference visit is only his second. The description of Paul's first visit in Acts 9:26-30 also contradicts that presented by Galatians 1:18-24. Another instance is found in the fact that in the letters Paul's central message is the doctrine of justification by faith. The Pauline speeches of Acts scarcely allude to this idea.

This evidence makes it questionable whether a companion of

Paul could have written Acts and suggests that the "we sections" represent a source used by the author. Nevertheless for convenience we may continue to refer to the writer as "Luke," realizing that the identification is questionable.

Date and Place of Composition
It is sometimes supposed that since the narrative ends without relating the death of Paul, Acts must have been composed before that event. This conclusion fails to realize that Acts was not written as a biography of Peter or Paul. Its intention is to describe the preaching of the gospel from Jerusalem "to the end of the earth" (1:8). When the good news is announced in Rome the climax of the story has been reached and the purposes of God have been fulfilled (28:28). Moreover, 20:25 and 21:10-14 suggest that the author knew about the death of Paul.

In any case the probability that he wrote Acts after his gospel practically rules out so early a date. The inconsistencies with Paul's letters indicate that he wrote before these letters were collected and given wide distribution sometime near the turn of the century. Probably, therefore, the best estimate for the date of Acts is between A.D. 90 and 100.

The place of composition of Acts remains unknown. The few traditions about it are based entirely on the assumption that the author was Luke, the companion of Paul.

Sources and Arrangement
Besides the material underlying the "we sections" other sources were no doubt used in the composition of Acts. Efforts have been made to identify two overlapping traditions in the early chapters. It is argued that since chapter 3 duplicates some of the narrative of chapter 2 the author had two different sources. Although it cannot be proved that these accounts are doublets, it is agreed that a variety of material, written or oral, underlies this section.

It is also held that chapters 6–15—usually accepted as more historical than the earlier material—embody tradition which grew up around important Christian centers such as Jerusalem and Antioch. A parallel development around the lives of outstanding church leaders like Peter or Stephen can be possible.

As in his gospel, Luke builds up his material in blocks. It is possible that he sometimes has more than one source for the same event. The blocks of source material are joined together by editorial summaries composed by the author. These summaries may present a key to the arrangement of Acts. It has been suggested that the summaries divide periods of five-year duration.

Most likely, however, the order is geographical rather than chronological. Acts 1:8 is not an outline of the book, but it does state the theme. It indicates that the order follows the expansion of the church—from Jerusalem to Samaria, Syria, Asia Minor, Greece, and finally Rome.

Acts is a unique composition. The only book of its kind in the New Testament, it displays a freedom and grandeur of style superior even to Luke's gospel. As the only source for much of the history of the early church it remains a document of extreme value despite its inaccuracies. Luke understands its story as the unfolding of the divine drama of redemption. The Lord has not yet returned, but in the meantime the word of God is being carried on by the church. The Gentile mission is itself the eschatological action of God.

PREFACE (1:1-5)

Like his **first book** Luke's second volume is dedicated to **Theophilus** (see Luke 1:1-4). The preface of Acts summarizes that gospel. It began with the ministry of Jesus (no reference is made to the birth stories) and ended with the account of Jesus' ascension. At that time **he had given commandment** that they should witness to these events (Luke 24:48-51). This reference to the gospel indicates that the history of Jesus is basic for Acts.

1:3-4a. Only Acts tells us of Jesus' **staying** (or possibly "eating"; the meaning of the Greek word is uncertain) with the disciples for **forty days** after his resurrection. This information conflicts with the view of the Ascension presented in Luke 24:51 and the number forty is a traditional symbol. Apparently Acts intends to connect the risen Christ with the beginning of the church. The charge **not to depart from Jerusalem** seems to acknowledge the contrary tradition of a return to Galilee (cf. Mark 16:7), but this has already been refuted in Luke 24:6. For Luke, Jerusalem is the messianic center. There the resurrection appearances occur, and there the mission of the church is begun.

1:4b-5. Probably **the promise of the Father** is a reference to Joel 2:28-32—a text which will be developed later (2:16-21). The promise has to do with the coming of **the Holy Spirit**. This has been predicted by John the Baptist (Luke 3:16; cf. Acts 11:16), and fulfillment will take place on Pentecost. The Spirit is of primary importance for Acts. The whole course of events is moved by its power.

I. THE BEGINNING OF THE CHURCH IN JERUSALEM (1:6–5:42)

A. THE TIME OF PREPARATION (1:6-26)

1:6-11. *The Promise of the Spirit.* Those who **come together** are probably the eleven listed in verse 13. The place of gathering is apparently the Mount of Olives (verse 12)—the traditional site of ascension. Since Jesus has mentioned the promise, the apostles suppose that he refers to the coming of **the kingdom**. Jesus, however, insists that the **times** of the end cannot be known, and instead of the kingdom the **Holy Spirit** is coming. Luke's typical interest in the delay of the Lord's return (see Luke 21:5-37) is seen. Rather than stressing the end he emphasizes the era of the church as the time of God's activity. During this time the leaders are to witness from **Jerusalem . . . to the end of the earth**. This shows that the message of Christ is not limited to **Israel** but is universal in character. The risen Lord is the founder of the Gentile mission.

1:9-11. Suddenly Jesus is **lifted up** into a **cloud,** much as Moses became invisible at his departure from the earth, according to Josephus. **Two men** dressed in the typical garb of heavenly messengers (cf. Luke 24:4) appear. They insist that the apostles must not keep **looking into heaven.** The Lord will return **in the same way** that he left, but the time of his return is in the distant future, after an extensive mission has been accomplished.

1:12-26. *The Restoration of the Twelve.* Returning to Jerusalem, the witnesses of the Ascension enter **the upper room** (cf. Luke 22:12). The list of the eleven, except for order, is identical with Luke 6:14-16. They pray that the promise will be fulfilled and are joined in **prayer** by the **women** (cf. Luke 8:2 and 24:10) and the family of Jesus. **Mary** is important to Luke's gospel, and James, Jesus' brother, will play a significant role in Acts (12:17; 15:13; 21:18). Those closest to Jesus are believed to be involved in the mission of the church.

1:15-20. In the days between the Ascension and Pentecost, **Peter** makes a speech to **about a hundred and twenty . . . brethren.** This number may result from the rabbinic notion that leaders of a community should compose a tenth of the total; 10 times 12 equals 120. Into this speech Luke has inserted information about the death of Judas—material not consistent with Matthew 27:3-10. Apparently early tradition devised a variety of stories about the fate of the betrayer. Although **Akeldama** may mean **Field of Blood,** it might be Aramaic for "Field of Sleep," referring to a burial place—or, as Matthew says, a "potter's field."

Peter believes Judas' place among the twelve must be filled, since scripture requires it. The first text, Psalm 69:25, predicts the desolation of **his habitation.** This means the desolation of the "field," or farm, which he has purchased, and thus implies Judas' death. The second, Psalm 109:8, insists that his apostolic office be filled.

1:21-26. Two candidates who meet the qualifications are put forth. To be an apostle one must have been a witness of the acts of Jesus from the Baptism until the Ascension. This would include the Resurrection, which is most important, for the apostle's primary task is to **become . . . a witness to his resurrection.** Those nominated are **Joseph . . . Barsabbas,** whose Latin name is **Justus,** and **Matthias,** whose name means "gift of the Lord."

Selection is made by casting **lots.** In this practice names are inscribed on stones, put into a container, and shaken until one falls out. In the mind of the primitive Christians, the method gives confidence that ultimately the choice is God's. Matthias is chosen, but never again mentioned in the narrative. The twelve are recognized as the divinely appointed leaders of the church; their number must be preserved. That Peter is their leader is obvious.

B. THE EVENTS OF PENTECOST (2:1-47)

2:1-13. *The Coming of the Spirit.* The disciples are gathered **all together**—whether the twelve or the 120 is not clear. The place is simply identified as **the house.** The feast of Weeks (see Leviticus 23:15-21; Deuteronomy 16:9-12) acquired the Greek name **Pentecost** because it was observed fifty days after Passover. Originally an agricultural festival, in Luke's time it commemorated the giving of the law.

The occurrence of a miracle is indicated by the **sound . . . of a mighty wind** and the appearance of **tongues** like **fire** which rest on each of those present. The latter is reminiscent of the "voice of the Lord" which "flashes forth flames of fire" (Psalm 29:7). The term "wind" is another translation for the Greek word "Spirit." John's prediction in Luke 3:16 has been fulfilled.

2:4. Further evidence that the Holy Spirit has been given is seen in the speaking in **tongues.** Although Luke interprets this as a miracle, the original was probably an outburst of emotional babbling like that discussed in I Corinthians 12 and 14. This seems to be the meaning of the expression elsewhere in Acts

7

(10:46; 19:6). The description of the disciples as **filled with new wine**—a wine which was recently produced but intoxicating—fits emotional speech and not proficiency in foreign languages. Actually no miracle was necessary; everybody in the audience spoke either Aramaic or Greek.

2:5-13. Luke has introduced verses 5-11 to offer a rational explanation of the miracle. Since it is a time of national festival, **Jews . . . from every nation under heaven** are **in Jerusalem**. That these verses are not part of the original source is clear from Peter's speech, which addresses primarily the **men of Judea**. Moreover the change of setting is abrupt and unnatural. In verse 2 the disciples are in the house, but in verse 6 a huge **multitude** is assembled **at this sound**. Whether the sound is of the Spirit (verse 2) or of the speaking is not clear.

If one omits the reference to **Cretans and Arabians** as an editorial addition, the listing of nations moves basically from east to west, terminating in Rome (on **Asia** see below on 16:6*b*-8). At any rate the point is clear: the gospel announced on Pentecost is universal. It is heard by representatives of the whole world. This is similar to the rabbinic notion that at the giving of the law all the nations of the world were offered an opportunity to accept God's revelation. When one notes that in Philo's description the giving of the law was accompanied by signs of fire and spirit, the parallelism is complete.

2:14-36. *Peter's Sermon.* Peter explains the ecstatic speech. The speakers **are not drunk**, for **it is only the third hour**; it is 9 A.M. and nobody is intoxicated that early. Instead the words of Joel 2:28-32 are being fulfilled: **the Spirit** has been poured out and **the day of the Lord** has come. For Joel the "Lord" was God and the "day" was the end. But for Luke the "Lord" is Jesus and the "day" is the time of preaching. Apocalyptic signs of **blood, and fire, and vapor of smoke** are interpreted to symbolize the importance of the event which has occurred in history.

That the speech in its present form was composed by Luke is indicated by the use of the Greek Septuagint. Peter would have employed an Aramaic version of the prophet.

2:22-36. The main body of the sermon emphasizes the act of

God through **Jesus of Nazareth**. The crucial events of his career are his death and resurrection. Although his death was according to the **plan** of God, the Jews (**you**) bear its guilt. It seems unlikely that Luke himself would refer to the Romans, the instruments of Jesus' crucifixion, as **lawless men**. This could indicate a genuine memory of Peter's speech, but more likely Luke understands "lawless" to mean "without the law"—a simple reference to Gentiles.

The Resurrection is the act of God which **David** predicted. The quotation (Psalm 16:8-11) speaks of one whose **soul** would not be abandoned in **Hades** (the place of death), and who would not **see corruption**. Since David is dead and **buried**, this text must refer to the one who has been raised. Moreover God swore an **oath** to David that one of his **descendants** would occupy his throne (Psalm 132:11), and David recognized the Christ as his **Lord** (Psalm 110:1). The conclusion is undeniable: Jesus is the one who was raised, whom God has made **both Lord and Christ**.

2:37-47. *Response to the Proclamation.* The crowd responds in chorus: **What shall we do?** Peter demands repentance and baptism. These were already linked by John the Baptist, but Luke adds **the gift of the Holy Spirit**. He seems to support a doctrine of baptismal regeneration and to present baptism as a prerequisite for receiving the Spirit. Actually the matter is more complex. Elsewhere he records incidents of conversion without mentioning baptism (9:35; 13:12, 48). Baptism does not always guarantee the Spirit's coming (8:17; 19:6); on one occasion the Spirit precedes it (10:47). Apparently Luke is presenting here an order of admission into the Christian community which is more uniform than the sources warrant.

2:39. The **promise** of forgiveness and the gift of the Spirit is universal. It is granted to those of later generations and distant places.

2:41. In response to this exhortation to salvation **three thousand** are **baptized** and **added** to the church. It would be difficult to administer the rite of baptism to this large number. It is no doubt idealized.

2:42-47. Two summaries of life in the community are given.

Verse 42 outlines the religious life of the believers; verses 43-47 present additional information. **The apostles' teaching** would involve instruction in the sort of doctrine contained in Peter's sermon. The term translated **fellowship** means "participation" and stresses the sharing of a common life under the leadership of the twelve.

The **breaking of bread**, observed **in their homes**, is the distinctive feature of early Christian worship. Although it involved a full meal, the breaking of bread is Luke's terminology for the Lord's Supper (cf. Luke 22:19 and 24:35). The idea of the supper as a sacrament arose perhaps in the Pauline churches. The distinctive character of the early Jerusalem practice is a partaking **with glad and generous hearts** and an observance **day by day**.

Other acts of worship include **prayers** at home and in the **temple** (cf. 3:1). The fellowship also involves a sharing of **possessions** (cf. 4:32–5:11). At **wonders and signs** an awesome **fear** comes on everyone, and **the Lord** is the one who adds **those who were being saved** to their number. Thus the church, like the young Jesus (Luke 2:52), finds **favor** with both God and man.

C. THE ACTS OF PETER AND JOHN (3:1–4:31)

3:1-10. *Healing a Lame Man.* Some scholars believe this section of Acts to be another—perhaps older—account of the beginning of the church. The story ends, like the Pentecost narrative, with a description of the receiving of the Spirit. Luke, however, understands this as a later event, as an illustration of the Spirit's work in empowering the church for its mission.

3:1. As loyal Jews **Peter and John** go **up to the temple at the hour of prayer**. The **ninth hour** is 3 P.M.—the traditional time of evening prayer. Although John Mark is possible, **John** is probably the son of Zebedee. The pair illustrate Luke's fondness for two witnesses; earlier they were joined in obeying the Lord's command (Luke 22:8).

3:2. The **gate . . . called Beautiful** cannot be positively identified. One of the eastern entrances to the temple was decorated with Corinthian bronze and noted for its beauty. If this gate is intended, the disciples, approaching from the east, may still be living in Bethany.

3:3-10. In relating the miracle Luke stresses the seriousness of the illness and the immediacy of the cure. The man has been **lame from birth**, but after the healing he is described as **leaping up** and **walking**. Luke's reference to **feet and ankles** is hardly medical language, but it does display his interest in details of this sort (cf. Luke 4:38).

The actual miracle is performed **in the name of Jesus Christ of Nazareth**. To the ancients the name carried the power and authority of the person. The miracle shows that the leaders of the church possess the power once operating through Jesus. This power has nothing to do with earthly authority, as evidenced by Peter's lack of **silver and gold**—poverty hard to square with 4:35. In any case the power to heal comes ultimately from God; it is he who is praised. The people are amazed and present evidence to support the miracle. They identify the healthy man as the beggar who used to sit at the gate.

3:11-26. *Peter's Address.* The miracle provides the occasion for a sermon. A crowd follows Peter and John to the **portico called Solomon's**—an eastern section of the great colonnade which surrounded the outer court of the temple. Peter insists that the healing was performed, not by some magical power of the apostles, but by God. He is the God of Israel, **the God of Abraham and of Isaac and of Jacob**. The miracle, however, is but a sign of the power of God which raised Jesus. This Jesus is the one whom the audience delivered to **Pilate** for execution, even though the Roman governor repeatedly found him innocent.

Here Jesus is interpreted as a fulfillment of the idea of the **servant** of Isaiah 53. The servant has been **glorified**, and he is called the **Righteous One**. Jesus is also contrasted with Barabbas (Luke 23:18-25). The latter was **a murderer**, while Jesus was **the Author of life**, the one whose resurrection heralds the raising of the faithful. It is to this death and resurrection of Jesus that the apostles **are witnesses**.

3:16. This verse is difficult to translate. Its major point is that the lame man was healed by the power of the **name** of Jesus (cf. verse 6), and it may simply repeat this idea in a parallel statement. In any case the **faith** that is involved is that of the healed man, and the Revised Standard Version's **faith which is through Jesus** is misleading. The New English Bible is clearer: "And the name of Jesus, by awakening faith, has strengthened this man, whom you see and know, and this faith has made him completely well, as you can all see for yourselves."

3:17-23. Peter now applies this message to the present situation. The crucifixion of Jesus was committed **in igno-rance**—a common Lukan theme (e.g. 13:27; Luke 23:34)—yet it was in accord with the plan of God. The idea that **Christ should suffer**, reflecting Isaiah 53, is also an emphasis of Luke (cf. 17:3). The sermon calls for repentance and conversion, though no mention of baptism is made.

Times of refreshing refers to the blessings of the end time, as the parallel reference to the sending of Christ indicates. This could suggest that the raising of the prophet like **Moses** alludes to the resurrection of Jesus, as does verse 26. At any rate verses 22-23 are a composite quotation based on Deuteronomy 18:15, 19 and Leviticus 23:29. This joining of biblical material may indicate an early collection of Old Testament texts used by early Christian preachers.

3:24-26. The idea of **all the prophets . . . from Samuel** seems strange (cf. 13:20). Luke probably understands Samuel as the next prophet after Moses. Also he may remember him as the anointer of David, the type of the messianic king. The **covenant** with **Abraham** refers to Genesis 22:18 and suggests that the blessing to **all the families of the earth** is granted through Jesus. The idea of the servant's being sent to Israel first is a typical Lukan theme (cf. 13:46).

4:1-12. *Arrest and Trial.* Peter's speech, like his Pentecost sermon, is "interrupted" after it is finished. Those who take the apostles into **custody** are **the captain of the temple and the**

Sadducees. The former is either the adjutant of the high priest or one of the lesser captains who commands the temple guard. The Sadducees are stereotyped opponents whose introduction into the narrative is not realistic. The concern of the hearing is not with an academic discussion of **the resurrection** but with the question of the authority for healing. Pharisees, who were talking about the resurrection all the time, ran no danger of being imprisoned.

4:3-4. The necessity of delaying the trial **until the morrow** indicates either that the sermon was long—it began shortly after 3 P.M.—or that the hearing is expected to run beyond sundown. At any rate Luke is anxious to show that the trial is legal and thereby presents a parallel to his account of the trial of Jesus (Luke 22:66-71). His summary notes that the preaching has evoked faith and that large numbers are being added to the church.

4:5-7. The hearing of the next day takes place before the council which has recently judged Jesus. The **rulers** hold official priestly positions, while the **elders** belong to the sanhedrin by ancestry, wealth, and religious prestige. **Caiaphas**, not **Annas**, is the official **high priest** at this time (see Luke 3:2). The words translated **high-priestly family** can mean either members of the high-priestly clan or men of rank among the priests. Since the charge has to do with the **name** by which the act of power has been accomplished, it is more a matter of Luke's theology than of Jewish jurisprudence.

4:8-12. Peter responds under the guidance of the **Spirit**. This reflects the notion that the Spirit comes sporadically to give inspiration. Peter again witnesses to the death and resurrection of Jesus. The Crucifixion is the act of men; the Resurrection is the accomplishment of God.

Jesus is described as the **stone which was rejected by you builders**—a reference to Psalm 118:22. Although this stone could be either the capstone or the cornerstone, the latter seems suggested in Luke 20:17-18. This foundation makes possible the superstructure of life. God's power extends beyond healing a lame man to giving **salvation** to the world. Indeed, **no other** means of salvation is possible.

4:13-22. *The Verdict.* The author presents the sanhedrin's estimate of Peter and John. **Uneducated** literally means "illiterate," and **common men** classifies the apostles among the "people of the land"—the ordinary folk of Palestine who do not know the niceties of Pharisaic piety. **Recognized that they had been with Jesus** may mean that the council has not previously known the identity of Peter and John. More likely, however, Luke stresses the council's recognition of the source of apostolic **boldness**, or courage, as residing in Jesus.

The **man that had been healed** is also present. It is not clear whether he too has spent the night in jail, or whether he is simply evidence introduced into the trial. The notice that the sanhedrin has **nothing to say in opposition** is fulfillment of Luke 21:15.

4:15-20. The council members go into secret session. They admit that a **sign** has been done, but hope to prevent further preaching **in the name of Jesus**. This section of the narrative lacks the ring of reality. How Luke could have received a record of the secret proceedings is far from clear, and the picture of Jewish leaders who recognize the power of God yet try to oppose it is artificial.

The charge to the apostles is a stage setting for the apostolic declaration of obedience to God. The first part of their response is perhaps proverbial, going back as far as Socrates, who said, "I shall obey God rather than you." The second part is more important to Luke, who hopes to stress the apostles' witness to **what we have seen and heard**. This includes God's acts of power through Jesus, especially his resurrection.

4:21-22. The trial results in release of the prisoners. Since there is **no way to punish** Peter and John it is clear that they are actually innocent. The people sympathize with the disciples as they earlier did with Jesus (Luke 19:48). The magnitude of the cure is again emphasized; the man who was lame from birth is **more than forty years old**.

4:23-31. *Report and Prayer.* After their release Peter and

John return **to their friends**, literally "their own." Though it is sometimes supposed that the friends would include the whole **company of those who believed** (verse 32), this number seems too large. Perhaps only the apostles, or possibly the 120 (1:15), are intended. The place of meeting is obscure, but it may be the upper room (1:13) or the house of John Mark's mother (12:12).

4:24. When they hear the report of the sanhedrin's warning the disciples **lifted their voices** in prayer. The resulting praise and petition is more an expression of the theology of witness than a prayer which meets the situation. In style the prayer has the quality of Semitic poetry reminiscent of the poems of Luke's birth narrative, and its address to God finds a background in passages like Isaiah 37:16-20. The title **Sovereign Lord** is based on a Greek term which our word "despot" transliterates. It stresses the mighty power of God and is found also in Luke 2:29.

4:25-30. The prayer quotes Psalm 2:1-2 and finds the fulfillment of this in the life of Jesus. The **Gentiles** have raged against the Christ, as the crucifixion by the Romans proves. **Herod** has fulfilled the prophecy that **kings of the earth** oppose the **Anointed** of God. **Pilate** represents the **rulers** who **gathered together** against him. Though God's plan has been accomplished through these leaders, Luke here emphasizes the guilt of Pilate and Herod, in contrast to his narrative of Luke 23.

The reference to Jesus combines two christological ideas: he is the **servant** of Second Isaiah; and he is the anointed Messiah. The anointing took place at baptism (Luke 3:22 and 4:18). For Luke the two ideas are one: Jesus is the Messiah, whose mission demands humble acceptance of the servant's role.

4:31. Just as Pentecost was accompanied by wind and fire, so this event is punctuated with a shaking of the ground. The concept of the sporadic coming of the Spirit (cf. verse 8) is again apparent, and Luke's view of the Spirit's coming is seen in the idea of being **filled** (cf. Luke 3:22).

Though the gift of the Spirit followed by a reference to speaking is parallel to the Pentecost events, Luke sees this occurrence as different. Here the Spirit's work becomes actualized in the life of the church. Its leaders do not speak in tongues but proclaim the gospel—**the word of God**.

D. LIFE IN THE CHURCH (4:32–6:7)

4:32-37. *Community of Goods.* Luke presents a summary of the church's life which parallels 2:42-47. The expression **heart and soul** is biblical (cf. Deuteronomy 6:5) and reveals the inner unity of the faithful. The major task of the leaders is to witness **to the resurrection**. The sharing of possessions is voluntary rather than required. There is no notion that a new economic order is being established. The laying of money **at the apostles' feet** is reminiscent of ancient customs in transfer of possessions or of religious dedication of an offering to the gods.

4:36-37. A specific illustration is **Barnabas**. His real name is **Joseph**, but the Aramaic original of his surname is elusive. Some think it is "son of Nebo," the Babylonian god. The name could mean "son of a prophet," as well as "son of exhortation," or **encouragement**. Luke's choice of "encouragement" is based on knowledge of Barnabas' later activity (cf. 11:22). Though he is a **native of Cyprus**, Colossians 4:10 says he is a cousin of John Mark, who was an inhabitant of Jerusalem.

5:1-11. *The Judgment of God.* In contrast to the generosity of Barnabas is the case of **Ananias** and **Sapphira**. Judgment as well as grace is operating in the community. The story seems to be a legend which makes this point. Its background is found in Old Testament passages like Joshua 7:1 and I Kings 14:1-20. The name **Ananias** can be translated "the Lord is gracious," while **Sapphira** means "beautiful."

5:1-3. According to the story Ananias sells **a piece of property** and gives the apostles a portion of the **proceeds**, holding back the rest for himself. Thus the statement that everything was held "in common" (4:32) is qualified. **Peter**, who seems to be endowed with a kind of prophetic power (cf. Luke 6:8; 19:30), rebukes Ananias for attempting to **lie to the Holy Spirit**. Here the Spirit seems to be a special possession of the church and its leaders, and lying to the Spirit is the same as lying to God.

5:4. This verse is apparently Luke's attempt to make clear that the sin of Ananias is not his failure to share his goods but his hypocrisy—his effort to appear generous when he is really miserly. The danger of wealth is a Lukan theme. The guilt is paradoxical: Ananias is charged with having **contrived this deed in your heart** even though **Satan filled your heart** to do it (verse 3; cf. Luke 22:3, 22).

5:5-6. It is possible to interpret Ananias' death as a coincidence or as the result of emotional shock. Luke understands the event as a miracle of God's judgment. The punishment seems radical, devoid of the Christian concept of forgiveness (Luke 17:4) and contradicting the divine forbearance in "times of ignorance" (17:30). Some have thought that the **young men** (literally "youngers") who perform the burial duties represent an official body within the church, parallel to the "elders." That this is a mere reference to those of youthful vigor is more probable.

5:7-10. Sapphira serves as a second witness to judgment against dishonesty. The implication that the church is still in session three hours after the death of Ananias is another element suggesting that the story is not real. Sapphira repeats the lie of her husband and is charged with conspiring with him to **tempt the Spirit**. Thus the Old Testament idea of testing God is taken up; here the emphasis is on going as far as possible before retaliation strikes. Sapphira's death could be attributed to the shocking news of her husband's fate, but Luke interprets it as a sign of God's wrath.

5:11. In view of the events, the news that **fear** fell on **all who heard** is not surprising, but the statement sounds a common Lukan theme (e.g. 2:43; 19:17). The term **church** appears here for the first time in Acts. In the Septuagint the same Greek word is used for the assembly of the people of Israel under the call of God. The Christians' use of the term indicates their understanding of themselves as the true people of God, called to do his work. In Acts the term can be used either for the whole body of believers (e.g. 9:31) or for a local group of God's people (e.g. 13:1).

5:12-16. *Acts of Power.* This is another of Luke's summaries. It expands the reference to "wonders and signs" of 2:43 and answers the prayer of 4:29-30. It is not clear whether those who are **together in Solomon's Portico** (cf. 3:11) included only the apostles or the whole church. If the latter, **the rest** who **dared** not **join them** would be people who refrained from association with the Christians for lack of courage. This interpretation would be in tension with verse 14, where the enthusiastic response of the community is recorded. It is better to understand those gathered as the apostles; they are the real subject of the text. Those who do not join them are ordinary members of the church who lack the power attributed to the leaders.

5:15-16. The carrying of **sick into the streets** for healing is reminiscent of Mark 6:56. Cure by the **shadow** of **Peter** is parallel to healings accomplished by handkerchiefs carried from the body of Paul (19:12). **Fall on** is literally "overshadow"—the same verb that is used for the cloud at Jesus' transfiguration (Luke 9:34). It is thus a symbol of the divine power. Here it is suggested that an apostle has this power working in his ministry—a power which emanates from his person without direct physical contact. This ministry draws people from towns beyond Jerusalem and successfully heals **all**.

5:17-26. *Imprisonment and Release.* This section involving a second arrest and trial of the apostles is parallel to 4:1-22. The miraculous release from prison anticipates 12:6-11. Though it is sometimes supposed that verses 17-22 are a doublet, the account may be historical. Jewish legal practice, at least at a later date, involved two steps, warning and legal action. In any case Luke understands this as a second legal encounter which reflects a heightening of the official opposition.

5:17-18. As the story goes, the **high priest** and the **party of the Sadducees** take action against the **apostles**, who, except for Peter (verse 29), are unidentified. The opponents are **filled with jealousy** apparently because of the growth of the Christian community. The **common prison** is literally the "public" jail, but the adjective could be an adverb—the apostles were thrown into prison "publicly."

5:19-21a. For Luke the **angel of the Lord** is the angel of God (cf. 7:30). The same sort of supernatural being protected Daniel during his imprisonment (Daniel 6:22). It is sometimes supposed that since the angel performs mundane acts the story suggests human complicity. Luke, however, understands the escape as a miracle.

The escape has taken place **at night**, but the apostles do not begin their teaching **in the temple** until **daybreak**. Though the temple is open during the night, worshipers do not come until morning. The message proclaimed is here described as **all the words of this life**. The expression means essentially the same as "the message of this salvation" (13:26).

5:21b-26. It is not clear whether Luke understands the **council and all the senate of Israel** as two separate bodies or, correctly, as two different ways to refer to one group. The report that the doors of the prison are **locked** and the **sentries** still in position indicates the magnitude of the miracle. That an angel could go unnoticed through locked doors is possible, but the escape of the apostles by this means is incomprehensible. Little wonder that a typical Lukan expression of amazement is repeated: What would this **come to?**

The **captain of the temple** is the chief of the temple police; the **officers** are his subordinates. Their fear of **being stoned** by the mob is perhaps unrealistic, but the point is clear. Though hated by the leaders, the Christians are loved by the people.

5:27-42. *Before the Council.* The apostles are brought before the sanhedrin. The previous prohibition **to teach in this name**—that is, in the name of Jesus (4:18)—has been ignored. In contrast to Matthew 27:25 this text presents the council as resisting responsibility for the **blood** of Jesus.

5:29-32. Peter's response is a sermon in miniature. Stress is placed on the church's witness to the death, resurrection, and exaltation of Jesus, as well as to the opportunity for **repentance . . . and forgiveness of sins** through him. The obligation to **obey**

God rather than men is more clearly stated than in 4:19. The activity of the apostles has confirmed their obedience. The reference to Jesus' **hanging . . . on a tree** is reminiscent of Deuteronomy 21:22; the same terminology appears in a later sermon of Peter (10:39).

The word translated **Leader** appears as "Author" (of life) in 3:15. Though it could carry a military connotation like "captain," the basic meaning is an originator. In this context Luke sees Jesus as the one who leads the way to salvation. The idea that the **Holy Spirit** participates in the witness of the apostles is seen in the boldness of their proclamation (4:31) and their acts of power (4:12-16).

5:33-37. The members of the council are **enraged** by the speech—literally "sawed through," or "cut to the quick." The reaction of **Gamaliel** is less violent. As a **Pharisee** he would be more sympathetic with the Christian doctrine of the resurrection. Jewish tradition holds him in high esteem, but his tolerance seems to have had little effect on his pupil, Saul of Tarsus (22:3).

Luke attributes to Gamaliel two historical errors. **Theudas** did not lead his revolt until some ten years after this speech; and **Judas**, who is said to have led a later insurrection, actually revolted at the time of the census of A.D. 6. Some scholars interpret these errors as an indication that Luke carelessly used Josephus' Antiquities of the Jews as a source.

While it is possible to acknowledge the essential historicity of Gamaliel's speech, clearly its real purpose is to support Luke's apologetic (cf. Luke 20:4). The officials of Judaism and Rome should let Christianity run its course. When it has reached its goal, it will be evident that God has been working in it. When Gamaliel is reported as saying, **if it is of God**, the form of his expressions assumes that this is so. His conclusion is Luke's: **You might even be found opposing God** or, as the Greek says in a terse adjective, "God-fighting."

5:40-42. The council takes Gamaliel's advice, but not without reservations. The apostles are beaten with the traditional "forty lashes less one" (II Corinthians 11:24) and charged to keep silent. However, the leaders of the church rejoice that they have been found **worthy to suffer dishonor for the name** of Jesus (cf. Luke 6:22). They continue their daily worship **in the temple and at home**, together with **teaching and preaching** literally "the Christ Jesus," which as Greek idiom may mean either "Christ Jesus" or **Jesus as the Christ**.

II. THE MISSION TO ISRAEL (6:1–9:31)

A. THE APPOINTMENT OF THE SEVEN (6:1-7)

Here Luke, apparently following a new source, turns to a new subject. Evidence of a change in source material is seen in the abrupt presentation of two groups, the **Hellenists** and the **Hebrews**, without explanation. The Christians are called **disciples** for the first time in Acts, and mention of **Antioch** could indicate the origin of this new source (cf. 11:26).

As to the identity of the Hellenists, two major theories have been proposed: (1) They are Greeks; (2) they are Greek-speaking Jews who have lived outside of Palestine but have returned. Luke supports the latter. He introduces Gentile converts into the narrative later on and with considerable emphasis (10:1–11:18).

6:1. The dispute between the Hellenists and the Hebrews concerns the administration of the dole. The care of **widows** was inherited from Jewish practice, but the method of **distribution** is not clear. It is not certain whether serving **tables** describes the role of a waiter at the common meal or refers to the money tables of the community's administration. At any rate the widows of the Hellenists seem to be **neglected**, perhaps supposing that they do not receive a fair share.

6:2-6. To solve the problem **the twelve** summon the whole church and propose the selection of **seven men** to supervise the distribution of food. It seems obvious that the apostles should not forgo **preaching the word of God** in order to wait tables or

21

administer finance. The men who are to be appointed should be filled with the **Spirit** and **wisdom**.

That a certain amount of worldly wisdom would be required is clear, but a special endowment with the Spirit does not seem necessary for such a mundane task. This, together with the use of the sacred number seven, suggests a more important sort of leadership. Whereas most texts assume that the selection is made by the church, at least one manuscript implies that the choice was made by the twelve. In any case the important action is performed by the apostles—the laying on of **hands**. This ceremony elsewhere in Acts is related to the conveying of the Spirit (8:17 and 19:6). Here it is understood in the Old Testament sense of transmitting authority (cf. Numbers 27:23). Luke interprets the ritual in terms of the ordination practice common to the church of his day.

Considerable debate has raged about the actual function of the **seven** in the early church. For example, it has been urged that they were the deacons of the Jerusalem community. But the title is lacking in the text, and the duties do not conform to the practices of that office in the later church. Most likely they represent a distinct faction within the Christian community. All their names are Greek. The absence of Hebrews from a rations committee seems difficult to explain.

Of the two Hellenists about whom we have information (**Stephen** and **Philip**) there is no record of their serving tables. We do have reports of their **ministry of the word** (6:7–7:60; 8:4-40; 21:8). It is surprising, too, that the persecution which Stephen provoked did not seriously affect the apostles (8:1). We can conclude that within the Jerusalem church were two groups: the Hebrews with the apostles as their leaders and the Hellenists under the guidance of the seven.

6:7. This summary refers again to the increase in the church's membership. It includes the only record of converts from the Jewish priesthood. Apparently the church had little impact on the religious leaders of the Jews and had little interest in the priestly tradition.

B. ACTS OF STEPHEN (6:8–8:3)

6:8–7:1. *The Arrest of Stephen.* The activity of one of the seven is here described. Possible doublets within the narrative have led to a theory of two sources. The charge against Stephen is repeated (verses 11, 13-14), and his stoning is presented as both mob violence (7:54, 57-58*a*) and legal action (7:1, 58*b*-59). The account of the glory of Stephen's **face** should probably be joined with the prayer of 7:59-60. Perhaps Luke has adapted sources to his own purpose, inserting Stephen's speech into a narrative which proceeds well without it.

6:8-10. Since Stephen is **full of the Spirit** (verse 3) acts of **power** are to be expected from him. Though Luke lists no specific miracles, Stephen's **wonders and signs** are probably similar to those attributed to the apostles. It is apparently his preaching which arouses opposition. Those unable to **withstand** Stephen's **wisdom** cannot be positively identified since the Greek is ambiguous. They certainly include members of a **synagogue** composed of Hellenistic Jews. But it is unclear whether Luke conceives of one synagogue that includes **Freedmen . . . Cyrenians . . . Alexandrians . . . those from Cilicia and Asia** or as many as five different groups. Most likely he means two: the synagogue of the Freedmen, which is composed of Cyrenians and Alexandrians, and a group from Cilicia and Asia.

The **Freedmen,** literally "Libertines," are usually identified as Jews who have been redeemed from slavery—perhaps desendants of those captured by Pompey. But some scholars accept the variant reading "Libyans" as a reference to the area from which the people of Cyrene and Alexandria come. Regardless of the interpretation, the opponents seem to be Hellenistic Jews—representatives of the background from which Stephen comes.

6:11–7:1. This group is able to arouse **the people**—in contrast to 5:26—and bring the case to the sanhedrin. The charge is reminiscent of that made against Jesus (Mark 14:58). **False witnesses** do not seem to be needed, since Stephen's speech confirms his opposition to **this holy place**, which is the temple. However, his view of **the law**, according to Luke, is true, so that the witnesses appear guilty of falsehood in this respect. The transformation of Stephen's face has its background in texts like Exodus 34:29-35. It reflects the early Christian trend toward glorification of the martyrs.

7:2-53. *Stephen's Speech.* Though the speeches of Acts often rest on valid tradition, they usually reflect Luke's own understanding of the events. This speech of Stephen's, since it goes beyond the idea of serving tables (6:2-3), may contain accurate historical information about the beliefs of the Hellenists. On the other hand it does not directly answer the charges, and it begins with a form of address identical with that of one of Paul's speeches (22:1).

It seems to have three main points:

(1) The major events of divine revelation have occurred outside Palestine.

(2) God's purposes are continually being misunderstood and rejected by Israel.

(3) True worship of God cannot be confined to the temple of Jerusalem. This last point proves Stephen's opposition to the temple; the whole sermon is based on Luke's understanding of the law.

7:2-8. *The Promise to Abraham.* Though this account is based on Genesis, Stephen appears to make two errors:

(1) The call of God is said to have come to the patriarch **when he was in Mesopotamia, before he lived in Haran**. But according to Genesis 11:27–12:5 God's command to go to the promised land occurred after Abraham was in Haran. This mistake could rest on texts like Genesis 15:7, where the impression is given that the call came in **the land of the Chaldeans**.

(2) It is said that Abraham did not move to the promised land until **after his father died**. Yet references to Terah's age in relation to the chronology of Abraham (Gen. 11:26, 32; 12:4) indicate that Terah lived sixty years after his son left Haran.

Both of these mistakes are found in Jewish writers—Philo, for example.

7:5-8. Luke emphasizes the fact that Abraham did not actually possess any of the **inheritance . . ., not even a foot's length** (cf. Deuteronomy 2:5). For **four hundred years** (430, according to Exodus 12:40) the Israelites were **aliens** and slaves in the land of Egypt. God's action in redeeming them was primarily not to give them a new land, but to provide them with valid worship at Sinai; Genesis 15:13-14 is interpreted in light of Exodus 3:12. Throughout this period the continuity of the people of God was preserved in the **covenant of circumcision**, which had been given outside Palestine and prior to the temple.

7:9-16. *Salvation in Egypt.* Stephen turns to **Joseph** and his brothers, **the patriarchs**. Some criticism of the patriarchs is implied in their being **jealous**, but the main point in the Joseph story is that **God was with him**. The purposes of God are accomplished in spite of ignorance and opposition. Two questions of accuracy can be raised:

(1) The **kindred** of **Jacob** who **went down into Egypt** are said to number **seventy-five souls**. The Hebrew text of Genesis 46:27 says "seventy"—evidence that Luke used the Septuagint, which reads "seventy-five."

(2) It is said that Jacob (or possibly Joseph) and the patriarchs were buried in **Shechem**. But, whereas Joshua 24:32 records the burial of Joseph there, Genesis 50:13 says that Jacob was buried at Hebron—the place where the traditional tombs of the patriarchs can be seen today. In any case the main meaning of the text is clear: the salvation of Israel occurred outside the Holy Land through a man who had been rejected.

7:17-34. *The Early Life and Call of Moses.* The account of Moses' career is based on the early chapters of Exodus. In verse 20 the word translated **beautiful** is found in the Septuagint of Exodus 2:2, but the idea that as an infant he was particularly pleasing **before God** is not recorded in the Old Testament. Luke may be suggesting a parallel to texts like Luke 2:52.

Similarly verse 22 has no basis in the Exodus narrative. Though **the wisdom of the Egyptians** was proverbial, the notion that Moses was **mighty in his words** is contradicted by Exodus 4:10. Perhaps Luke is presenting him as a type of Jesus, who was "mighty in deed and word before God" (Luke 24:19).

7:23-29. The information that Moses was **forty years old** when he attempted to deliver his **brethren** is lacking in the Old Testament, but the division of his life of 120 years (Deuteronomy 34:7) into three periods of forty years (cf. verse 30) is found in Jewish tradition.

The content of verse 25 is also missing from the Exodus account, though Jewish writers sometimes excused Moses for his good intentions. Luke, in presenting the failure of Moses to be understood, is probably following the theme of the prophet who is rejected by his own (cf. Luke 4:24).

Though the account of the quarrel between the **two sons of Israel** is slightly different from Exodus 2:13, the important feature is the reason for Moses' flight from Egypt. Whereas in Exodus 2:15 Moses flees from Pharaoh, in Acts he goes into exile because his people reject him.

7:30-34. Again, it is on foreign soil that God speaks to Moses. Though Luke refers to the place as **Mount Sinai** in contrast to "Horeb" (Exodus 3:1), the two terms are used interchangeably to refer to the same mountain. Luke presents the command for Moses to remove his **shoes** as coming after the words of revelation. By putting the command in a position of climax Luke may hope to stress the fact that, as in the case of Abraham, the **holy ground** of God's call is located outside the Holy Land.

7:35-43. *Opposition to Moses.* The one who was repudiated as **a ruler and a judge** (cf. verse 27) has been chosen by God as **ruler and deliverer.** This both parallels the rejection of Joseph (verse 9) and anticipates the redemption through Jesus (Luke 24:21). Moses is also a type of the miracle worker, as the plagues of Exodus 7–12 show. The reference to a **prophet** like Moses, based on Deuteronomy 18:15, is a typical Lukan theme.

The congregation in the wilderness is reminiscent of the assembly of the people to receive the law. Though possibly based on Deuteronomy 33:2, the idea that the law was mediated through angels (cf. verse 53) developed in Jewish tradition. The description of the law as **living oracles** suggests that its content is divine utterances which give life to the hearer.

7:39-42a. Even though Moses and the law have been glorified by tradition, his contemporaries **thrust him aside**. Almost no blame is placed on **Aaron** for the golden **calf** (cf. Exodus 32:2-4, 25); the burden of guilt must be borne by the people. **The works of their hands** is a typical phrase of the Jewish polemic against idolatry (cf. Psalm 115:4). **The host of heaven** refers to the astral deities of Babylonian and Assyrian religion, whose worship involved the adoration of idols.

7:42b-43. The quotation from **the book of the prophets** is from the Septuagint of Amos 5:25-27, which varies in some respects from the Hebrew text. Both the Septuagint and the Hebrew, however, read "beyond Damascus," referring to Assyria, rather than **Babylon**. Luke understands the Babylonian captivity as the punishment for abandoning God in the desert. For Amos the time of wilderness wandering was a golden age, but Luke sees it as a time of idolatry.

7:44-53. *Building the Temple.* At last the charges against Stephen are taken up. The indictment that he speaks **against this holy place** is confirmed, though his attack on the temple is based on **the law** (6:13).

The narrative which makes these points is not without problems. Verse 44 does not logically follow verse 42. The approval of the tabernacle contradicts the opposition to the worship in the wilderness. Possibly verses 38-48 represent another source which has been inserted here.

7:44-47. Luke's description of the tabernacle as the **tent of witness** employs the typical Septuagint substitute for the Hebrew "tent of meeting." The information that God presented **Moses** with a **pattern** of the portable sanctuary is found in Exodus 25:40. The tabernacle is thereby contrasted with the temple **made with hands.** From the time of **Joshua** to **David** this tabernacle served as the place of worship. It was David who asked permission to **find** a permanent **habitation** for God.

Actually, although the following verses indicate that "habitation" refers to the temple, the best manuscripts say it was "for the house of Jacob." If this reading is original, it may reflect the reference to the house of David in II Samuel 7:26. Perhaps Luke views the place of worship as a dwelling for both God and the people. Or perhaps the substitution of "house of Jacob" for "Mighty One of Jacob" in his allusion to Psalm 132:5 is a subtle criticism of the temple implying the same idea as verse 48.

7:48-50. The title **Most High** is used in the Old Testament to express the recognition of the true God by foreigners; it is a favorite phrase of Luke. When Stephen says that God **does not dwell in houses made with hands,** he implies that heathen gods do, but that God cannot be confined to the temple. The idea that neither earth nor heaven can contain God is found in Solomon's prayer of dedication (I Kings 8:27), but the quotation which Stephen uses is the Septuagint of Isaiah 66:1-2.

7:51-53. Stephen's final word is a collection of judgments based on the Old Testament. They are **stiff-necked people** (Exodus 33:3), **uncircumcised in heart** (Leviticus 26:41) **and ears** (Jeremiah 6:10). **The Holy Spirit,** which they have resisted, is the spirit of prophecy which has been speaking to them through **the law.** Israel's failure to understand the law has led to its distortion of worship. The notion that all the prophets were persecuted and **killed** cannot be supported by the Old Testament but had become traditional. According to that tradition it is not surprising that the descendants of the **fathers . . . murdered** Jesus, who is here called **the Righteous One.**

7:54-8:3. *The Stoning of Stephen.* The stern words of Stephen's conclusion provoke a bitter reaction. On **enraged** see above on 5:33-37. The gnashing of **teeth** is a biblical figure describing the hostility of the wicked against the righteous. By way of contrast Stephen is presented as possessing the Spirit and seeing **the heavens opened.** Possession of the Spirit was a normal feature of his religious life (cf. 6:5), but here **the Holy Spirit** seems to be a special gift which makes possible this unique experience. The theme of visionary experience preceding martyrdom is found in Jewish literature.

7:56. Two features are important:
(1) Stephen refers to Jesus as the **Son of man**—the only such

usage outside the gospels. The prediction of Luke 22:69 is fulfilled, and Jesus is now to be recognized as the supernatural Messiah of Jewish eschatology.

(2) The Son of man is portrayed, not as sitting (Luke 22:69), but as **standing at the right hand of God**. Perhaps this symbolizes the one who stands as advocate of the righteous in the time of judgment (Job 16:19). Or possibly Luke is depicting Jesus as standing to welcome Stephen into heaven. If so, Luke's note of ascension immediately after death is again sounded (cf. Luke 23:43).

7:57-58. It is not clear whether Luke imagines a lynching or a legal process (see above on 6:8–7:1). The information that they (the council or the people?) **rushed together upon him** and threw him **out of the city** suggests mob violence. But the reference to stoning by **the witnesses** reflects judicial procedure, since witnesses were customarily the executioners.

Stoning was normally performed outside the city and was the regular punishment for blasphemy (Leviticus 24:10-23)—a charge perhaps reflected in **stopped their ears**. The victim was usually put in the bottom of a pit and heavy stones were pushed upon him. No record is found of the executioners' removing **their garments**, although the victim was stripped of his clothing.

7:59-60. The death of Stephen reflects motifs from the passion of Jesus: he too committed his spirit to God (Luke 23:46); he too prayed for the forgiveness of his executioners (Luke 23:34).

8:1a. The name **Saul** is used for Paul until 13:9. It is a Hebrew name meaning "asked"; Paul is Latin and means "little." That Paul **was consenting to** Stephen's **death** has been interpreted as hinting that he participated in the official action of the sanhedrin (cf. 22:20; 26:10).

8:1b-3. The effect of the execution was **persecution . . . against the church**. The idea that **all** were **scattered** is modified by Luke's indication that the persecution did not disturb the **apostles**. As some manuscripts say, these leaders "remained in Jerusalem." The opposition was directed against the Hellenists (see above on 6:1-7) just as the stoning was aimed at one of the their number, Stephen. There is abundant evidence that Paul persecuted the church. Since he was from Tarsus of Cilicia, he could have been one of the Cilicians who originally opposed Stephen (6:9).

C. THE ACTS OF PHILIP (8:4-40)

8:4-13. *The Mission to Samaria.* Perhaps following a new source, Luke now presents the extension of the mission beyond Judea. The leader of this movement is **Philip**, one of the Hellenists (see above on 6:1-7). He goes to **a city of Samaria** which is unnamed, but later tradition connects Simon the magician with Gitta, halfway between the Samaritan capital Sebaste, which was the Old Testament Samaria, and Caesarea. Though the narrative finds the impetus for this expansion in the persecution of verse 1*b*, the Hellenists believed a mission beyond the shadows of the temple to be of the essence of Christianity.

To be sure, the Samaritans were similar to the Jews, worshiping the same God and following the first five books of the Law. Yet they were considered by the Jews to be inferior and therefore were a step toward the Gentiles. Possibly Luke sees the evangelizing of Samaria as fulfilling the unrealized intention of Jesus (cf. Luke 9:51-56).

8:4-8. Philip's mission is described in general terms. His primary activity is to proclaim Jesus as **the Christ**. Jesus is the triumphant Messiah through whom God has acted to offer salvation. This is especially seen in the later reference to preaching **good news about the kingdom of God** (verse 12). God's rule has broken into history with Jesus and now operates in the church. The power of God so worked in him that healing was done in his name and now that power is operating in the church's proclamation, **the word of God** (verse 14). The potency of this message is confirmed by **signs**. Like Stephen, Philip is able to cast out demons and cure the sick. The mission evokes an enthusiastic response.

8:9-11. In the tradition of the later church **Simon** the magician became the arch heretic—the father of Gnosticism, which was a leading heretical movement. Soothsayers and astrologers were common in the ancient world, but Simon is unusual in demanding special loyalty to himself. Indeed all the people **from the least to the greatest** acclaim him to be the **power of God**. This seems to suggest that his followers worship him as a divine being—the supernatural power which stands between a person and the high God as mediator.

8:12-13. The power of Christianity is greater than the power of magic. The Samaritans believe the preaching of Philip and confirm their faith by baptism—a baptism which does not convey the Spirit (verse 16). Simon too is **baptized**, apparently more impressed by the miracles than by the message. He continues **with Philip**, becoming a kind of disciple.

8:14-25. *Apostolic Confirmation.* This text affirms the authority of the **apostles** in supervising the mission of the church. Such close cooperation between the Hellenists and the Jerusalem leaders seems unlikely, and the power to confer the Spirit does not appear to be the special prerogative of the twelve. The account of the sending of **Peter and John** indicates Luke's typical interest in two witnesses. Though it is possible that the second man is to be identified as John Mark, more likely the companion of Peter is John the son of Zebedee. The two are often associated in Luke and Acts.

8:14-17. The notion that the Spirit is not conveyed through baptism is also found in 19:1-6. There those who do not receive the Holy Spirit have been baptized in John's baptism, while here the rite has been performed **in the name of the Lord Jesus**. Luke is not describing some practice of baptism which differs from that of 2:38. He is stressing the apostolic leadership of the church.

Apparently laying on of hands was a regular feature of early baptismal practice. At Ephesus emphasis is put on rebaptism of the converts, with laying on of hands as a normal conclusion of the ritual (19:5-6). The Christian rite involved a combination of John's baptism and baptism with the Spirit (1:5). Possibly immersion in water symbolized the former, while laying on of hands portrayed the latter. Earlier the laying on of hands indicated the commission to special service (6:6). Here it confers to Samarian converts the right to be a part of the church.

8:18-24. While the narrative suggests that Simon wants the authority to confirm Christians, he is really interested in gaining the power to perform miracles. His attempt to purchase this power which belongs to the apostles has given birth to the term "simony"—the attempt to obtain church office by money. Peter makes it clear that the authority to convey the Spirit is a **gift of God**. His stern rebuke of Simon is based on Old Testament allusions (cf. Deuteronomy 12:12; Psalm 78:37; Deuteronomy 29:18).

It has been debated whether **if possible** means if Simon repents or if God wills—the latter implying that God remains free in his right not to forgive. The remorse of Simon is perhaps a polemic against Simonians of Luke's day.

8:25. The apostles go back **to Jerusalem**, the seat of authority. On their way they preach to Samaritan **villages**. Here **the gospel** is called **the word of the Lord** (cf. verse 14).

8:26-40. *Mission to a Eunuch.* The narrative returns to the activity of **Philip**. Revelation through an **angel** is a common Lukan motif, and here the heavenly messenger performs the same function as **the Spirit** (verse 29).

Gaza, the ancient city of the Philistines, is southwest of Jerusalem on the route to Egypt. The **Ethiopian** is a Nubian from an area south of Egypt, not an Abyssinian. As a **eunuch** he cannot be admitted to the Jewish congregation (Deuteronomy 23:1), despite the more tolerant attitude found in Isaiah 56:3. Luke shares the latter views, since he considers the Ethiopian to be not a Gentile but a proselyte—he has been **to Jerusalem to worship** and is reading one of the prophets.

The first Gentile convert, according to Luke, is Cornelius (10:44-48); Philip's mission only prepares the way. In the mind of the Hellenists, however, the eunuch may have represented a non-Jew. At best he is on the fringes of Jewish religion. **Candace** is the title of the **queen**, not her name.

8:29-31. Under the guidance of the Spirit, Philip runs after the Ethiopian's **chariot** (or carriage). He hears the eunuch **reading**, for in the ancient world reading was done aloud.

8:32-33. The text is Isaiah 53:7*b*-8*a*. Since this is one of the first clear uses of this important passage in reference to Jesus, the question can be raised whether this usage appeared so early in the life of the church.

Of course it is possible that the earliest Christians interpreted the meaning of Christ in view of the servant poems of Second Isaiah. Some scholars hold that Jesus understood his own role in light of these passages. However, the term "servant" is not applied to Jesus here, and the references to one who has borne our sins are lacking. Luke is simply emphasizing his conviction that Old Testament expectation has been fulfilled in the suffering and resurrection of Jesus (cf. Luke 24:25-27, 44-47).

The **lamb** which is **dumb** refers to the silence of Jesus at his trial and the denial of **justice** to his unjust execution. His **generation** has been destroyed by his crucifixion. The prediction that **his life is taken up from the earth** has been fulfilled in his resurrection, ascension, and exaltation.

8:34-38. Philip preaches **the good news of Jesus**. His sermon apparently includes the demand of 2:38 to repent and be **baptized**. Some manuscripts add a call to confession by Philip and the eunuch's response, which is given in a footnote in the Revised Standard Version. This addition seeks to moderate the abruptness of baptism without instruction and evidence of faith.

8:39-40. After the baptism, the Spirit sends Philip on his mission. Here some manuscripts say that the Spirit came on the eunuch and an angel caught up Philip. This would indicate that the Ethiopian has received the Holy Spirit at baptism. Philip proceeds to **Azotus** (the Old Testament Ashdod), preaching in towns on the way to **Caesarea**.

D. THE CONVERSION OF PAUL (9:1-31)

9:1-9. *The Heavenly Vision.* The account now picks up the narrative of 8:3. The conversion of Saul (Paul) had been prepared for. He had witnessed the stoning of Stephen as well as the persistence of his victims. The actual conversion is described three times in Acts (9:3-19; 22:6-16; 26:12-18), all with minor variations.

9:1-2. It is sometimes supposed that the **high priest** had the right to extradite criminals who had fled to another country. However, recognition of that right by the authorities of **Damascus** in Syria in Paul's day seems unlikely. A writing called the Damascus Document confirms that a group of unorthodox Jews flourished in Damascus. Paul plans to persecute those **belonging to the Way**—an early designation for the Christians.

9:3-7. Paul's vision is presented in the form of ancient symbolism. The **light from heaven** signifies divine revelation, and the heavenly **voice** is reminiscent of the supernatural word heard in rabbinic debate (cf. Luke 3:22). The charge against Paul makes it evident that persecuting the church is the same as persecuting Christ (cf. Luke 10:16). In this account Paul seems to hear, but not see, the heavenly spokesman (cf. **when his eyes were opened**, verse 8). His own writings assert that he has "seen Jesus our Lord" (I Corinthians 9:1).

The command that he go to **the city** to receive instruction conflicts with his own statement that he did not receive his commission to preach from men (Galatians 1:11-16), and the information that his companions **stood speechless** is not in harmony with 26:14. Similarly Luke's statement that these companions were hearing **the voice** is contradicted by his later declaration that they "did not hear the voice" (22:9). On the one hand he wants to present witnesses to the event. On the other hand he is anxious to interpret the vision as an experience of Paul.

9:8-9. Paul's blindness is probably to be viewed, not as punishment, but as a result of the radiance of the vision (cf. 22:11). His failure to eat and drink may be interpreted either as penitent fasting or as the effect of the vision's impact. In general the Acts accounts focus on the externals of the conversion, while Paul himself emphasizes the inward character of the experience. For him the conversion has two main elements: Christ appeared to him (I Corinthians 15:8); God called him to preach (Galatians 1:16).

9:10-19. *Acceptance into the Church.* The scene shifts to **Ananias**; the traditional site of his house can be visited in Damascus today. The parallel of this narrative is found in 22:12-16. There Luke records that Ananias was respected by the Jewish community. It must have been converted to Christianity out of that background. How Christianity came to Damascus is unknown, although Ananias may have been won to the church by the Hellenist mission (8:1; 11:19).

9:10-16. Just as **the Lord** has appeared to Paul on the road, so he speaks to Ananias **in a vision.** The vision instructs him to find Paul, who is residing on **the street called Straight**—a main east-west artery of ancient and modern Damascus. At this very time Paul is praying and seeing a vision which corresponds to that of Ananias (for similarly corresponding visions cf. chapter 10).

Ananias resists this instruction, recalling the persecution which Paul has promoted in Jerusalem and proposes here. **Saints** and those **who call upon thy name** are typical biblical terms for the Christians. Ananias' reluctance, which appears to be an affront to the risen Christ, serves to emphasize the greatness of Paul's conversion. In spite of his past he is to be **a chosen instrument** (literally "vessel"; cf. II Corinthians 4:7) to carry the Lord's name to **the Gentiles and kings and the sons of Israel**—a prediction which will be fulfilled later.

9:17-19. Ananias goes to the place Paul is staying and addresses him as **Brother.** He lays hands on him so that the power of God can return his sight and convey **the Holy Spirit** (cf. 8:17). The mention of **something like scales** falling from **his eyes** may be simply a symbolic way to describe the miracle. Though the sequence of events is not clear, receiving the Spirit seems to precede baptism. The suggestion that Paul has something to eat demonstrates the completeness of his recovery.

For Luke this episode incorporates Paul into the church and implicitly commissions him to mission (cf. 13:3). Paul says he made a trip to Arabia at this time (Galatians 1:17), but Luke does not mention it. Instead he represents the convert's eagerness to preach in Damascus. According to Paul himself the Gentile mission was of the essence of his conversion, and his commission to preach was not conferred through "flesh and blood" (Galatians 1:16).

9:19b-31. *From Damascus to Jerusalem.* Paul enters the **synagogues** of Damascus as a preacher instead of a persecutor. His message presents Jesus as **the Son of God**. This title is unique in Acts but typical of Paul. For Luke the title presents Jesus as the promised Messiah (cf. Luke 22:70), who stands in special relationship to God (cf. Luke 1:35). The **Jews** of the city can offer no answer to Paul's proof that Jesus is **the Christ**.

9:23-25. Paul's escape from Damascus is described also in II Corinthians 11:32-33. There "the governor under King Aretas" is identified as the one who is attempting to seize him. This ruler would be Aretas IV, who ruled Nabatea, an Arabian region southeast of Damascus and of Palestine, from 9 B.C. to A.D. 40. Just what authority he had in Syrian Damascus is not clear.

Luke presents the Jews as the stereotyped opponents of the gospel (cf. 13:50; 14:19). The description of Paul's escape **over** (literally "through") **the wall** is confirmed by his own account of his flight "through a window in the wall" (II Corinthians 11:33). The traditional window, a popular tourist attraction in Damacus has been constructed at a later time, yet windows are still visible in sections of the older wall nearby.

9:26-30. Paul's difficulty in joining the **disciples** in **Jerusalem** is not surprising. The account of Barnabas' mediation, however, is dramatic and possibly reflects knowledge of his later association with Paul. Here the disciples are distinguished from the **apostles**, but later (14:4, 14) that title is applied to them.

According to Paul's own account this visit occurred three years after his conversion (Galatians 1:18-23). Paul also swears that he saw only Cephas (Peter) and James the Lord's brother during this visit and that he "was still not known by sight to the churches of Christ in Judea." This is difficult to square with Luke's statement that **he went in and out among them . . . preaching boldly**. Apparently Luke is anxious to present Paul as filling the role of Stephen, who also **disputed against the Hellenists** (cf. 6:8-9). Paul's departure to **Tarsus** in Cilicia, his home town, is confirmed by his own reference to going to Syria and Cilicia (Galatians 1:21).

9:31. Again Luke summarizes the mission. He refers to the church **throughout all Judea and Galilee and Samaria** in the singular; the whole church is understood as a unity.

III. THE MISSION TO THE GENTILES (9:32–12:25)

A. THE MISSIONARY ACTIVITY OF PETER (9:32–11:18)

9:32-43. *To Lydda and Joppa.* Peter was last mentioned in 8:25. Thus his going **here and there among them all** may refer to his visit to Samaritan villages. His purpose is to confirm **the saints** who have been converted, probably by Philip's mission (8:40). At **Lydda**, a town some twenty-five miles northwest from Jerusalem in the coastal plain of **Sharon**, Peter heals **Aeneas**. As is typical of the miracle stories in Acts, the name of the patient and the duration of the illness are given.

9:34-35. The verb translated **make your bed** could also mean "spread your table." Either meaning would stress the completeness of the cure. The intention of this narrative is to present Peter in parallel to Jesus, in whose power the healing has been performed. The notion that **all the residents** of the region **turned to the Lord**—that is, were converted—is exaggerated. According to Luke's own understanding of the course of events no Gentiles were added to the church at this time.

9:36-42. The port of **Joppa** is on the Mediterranean some eleven miles beyond Lydda. **Tabitha** is an Aramaic name for which Luke gives the Greek equivalent, **Dorcas**; the English translation is "gazelle." The lady who bears this name seems to be one of the **widows** of the Joppan church. In later times widows were a special class in the church who directed programs of **charity**; the **tunics and other garments** are probably evidence of such a project. After her death the body of Dorcas is **washed** according to the ancient customs of purification.

The summoning of Peter by **two men** reflects Luke's fondness for two witnesses. The description of the miracle is reminiscent of I Kings 17:17-24 and II Kings 4:32-37. Peter's action is parallel to the raising of Jairus' daughter (Luke 8:49-56; cf. Mark 5:40). In both Lydda and Joppa conversion is accomplished by deed rather than word. God's action participates in the mission of the church.

9:43. Peter stays at Joppa with **Simon, a tanner**. The hosts of the missionaries are frequently mentioned by Luke. As a tanner Simon belongs to a profession despised by the Jews.

10:1–11:18. *To Cornelius.* It is often supposed that this material is out of place. Perhaps it belongs after Peter's escape from prison (12:19). A Roman garrison was not established in Caesarea until after the death of Herod Agrippa I (12:20-23).

The importance of this narrative for Luke cannot be overestimated. It describes the beginning of the Gentile mission and prepares for the Jerusalem conference of chapter 15. However, the historicity of the passage is debatable. If it is taken literally, the conduct of Peter described in Galatians 2:11-12 is difficult to explain, and the significance of Paul as leader of the Gentile mission (Galatians 2:7) is minimized. Apparently Luke has taken a simple conversion story and expanded it into a pivotal event. The many repetitions reflect the Semitic style of emphasis.

10:1-8. *Cornelius' Vision.* The city of **Caesarea** was the beautiful seaport rebuilt by Herod the Great in honor of Augustus. After Herod's death it became the official residence of the Roman governor. The ruins of a forum, an aqueduct, and a Greek theater, set on the edge of the azure Mediterranean, are still visible.

Cornelius is a common Roman name. The **Italian Cohort**, a detachment of troops containing theoretically six hundred or perhaps a thousand men, was stationed in Syria at a later time. Cornelius may be in Caesarea in retirement, as the reference to **his household** could indicate. However, he seems to have soldiers in his command. Luke views him as a "God-fearer"—that is, a Gentile who attended the synagogue, accepted Jewish monotheism and ethics, but did not convert to Judaism. His piety is demonstrated by generosity in giving **alms liberally to the people** (the Jews).

10:3-8. Like a pious Jew, Cornelius follows the prescribed hours of prayer. **The ninth hour** is 3 P.M. Vision at the time of prayer is not surprising and the **angel** is a typical mediator of revelation. The idea that Cornelius' prayers have **ascended as a memorial** is reminiscent of the meal offering described in Leviticus 2. A memorial **before God** means that God will remember this offering with action. Cornelius is told to send for **Simon . . . Peter**. The drama is heightened by the fact that nothing more is hinted concerning his identity (but cf. 11:14). Joppa is some thirty miles distant.

10:9-16. *Peter's Vision.* The **next day** after Cornelius has sent for him Peter is praying **on the housetop**. Palestinian houses were flatroofed with an outside stairway. Although noon (**the sixth hour**) is not one of the regular times of daily prayer, it is recommended by Psalm 55:17. Luke's purpose is to present Peter's hunger at lunchtime. While food is being prepared he falls **into a trance**—literally "a trance fell on him," indicating the initiative as God's. A trance, literally "ecstasy," is common at time of prayer and indicates readiness for divine revelation.

10:11-16. Various efforts have been made to discover psychological stimuli which aroused the vision. It has been suggested that Peter has been wrestling with the problem of Gentile mission, or that he has seen in the distance a sailboat suggesting the **sheet** of his vision. More likely we have a religious picture constructed out of Old Testament material. The **animals** of the sheet are reminiscent of the passengers of the ark, while Peter's protest is parallel to the words of Ezekiel 4:14.

A **voice**, which is later identified with the Spirit, commands Peter to eat unclean beasts (cf. Leviticus 11) because **God has cleansed** them. The message is repeated a third time for emphasis. It is evident that the point of the vision is not Gentile inclusion in the church but the question of ritual regulations concerning food.

10:17-35. *The Meeting with Cornelius.* As Peter is **pondering the vision** the men from Cornelius arrive. The coincidence of their arrival makes the meaning of the vision clear to the reader, although Peter does not discover it until verse 28. Now it is **the Spirit** that addresses the apostle and goes on to say, **I have sent them**; perhaps Luke identifies the Spirit as the risen Christ. In any case the Spirit informs Peter of the men who are seeking him.

10:22-23a. The visitors describe Cornelius and refer to his vision. Receiving Gentiles as **guests** might have been strange among orthodox Jews, but the Jews of the Diaspora were more liberal. Peter is already prepared for social intercourse with non-Jews.

10:23b-29. On the **next day** Peter goes with these emissaries to **Caesarea**, taking with him **brethren from Joppa** as witnesses; according to 11:12 there are six of them. Cornelius, though knowing nothing about Peter, collects his **kinsmen and close friends** in great expectation. The way is prepared for the household conversion of 11:14. The attempt of Cornelius to worship the apostle is a typical Lukan motif (cf. 14:15). The word **unlawful** which Peter uses of associating with Gentiles does not mean "contrary to the Mosaic law," but "improper" or "taboo." His reference to his vision clarifies its meaning, but a change has been made. In verse 15 it is things (animals) which are no longer unclean, while here no **man** is to be called **common or unclean**.

10:30-33. Cornelius recounts his visionary experience. **Four days ago** means three days by our way of reckoning. As the various references to time indicate (verses 9, 23, 24), Cornelius' speech falls on the fourth day. It is possible to interpret the phrase to suggest that he has been praying constantly since the vision occurred. His conclusion reaches a climax of expectation and focuses on the speech of Peter.

10:34-43. *Peter's Sermon.* In presenting the speech Luke employs Semitic style. It offers a summary of his understanding of early Christian preaching. The belief that **God shows no partiality** is also found in Romans 2:11. No notion of salvation apart from Christianity is implied in the statement that the righteous **in every nation** are **acceptable** to God. Instead the way is cleared for the Gentile mission.

10:36-38. The content of the gospel is **Jesus Christ**. That the associates of Cornelius really **know** this **word** seems unlikely. The comment that Jesus is **Lord of all** is perhaps an editorial addition by Luke. The expression is used in Hellenistic Judaism to extol the cosmic might of God, but here it suggests the universality of salvation through Christ.

The idea that the ministry of Jesus began after the **baptism of John** and progressed from Galilee to the Holy City reflects Lukan motifs (cf. Luke 23:5). The presentation of Jesus' ministry as the content of early Christian preaching is not frequent, but Luke understands his gospel as a commentary on this idea. Basic to it is the conviction that the ministry of Jesus resulted from his being **anointed . . . with the Holy Spirit** (cf. Luke 4:18).

10:39-43. The witness of the disciples is essential to the proclamation (cf. 1:21-22). They have observed the crucial events in the career of Jesus—his death and resurrection. Reference to **death by hanging him on a tree** is typically Lukan (cf. 5:30). In contrast to Mark's resurrection "after three days" (Mark 8:31) Luke describes the raising of Jesus as occurring **on the third day** (cf. Luke 9:22). The fact that disciples ate with the risen Christ (Luke 24:42-43) witnesses to the reality of his resurrection. His command **to preach** is being obeyed here, and this proclamation testifies to his position as **judge** of the future. Thus the risen Christ fulfills the role of the triumphant Son of man (Luke 22:69)—the eschatological judge, the vicegerent of God.

10:44-48. *The Gift of the Spirit.* Peter's speech results in the Spirit's falling **on all who heard.** This event is described as an interruption—in fact 11:15 asserts that it came at the very beginning of his remarks—but as usual (e.g. 2:37; 4:1) the sermon has been completed. The gift of the Spirit preceding baptism is unique (see above on 2:37-47). The usage here is a special sign to demonstrate God's acceptance of the Gentiles. Proof of this is seen in their **speaking in tongues**—an external display of the Spirit's presence (2:1-13). The companions of

Peter, who are Jewish Christians, express amazement that God's gift is conveyed to **Gentiles**. The experience of Cornelius and his household is generalized.

10:47-48. Baptism of course cannot be withheld from those who have received the Spirit. The Christian rite is understood, as in the experience of Jesus (Luke 3:21-22), to involve both water and Spirit. Peter does not perform the baptism himself, but is presented as the apostolic supervisor. The baptism is **in the name of Jesus Christ** rather than by the trinitarian formula of Matthew 28:19.

11:1-18. *The Report to Jerusalem.* Although Peter's report to Jerusalem is highly repetitious, it is completely clear only to the reader of chapter 10. The charge of the **circumcision party**—that he had eaten with **uncircumcised men**—is reminiscent of criticism leveled at Jesus (Luke 15:2).

11:4-17. Peter's response recounts his vision with minor variations (e.g. the addition of **beasts of prey**) and summarizes his trip to Caesarea and the events at Cornelius' house. The report that the angel told Cornelius that Peter would **declare . . . a message** of salvation differs from the original narrative (see above on 10:3-8). The reference to **the Holy Spirit** falling on Peter's hearers **at the beginning**—another variation—no doubt remembers Pentecost. In the gospels the promise **John baptized with water, but you shall be baptized with the Holy Spirit** is attributed, not to Jesus, but to John (Mark 1:8; Matthew 3:11; Luke 3:16); but Luke has already reported the same words as spoken by the risen Christ (1:5).

11:18. Peter's report silences all opposition. The audience gives glory to God, since **repentance unto life** has been **granted** to the **Gentiles**. This conclusion prepares for the Jerusalem council of chapter 15.

B. THE CHURCH AT ANTIOCH (11:19-30)

At **Antioch** the congregation includes both Jewish and Gentile Christians. The evangelization of the Gentiles is described unobtrusively in verse 20. Luke seems to be following another source here, which avoids the emphasis of the Cornelius story. Evidence for an earlier use of this source is seen in 8:4, where **those who were scattered because of the persecution** are mentioned. It may have had its origin in Antioch.

In Luke's mind the geographic expansion of Christianity is a slow process moving out from Jerusalem to Samaria, to the Palestinian cities of Joppa and Caesarea. Now it reaches a great center of Greek culture, Antioch on the Orontes. The third largest city of the empire, Antioch boasted a population of 800,000. It was a prominent commercial city, noted for its blatant paganism.

11:20-21. The **men of Cyprus and Cyrene** are not identified, although they may include those mentioned in 13:1. In 4:36 we have been told that Barnabas was a "native of Cyprus."

Some manuscripts read "Hellenists" rather than **Greeks** (cf. 6:1). It is clear, however, that the author is referring to Gentiles, since the action of the Cypriots and Cyrenians is in contrast to **speaking the word to none except Jews**. The content of their message is **the Lord Jesus**. The Greek idiom here, which is the same as in 5:42 may mean that they are preaching "Jesus as the Lord"—that is, the Lord of their lives in contrast to the lords of the Hellenistic cults. The title "Lord" is employed three times in the passage.

The notice that **the hand of the Lord was with them** is a typical Old Testament expression which recognizes divine assistance and support. The Jewish and Gentile converts apparently participate in the common life of the church, at least at this time, without incident (contrast Galatians 2:11-14).

11:22-26a. According to Luke, **Barnabas** is sent from Jerusalem to supervise the Antioch church. Thus he plays a role similar to that of Peter and John in Samaria (8:14-24). Elsewhere he is given the title "apostle" (14:14). The reader receives the impression that **Saul** (Paul) has dropped into obscurity, but not that a great amount of time has elapsed since 9:30 (contrast Galatians 2:1). Actually Paul has been busy in Syria, Cilicia, and

perhaps farther west promoting a mission similar to that in
Antioch (Galatians 1:21).

11:26b. The fact that **the disciples were . . . first . . . called
Christians** in Antioch has led to debate. The name appears in a
variety of forms in the manuscripts, but its ending is the familiar
Latin "-ian." This ending suggests that the name describes its
bearers as followers of Christ (taken as a proper name) or, in a
frequent variant, of Chrestus (a common Greek name meaning
"good" or "worthy"). It is not clear, however, whether the
Christians devised this name for themselves, or whether
outsiders—perhaps the people of Antioch or the police of
Rome—used it as a nickname.

11:27-30. Even more problematic is the sending of **relief** to
Jerusalem **by the hand of Barnabas and Saul**. Though famine
did occur in various parts of the empire during the reign of
Claudius (A.D. 41-54), the possibility of a **famine over all the
world** seems excluded by the text. Such a famine would affect
Antioch too.

Moreover a trip to Jerusalem by Paul is contradicted by his
own record. It is probable that the conference described in
chapter 15 is the same as that mentioned in Galatians 2. If so,
then Paul's attendance at the conference constitutes his second
(Galatians 1:18; 2:1), not his third (9:26; 11:30; 12:25; 15:4), visit
to Jerusalem after his conversion.

Among the many possible solutions two seem reasonable:

(1) The "famine visit" is a doublet with the "conference visit."

(2) The "famine visit" is a doublet with the "offering visit"
(21:15; cf. Romans 15:25).

Both solutions assume that Luke had more than one source for
the same event but misunderstood these as representing two
different events. The second solution is preferable since in 21:10
Agabus appears again as prophet.

The passage introduces two classes of church official. The
prophets were not ecclesiastical functionaries but charismatic
leaders—men moved by the Spirit (I Corinthians 12:28; 14:5-6).
Though associated with Jerusalem and Antioch (cf. 13:1) the
prophets were not restricted to a local church. The **elders**, on

the other hand, seem to have been local officials (cf. 14:23). They find their background in Judaism (cf. 4:5, 8) and may have been appointed by the apostles, as were the seven (6:3), to administrative duties.

C. PERSECUTION OF THE CHURCH (12:1-25)

12:1-19. *The Escape of Peter.* Chapter 12 is presented as an interlude between 11:30 and 12:25. Though Paul and Barnabas are supposed to be in Jerusalem during this time, no mention is made of them. Since the Jerusalem visit of 11:30 is possibly a doublet with the offering visit of 21:15 (see above on 11:27-30) it is likely that material has been misplaced. Perhaps Peter's departure **to another place** refers to his mission to Lydda, Joppa, and Caesarea (9:32-43).

12:1-5. Since the ruler of Palestine is anxious to please the Jews, his opposition to the church is to be expected. **Herod the king** is Agrippa I, grandson of Herod the Great. Reared in Rome, he was given the title "king" and the territory of Philip (cf. Luke 3:1) by Caligula in A.D. 37. By 44, under Claudius, he became the ruler of all Palestine. Herod's first victim was **James the brother of John**, the son of Zebedee, one of the twelve. It is sometimes supposed that his brother John was also martyred on this occasion (cf. Mark 10:39).

12:3-5. Peter's imprisonment and miraculous escape find a parallel in 5:18-23. Herod's intention to avoid drastic action during the feast is reminiscent of Mark 14:2. As in Jewish folk tradition, the **Passover** and **Unleavened Bread** are confused (cf. Luke 22:1).

A squad was normally composed of four soldiers—one for each of the watches of the night. The assignment of **four squads** to Peter implies four men for each watch, so that the magnitude of the miracle is emphasized. The term **earnest prayer** of the church is similar to that describing Jesus' prayer in Luke 22:44.

12:6-11. Because of the mention of seven steps in some manuscripts it is sometimes assumed that the place of Peter's confinement was the Tower of Antonia. The practice of chaining the prisoner to a guard is described in Roman literature. The appearance of the **angel** with accompanying **light** is a Lukan theme. The opening of doors by their **own accord** is a motif of Hellenistic legend.

Four guards, the whole squad, have apparently fallen asleep. The story has a strange mixture of realism (the waking of Peter, the conversation of the angel) and the miraculous (the falling **chains**, the idea of a **vision**).

12:12-16. According to later tradition **the house of Mary, the mother of John . . . Mark** is the place of the Last Supper and the headquarters of the Jerusalem church. Peter knows this as a gathering place of the Christians. He knocks **at the door of the gateway**, which is the door which opens from the street into the courtyard of the house. **Rhoda**—meaning "Rose," a typical name for slave girls—is the doorkeeper. While she is convinced by **Peter's voice**, those inside the house suppose her **mad** or believe that she has heard Peter's **angel**. This refers, not to the angel of the Lord which has accomplished his escape, but to Peter's guardian angel (cf. Tobit 5:21; Matthew 18:10). The picture of Peter continuing to knock at the gate is a dramatic feature of the story.

12:17. In contrast to chapters 1-5, **James** is now clearly the leader of the Jerusalem church. Perhaps he is so well known that Luke does not think to identify him as "the Lord's brother" (Galatians 1:19; cf. Mark 6:3). James is not present at this gathering. Perhaps he is worshiping at some other one of the Jerusalem household churches. Or he may be in hiding because of the persecution.

12:18-19. Herod is disturbed by Peter's escape. Though the Greek simply says that the **sentries** were "led away," **put to death** is probably an accurate translation. The guard, according to Roman law, was responsible for the life of his prisoner. Herod (or possibly Peter) goes to **Caesarea**, so that the events of the following verses occur there.

12:20-23. *The Death of Herod.* We are not told why Herod is **angry with . . . Tyre and Sidon** or what has persuaded **Blastus**

to intercede. The dependence of these Phoenician cities on Galilean grain goes back to Old Testament times.

12:21-23. Another account of Herod's death is found in Josephus' Antiquities of the Jews. There it is said that the occasion for his appearance in Caesarea was a celebration in honor of the emperor. Herod's **royal robes**, according to Josephus, were made "wholly of silver," and it was his appearance which led **the people** to acclaim him divine. The **angel** of retribution is a feature of Old Testament religion. Josephus says that the appearance of an owl, taken as an evil omen, signified Herod's death. Failure to give **glory** to God is understood as evidence of sinful pride. To be **eaten by worms** was a typical mode of death for tyrants (cf. II Macc. 9:9). Josephus says that Herod was stricken with a severe pain in the abdomen and died five days later.

12:24-25. *Growth of the Church.* These verses provide a summary. Luke evidently intends that verse 25 describe Paul and Barnabas' return from the famine visit (11:30). Actually the best manuscripts read **returned to Jerusalem**, implying still another trip to the Holy City. However, the term "return" suggests a coming back to Antioch, and the reference to bringing **John . . . Mark** implies the same.

IV. THE MISSION TO ASIA MINOR (13:1–15:35)

A. CYPRUS (13:1-12)

Here Luke presents the first of Paul's "three missionary journeys." Though the narrative may be based on adequate sources (possibly a travel itinerary) the concept of three journeys is largely Luke's construction. The first journey introduces problems which are to be solved at the Jerusalem conference in chapter 15. Antioch is understood as the instigator of this mission, since it is both the point of departure and the goal.

13:1-3. Paul and Barnabas are commissioned by **prophets and teachers** of the Antioch church. In contrast to 11:27, these prophets seem to function only in the local church. Except for Barnabas nothing is known of those listed. Efforts have been made to identify **Simeon . . . Niger** with Simon of Cyrene (Luke 23:26) and **Lucius of Cyrene** with Luke. The Greek word used of **Manaen** means literally "one reared with" the ruler but had come to be a conventional term for a **member of the court**. His patron **Herod the tetrarch** was Antipas, who governed Galilee during Jesus' ministry.

Actually Paul and Barnabas are **set apart** by **the Holy Spirit**, whose action has been awaited by **fasting and praying**. Luke seems to understand the laying on of hands as a kind of ordination (cf. 6:6), since the title "apostle" is applied to Paul and Barnabas only after this event (14:4). Paul refutes this idea in Galatians 1:1.

13:4-5. The departure for the mission is from **Seleucia**—the seaport of Antioch, some fifteen miles to the west. They sail to **Cyprus**, landing at **Salamis**, an important city on the eastern coast. According to Luke's pattern (13:14; 14:1) preaching begins in **the synagogues**. It is said that **John** Mark serves as an assistant or helper, but the nature of his service is not described.

13:6-10. The missionaries move across the island to **Paphos**, the provincial capital. The ruler of this province is **Sergius Paulus**, who is accurately described as **proconsul**.

Since **Elymas** cannot be a translation of **Bar-Jesus**, some have supposed that two different individuals, a Hellenistic **magician** and a **Jewish false prophet**, have been combined in the tradition. Others have attempted to show that some form of Elymas may be the Aramaic or Arabic equivalent of Bar-Jesus. Possibly it is simply a nickname. Paul's epithet **son of the devil** is the exact opposite of Bar-Jesus, which means "son of salvation."

The change from **Saul** to **Paul** at this point may indicate that as he moves west Paul increasingly employs the Roman version of his name. The appearance of the Roman Sergius Paulus in the narrative may provide the literary device for the introduction of the Roman name here.

13:11-12. The idea of **mist** falling on the magician is an expression as old as Homer, who used it to describe the darkness which covers a dying man's vision. The miracle of judgment convinces the proconsul that Christianity is superior to magic.

B. ANTIOCH OF PISIDIA (13:13-52)

13:13-15. *Arrival.* Leaving Cyprus, the missionaries sail to the southern coast of what is now Turkey. Though the coastal town of **Perga** is the first stop, **Paul and his company** (he is clearly the leader of the group) go immediately inland to Galatia. This may indicate a sudden change of plans, possibly supporting the notion that Paul went to Galatia for his health (cf. II Corinthians 12:7 and Galatians 4:13). **John** Mark's departure might also be explained by this decision to travel the difficult road to a more remote area. That Paul is displeased with John's defection is clear from 15:38.

13:14-15. The main city of the southern part of the province of Galatia was **Antioch of Pisidia.** Most scholars believe the churches founded in this area are those addressed by Paul in Galatians. The service of the **synagogue** included **reading of the law and the prophets**—the two most important sections of the Old Testament—followed by exposition. **The rulers of the synagogue** (cf. Mark 5:22) were responsible for the oversight of worship. Perhaps Paul's bearing marked him as a Pharisee, but any visiting teacher might be allowed to address the congregation.

13:16-41. *Paul's Sermon.* Like other speeches of Acts this sermon is largely the composition of Luke. It contains reminiscences of the speeches of Peter and Stephen. Though some hints of Pauline doctrine may be discovered (verse 39), the main elements of Paul's preaching as summarized in Romans are lacking. Luke understands this sermon as a model of the preaching which was offered to the Hellenistic synagogue. The normal pose of the Jewish speaker was sitting. Paul speaks like a Hellenistic rhetorician who stands and gestures. The sermon is addressed to Jews and "God-fearers" (see above on 10:1-8).

13:16-22. The main theme of this sermon is Jesus as the son of

49

David. Perhaps this is why the acts of Moses, emphasized in Stephen's speech (7:20-44), are ignored. The Exodus, accomplished by God's **uplifted arm**, is a type of the salvation granted through Jesus. Because of a variation of one letter in the manuscripts it is not certain whether the translation should say that God **bore with** or "cared for" (cf. Deuteronomy 1:31) Israel during the **forty years . . . in the wilderness**. The **seven nations . . . of Canaan** are listed in Deuteronomy 7:1.

After that (literally "these") appears to refer to **about four hundred and fifty years** and thus to indicate that this period elapsed between the occupation of the land and the judges. But more probably "that" is intended to point back to the occupation at the beginning of the four hundred and fifty years, in conformity with traditional Old Testament chronology (I Kings 6:1). The King James Version, which is based on the Western text of Acts, reads: "And after that he gave unto them judges about the space of four hundred and fifty years." As in Peter's speech (3:24), **Samuel** is the first of the prophets. **Saul**, whose reign according to Josephus was **forty years** (cf. I Samuel 13:1), was **removed** from the throne by God's rejection. God's word about **David** is a composite quotation based on Psalm 89:20, I Samuel 13:14, and Isaiah 44:28.

13:23-25. Fulfillment of the promises concerning the son of David (II Samuel 22:51; Psalm 132:11, 17) began in **John** the Baptist. His distinctive act was a **baptism of repentance**, but he denied any messianic pretensions for himself.

13:26-31. The concept of **salvation** is suggested by the name "Jesus." Israel's failure to recognize this one prophesied in the **sabbath** readings is another sign of her ignorance. As Pilate repeatedly said, Jesus did **nothing deserving death**. The actual crucifixion is not described here, and the cryptic reference to **the tree** (cf. 5:30 and 10:39) might not be clear to hearers unfamiliar with Luke's narrative. **Many days** and **those who came . . . from Galilee** are Lukan motifs. The speaker seems to distinguish himself from the **witnesses** of the Resurrection—a concept foreign to Paul (cf. I Corinthians 9:1 and 15:8).

13:32-41. The three texts cited in verses 33-35 are taken as proof that David's son was to be raised from the dead and that Jesus is the son of David, heir of the promises. Psalm 2:7 indicates that the son of David is actually the **Son** of God whose eternal nature and divine power is revealed in the Resurrection. Isaiah 55:3 and Psalm 16:10 are held together by the term **holy.** The former shows that the **blessings of David** are applied to his son, and the latter indicates that the son will **not . . . see corruption.** Since David's activity was confined to **his own generation,** since he **fell asleep** (died) and **saw corruption,** the promise cannot be fulfilled in him. Instead it is fulfilled in David's son, whom **God raised up,** who **saw no corruption**— Jesus Christ.

The idea that **forgiveness of sins is proclaimed** through him is typically Lukan. Verse 39 does contain superficial Pauline elements, although the depth of faith and the paradox of **the law** is lacking. A final warning to the anticipated opponents is sounded in verse 41 from Habakkuk 1:5—a text understood sometimes as referring to events of the last days.

13:42-52. *Turning to the Gentiles.* Paul's sermon creates a favorable response. According to some manuscripts it is the Gentiles who request a similar sermon for **the next sabbath.** Luke, however, is not anxious to introduce them into his narrative until verse 46.

The mention of **devout converts** is confusing, since the two terms describe different groups. The **devout** are the "God-fearers" (verses 16, 26), while the word translated **converts** is literally "proselytes." Perhaps Luke is describing the former in an imprecise way. **Paul** and **Barnabas,** who is now mentioned for the first time in the Antioch of Pisidia narrative, urge those who follow them from the meeting **to continue in the grace of God.** They are suggesting that these followers maintain a relationship with God wherein his favor and help are effective.

13:44-46. The description of **the next sabbath** is exaggerated. The synagogue could hardly accommodate **almost the whole city.** At first Jewish opposition comes from **jealousy,** but the fact that they contradicted Paul's message implies a dispute over doctrine. The word translated **reviled** means "blasphemed."

Luke may understand opposition to the **word** as blasphemy against God.

The idea that salvation was offered **first** to the Jews is both historical and true to the early Christian understanding of the drama of redemption (cf. Romans 1:16). The **turn to the Gentiles**, on the other hand, is basically a pattern constructed by Luke (cf. 18:6). That Paul, this late in his career, directed his mission for the first time to the Gentiles is at variance with both Acts 22:21 and Galatians 1:16.

13:47-52. The text cited to support this action is Isaiah 49:6. Originally the words were directed to the servant of the Lord, and in Luke 2:32 Simeon applies them to the child Jesus. Here they are addressed to the missionaries. The observation that some were **ordained to eternal life**—that is, life in the age to come—could imply a concept of predestination, but Luke's stress on their belief qualifies his determinism. **Shook off the dust from their feet** (cf. Luke 9:5; 10:11) symbolizes either scorn or disavowal of responsibility.

C. ICONIUM (14:1-7)

Iconium was an important commercial center located some eighty miles east of Antioch of Pisidia. Though its inhabitants considered themselves Phrygians, the city had been part of **Lycaonia** and now belonged to the Roman province of Galatia.

Luke presents only a generalized picture of the mission. The pattern of entering the synagogue first is repeated, although 13:46 would seem to contradict this. The word translated **together** can also mean that they carried on the mission "after the same manner" as in Antioch. That they **remained for a long time** is surprising in view of the action of **the unbelieving** (literally "disobedient") **Jews**.

14:3-7. Luke presents Paul and Barnabas as doing the **signs and wonders** attributed to the **apostles** (cf. 5:12). In fact he applies that title to them here and in verse 14. Since Luke normally thinks of the apostles as Jerusalem officials, it may be that his use of the term here depends on the source which underlies 14:14. Or possibly he is using the word in a general way, meaning "those who are sent." The proposal to **stone** the missionaries anticipates 14:19.

D. LYSTRA (14:8-18)

The missionaries flee to **Lystra**, twenty miles south. Formerly a part of Lycaonia, this city had been incorporated into the province of Galatia. The narrative of the mission does not follow the Jew-Gentile pattern, and its vividness of detail may suggest eyewitness sources. However, parallels to other sections of Acts betray the hand of Luke. The healing of the **cripple** is similar to Peter's cure of the man at the temple (3:2-10). Both had been lame **from birth**, the healer looked **intently** at them, and they **sprang up and walked**.

14:11-12. The effort to identify the apostles as gods in the **likeness of men** rests on a legend in which Zeus and Hermes once descended to this area. The notion that Paul refers to this incident in Galatians 4:14 is unconvincing. The identification of **Barnabas** as **Zeus** could suggest that something about his bearing suggests that he is leader of the mission. More likely stress is placed on **Paul** as **Hermes**, the patron of oratory, so that Paul can be presented as **the chief speaker**—an emphasis which provides the occasion for his sermon. The missionaries do not understand **Lycaonian**—a dialect employed in this region until the sixth century A.D. This allows time for the people to organize the **sacrifice**.

14:13-14. The Greek reads literally "Zeus before the city," but reference to the **temple** is probably intended. Unfortunately no archaeological efforts have been made at Lystra to recover this building at whose **gates sacrifice was to be made**. **Oxen** or bulls were typical victims of pagan sacrifice, symbolizing power and fertility. The **garlands** consisted of wool and sometimes flowers. Tearing of **garments** was the prescribed Jewish reaction to blasphemy (cf. Mark 14:63).

14:15-18. Paul's speech is a preview of his sermon in Athens (17:22-31). The protest that **we also are men** is reminiscent of 10:26. The word translated **of like nature**—literally "of like feelings"—reflects the pagan belief in the lack of feelings of the gods. Paul's answer to these pagan ideas is not philosophical argument but proclamation of Old Testament faith in God as creator. To **turn from these vain things to a living God** has a Pauline ring (cf. I Thessalonians 1:9). So does the reference to God's providential care as a **witness** to him (cf. Romans 1:20). More important is the Lukan emphasis on God's allowing **the nations to walk in their own ways** (cf. 17:30).

E. RETURN TO ANTIOCH (14:19-28)

14:19-20. The sudden change of the Lystrans, who have been **persuaded** by **Jews** from out of town, is difficult to explain. The stoning of Paul, however, is possibly supported by II Corinthians 11:25. Some manuscripts add that the companions of Paul stayed by him until evening, when he was revived. This would have made entry into the hostile town easier. In any case the persecution was unbelievably brief.

Derbe is some thirty miles to the southeast. The mention that they **preached the gospel** picks up the narrative of 14:7. The material about Lystra is perhaps from a separate source.

14:21-24. The **strengthening** of churches already established follows a Lukan pattern (cf. 9:32-43). It is possible that the material following 16:5 belongs here and that Paul goes on from this area to northern Galatia and the west.

At any rate the concept of **faith** expressed in this text (meaning "Christianity" or "orthodoxy") is not Pauline. The **kingdom of God** here refers to the realm which the faithful will enter after death (cf. Luke 23:42), and the idea that **tribulations** are a prerequisite is typically Lukan (cf. Luke 24:26). The term **elders** never appears in the authentic letters of Paul. Luke understands the church's organization as following the pattern of the synagogue (cf. Luke 7:3).

14:25-28. The city of **Attalia**, near **Perga**, was the principal port of the region of **Pamphylia**. From there the missionaries could sail directly to Syria. Why they did not return to strengthen the churches of Cyprus is not explained.

On returning to **Antioch** of Syria, Paul and Barnabas report on the mission, which is understood as the work of God. The reference to a **door** which has been **opened** reflects Pauline language (I Corinthians 16:9). The object of the mission has been the **Gentiles**, whose role in the church must now be decided.

F. THE CONFERENCE AT JERUSALEM (15:1-35)

The report of this conference contains some of the most problematic material of Acts. Two questions should be faced at the outset: What is the relation of this council to that described in Galatians 2:1-10? What was the topic discussed at the conference?

To the first question two major solutions have been proposed:

(1) That the meeting described in Galatians 2:1-10 occurred during Paul's visit to Jerusalem which Luke mentions in 11:30. This would mean that the conference Luke now describes took place after Galatians was written. It would also mean that the beginning of the controversy discussed here is seen in Galatians 2:11-14, and that the men who **came down from Judea** can be identified with the men "from James" (Galatians 2:12). This theory has been devised primarily to harmonize Acts and Galatians—a harmonizing which puts the conference of Galatians 2 too early in Paul's career.

(2) That verses 1-19 of this chapter and Galatians 2:1-10 represent different accounts of the same event. Antioch and Jerusalem are the places of conflict in both narratives. In both Paul and Barnabas go to Jerusalem for the discussion of the issues. This would mean that the dispute described in Galatians 2:11-14 occurred after the conference. Thus Luke's account in verses 20-29 represents a later attempt to settle this second dispute after Paul has left Jerusalem.

It is unlikely that the apostolic letter in verses 23-29 was composed with Paul's concurrence, since in 21:25 he is told of it as if for the first time. Also his treatment of the question of meat offered to idols in I Corinthians 8 shows no knowledge of it. The men from James in Galatians 2:12 are perhaps to be identified with the delegation which brings the "letter" to Antioch. This second theory is the more widely accepted.

The debate about the topic of discussion is best answered by Paul's own account (Galatians 2:1-10). There it is clear that the real question of the conference is circumcision or, better, the validity of the mission to the uncircumcised. The question of social intercourse between Jewish and Gentile Christians arises in Antioch later, after Peter and the men from James come from Jerusalem (Galatians 2:11-14). Though Luke's account here gives the impression that circumcision is the question, the settlement in verse 19 does not explicitly mention this issue. The concluding apostolic decree (verses 20-29) deals with the other question. Luke has confused the two issues earlier in his narrative (10:1–11:18).

The discrepancies in Acts are perhaps due to inadequate sources which have been misplaced, although theological motifs are apparent. The council is presented at the midpoint of the narrative. It symbolizes the movement from Jerusalem to the west. The apostles drop out of the story, and the Gentile mission is the central concern. The transition from Jewish to Gentile Christianity, however, occurs without conflict. The decision is made in Jerusalem, the source of the church's mission.

15:1-5. *The Controversy.* The **men . . . from Judea** are converts **who belonged to the party of the Pharisees.** Coming out of a legalistic background they believe **the law of Moses** must be obeyed by Christians. Their program in Antioch does not have authorization from Jerusalem (verse 24). Whereas verse 1 presents them as demanding circumcision for salvation, verse 5 might mean that it is a prerequisite for social participation in the Christian community. Those on whom they lay this requirement could include Titus (Galatians 2:3), who may be one of **the others** accompanying **Paul and Barnabas.**

15:2-5. Our text implies that Paul and Barnabas are **appointed** by the Antioch church, but some manuscripts suggest appointment by the men from Judea—an authority which Paul would not attribute to Jerusalem (Galatians 2:2). Luke understands the officials of Jerusalem as consisting of two groups: the **apostles**—that is, the twelve—and the **elders**, who exercise an authority parallel to that of the Jewish sanhedrin. The conversion of **Samaria** has been described in 8:4-25. Though no work in Tyre and Sidon has been recorded, a mission to **Phoenicia** is implied in 11:19.

15:6-21. *Discussion and Decision.* In Galatians 2:2 Paul implies both a larger and a private hearing. It is sometimes supposed that the meeting with the **apostles and the elders** refers to the private hearing while **the assembly** describes the larger audience. Though Luke may think of the conference as involving a plenary session of the whole church, the reference to **all** the assembly may mean only the total group of apostles and elders. In any case his narrative does suggest a presentation to the church (verse 4) and to a group of its leaders (verse 6).

15:7-11. Peter's role in the conference seems to conflict with the description of him in Galatians 2:7. God's **choice** in **the early days** refers to the conversion of Cornelius (10:1–11:18), and the gift of the **Holy Spirit** is reminiscent of 10:44 and 11:15. **God who knows the heart** is a Lukan expression associated with Peter in 1:24. The idea of **no distinction** is a reference to Peter's vision (10:15, 28). To **make trial of God**, an Old Testament expression, means to try God's patience after God's will has been revealed. Actually this latter part of the speech is more typical of Paul than of Peter. The **yoke** is reminiscent of Galatians 5:1-3, and the idea of salvation through **grace** is a typical Pauline theme.

15:12-18. Paul and Barnabas are presented in a passive role (contrast Galatians 2:2-10). They simply relate the events of their mission, notably **signs and wonders** which confirm God's participation.

The decision is rendered by **James** the Lord's brother, who has become the leader of the church. He supports the testimony of Peter and becomes a second witness to the validity of the

Gentile mission. James's speech has a Jewish quality. He speaks of Peter as **Simeon**, using the Semitic form of his name. In referring to the conversion of Cornelius he uses the Old Testament idea that God **visited** his people. However, his quotation from **the prophets** (Amos 9:11-12) uses the Septuagint; his argument is not supported by the Hebrew text. It seems unlikely that James himself, a Palestinian Jew, would use the Greek translation, particularly in a passage which misrepresents the original.

15:19-20. James's **judgment** embodies the authoritative conclusion of the church. That Jewish Christians **should not trouble** the Gentile converts refers to the yoke (verse 10) and implies that circumcision is not to be required. The requirements which are made (verse 20; cf. verse 29) constitute the "apostolic decree." It present two problems:

(1) What is its proper text? Some manuscripts omit **what is strangled** and add a negative form of the Golden Rule.

(2) What is its meaning? If we accept the best text, which includes the four prohibitions, the meaning is cultic. The decree contains ritual requirements regarding food (Leviticus 17). The **pollutions of idols** means meat which has been "sacrificed to idols" (verse 29; cf. I Corinthians 8). **Unchastity** describes immoral aspects of pagan worship. Eating **what is strangled** or contains **blood** is forbidden to Jews. The manuscripts which omit "what is strangled" and add the Golden Rule have attempted to change cultic requirements into ethical instructions.

15:21. The fact that the law **is read every sabbath** throughout the empire may be taken either to support the Gentile mission or to confirm the decree. In any case the result of the conference (in contrast to Galatians 2:6-10) is a compromise. Circumcision is not required for salvation, but Jewish ritual requirements are essential to fellowship.

15:22-29. *The Apostolic Letter.* The decision of the conference is put into the form of a letter. The device may be, after the style of Hellenistic historians, a composition of Luke. The emissaries who bring this letter **to Antioch** are **Judas . . . Barsabbas** (possibly some relation to Joseph Barsabbas, 1:23) and **Silas**, later to become a companion of Paul. Luke seems to identify Silas as a Roman citizen (16:37). New Testament letters prefer the Latin form of his name, Silvanus (I Thessalonians 1:1; II Corinthians 1:19; I Peter 5:12).

15:23-29. In sending the letter the Jerusalem leaders assume authority over a wide area. Actually it is addressed only to the Christians of **Syria and Cilicia**, but Paul delivers its decisions to the churches founded on his earlier mission (16:4), and James considers it directed to all Gentile Christians (21:25).

The letter denounces the Judaizers of verse 1 and commends its bearers as **men who have risked their lives** for the Lord's sake. The decision of the conference is said to have been moved by the **Holy Spirit**. On verse 29 see above on verses 19-20.

It is unlikely that Paul would have approved this letter or brought it to Antioch. If it is historical, it must have been composed after Paul and Barnabas left Jerusalem. This is hinted in the fact that James's speech makes no mention of them.

15:30-35. *Return to Antioch.* The Christians at Antioch rejoice at receiving the letter. Apparently they are happy that so few requirements are placed on them. Actually the decree would be a restriction of their previous practice (11:19-26). The seriousness of the dispute about table fellowship is obscured (cf. Galatians 2:11-14). **Judas and Silas** are now identified as **prophets**, whose essential task is exhortation. Since their being **sent** back to Jerusalem in verse 33 contradicts verse 40, there was added in some manuscripts a decision by Silas to remain in Antioch (verse 34; see the footnote in the Revised Standard Version).

V. THE MISSION TO GREEK LANDS (15:36–19:41)

A. RETURN TO ASIA MINOR (15:36–16:5)

15:36-40. Here begins the narrative of the "second missionary journey" (see above on 13:1-12). New territory is not reached until 16:6-7. In contrast to 13:2 Paul is presented as the instigator of the mission. The **sharp contention** between Paul and Barnabas is attributed to the defection of **John . . . Mark** in Pamphylia (13:13). More likely their dispute concerned the question of table fellowship with Gentile Christians (Galatians 2:13).

Barnabas is not mentioned again in Acts (but cf. I Corinthians 9:6), while Mark seems to have been restored to Paul's good favor (Philemon 24). With Mark, Barnabas sails to **Cyprus**—his native land, where both have worked. When last mentioned previously in the narrative Mark (13:13) and Silas (15:33) were in Jerusalem.

15:41–16:3. After passing **through Syria and Cilicia** (cf. 15:23) Paul and Silas revisit the churches of the previous mission (14:6-23). I Corinthians 4:17 implies that **Timothy** was a convert of Paul. Marriage with Gentiles was contrary to Jewish custom, but the offspring of such a marriage were accepted as Jews. Timothy's association with Paul is well attested in the letter, although the Pastoral Epistles addressed to him are probably not authentic Pauline letters.

That the circumcision of Timothy actually took place is questionable on three grounds:

(1) The Jerusalem conference decided not to require it.

(2) Paul refused to submit Titus to the requirement (Galatians 2:3).

(3) Paul was opposed to the demand of circumcision (Galatians 5:2-6).

Actually the issue is not circumcision as a prerequisite for church membership; Timothy apparently was a member already. Luke understands Paul's action according to the pattern of missionary activity. Since the missionaries go first to the synagogue (13:14) Timothy must be prepared for social relations with the Jews (cf. I Corinthians 9:20).

16:4-5. In contrast to what is historically probable (see above on 15:1-35) Paul informs the churches of Jerusalem's **decisions**—a term used for official decrees of the emperor.

B. The Call to Macedonia (16:6-10)

The mission moves west under the guidance of the **Holy Spirit**.

16:6a. The effort to determine Paul's route has resulted in the South and North Galatia theories. The South Galatia theory supposes that **the region of Phrygia and Galatia** refers to the Phrygian region of the province of Galatia—that is, to the area visited on the "first missionary journey." The North Galatia theory interprets the phrase as mentioning two regions, **Phrygia** and **Galatia**, thus meaning that after Paul passes through Phrygia he proceeds into North Galatia—the original Galatian region.

16:6b-8. The Roman province of **Asia** in New Testament times consisted of the entire western coast of Asia Minor. The hinterland extended to **Galatia** on the east and **Bithynia** on the northeast. The region of **Mysia** was the northern part of this province. In it was located the important port of **Troas**, some ten miles south of the site of ancient Troy. Apparently Luke, however, uses the name "Asia" to mean, not the whole province, but the territory around the capital city, Ephesus (see below on 18:19-21).

Thus Paul, being forbidden to preach around Ephesus, moves north toward Bithynia. Then, being forbidden again, he turns west to go through Mysia (**passing by** evidently means not preaching) to Troas. Is the **Spirit of Jesus** which prevents Paul's entrance into Bithynia to be understood as implying a vision of the risen Lord? Cf. 23:11.

16:9-10. It is sometimes supposed that the **man of Macedonia** is Luke himself, since a "we section" (see Introduction) begins in the next verse. Luke, however, understands this as a **vision** communicated to Paul in a dream (cf. 18:9).

C. Philippi (16:11-40)

16:11-15. *Conversion of Lydia.* From Troas, Paul and his company sail to **Neapolis** (modern Kavalla), stopping overnight on the island of **Samothrace**. To make this journey in two days required favorable winds. Taking the Via Egnatia (the Roman road to the west) they travel inland some nine miles to **Philippi**. Since Philippi was not **the leading city** of the province of **Macedonia** (see below on 17:1), perhaps the text should read: "Philippi, a city of the first district of Macedonia." Inhabitants of a **Roman colony** enjoyed self-government and the right of citizenship.

16:13-15. The word translated **place of prayer** is a synonym for "synagogue." However, just west of the Roman arch which may mark the pomerium—the area around the city from which foreign cults were excluded—the river makes a bend providing a small natural amphitheater.

Since Paul makes no mention of **Lydia** in Philippians her name may be a title; **Thyatira** was a city of the region of Lydia noted for its industry of **purple** cloth. Lydia has been a "God-fearer" (see above on 10:2), and **the Lord opened her heart** to receive the gospel. Her conversion involves the baptism of her relatives and slaves, since the decision of the master is valid for the whole **household**. The church which resulted from this conversion maintained good relations with Paul (Philippians 1:3-5 and 4:10, 15-16).

16:16-18. *An Exorcism.* Again the church encounters sorcery (cf. 8:9 and 13:6). That Paul could perform signs and wonders is known by his own writing (II Corinthians 12:12; Romans 15:19). The **spirit of divination** which the **slave girl** possesses is literally "a python spirit"—a term which originated in the legend of Apollo's slaying the dragon at Delphi. It was later applied to ventriloquism and soothsaying in general. To her **owners** she brings economic **gain**.

The demon's recognition of the **servants of the Most High God** is reminiscent of the exorcisms of Jesus (cf. Luke 8:28). Paul, who seems to act without interest in the girl, is not portrayed in his best light. A miracle performed **in the name of Jesus Christ** is a familiar theme.

16:19-34. *Imprisonment and Escape.* Paul and Silas are **dragged . . . into the market place**—an action implying a sizable group of opponents. **Rulers** and **magistrates** are apparently two terms used to describe the same leaders. The latter means "praetor"—a title higher than the officials in Philippi deserved, though it appears in inscriptions.

The agora of a Greek city, like a Roman forum, was both **market place** and judicial center. The ruins of the agora at Philippi include a platform used for public speeches and trials. The missionaries are charged with being **Jews** who have disturbed the **city**. Since Judaism was a tolerated religion under Roman law, a charge against Jews would have to be based on an illegal attempt to make converts. Perhaps Luke wants to show that the charges are utterly false. The missionaries are not Jews and have done nothing contrary to Roman custom.

16:22-24. The victims are stripped as a preparation to beat them with rods. Paul's suffering at Philippi is attested by I Thessalonians 2:2 (cf. Philippians 1:30). The **jailer** is probably the warden of the prison, holding perhaps the rank of centurion. The **inner prison** may have been underground; the traditional site can be visited today. The description of **feet** being put in **stocks** (literally "wood") and the other extreme security measures serve to enhance the miracle of escape.

16:25-26. There are evidences that legendary material has been inserted into the story of the escape:

(1) The narrative of verses 35-40 proceeds as if the **earthquake** and escape have never happened.

(2) The other **prisoners** apparently do not escape and are ignored by the jailer.

(3) The account has parallels to the escape of Peter (12:6-11).

(4) Typical details of Hellenistic escape legends (the automatic opening of **doors**, the **singing** of the prisoners) are included.

16:27-31. The jailer's attempt on his own life is an effort to avoid humiliating judgment by his superiors (cf. 12:19). His question, which historically would be no more than a call for help, becomes the cry of one ready to obey the gospel: **What must I do to be saved?** The answer is a simple confession of the Pauline faith (Romans 10:9). The prediction in verse 17 that Paul and Silas **proclaim . . . the way of salvation** is fulfilled. The call for **lights** may be symbolic.

16:32-34. Apparently the jailer takes the prisoners to his **house** for further preaching of the gospel. Then the whole group goes to a place where the **wounds** can be **washed** and the entire **family** can be **baptized** (cf. verse 15). The setting of food before Paul and Silas is probably not a reference to the Lord's Supper but an act of kindness like the washing of their wounds. Two late manuscripts give the name of the jailer as Stephanas (cf. I Corinthians 1:16).

16:35-40. *Apology of the Magistrates.* The **magistrates** send **police** to release the prisoners. The police are "lictors" (literally "rod bearers")—men who carry the fasces (an ax bound with rods), which symbolizes their power to execute judgments of the magistrates. Paul is told of his release by the jailer, who employs the biblical admonition **Go in peace.** Paul is incensed, insisting that officials who have **beaten . . . publicly . . . Roman citizens** must **come themselves** and release them. His charge that they are **uncondemned** probably means that they have been condemned without adequate investigation.

16:38-40. Since Roman citizens were exempt from scourging, the **magistrates** fear repercussions, perhaps removal from office. Perhaps Paul had no opportunity to reveal his citizenship earlier (cf. 22:24-25), or possibly Luke has saved this revelation for the climax of his story. Paul is casual about leaving, stopping to visit the church which meets at the house of **Lydia.**

D. THESSALONICA (17:1-9)

17:1. Paul and his companions travel west to **Thessalonica** by way of the Via Egnatia through **Amphipolis** and **Apollonia.** The total trip is over 100 miles. Thessalonica is the most important city of Macedonia. Although the seat of the Roman provincial government, it had become a free city with its own administration.

17:2-4. According to Luke's scheme, the mission begins in the **synagogue.** A period of more than **three weeks** (literally "three sabbaths") is suggested by Paul's claim that he worked in the city to support his mission (I Thessalonians 2:9) and that he received two offerings from Philippi while there (Philippians 4:16).

The theme of the preaching is Lukan. **The scriptures** are used to prove that **the Christ** must **suffer**; since **Jesus** suffered, he must be the Christ. In I Thessalonians 1:5 and 2:8, 13 Paul describes his message as the powerful word of God. The letter also indicates that the majority of converts were from paganism (I Thessalonians 1:9). This is supported by Luke's reference to **devout Greeks** (God-fearers; see above on 10:1-8) and **leading women** (cf. verse 12), implying a mission beyond the synagogue.

17:5. Opposition to the mission is confirmed by I Thessalonians 1:6 and 2:14, although the latter identifies the opponents as "your own countrymen." Luke's picture of the **Jews** as **jealous** may reflect their view of the God-fearers as potential proselytes. **Rabble** from the market place are enlisted to stir up the city; opposition to the church is from the disreputable, not the law-abiding. Apparently the missionaries are staying at the house of **Jason** who is at least sympathetic to the Christian cause.

17:6-9. Jason and **some of the brethren** (Christians) are **dragged** before the **city authorities** (literally "politarchs"—a title used exclusively in Thessalonica). The charge is ironic. The rabble rousers have the audacity to accuse the Christians of disturbing the order, of having **turned the world upside down**. Jason is charged with guilt by association, while the Christians are thought to be guilty of insurrection. Taking **security** means demanding bond—a fee which will be forfeited if the Christians cause difficulty again.

E. BEROEA (17:10-15)

17:10-12. With a measure of secrecy the Christians send Paul and Silas to **Beroea**, about fifty miles southwest of Thessalonica. In that day it was an important city, and the success of Paul's mission is shown by the presence of Sopater of Beroea among his companions in 20:4. The mission begins as usual in the

synagogue, but the Jews are **more noble** (a term which can refer either to status or to character) than those of Thessalonica. They accept **the word with all eagerness**, studying the Old Testament to see if Paul's claims are valid. Again **Greek women** of high position (or character) are converted in large numbers.

17:13-15. As at Thessalonica, converts among prominent people cannot prevent opposition to the church. Jews come from Thessalonica to stir up **the crowds**, so that Paul is again hurried out of town. Most manuscripts seem to assume a route to **Athens** by **sea**. The **command** for Silas and Timothy (mentioned for the first time since 16:3) to **come to him as soon as possible** appears to be answered in 18:5 with the arrival of Silas and Timothy in Corinth. However, Paul himself (I Thessalonians 3:1-6) implies that Timothy hás accompanied him to Athens, returned to Macedonia, and rejoined him before the writing of I Thessalonians.

F. ATHENS (17:16-34)

17:16-18. No longer of political importance in New Testament times (Corinth was the capital of the province of Achaia), **Athens** remained an intellectual center. Paul is **provoked** into mission by the city's paganism. He begins in the **synagogue**, where he encounters **Jews** and God-fearers (see above on 10:1-8). The agora, or **market place**, is located northwest of the Acropolis. The **Epicurean and Stoic philosophers** represent the two leading philosophical schools of the day. Some of their views may be expressed in Paul's speech.

Babbler is literally "seed picker" and was used to describe birds. Perhaps Paul is viewed as an intellectual scavenger. The assumption that he is preaching **foreign divinities** could result from his proclamation of **Jesus and the resurrection**. The Greek word for "resurrection" is *anastasis,* which Paul's hearers may have construed as the name of a goddess. More likely, however, Luke's use of these terms sounds the major theme of Paul's sermon (cf. verse 31).

17:19-21. The identification of the **Areopagus** is debated. There are two theories:

(1) It is the hill of the god Ares—Mars Hill—a knoll west of the Acropolis.

(2) It is a court which originally met on the hill but in Paul's time may have met in a building of the agora. This view is supported by the information that Paul stood **in the middle of** it (verse 22) and that he **went out from among them** (verse 33). Apparently this court supervised educational policies, possibly investigating the credentials of foreign lecturers. Luke's notion that the Athenians were always anxious to hear **something new** is confirmed by Hellenistic authors.

17:22-31. Much discussion has raged about Paul's sermon. Two questions call for consideration:

(1) What is the relation of this sermon to the preaching of Paul? Though there may be points of contact with Romans 1–2, the main elements of Pauline theology are lacking. Probably the speech is a composition of the author of Acts, expressing his understanding of Christian preaching to pagans.

(2) What is the religious background of the speech? While some features of Hellenistic philosophy are found in the sermon, its main background seems to be Hellenistic Judaism. The speech is a Christian adaptation (verses 30-31) of the typical missionary preaching of the Hellenistic Jews.

17:22b-23. The reference to the Athenians as **very religious** is probably intended in a positive sense, although the term can mean "superstitious." While no inscription reading **To an unknown god** has been discovered, inscriptions which mention unknown gods have been unearthed in the vicinity of Athens. Perhaps Luke has modified the reference so as to give a monotheistic basis for Paul's proclamation of the unknown God. The theme of the sermon seems to be: knowledge of the one God, Creator of all, demands the Christian faith.

17:24-29. Such a God **does not live in shrines made by man** and does not need the service of **human hands**. He has created all **men from one** (some manuscripts add "blood")—that is, from Adam—so that a universal revelation is implied. The idea of

allotted periods and **boundaries** reflects apocalyptic motifs and shows that the Creator is also ruler of history. The belief that all **seek** this God, feeling or groping **after him**, is Stoic. That all persons find their being in God—**in him we live and move and have our being**—may reflect a Hellenistic poem, although the idea is not lacking in Judaism. **For we are indeed his offspring** is a quotation from Aratus, a Cilician, born about 310 B.C. The speech employs these themes to disqualify pagan religion, specifically its idolatry. Since people are offspring of a living God, it is folly to suppose **the Deity is like gold, or silver, or stone**, shaped by human hands.

17:30-31. The specifically Christian material is now introduced. It makes the point that the unknown God, who is creator of heaven and earth, is revealed in Jesus Christ. The idea that **ignorance** is **overlooked** by God is a Lukan theme found also in Paul (Romans 3:25). The call to **repent** is typical of early Christian preaching. The idea of judgment through a **man** may represent the Son of man Christology of the gospels (cf. Luke 22:69).

17:32-34. In any case the **resurrection** is the main theme of the message. That resurrection is not to be identified with the Greek doctrine of immortality is seen in the reaction of the audience, although any concept of life after death was rejected by the Epicureans.

While Paul suffers no persecution in Athens, he founds no church. **Dionysius the Areopagite** becomes a fanciful figure in later tradition. About **Damaris** nothing is known. Paul's assertion that "the household of Stephanas were the first converts of Achaia" (I Corinthians 16:15) seems to deny any result in Athens.

G. CORINTH (18:1-17)

18:1-4. Located on the isthmus between northern Greece and the Peloponnesus, **Corinth** was a busy commercial center. It had imported a host of pagan cults and was noted for immorality. There Paul met **Aquila** and **Priscilla**, recently driven from **Rome**

by the Emperor **Claudius'** decree (mentioned by the historian Suetonius). While Paul makes several references to supporting himself by his work, Luke is the first to identify his **trade**. Some scholars maintain that the word for **tentmakers** in New Testament times had come to mean "leather workers."

Since Paul makes no mention of their conversion, Aquila and Prisca, as he calls her (I Corinthians 16:19), were probably Christians when he met them. Later they travel with him to Ephesus, perhaps returning eventually to Rome (Romans 16:3). The **synagogue** may have been near the gateway into the Corinthian agora, where an inscription has been found reading "Synagogue of the Hebrews."

18:5-6. The arrival of **Silas and Timothy** seems to allow Paul to concentrate on **preaching**. Perhaps they bring a financial contribution (cf. II Corinthians 11:9) which alleviates the burden of self-support. Paul's message, **that the Christ was Jesus**, represents Luke's typical understanding of early Christian preaching to **Jews**.

Since Paul has already turned to the Gentiles (13:46) and since he will return to the synagogue in Ephesus (18:19), Luke seems to see this turning take place at every point of the mission. It illustrates the movement of the history of salvation from the Jews to the Gentiles. Here the rejection of the Jews is graphically portrayed. Shaking out **his garments** is reminiscent of 13:51; it symbolizes casting guilt on those who reject Jesus. The idea of **blood . . . upon your heads** is an Old Testament expression (II Samuel 1:16; cf. Matthew 27:25).

18:7. Some manuscripts suggest that when Paul moves to the house of **Titus Justus** he leaves the shop of Aquila. The reading "Titus" in some manuscripts is probably an error. Paul's host can hardly be identified with the Titus of the Pauline letters (Galatians 2:1; II Corinthians 2:13).

18:8-10. Among Paul's **many** converts is **Crispus, the ruler of the synagogue** (cf. 13:15), who **with all his household** (cf. 16:15) is **baptized** by Paul. Paul's **vision** portends trouble **in this city**. He should **not be afraid**, a typical admonition of ancient visions, since God guides the mission.

18:11. Paul's **year and six months** in Corinth can be dated with some accuracy. According to an inscription **Gallio** became governor of Achaia in A.D. 51 or 52. If Paul's appearance before him occurred at the end of the apostle's stay in Corinth, the mission must have begun in 50 or 51.

18:12-17. Luke accurately identifies **Gallio** as the **proconsul of Achaia**. He was the brother of the philosopher Seneca. The **tribunal** (literally "step"; cf. English "bench") was probably a large marble platform which has been excavated in the center of the agora at Corinth.

Though the charge may suggest that Paul has violated either Roman or Jewish law (cf. Gallio's response in verse 15) Luke probably intends to suggest simply that the Christians are disturbing the order. However, the proconsul declares that the Christians are guilty of no **wrongdoing or vicious crime. Sosthenes** has been understood by some as a Jew (**ruler of the synagogue**) beaten by the crowd. Others see him as a convert to Christianity (cf. I Corinthians 1:1) beaten by the Jews.

H. EPHESUS (18:18–19:41)

18:18-23. *A Trip to the East.* Paul leaves Corinth casually (cf. 16:40) and sails **for Syria**. Perhaps Luke continues to view **Antioch** as Paul's missionary base. That **Priscilla and Aquila** cross the Aegean and found a household church at Ephesus is confirmed by I Corinthians 16:19. Apparently Paul (not Aquila) has made a Nazirite **vow**, which normally was terminated by shaving the head (Numbers 6:5, 18). At **Cenchreae**, the eastern port of Corinth, a suburban church had been established (cf. Romans 16:1).

18:19-21. An important port at the terminus of trade route from the East, **Ephesus** was the capital of the Roman province of Asia (see above on 16:6*b*-8). The temple of Artemis, one of the seven wonders of the world, had been built outside its walls (see below on 19:26-27). Paul's preaching in **the synagogue** probably represents an effort to present the apostle as founder of the Ephesian church (cf. 18:27).

18:22-23. After landing **at Caesarea**, Paul goes up and greets **the church**. The terminology implies a visit to Jerusalem. Since no mention of this visit is made in the Pauline letters two theories have been devised:

(1) It is a doublet with the conference visit (15:1-35; see comment). Paul (Galatians 2:1) seems to date the conference later in his career than Luke places it, and parallels can be found in 16:6 and 18:23.

(2) It is a doublet with the collection visit (chapter 21). Both are made via Caesarea (21:8), involve a vow (21:23), and predict danger in the city (18:21; 21:14).

18:24-28. *The Mission of Apollos.* The activity of **Apollos** is the only non-Pauline mission described in Acts 16–28. He is said to be an **eloquent** (or learned) man, **well versed** in the Old Testament. Perhaps he is steeped in the philosophy of **Alexandria**. Luke views him as a Christian whose understanding of the faith is incomplete. He is familiar with the life and teachings of **Jesus** but knows **only the baptism of John**—a baptism which does not convey the Spirit (19:1-7). After instruction from **Priscilla and Aquila**, Apollos preaches Jesus as the Messiah—a message identical with Paul's.

18:27-28. Apollos' mission to **Achaia** is supported by a letter of recommendation from the Ephesian church (cf. II Corinthians 3:1-3). His presence in Corinth is attested by I Corinthians 1–4. Though Luke records no meeting of Paul and Apollos, their personal contact is affirmed by I Corinthians 16:12.

19:1-7. *Paul and the Disciples of John.* Paul returns to **Ephesus** by way of **the upper country**. This means he went overland through the interior of Asia Minor, the **region of Galatia and Phrygia** (18:23). Though Luke's account of Paul's Ephesian ministry is detailed, events known from the letters are lacking. For example, Paul's difficult relation with the Corinthians involved a hasty trip to Corinth (II Corinthians 12:14; 13:1) and the writing of three letters (I Corinthians 5:9; II Corinthians 7:8). Luke nowhere mentions Paul's literary activity. The apostle had various difficulties in Ephesus (II

Corinthians 1:8). Some have claimed that he was thrown into the arena (I Corinthians 15:32) or imprisoned.

19:1b-7. Paul encounters **disciples** who have not received the **Holy Spirit**. Luke assumes that these **twelve** are Christians who, like Apollos (18:26), need fuller instruction. However, Christians who **have never even heard that there is a Holy Spirit** would be very strange. These are more likely members of a sect of John the Baptist. Paul characterizes John's baptism as a ritual of **repentance** (cf. Luke 3:3). He interprets John's message as proclaiming the coming one (cf. Luke 3:16).

These disciples are rebaptized **in the name of . . . Jesus** and after the laying on of **hands** receive the Spirit. Luke sees them as similar to the converts of Samaria (cf. 8:14-17) and attributes to Paul the apostolic power to convey the Spirit. Proof of its presence is their speaking in **tongues** (cf. 2:4; 10:46) and prophesying—manifestations of the Spirit which the author considers identical (cf. 2:17).

19:8-22. *Preaching the Word and Acts of Power.* Again Paul preaches in the **synagogue.** In Acts **the kingdom of God** seems similar to the church (cf. 8:12), but the idea that God's rule will be consummated in the future is not lacking (cf. 14:22). Paul's withdrawal from the Jews fits the Lukan pattern.

The **hall** (or school) **of Tyrannus** is a lecture room rented to visiting philosophers. Tyrannus could be either a philosopher who used the hall or its owner. According to some manuscripts Paul preaches from 11 A.M. to 4 P.M.—the time of leisure when an audience is available. The **two years** are in addition to the **three months** in the synagogue (cf. 20:31). The reference to **all the residents of Asia** is an exaggeration, but Luke may be suggesting a mission into other cities.

19:11-13. Paul's encounter with the Jewish **exorcists** is probably legendary. The story has parallels to the miracles of Peter (5:12-16). Paul's power to perform signs and wonders is claimed in his own writings (Romans 15:18-19; II Corinthians 12:12). However, the notion that **handkerchiefs or aprons** carried a healing power which exuded from Paul's **body** (literally "skin") borders on magic.

The existence of Jewish exorcists is attested by the appearance of Semitic names in Greek magical texts which have been discovered, and the incantation "I adjure you by Jesus the God of the Hebrews" is also found in this literature.

19:14-20. The story of the **seven sons of . . . Sceva** is humorous. Actually no **Jewish high priest** with this name is known; perhaps these men are impostors. **Seven** heightens the miraculous—one person possessed with a demon can overcome seven men. The demon's response, **Jesus I know, and Paul I know; but who are you?** indicates that the name of Jesus is powerful but dangerous. Only those who have accepted the name dare use it. This point of view is not entirely consistent with the words of Jesus (Luke 9:49-50).

News of this bizarre incident brings about conversions among the magicians. **Divulging their practices** may mean that they reveal their secret spells and incantations. The **books** (scrolls) which are **burned** probably record their charms and spells. Ephesus was famous for magical writings, some of which were called "Ephesian scripts." A precedent for burning unfavorable books had been established by Augustus. The total value of the literature is said to be **fifty thousand pieces of silver**—presumably drachmas.

19:21-22. Paul's travel plans are disclosed in what is almost an outline of the rest of the book. His trip to **Macedonia and Achaia** takes place in 20:1-2 and his journey to Jerusalem in 21:17. The purpose of the latter is to take an offering to the Jerusalem church (Romans 15:22-29), but this is barely mentioned by Luke (24:17). **Rome** is the goal of his entire book (28:14).

The travels of **Timothy** are confirmed by I Corinthians 4:17 and 16:10. **Erastus** may be the same man mentioned in Romans 16:23. No mention is made of Titus, who figured prominently in Paul's mission at this time (II Corinthians 2:12-13; 7:6; 8:16-24).

19:23-41. *Conflict with Paganism.* This narrative is full of local color. It rests on accurate information. **Demetrius** is presented as **a silversmith, who made silver shrines of Artemis.** An inscription has been found which refers to a certain Demetrius as a "temple maker," which was one of the officials of the

Artemision, the ruling body of the temple. No silver **shrines**, presumably replicas of the temple, have been found at Ephesus, but small souvenir temples used as amulets have been discovered elsewhere. Possibly, however, Demetrius makes miniature images of the goddess. **Artemis**, while bearing the name of the Greek virgin huntress, is actually a form of the Asian "Great Mother"—a fertility deity widely worshiped in this section of the empire.

19:26-27. Christianity challenges pagan business practices—a fact confirmed by Pliny's letter to the Emperor Trajan (A.D. 112). Demetrius' charge that **Paul has persuaded** many **people** would be understood by the Christian reader as proof of the mission's power. Luke certainly believed that Paul attacked idolatry (cf. 17:29), but no pagan believed that **gods made with hands** were really **gods**.

The **temple of . . . Artemis** was the sign of Ephesus' greatness (see above on 18:19-21). About 340 by 160 feet in dimension, it displayed over 100 columns some 60 feet high. Its marble blocks, according to some reports, were cemented together by gold instead of mortar.

19:28-34. The cry of the rioting populace, **Great is Artemis of the Ephesians**, has been found in inscriptions. Ruins of the **theater** where they gathered are still clearly visible to the modern traveler. On Paul's **companions** who are dragged into the **confusion** see below on 20:4.

Paul is prevented from entering the theater by **friends** who are among the most prominent people of the province—the **Asiarchs**. Although their exact function is not known, these wealthy officials of Asia were patrons of public events and supervisors of religious festivals. The role of **Alexander** is not clear. He may be a Jew who hopes to distinguish his people from the Christians, or he may be a convert who is attempting to defend Paul. According to the Pastoral Epistles a certain "Alexander the coppersmith" is an opponent of the apostle (II Timothy 4:14; I Timothy 1:20).

19:35. The **town clerk** is the executive officer of the civic assembly—the governing body of this free city. His speech is a composition of Luke. The title **temple keeper** (literally "temple sweeper") was given to cities which were centers of emperor worship. Inscriptions have been discovered which show that Ephesus was noted both for this honor and also as the temple keeper of Artemis. The reference to **the sacred stone that fell from the sky** is obscure. Perhaps the temple contained an image which was supposed to have had a supernatural origin, or possibly the statue of the goddess had been a meteorite. Images of Artemis, standing with high crown and upper body covered with breasts, have been found at Ephesus.

19:36-41. The main point of the speech is that Paul and his companions are guilty of no civil offense. They are not **sacrilegious** or **blasphemers** of the goddess. If Demetrius and the members of his guild have valid charges, let them follow legal procedure (cf. 24:19). Ephesus, as a provincial capital, is the seat of the proconsul and his court. **The courts are open** on stated days. If this is not satisfactory they can appear before one of the three **regular** monthly meetings of the municipal **assembly**. The real **danger** (cf. verse 27) is that the citizens could be charged with rioting—a crime not tolerated by the Romans. Charges against the Christians are made by a riotous mob, but legal process would vindicate them.

VI. THE JOURNEY TO ROME (20:1–28:31)

A. RETURN TO JERUSALEM (20:1–21:14)

20:1-6. *A Visit to Greece.* Paul's trip to **Macedonia** and **Greece** fulfills the plans of 19:21 (cf. I Corinthians 16:5). His route is via Troas (II Corinthians 2:12-13) to Philippi (II Corinthians 7:5-7) and through Macedonia to Corinth. During his stay of **three months** in Achaia he writes Romans.

Paul's original plan seems to have been to sail from Corinth directly to Palestine to take the collection from his churches to Jerusalem (see above on 19:21-22). Since Macedonia and Achaia have already made their contribution (Romans 15:25-26) a trip

75

through these provinces is not needed. The nature of the **plot** against Paul is not explained; perhaps the large amount of money offered a temptation. Luke seems to assume that the representatives of the churches have gathered at Corinth. But it is possible that Paul changes his plans because of difficulties involved in the collection (cf. I Corinthians 16:1-5; II Corinthians 8–9) and that he gathers the delegation on the way to the east.

20:4. Seven representatives are named; no delegation from either Corinth or Philippi is mentioned. Some have wanted to identify **Sopater** with Sosipater of Romans 16:21, but there is no evidence for a connection. **Aristarchus** appears also in 19:29; 27:2; Colossians 4:10; and Philemon 24.

How is **Gaius of Derbe** in Galatia to be reconciled with "Gaius and Aristachus, Macedonians" in 19:29? Possible solutions are:

(1) Two different men are intended (cf. others of this name in Romans 16:23; I Corinthians 1:14; III John 1).

(2) **Of Derbe** (literally "Derbean") is the identifying surname of a Macedonian who came originally from Derbe.

(3) **Of Derbe** is a scribal error for "of Doberus," a town near Philippi.

(4) **Gaius** belongs with **the Thessalonians**, while **of Derbe** goes with **Timothy** (cf. 16:1).

(5) A whole line of text has been lost between **Gaius** and **of Derbe**, reading "and of the Galatians" followed by one or more names, the last being a Derbean.

Probably only **Tychicus** (cf. Colossians 4:7) and **Trophimus** (cf. 21:29; II Timothy 4:20) wait for Paul **at Troas**. Either this is the place where they join the group or they have been sent ahead to make travel arrangements.

20:5-6. Here another "we section" begins (see Introduction). Since this usage appeared last in **Philippi** (16:16-17) it is possible that the writer of the "we" source joined the company again at that place. The celebration of **the days of Unleavened Bread** at Philippi is not explained. Is this some early form of an Easter service, or are the Christians observing Jewish ritual? (cf. verse 16). At this season sailing conditions are not good. The trip from

Neapolis to Troas takes **five days** instead of the two days described in 16:11.

20:7-12. *Preaching in Troas.* At Troas (see above on 16:6*b*-8) Paul participates in the weekly worship of the church. The **first day of the week** is Sunday. It is not clear whether the meeting takes place on Sunday or Saturday evening—that is, whether Luke follows the Greek or Jewish method of reckoning time. Probably the former, since the **morrow** seems to occur at **daybreak** and not at sundown. The breaking of **bread** is apparently the primary act of worship. Its observance included a whole meal—an early form of the love feast—but the breaking of bread seems to have been a distinct part of the meal which had eucharistic meaning.

20:9-12. Like 19:13-17 the story of **Eutychus** is not without comic elements. The reference to **many lights** could explain the stuffiness of **the upper chamber** or suggest that the **young man** (a **lad** or boy in verse 12) fell asleep in spite of the light. After the fall **from the third story** Eutychus is **taken up dead.** Though Paul says that **his life is in him,** Luke intends to describe a miracle of resurrection. Its background is found in I Kings 17:21 and II Kings 4:34-35. It is parallel to a miracle performed by Peter in 9:36-41.

20:13-38. *Farewell at Miletus.* Paul's trip from Troas to **Miletus** is sketched in a "we section" (see Introduction). While his companions sail around Cape Lectum to **Assos,** Paul takes the more direct route by land—a distance of about twenty miles. There he joins his company, and together they sail south to **Mitylene,** the chief town of the island of Lesbos. Their ship then passes between the island of **Chios** and the mainland, coming eventually to Miletus. It is not clear whether they actually stop at **Samos** on the way or simply come near.

Some manuscripts add that they landed at **Trogyllium**—a port on the mainland opposite Samos. This would have been a more convenient place for Paul's meeting with the Ephesian elders. **Miletus,** however, was an important port in Paul's day. Its impressive ruins, especially the magnificent theater, can still be seen.

20:16. According to Luke, Paul sailed **past Ephesus** because **he was hastening** on to **Jerusalem** in order to arrive by **Pentecost**. No mention is made of this, however, in the narrative of his arrival in Jerusalem, and there is time to tarry at both Tyre (21:3-4) and Caesarea (21:10). Moreover, the round trip from Miletus to Ephesus to summon the elders must have required at least four or five days. Therefore the reason for missing Ephesus was more likely the danger involved in facing the opposition there (cf. II Corinthians 1:8-10).

20:17-18a. The speech to the Ephesian **elders** (cf. 14:23) is the only Pauline sermon to Christians recorded by Luke. It contains prophecy after the event (verses 23, 25) and contradicts Paul's own anticipation of this journey (Romans 15:28, but cf. verse 31). Thus the speech is essentially a composition by Luke. Its purpose is to present the goal of Paul's entire mission. It is written in the style of a farewell address.

20:18b-21. First the speech recalls Paul's missionary activity in the past. He has served **the Lord with all humility and with tears** (cf. verse 31; II Corinthians 2:4). Although no **plots** have been mentioned in connection with the Asian mission, there was one at Corinth (verse 3). The idea that Paul **did not shrink from declaring** his message is a theme of the speech. Perhaps Luke has in mind some specific opponents, or heretics who did not proclaim **the whole counsel of God**. The content of the message—**repentance** and **faith**—is typical of Luke's summaries of the gospel (cf. 17:30 and 16:31). So is the notion that Paul repeatedly made converts among both **Jews** and **Greeks**.

20:22-27. Next Paul's future is revealed. He will **go to Jerusalem, bound in the Spirit**—that is, under the guidance of God (cf. 19:21). Up to this point the reader has not been told of the spirit's prediction that **imprisonment and afflictions await** Paul; this will be disclosed in 21:4, 10-14.

Although the Greek construction of verse 24 is confusing, the meaning is basically clear: Paul is ready to lay down his life **to testify to the gospel**. This idea, together with the statement that **they should see his face no more** (verse 38) betrays the author's knowledge of Paul's death.

Only here does Luke report Paul's using the term **gospel**, although it is common in his letters. On **the kingdom** see above on 19:8-22. That Paul is **innocent of the blood** of his hearers means that he has faithfully proclaimed the message which offers life.

20:28-31. Next Paul's admonition to the elders is presented. The understanding of church organization here is later than that of apostolic days. Paul's charismatic leaders (cf. I Corinthians 12:27-31) have been replaced by the officials of the Pastoral Epistles; the **Holy Spirit** functions through the institution.

The elders are called **overseers**—or, according to the English adaptation of this Greek term, "bishops." These leaders are presented as shepherds of a flock of sheep (cf. John 10:7-18)—a typical representation of the bishop and the church in later Christian literature.

20:29-31. Paul's warning to the church might suggest dangers both from without (persecution) and from within (heresy). However, the use of **wolves** to describe false teachers is common in early Christian authors. That heresy actually arose in Ephesus is attested by I Timothy 1:3-7.

20:32-35. Finally Paul speaks his farewell in the form of a last will and testament. He commends the church to the **grace** (favor) of God. His own self-support (see above on 18:1-4) is an example of how the elders should work to **help the weak**. The phrase **remembering the words of the Lord Jesus, how he said** has become a formula (cf. 11:16; Luke 22:61). The words **it is more blessed to give than to receive** may represent an authentic saying of Jesus not preserved in the Synoptic gospels, although the words were proverbial in the Hellenistic world.

20:36-38. The farewell scene is portrayed with affection. After prayer the elders **embraced** Paul, literally "fell on his neck"—an Old Testament expression used in the parable of the lost son (Luke 15:20).

21:1-14. *The Trip to Palestine.* Though this material is part of a "we section" (see Introduction), only the stations of Paul's journey between Miletus and **Tyre** are mentioned. His course is south to **Cos**, the main city of the island of that name, and then to

Rhodes, coming finally to **Patara**—a town on the southwest corner of what is now Turkey. Some manuscripts add that he goes a short distance east to Myra—a more important port (cf. 27:5-6). From there it may have been easier to find a **ship** sailing directly to **Phoenicia**. The distance to **Tyre** is about 350 miles. **Cyprus** is sighted, but the course is to the west and south of it, supported by the prevailing winds from the northwest. Because of commercial red tape **seven days** would not be an inordinate length of time to **unload** the **cargo**.

21:3-6. No information about the founding of a church in **Tyre** has been recorded. Paul seems to know of its existence and seeks out **the disciples**. Probably Luke does not intend to suggest that the **Spirit** warned **Paul not to go on to Jerusalem**, since that journey is according to the will of God (verse 14). Instead the Christians have received a revelation of the future tragedy and on their own behalf urge Paul not to proceed. The phrase **when our days there were ended** could be interpreted to mean "when the ship was fitted out for the journey" (but see below on verse 7). The farewell scene parallels that of 20:36-38.

21:7. The meaning of this verse is not entirely clear. It could read: "After we had completed the voyage, we arrived at Ptolemais from Tyre"—suggesting an overland trip of about twenty miles. At **Ptolemais**, which is south of Tyre, Paul meets the church and presumably says farewell. The distance to **Caesarea** (see above on 10:1-8) is about forty miles. **Philip** was last mentioned in 8:40 at Caesarea. The title **evangelist** is used in the New Testament only in Ephesians 4:11 and II Timothy 4:5. Here it seems to refer to the preaching activity of Philip—one of the seven (6:5). Though the content of their prophecy is not related, the **unmarried** (virgin) **daughters** of Philip no doubt confirm the word of the Tyrians in verse 4 and anticipate the prediction of Agabus in verses 10-14.

21:10-14. Luke has **Agabus** foretell in 11:28 the famine that occasioned a trip by Paul to carry relief to the Jerusalem church. Since that visit is probably the same as this one (see above on 11:27-30) Agabus plays his only role here. The binding of **his own feet and hands** with **Paul's girdle** represents the symbolic action of the Old Testament prophets (cf. Isaiah 20:2; Jeremiah 13:1-7). Though the Jews themselves will not actually bind Paul (verse 33), they are, as in the case of Jesus, ultimately responsible for delivering him **into the hands of the Gentiles**.

While he is moved by the concern of the Christians, Paul is **ready not only to be imprisoned but even to die at Jerusalem for the name** (or "sake") **of the Lord Jesus**. Paul, like Jesus, determines to follow the **will** of God. A paradox of the necessity of Paul's journey and the freedom of his own decision is maintained.

B. Jerusalem Events (21:15–23:30)

21:15-26. *Church and Temple.* Jerusalem is about sixty-five miles from Caesarea. Since the journey cannot be made in a day, **the house of Mnason** is probably a convenient stop on the way. It is possible, of course, that Mnason lives in the environs of Jerusalem and that Paul considers him more sympathetic to the Gentile mission. Like Barnabas (4:36) Mnason may have been one of the **early** converts from **Cyprus** (cf. 11:20).

21:17-19. In Jerusalem the church receives Paul **gladly**. No mention is made of his delivering the offering (Romans 15:25-27). On the next day Paul appears before **the elders**. The apostles are not mentioned, and **James** is the leader (see above on 12:17). Paul's report is reminiscent of 15:4, 12; the response suggests Jerusalem's enthusiastic support of his mission.

21:20-25. This is a "collective speech"—the leaders speak in chorus. Their point is that Paul should prove his loyalty to Judaism by participating in Jewish ritual. **Thousands** is literally "myriads"—"ten thousands"—an exaggeration. These Jewish Christians charge that Paul teaches the Jews of the Dispersion to **forsake Moses**, abandon circumcision, and neglect **the customs**. The reader of Paul's letters knows that these charges are essentially true (cf. Romans 10:4 and Galatians 5:6), but the reader of Acts is confident that they are false. Paul has insisted on the circumcision of Timothy (16:3) and has been scrupulous about ritual (18:18).

21:23-24. The elders advise Paul to support **four men** in fulfilling their **vow**. Since they are going to **shave their heads** a Nazirite ritual is in view (Numbers 6:5, 18). The **expenses** included the cost of sacrifices which completed the vow (Numbers 6:13-20). To pay this for another was considered a meritorious act.

What the elders mean by suggesting that Paul **purify** himself (cf. 24:18) is not clear. Since the Nazirite vow required thirty days Paul could not have become involved. Perhaps Luke thinks of some special defilement which required **seven days** (verse 27) of purification, or possibly he has misunderstood the length of the Nazirite vow on the basis of Numbers 6:9.

21:25-26. The **letter** to Gentile converts (see above on 15:20-21, 23-29) is mentioned as if Paul has never heard of it. While the apostle is able to make concessions to the Jews (cf. I Corinthians 9:20), participation in a ritual to prove his loyalty to the law would be out of character.

21:27-40. *Paul's Arrest.* The arrest and imprisonment of Paul are narrated in detail. Parallels with the passion of Jesus are apparent. The trouble is instigated by **Jews** who have come from **Asia** (i.e., Ephesus; see above on 16:6*b*-8), perhaps for Pentecost. They have seen **Trophimus**, a Greek of their own region (20:4), in Jerusalem with Paul and assume that Paul has taken him **into the temple**. Their charge is reminiscent of 6:13. Gentiles were debarred from the temple. As inscriptions which marked the barrier between the court of the Gentiles and the court of Israel show, they entered at the cost of their lives.

21:30-36. Paul is **dragged . . . out of the temple** and the **gates** are **shut**, presumably to prevent rioting within the holy precincts. Report of the commotion comes to the **tribune of the cohort** who commands a garrison of theoretically a thousand men. Taking with him **centurions** (the plural suggests at least two) and their commands (no less than two hundred men), the tribune saves Paul from lynching by the mob. Paul is **arrested** and chained between **two** soldiers. The officer considers him the cause of the disturbance (verse 38).

21:34-36. The confusion of the crowd makes it impossible for the tribune to **learn the facts**—a theme of Luke's imprisonment narrative (cf. 22:30; 25:26). Paul is brought to the **barracks**, which are probably in the Tower of Antonia located in the northwest corner of the temple area. The fact that he has to be **carried** to the **steps** which led into the tower may hint that Paul has been beaten into unconsciousness. Luke may have ignored this detail in order to make possible Paul's speech.

21:37-39. The tribune notes that Paul can speak **Greek**. Not only is he a cultured man, he is not to be mistaken as **the Egyptian**. According to the historian Josephus this insurrectionist led a group of people from **the wilderness** to the Mt. of Olives in a revolt. Though they were defeated, their leader disappeared. Josephus also mentions the **Assassins** (the Sicarii, or "dagger bearers"), though not in connection with the Egyptian.

Paul's response makes two points: (1) He is a Jew and therefore has a right to enter the temple. (2) He is a **citizen** of **Tarsus** and thus not an Egyptian. **No mean city** is a typical Hellenistic expression.

21:40. That a Roman officer would allow a prisoner responsible for a riot to speak to the crowd which has been rioting is unlikely. Paul motions **with his hand** to quiet the crowd and speaks in Aramaic, popularly called **Hebrew**.

22:1-21. *Paul's Defense Before Israel.* This speech has been composed by Luke. Not only is its setting improbable; the speech makes no contribution to the progress of the narrative (cf. 21:34 with 22:24). The purpose of this **defense**, or apology, is to prove that Paul's mission is motivated by the God of Israel. The address **Brethren and fathers** is the same as that used by Stephen before the sanhedrin (7:2). Although **a great hush** has already come over the crowd (21:40), they become even **more quiet** at hearing Paul's "Hebrew," which is actually Aramaic.

22:3. This verse is subject to a variety of interpretations. Instead of the translation adopted by the Revised Standard Version, the text may mean, "I was born at Tarsus, brought up in this city, educated at the feet of Gamaliel." Luke may accept the tradition that Paul's parents moved to Jerusalem when he was quite young (cf. 23:16; 26:4).

83

It is also not clear whether Paul is supposed to have been educated in a **strict manner** or in the strict interpretation **of the law**. The former would allow as a further alternative that he was **zealous** for the law (cf. 21:20) rather than **for God** (cf. Romans 10:2). Sitting **at the feet** of a rabbi is the typical posture of the Jewish learner. On **Gamaliel** see above on 5:34.

22:4-5. Paul's conversion has been discussed in connection with 9:1-22. Both accounts set the narrative in the context of Paul's persecuting. Here it seems implied that **the high priest** at that time was the same as the current one, Ananias (23:2). In fact, it was probably Caiaphas (see above on 4:5-7). The **council of elders** is the sanhedrin. The wording of verse 5 may suggest that those persecuted in **Damascus** had fled there, perhaps from Jerusalem.

22:6-11. In the narration of the conversion experience the major differences in the two accounts are:

(1) Here mention is made of the time of Paul's vision as **noon** (cf. 26:13).

(2) Jesus is called **Jesus of Nazareth**.

(3) Paul's companions are said to have seen **the light** but not heard **the voice**.

22:12-16. The account of **Ananias**, though similar to 9:10-19, makes a different emphasis. Ananias is a **devout** Jew, highly regarded **by all the Jews** of Damascus. No mention is made of his vision. The content of his speech has an Old Testament flavor. Christ is described as the **Just** (or "Righteous") **One** (cf. 3:14). The question **Why do you wait?** may represent an early formula used in baptismal liturgy. Stress is placed on Paul's role as a **witness** (cf. 1:22).

22:17-18. The narrative of Paul's first visit to Jerusalem after his conversion differs from 9:26-30. For one thing the impression is given that Paul returns to the Holy City immediately after his baptism (contrast Galatians 1:17). The description of this **trance** has no parallel in Acts. Though Paul did have ecstatic experiences (cf. II Corinthians 12:2-4), the notion that his Gentile mission is motivated by a vision in the temple is inconsistent with Galatians 1:16. Luke is anxious to present Paul as a loyal Jew who is found **praying in the temple** and receives his commission from the Jerusalem temple (cf. Luke 24:47-48). The narrative also fits Luke's pattern of a Gentile mission following Jewish rejection (cf. 13:46; Luke 14:16-24).

22:19-21. Again reference is made to Paul's career as a persecutor and to his role in the death of **Stephen**. The mention of Stephen's **witness** even to the shedding of **blood** shows the trend toward the early Christian emphasis on martyrdom as the supreme form of witnessing. In contrast to verse 19 Paul's past probably made him a more effective witness to the Jews.

22:22-29. *Jewish Mob and Roman Citizen.* Paul's speech is "interrupted" after it is finished (cf. 4:1; 7:54). Apparently the mention of **Gentiles** sets the crowd into an uproar. A mission to Gentiles should not have troubled the Jews, but Paul is claiming divine inspiration for a heretical mission.

The cry **Away with such a fellow!** is reminiscent of the mob's reaction to Jesus (Luke 23:18). It is not clear from the Greek verb used whether the **garments** are thrown off or brandished; the typical response would have been tearing their clothing (cf. 14:14). Throwing **dust into the air** has no known ancient parallel, but it evidently symbolizes extreme wrath.

22:24-26. Again the **tribune** commands Paul **to be brought into the barracks** (cf. 21:34). To examine **by scourging** means to obtain a confession by torture. Verse 25 can mean either that they **tied him up with the thongs** in preparation for scourging or that they put him forward to receive the thongs—that is, the lash, which was made of leather thongs.

Paul's failure to reveal himself as a **Roman citizen** earlier seems strange, but it probably displays Luke's ability to build a climax. The word **uncondemned** could mean either that Paul is about to be punished without a trial or that he is about to be scourged without legal sentence. Citizenship made one immune from either examination by scourging or from punishment without trial.

22:27-29. The tribune has purchased his **citizenship for a large sum**—a practice common during the reign of Emperor

Claudius. This is confirmed by the tribune's name, Claudius Lysias (23:26), since a new citizen normally took the name of his emperor. Perhaps Paul's father received Roman citizenship from Mark Antony, who granted the privilege to whole peoples in the East.

22:30–23:11. *Paul Before the Sanhedrin.* This scene is of doubtful historicity. It is unlikely that a Roman tribune would keep a citizen bound overnight and then bring him before a Jewish court instead of hearing his own explanation as to **the real reason why the Jews accused him**. No progress is made in the narrative. For the third time Paul is ordered brought **into the barracks**.

Paul's claim that he has **lived before God in all good conscience** seems to ignore confessions like I Corinthians 15:9. While the term "conscience" is common in Paul (e.g. Romans 2:15; II Corinthians 1:12), this notion of a "clear conscience" (24:16; I Timothy 1:5) represents a different meaning.

23:2-5. According to Josephus, **Ananias** was appointed **high priest in** A.D. 48 and was an insolent man of bad temper. Perhaps he is enraged by Paul's consistent plea of innocence. The striking of Paul is parallel to that of Jesus (John 18:22). Paul's rebuke, that the high priest is a **whitewashed wall**, is reminiscent of Matthew 23:27 and Ezekiel 13:10-11. Possibly Luke knows of the assassination of Ananias, which took place in A.D. 66.

Why Paul is not able to recognize the presiding officer is not explained. Luke's purpose is to present the high priest as acting **contrary to the law**, while Paul, even in criticizing himself, quotes the Old Testament (Exodus 22:28).

23:6-7. That Paul would use his former position as a **Pharisee** to escape the judgment of the council seems out of character and in conflict with texts like Philippians 3:2-11. In spite of 24:21 belief in **the resurrection of the dead** is not the charge which has been leveled against Paul (cf. 21:28). Moreover, the translation **the hope and the resurrection**, as if Paul were talking about two different things, is misleading. The meaning is probably "the hope of the resurrection." Luke is apparently indicating that the bond between Christianity and true Judaism is belief in resurrection.

23:8-10. That the **Sadducees** rejected the idea of **resurrection** is supported by both the Synoptic gospels and Josephus; that they did not accept **angels** or **spirits** is attested only here. Luke gives the impression that the Sadducees do not reject these beliefs because of their adherence to the Pentateuch; rather, they are guilty of skepticism.

While **the scribes of the Pharisees' party** are presented as Paul's defenders, Judaism is discredited by its divisiveness. The Pharisees acknowledge that Paul may have received revelation. This implies their acceptance of either his conversion experience (22:6-11) or his vision in the temple (22:17-21). Some manuscripts, in the spirit of 5:39, add: "Let us not fight against God."

23:11. At this time of crisis Paul has another vision (cf. 18:9-10). His purpose since 19:21 has been to go to Rome. Now divine sanction is given to this intention in spite of human opposition.

23:12-22. *A Plot Against Paul.* According to Luke, Paul is removed to Caesarea in order to escape a plot; his Roman citizenship would guarantee the transfer anyway. The theme of destroying the apostle by an ambush is repeated in 25:3. Though the Jews had ways to find release from an oath, the reader is left wondering whether the **more than forty** starved to death. Since only **the chief priests and elders**, not the Pharisees, are mentioned, the plotters may be making their request of the Sadducees in the sanhedrin. The wording of the proposed request could mean either that the council members wish to know more about the case or that they hope to reach a verdict.

23:16. The reference to **the son of Paul's sister** may represent a tradition that Paul grew up in Jerusalem (cf. 22:3; 26:4). How the **young man** learns of the plot is not clear. Perhaps Paul's sister has connections with the hierarchy, or possibly the boy has stumbled onto the information by accident. Prisoners were allowed visitors. The mention of **Paul the prisoner** need not imply that the apostle is still in bonds.

The young man's interview with the tribune is related with a relish for artificial personal detail. He repeats the vow of Paul's enemies with unnatural accuracy (cf. verse 12). Depending on manuscript variants verse 20 can mean either that **they** (the sanhedrin) or "you" **were going to inquire**; verse 15 argues for the former.

23:23-35. *Removal to Caesarea.* While it is certain that Paul was taken from Jerusalem to Caesarea, the details of this narrative are questionable. For one thing the number of troops in Paul's escort—a total of 470, or about half the Jerusalem garrison—is exaggerated. The meaning of the word translated **spearmen** is uncertain; later it came to mean "light armed soldiers." **The third hour of the night** was about 9 or 10 P.M. Luke seems to have ignored the fact that secrecy would be prevented by the size of the escort.

23:24. Antonius **Felix** was the brother of Pallas, a favorite of the Emperor Claudius. The length of his rule in Palestine is debated; he gained power in A.D. 52 or 53, but the estimates of his recall range from 55 to 60. Ancient historians are agreed in judging him an evil man, guilty of maladministration.

23:25-30. The **letter** from the tribune to the governor is a composition of Luke. The address follows the form of 15:23. The **accusers** certainly would not have been ordered to bring their charges before the governor until after Paul had been slipped out of town. Felix is addressed as **Excellency**, the same title used for Theophilus (Luke 1:3) and Festus (26:25).

The letter presents Lysias' version of the rescue of Paul (21:31-40). No mention is made of his intention to scourge him (22:24-29). Throughout the letter legal terms are used, and its purpose is to prove that the first Roman official to view the evidence finds Paul guilty of no crime **deserving death** (cf. Luke 23:4, 14, 22). Like Gallio (18:15), Lysias concludes that the charges against the Christians are matters of Jewish religion which are of no concern to Roman authority.

23:31-35. The soldiers bring Paul as far as **Antipatris**, a Roman military relay station some thirty-five miles from Jerusalem. Only the cavalry accompany him the final thirty miles to

Caesarea. Felix's question tries to determine venue; Paul can be tried in either the **province** where the alleged crime has been committed or in his native province. The governor can hear the case either as procurator of Judea or as the deputy of the legate of Syria and **Cilicia**. His attempt to delay matters is consistent with the character. **Herod's praetorium** is apparently the palace built by Herod the Great, now used as the governor's residence or administrative headquarters.

C. Paul in Caesarea (24:1–26:32)

24:1-9. *The Case Against Paul.* Luke's narrative of the judicial proceedings against Paul continues. Throughout this passage legal terms are used frequently. After Paul has been in Caesarea **five days** (see below on verses 10-21), **the high priest** and representatives of the sanhedrin appear **before the governor**. Their charges are presented by **Tertullus**, their **spokesman**, or attorney—a professional counsel for the prosecution. The notice that Paul is **called** suggests that he has received a legal summons.

24:2b-4. Tertullus begins the accusation with the conventional attempt to secure the judge's favor. The use of **we** and **this nation** does not imply that Tertullus (a Latin name) identifies himself with the Jews or that he distinguishes himself from them. He simply represents his clients. The word **nation** can refer to the Jews (cf. Luke 7:5; 23:2) or possibly to the province of Judea. Since this praise is conventional, the references to **much peace** and **reforms** reveal little about the actual conduct of Felix's adminstration (see above on 23:24). The promise of brevity is typical of speakers ancient and modern.

24:5-9. The charge against Paul is three-fold:

(1) He is guilty of sedition, because he is a **pestilent** (troublesome) **fellow** who has upset order throughout the empire (cf. 17:6). To the Romans this would be a significant charge.

(2) He is the **ringleader** of a heretical **sect** (cf. verse 14; 28:22). The term **Nazarenes**, used in the plural only here,

indicates that the Christians are followers of Jesus of Nazareth. Though Luke assumes that this sort of charge means little to the Romans, he may be presenting Paul's opponents as arguing from Judaism's status as an "approved religion"—a status which Christianity does not enjoy.

(3) Paul has **tried to profane the temple** (cf. 21:28). While the Romans are not concerned with the niceties of Jewish religion, they recognize the right of the Jews to regulate their own practices. Some manuscripts add verses 6*b*-8*a*, which suggest that Lysias overstepped his authority in interfering with the Jewish right to judge Paul (see the footnote in the Revised Standard Version). The Jews are convinced that an examination of Paul will confirm their charges.

24:10-21. *Paul Before Felix.* Like Tertullus in verses 2 and 3, Paul begins his speech with an attempt to gain the governor's favor. The reference to **many years** is conventional, so that little is disclosed about the length of Felix's rule (see above on 23:24). Paul's observation that **it is not more than twelve days since I went up to . . . Jerusalem** seems to suggest that the events are recent enough for Felix to conduct a careful investigation. Actually the events which have occurred since Paul's arrival in Jerusalem demand at least sixteen or seventeen days. Luke's twelve apparently results from adding the seven of 21:27 and the five of 24:1. Paul's **defense** has two parts (verses 10-16 and 17-21); both make essentially the same points.

24:11, 17. First he went up to Jerusalem **to worship** or, as he says in verse 17, **to bring to my nation alms and offerings**. This may be a reference to Paul's offering at the completion of religious vows (cf. 21:26). Or it could be a hint of Luke's knowledge of Paul's offering for the Judean Christians (see above on 20:1-6). If so, Luke has misunderstood Paul's collection as intended for the temple.

24:12, 18*a*. Since Paul has gone to Jerusalem for religious purposes he is not guilty of **stirring up a crowd**. Instead he was found **in the temple, without any crowd or tumult**. In fact, rather than being guilty of profaning the temple, he has participated in a ritual of purification (cf. 21:26).

24:13, 18b-19. His opponents can **prove** none of their charges against him. **Some Jews from Asia** (not a large crowd) falsely understood his purpose in the temple, but if they had any valid charges, they should be present to make them.

24:14-15, 21. Rather than being the leader of a heretical sect (verse 5), Paul is a follower of **the Way** (cf. 9:2)—the culmination of true Judaism. Although actually Paul did not believe **everything** in the **law** and **prophets** (cf. Galatians 3:25 and Romans 10:4), Luke sees Christianity as fulfillment of the Old Testament (cf. Luke 24:44). This is seen in the **hope** of a **resurrection**, which is common to Paul and the best of Judaism (cf. 23:6-9). While both Paul (I Corinthians 15) and Luke (Luke 14:14; 20:35) stress the resurrection of the righteous, the belief in **a resurrection of both the just and the unjust** may be implied in Luke 16:19-31.

24:20-21. It is sometimes supposed that Paul here confesses that his strategy in 23:6-9 involved **wrongdoing**. More likely the statement involves irony. **The resurrection of the dead** is a truth recognized by the Jews which is of no concern to the Romans.

24:22-27. *The Indecision of Felix.* The governor delays a decision under the excuse that the **tribune** can bring additional evidence. How Felix has acquired **knowledge of the Way** is not explained—perhaps through his **wife**, who is a **Jewess**. Paul is kept in custody, but not in a public prison; he has **some liberty** and is allowed visitors. Luke shows that Roman officials understand Christianity and treat its leaders well.

24:24-25. According to some manuscripts it is **Drusilla** who instigates the interview with Paul. She was the youngest daughter of Herod Agrippa I (chapter 12) and was noted for her beauty. According to Josephus, Felix lured her away from her husband with the help of a pseudo magician.

The governor is **alarmed** at Paul's stress on the ethical implications of **faith in Christ Jesus** and the concept of a **future judgment**. **Self-control** is one thing Felix lacks. Paul is dismissed without decision. This story bears a slight resemblance to the account of John the Baptist's execution in Mark 6:17-28—material which Luke has not included in his gospel.

24:26-27. Felix hopes to get **money** from Paul. He heard of the offering in verse 17. This avarice, though true to the character of Felix, explains to the reader why Paul is kept in custody though innocent. The reference to **two years** apparently describes the length of Paul's imprisonment, though it could refer to the duration of Felix's rule (see above on 23:24).

25:1-12. *Paul Before Festus.* Almost nothing is known of **Porcius Festus.** Estimates of the date of his assumption of power range from A.D. 55 to 60. Apparently he was a man of higher character than his predecessor. The Greek word used for Festus' coming **into his province** may mean entering "into his office."

In order to create cordial relations with the Jews the new governor goes immediately **to Jerusalem. Since Festus desires cordiality the Jewish leaders ask a favor** (cf. verse 9)—that Paul be sent to Jerusalem. Probably they intend to have his case commuted to their jurisdiction. The idea of an **ambush** is secondary and thematic (cf. 23:12-15). Festus refuses a change of venue but provides for the reopening of the case in **Caesarea.**

25:6-8. After returning to his capital Festus takes **his seat on the tribunal** (judgment bench; see above on 18:12-17), and sends for Paul. The **serious charges** are not enumerated, but they are well known to the reader. Paul's **defense** names the major issues: disregard of **the law of the Jews** (21:21), profanation of **the temple** (21:27-28), and offenses **against Caesar** (24:5). In this defense Paul distinguishes himself from Judaism (contrast 24:14-15). The real issue is the charge of offenses against the state.

25:9. In view of the mention of **Caesar** it seems unlikely that Festus would suggest a trial in Jerusalem. Though the governor does not intend to relinquish Roman jurisdiction, it is clear that Paul should resist this suggestion; Festus is anxious to do a **favor** for the Jews. Here Luke gives his most critical estimate of a Roman official. Except for Festus' effort to please the Jews the innocent apostle could be acquitted.

25:10-11. The Roman practice of **appeal to Caesar** is not clearly understood. Apparently a Roman citizen, when charged with a capital crime, could appeal to the imperial court as a sort of supreme tribunal. It is not clear whether this appeal was made before or after a verdict was rendered in the lower courts. While there is no evidence that a defendant could not be released after he had made an appeal (26:32), a matter referred to the emperor would be modified with reluctance.

Paul's reasons for appealing at this point are probably: (1) his intention to avoid a trial at Jerusalem; (2) his belief that Festus has a negative view of his case—a view more hostile than Luke is willing to admit. Luke does admit, however, that Paul's case is more than a matter of Jewish religious dispute (contrast verse 19). It is a case for **Caesar's tribunal**—a somewhat inaccurate way to describe the Roman court at Caesarea.

25:12. Festus' conference **with his council** indicates that the appeal is not automatically granted. His legal advisers probably check Paul's credentials of citizenship and the seriousness of the case.

25:13–26:32. *Paul Before Agrippa.* This narrative seems historically improbable. Not only are some of the events related in an artificial manner (25:23–26:32), but there is included a private conversation between governor and king (25:14-22) which would not be available to the author. The notion that Festus would need Agrippa's help in formulating charges is out of character with a Roman governor, who would have adequate opportunity for investigation. The purpose of the narrative is to present a parallel to Luke 23:6-12 and to fulfill the prophecy of 9:15.

25:13-27. *Festus Presents Paul.* Herod **Agrippa** II was the son of Herod Agrippa I (chapter 12). Reared in Rome, he was gradually granted power until he ruled the areas of Philip and Lysanias (cf. Luke 3:1) and controlled some Galilean and Perean towns. He had custody of the temple treasury in Jerusalem and authority to appoint the high priest. According to rumor Agrippa was guilty of incestuous relations with his sister **Bernice**—the oldest daughter of Herod Agrippa I. Though a widow at the moment, Bernice was married a total of three times and eventually became the mistress of the Emperor Titus.

However, on one occasion she appeared barefoot before the procurator Florus as a penitent interceding for the Jewish people.

25:14-17. Festus' reason for presenting Paul's case to the king is to be explained in verse 26. While the reader knows that he has been subject to political pressures (see above on verses 1-12), Festus depicts himself as a champion of Roman justice. The idea that **the accused** has the right to meet his **accusers face to face** was an established principle of Roman law. Unlike Felix (24:22), Festus has heard the case with **no delay**.

25:18-19. The charges, however, are matters of Jewish religion rather than Roman law. Most modern translators use "religion" rather than **superstition** since Festus would not have offended his guest, who was a member of the Jewish faith. If the Greek word actually bore this negative connotation, then **their own** (literally "the own") perhaps should be understood as "his own," i.e. Paul's, "superstition." It is clear here that the resurrection question has to do with the raising of **Jesus** (contrast 24:15).

25:20-22. Festus admits that Roman officials are not competent to **investigate** such matters. His implication that he proposed a **Jerusalem** trial in order to amass more evidence is at variance with the motive of verse 9. On Paul's appeal **to the emperor** see above on verses 10-11. Agrippa's desire to **hear** Paul is reminiscent of Luke 23:8.

25:23. The vivid picture of Paul's appearance before important people portrays Christianity as well known in significant circles. The **audience hall** is probably a large room of Herod's palace used for important judicial proceedings. The **military tribunes** would be the commanders of the five cohorts (see above on 10:1-8) stationed at Caesarea. Some manuscripts say that **the prominent men of the city** are the leaders of the province.

25:24-27. The **whole Jewish people**, of course, have not **petitioned**, but only their leaders. The petitioning has occurred in **Jerusalem** and **here**. The **shouting** of the Jews may echo the mob scene of 22:22. Again Paul is judged guilty of **nothing**

deserving death (cf. 23:29; also Luke 23:22). The recognition of the emperor as **lord** had been employed since the time of Caligula. As a matter of fact the governor was required to send formal **charges** with the prisoner.

26:1-23. *Paul's Defense.* The author understands the speech before Agrippa as the high point in Paul's defense. While it is evident to the historian that the political charges were the primary concern of the Romans, Luke has been insisting that Paul has committed no crime against the state. Christianity is no threat to good order; it is a religion of resurrection, fulfilling the hopes of Jew and Gentile. Now the reader is told that Paul's mission to the Gentiles is the cause of the whole process against him.

26:1-3. The style of the speech imitates classical forms. Paul **stretched out his hand** like a Hellenistic rhetorician (cf. 13:16 and 21:40). He begins with the conventional attempt to win the hearer's favor (cf. 24:2-3, 10). Like Felix, Agrippa is said to be **familiar with all customs and controversies** (or questions) **of the Jews.** In the Greek **especially** falls between verses 2 and 3, so that it may mean either that Paul is especially fortunate to appear before Agrippa or that the king is especially familiar with Jewish customs. While Agrippa was pro-Roman, he considered himself king of the Jews.

26:4-8. As in 22:3-16 Paul describes his early life. Details told there are not repeated; the earlier material is known to the reader. The main point is that Paul has been a Jew of **the strictest party** (literally "sect"; cf. 24:5) and that this fact is **known** to the Jews. The Revised Standard Version seems to suggest a contrast between **nation** and **Jerusalem**, as if the former means "province" and refers to Paul's days in Cilicia. More likely "nation" stands for the Jews without reference to the time of Paul's move to Jerusalem (see above on 22:3).

As a former **Pharisee** Paul sees the resurrection **hope** as the fulfillment of ancient **promise** (cf. Luke 24:44-49)—the hope of all Israel (the **twelve tribes**). At verse 8 the defense is turned into a missionary appeal.

26:9-11. Paul's testimony is confirmed by his earlier role as a persecutor. The picture of his opposition to Christianity is sterner here than in 22:3-5. He not only imprisoned the believers but advocated a sentence of **death**. While the phrase **I cast my vote against them** does not prove that Paul was a member of the sanhedrin, Luke seems to suppose that Paul played some official role in the execution of Christians. His effort to **make them blaspheme** may anticipate the persecutions of the second century where Christians were compelled to curse Christ.

26:12-14. Paul's conversion has been described in 9:1-9 and 22:6-11. While this account is not entirely consistent with the others (cf. verse 14 with 9:7), it is easier to harmonize with Paul's own description in Galatians 1:12-17. The time of the event, as in 22:6, is **midday**. The address **Saul, Saul** (in all three accounts) is explained—the voice speaks **Hebrew** (actually Aramaic; cf. 21:40). Strangely, the voice announces a Greek proverb: **It hurts . . . to kick against the goads** (prods used on unruly animals). The saying was used by the Greeks to depict those who resisted the will of the gods.

26:15-18. Most important, Paul's commission to preach to the **Gentiles** is given in his conversion experience (cf. Galatians 1:16). The material about Ananias and Paul's blindness is omitted. The commission of Paul is presented under the motif of the prophetic call (cf. Ezekiel 2:1; Isaiah 35:5; 42:7, 16). This use of Old Testament allusions makes it clear that Paul's mission is under the direction of the God of Israel. Verse 16 is difficult; the New English Bible is clearer: "to appoint you my servant and witness . . . to what you have seen and to what you shall yet see of me."

The promise that Paul will be delivered does not imply that Luke believes the trial will end in acquittal. Paul is to be "delivered" in the sense that his witness will be accomplished.

26:19-21. The mission involves obedience. The notion that Paul began an extensive mission in **Damascus** and **Jerusalem** immediately after his conversion enlarges on 9:28-29. The idea that he preached **throughout all the country of Judea** contradicts Galatians 1:22. The theory that Paul was sent to both

Jews and Gentiles, though not consistent with Galatians 2:7, is a Lukan motif.

The word translated **to kill** was used in 5:30; literally it means "to lay hands on violently" and refers to the mob action of 21:30-32.

26:22-23. Paul's gospel is nothing more than **what the prophets and Moses** predicted. While the Jews did not expect a suffering Messiah, the Christian experience of the Crucifixion and Resurrection led to a messianic interpretation of texts like Isaiah 53. The idea that Christ was **the first to rise from the dead** finds parallels in I Corinthians 15:20 and Colossians 1:18.

26:24-32. *Verdict of Governor and King.* Paul is again "interrupted" after he has finished (cf. 22:22). The cry of Festus accentuates the inability of Romans to prosecute Christians and the greatness of Paul's **learning.** The phrase **turning you mad** is a common Hellenistic saying. Paul replies that what he is saying is **the sober truth**—literally "words of truth and reasonableness."

26:26-27. Agrippa's knowledge (cf. verse 3) emphasizes the Lukan notion that Christianity is appreciated by important people. This is also expressed by the claim that **this was not done in a corner**—a Greek proverbial saying which displays the whole program of Acts. Paul's appeal to the king's belief in the **prophets** assumes Agrippa's role as Jewish monarch.

26:28. Agrippa's response involves sarcasm, but its exact meaning is obscure. Using the best manuscripts the sentence reads literally: "In little [literally "time," or perhaps "effort"] you are persuading me to make ["play" (act)] Christian." The Revised Standard Version's **think to make me a Christian** rests on a manuscript variant, and another manuscript variant allows the translation "you are persuading me to become a Christian." On **Christian** see above on 11:26.

26:29. Paul's reply plays on Agrippa's words—**whether short or long** (literally "in little and in big")—and makes a missionary appeal to the whole audience. The **chains** symbolize Paul's status as a prisoner; a literal understanding is not entirely consistent with 24:23.

26:30-32. As in Luke 23:14-15, king and governor agree that

the accused deserves neither **death** nor **imprisonment**. On
Paul's appeal see above on 25:10-11. It is sometimes supposed
that verse 32 betrays Luke's knowledge of Paul's conviction in
the imperial court. Actually Luke may be suggesting that the
divine intention of a mission to Rome must be fulfilled (cf.
23:11).

D. Voyage to Rome (27:1–28:16)

27:1-12. *To Crete.* Along with other prisoners Paul is sent to
Rome. He is in the custody of **Julius,** a **centurion of the
Augustan Cohort** (see above on 10:1-8), which was stationed in
Caesarea about this time. Paul is **accompanied by Aristarchus,**
who is mentioned in 19:29; 20:4; Colossians 4:10; and Philemon
24. Presumably "Luke" also goes, since 27:1–28:16 is the last
and longest of the "we sections" (see Introduction).

27:2-4. Ships sailing from Caesarea directly to **Italy** are not
available. Instead the prisoners are put on a vessel of
Adramyttium, a port near Assos. It is about to embark for
important **ports** of the province of **Asia.**

The course is north along the coast to **Sidon.** There Paul is
permitted to visit **his friends,** literally "the friends"—perhaps
meaning the Christians, since no trip to Sidon by Paul has been
recorded. Because the prevailing **winds** are from the northwest
the ship sails on the east and north of **Cyprus.** After hugging the
coast of **Cilicia,** it sails **across** the bay which is off the coast of
Pamphylia. Some manuscripts add that this short journey
required fifteen days.

27:5-8. At **Myra,** a port for grain ships sailing from Egypt to
Rome, the prisoners board an Alexandrian vessel hauling wheat
(verse 38) and passengers (verse 37) to the capital. Head winds
make the trip to **Cnidus** difficult. Turning south, the ship sails
around the east point of Crete, Cape **Salmone,** and arrives at
Fair Havens—a small bay on the southern shore of the island.

27:9-11. It is now evident that the trip is being made too late
in the year. Travel on the Mediterranean was closed from

November 11 to March 10, and any trip after September 14 was considered **dangerous**. The **fast** was probably the Day of Atonement, which would be observed in late September or early October.

Though Paul has had considerable experience in sailing (II Corinthians 11:25) it is unlikely that a prisoner would be consulted about nautical affairs. At any rate the **centurion** accepts the advice of the **captain** and the **owner**. What authority the centurion might have is not clear. The **majority** decision is perhaps that of the leading men on board. Luke is anxious to stress Paul's importance, his prophetic power, and his right to say "I told you so" (verse 21).

27:12. The location of **Phoenix** is debated. It is clearly a better harbor, farther west, on the southern shore of Crete.

27:13-44. *Shipwreck.* This narrative is written in fine literary style. The details are vividly described, and nautical terms are frequently used. The author may be following a written source or copying the pattern of Hellenistic sea romances.

27:13-16. When the **south wind** begins to blow **gently**, the crew assume that the voyage around Cape Matala and northwest across the Gulf of Messara to Phoenix can be readily accomplished. They sail west along the southern coast of Crete, cautiously hugging the shore. No sooner are they beyond the cape and exposed to the open sea than a mighty **wind** sweeps **down from** Mt. Ida, seven thousand feet high. The term translated **tempestuous** suggests a typhoon or hurricane. In sailors' jargon this wind is called *Euraquilo*—a combination of Greek and Latin which means **northeaster**.

Driven into the open sea, the ship sails south of **Cauda** (or Clauda), a small island some twenty-five miles south of Crete. The **boat** which **we . . . secure** is the ship's dinghy, used in boarding and escape. It is apparently being towed but, when it becomes filled with water, it is hoisted on deck.

27:17-20. What it means **to undergird the ship** is debated. Some scholars suggest that the vessel is bound together from side to side, either by ropes which go under the keel, or by chains which are stretched across the beam below deck. Others believe the ship is bound from stem to stern, either around the outside, or by lines which run longitudinally over the deck supported by props. **Took measures** is literally "used helps," which could mean props.

The **Syrtis** is a gulf along the coast of Africa west of Cyrene where shifting sands create a dangerous shallows. Since the direction of the wind could drive the ship south into this hazard, the words **lowered the gear** suggest some maneuver which either assured a more westerly course or slowed the ship's progress. Thus some suppose that the sails are set to tack, while others believe the main sail is taken down or an anchor lowered. The **cargo** and surplus **tackle** are thrown overboard—an action not completed until verse 38—in order to ease the storm's strain on the ship. The disappearance of **sun** and **stars** leads to loss of **hope**, since navigation is dependent on them.

27:21-26. Paul comes forward in the time of crisis. As a speech in the midst of a hurricane seems unlikely, verses 21-26 (as well as verses 33-36 or 38) may have been inserted into the narrative. Paul points out that his advice should have been heeded, but no one had actually recommended sailing away **from Crete** (cf. verse 12). During the night Paul has seen **an angel of . . . God** (cf. 10:3) in a vision and has been told that it is God's will for him to **stand before Caesar** (cf. 23:11). The apostle also predicts what will be described in verses 40-41.

27:27-28. On **the fourteenth night** after leaving Crete the ship is **drifting across the sea of Adria**. Experts conclude that the rate of a ship's drift in this kind of weather would require about fourteen days to reach Malta (28:1). Though the main body of the Adriatic lies between Italy and Dalmatia, the ancients considered that it reached south to North Africa. At **midnight** the **sailors** believe the ship is approaching **land**—literally "land was drawing near." This is surmised, perhaps, by the drag of the anchor or the sound of breakers; some manuscripts say that the "land was resounding." Soundings of **twenty** and then **fifteen fathoms** (120 and 90 feet) correspond to the eastern approach to St. Paul's Bay, which is located in the northwest part of Malta.

27:29-32. Throwing out **four anchors** is prompted by the violence of the storm. Anchoring **from the stern** is essential to keep the bow toward the beach, preparing to run aground. It is unlikely that sailors would attempt to **escape** during the night in a fierce storm on a foreign shore; **laying out anchors from the bow** to secure the ship is precisely what the situation demands. Both Paul and the **centurion** misunderstand this maneuver. **The soldiers** in the latter's command **cut away . . . the boat** which the sailors are preparing to use. Though Paul is presented as the prophet who can announce the salvation of all who remain on board, securing the ship might have prevented the wreck, and the dinghy could have provided the means of escape.

27:33-34. With a captive audience Paul makes another improbable speech. The failure to eat was not from lack of provisions (cf. verse 38), but from seasickness or fear. Paul urges taking **food** for **strength** and promises that **not a hair is to perish from the head of any** of his hearers—an Old Testament expression.

27:35-38. The **giving** of **thanks** and breaking of **bread** is probably only a picture of Christian conduct at table, although eucharistic language is used (cf. Luke 22:19). Some manuscripts add that Paul "distributed" the food "to us," reflecting an observance of the Lord's Supper.

The number of people on board is perhaps mentioned because of the problem of rationing the provisions. A total of **two hundred and seventy-six** passengers and crew is not impossible, but some manuscripts read the more conservative "seventy-six." A slight change in Greek letters could account for the difference. The ship is **lightened** as the last of the cargo is thrown overboard. A lightened vessel would be able to run aground higher up the beach.

27:39-41. When **day** comes the crew see that the ship is situated off an unfamiliar **bay**. The **anchors** are **cast off**, and **the rudders**—normally two—are loosened; they would have been previously lashed to the stern to help secure the ship. An ancient vessel also had two sails: a large mainsail (already removed either at verse 17 or at verse 29) and a small **foresail** attached to a mast which slanted forward. The foresail, like the rudders, was used in maneuvering the ship. The **shoal**, sometimes translated "cross currents," is probably a promontory or sand bar extending into the bay. **Stuck** on this shallow ground, the ship breaks in the **surf**.

27:42-44. The soldiers would prefer **to kill the prisoners** rather than have them **escape**, but the **centurion**, recognizing the importance of Paul, intervenes. Passengers who can swim **make for the land**. Others float to shore **on planks** or **pieces of the ship**—literally "some of those from the ship," which could refer to members of the crew, possibly providing an ancient picture of lifesaving. Paul's prediction is fulfilled; **all** make their way **to land**.

28:1-10. *At Malta.* It is generally agreed that Paul's shipwreck occurred at Malta. This small island is located some sixty miles south of Sicily. The **natives** (literally "barbarians," or non-Greeks) were descendants of the Phoenicians. They spoke a Punic dialect, but Luke's narrative presents them as speaking Greek. The word for **welcomed** (literally "took forward") could mean merely that they brought Paul and his companions (no mention of soldiers or crew) to **the fire**. A variant text reads instead that they "revived" them. In October low temperatures on Malta are in the 50's, while five to twelve days of **rain** may be expected.

28:3-6. Paul's encounter with the **viper** has Hellenistic parallels. An epitaph has been discovered which tells of a man who survived shipwreck only to be killed by snakebite. Actually there are no poisonous snakes on Malta, and a viper does not fasten on when it bites. The natives, however, are convinced of the snake's deadly power and assume that Paul will **swell up or . . . fall down dead**.

His escape **from the sea** followed by this terrifying fate proves that he is guilty of some serious crime. The word translated **justice** is *Dike*—the goddess of vengeance and justice. When Paul escapes misfortune the observers **changed their minds** completely and suppose him to be **a god**. In contrast to 14:11-15 this conclusion is not rejected, and the recognition of Paul's divine power is made the climax of the story.

28:7-10. Paul arouses interest among important people. On Malta his host is **Publius,** the **chief man** (literally "first") of the island. This official title has been found in inscriptions, but it is not clear whether it means a native ruler or the representative of Rome. Paul's cure of Publius' **father** is reminiscent of Luke 4:38-40. The word **fever** appears in the plural, perhaps suggesting repeated attacks. Laying on **hands** as a means of miraculous cure finds a parallel in 9:17. The healing of this man leads to the cure of **the rest of the people on the island who had diseases**—an exaggeration. The response of the people is literally that they "honored us with many honors," which probably means that they **presented many gifts** and contributed provisions for the journey to Rome.

28:11-16. *Arrival in Rome.* If he leaves Malta **after three months** Paul apparently sails to Italy in January or February (cf. 27:9, 27). The sailing season did not open until March, though travel was sometimes attempted in February. The **ship,** probably another grain vessel of **Alexandria,** has also **wintered in the island.** The **Twin Brothers** are Castor and Pollux, sons of Zeus and patrons of sailors, whose images are carved or painted on the prow.

28:12-14. The ship spends **three days** at **Syracuse,** the beautiful port on the eastern coast of Sicily. To make a **circuit** suggests sailing along the curved shore of Sicily north to **Rhegium** (Reggio di Calabria) on the toe of Italy's boot.

Reaching **Puteoli** in two days would require an average speed of five knots—almost as fast as an ancient sailing vessel could travel. This port on the Bay of Naples was Italy's best harbor and the destination of most grain vessels from Egypt. Paul spends **seven days** there with the **brethren** (Christians) to allow time for the Roman Christians to meet him on the way.

28:15. The Christians of Rome meet Paul **at the Forum of Appius,** a town forty-three miles from the city, and at **Three Taverns,** a station at an important crossroad ten miles nearer the capital. Both are on the Appian Way. The church at Rome is not mentioned again in the narrative. Luke presents Paul almost as if he were the pioneer preacher of Christianity there.

28:16. In Rome, Paul is held under "household arrest" with a single guard and considerable freedom (but cf. verse 20). Some manuscripts add that the centurion delivers the prisoners over to a Roman official. No mention has been made of Paul's military escort since 27:43. The use of "we" drops out of the narrative at this point. Paul has reached his destination.

E. The Gospel Is Preached in Rome (28:17-31)

Luke's narrative has reached its climax. The Christian message has been proclaimed in Rome, and thus, symbolically, "to the end of the earth" (1:8). Throughout this section the Roman church (verse 15) is ignored. As always the mission begins with preaching to **the Jews**. The turning to **the Gentiles** reaches its high point: Jewish rejection is fulfillment of prophecy, and Gentile Christianity is the heir of the Old Testament faith.

28:17-19. Shortly after arriving in the city Paul summons the **leaders** of the Roman **Jews**. He addresses them in the same terminology used by Peter in 2:29. Paul argues that, although he has **done nothing against** the Jews or **the customs of our fathers**, he has been **delivered . . . into the hands of the Romans**—words reminiscent of the passion story (cf. Luke 9:22; 24:7). They found no grounds **for the death penalty**. Paul's **appeal to Caesar**, somewhat in contrast with 25:9-12, has been due to the Jewish objection to his release. In this passage Paul is distinguished from **the Jews** as if they were not his **brethren** at all.

28:20-22. Paul has summoned the Jewish leaders to set the record straight. He has not betrayed the ancient faith but is **bound with this chain** (see above on 26:29) **because of the hope of Israel**—a hope realized in the resurrection of Jesus. The Jews reply that they have received no negative report about Paul either by **letters or by visitors from Judea**. They are anxious to hear Paul's **views**, since **this sect** (cf. 24:5) **. . . is spoken against** everywhere.

The impression given—that the Roman Jews know nothing

about Christianity—is misleading. The church has been established in Rome for some time and includes among its membership converts from Judaism (Romans 2:17 and 4:1).

28:23-24. On an **appointed . . . day** Jews **in great numbers** come to Paul's **lodging** to hear his proclamation. How a prisoner living **at his own expense** (verse 30) is able to provide a room large enough for such a crowd is not explained. The apostle's message has been summarized throughout Acts: **the kingdom of God** and **Jesus** as the Messiah—a message which fulfills Old Testament expectation (cf. Luke 24:27).

28:25-29. Paul quotes Isaiah 6:9-10; the Septuagint is followed almost verbatim. Luke has used this text in his gospel (8:9-10) to explain the misunderstanding of the parables. Here, however, the point is that Jewish rejection of the gospel is final and is according to the will of God. **Salvation . . . has been sent to the Gentiles**—a point not entirely consistent with Romans 9–11. Verse 29, which describes the departure of the Jews, is not found in the best manuscripts (see the footnote in the Revised Standard Version).

28:30-31. Paul lives on in Rome **at his own expense**—the word is regularly used of money rather than of a house, as in the Revised Standard Version footnote. The picture of the apostle continuing in the capital city with much freedom and able to preach the **kingdom** and **the Lord Jesus Christ . . . openly and unhindered** proves that the Romans have nothing against Christianity.

Luke hints that after **two whole years** a change in Paul's situation occurs. There has been much debate over why the narrative ends without reporting this event. Efforts to show that Paul was released, or that Luke projected a third volume to complete the story, remain unconvincing. The careful reader will come to the conclusion that Paul was finally executed (cf. 20:25, 38), and that Luke deliberately chose not to include this result in his book—quite apart from the fact that it would detract from his apologetic to the Romans. The real interest of Acts is not with the ultimate end of its heroes, but with the triumph of the message they delivered to the world.

THE LETTER OF PAUL
TO THE ROMANS

Edwin Cyril Blackman

INTRODUCTION

The letter to the Romans is Paul's most mature writing. It has probably influenced Christian thought more than any other New Testament document. It is difficult to understand because it deals with objections and misunderstandings arising out of Jewish opposition which was part of Paul's situation but is not part of the situation today. Paul's intellectual vitality also causes difficulty. His quick-moving mind does not always provide a chain of argument with as many links as his interpreters would like.

But wrestling with his work is rewarding because of the majesty and continued relevance of his theme: God's judgment and mercy addressed to human disobedience. Romans is a restatement, in the light of Christ, of the biblical insights into God's righteousness applied to the moral failure of people and society, both then and now.

Occasion and Purpose

Paul wrote in the first instance to introduce himself to the Roman church and to acquaint its members with his desire to

106

visit them and his plan for a journey farther west. But self-introduction was no merely personal matter for him. It meant more than explaining his movements and his strategy as a church builder. It meant no less than an exposition of God's good news as he understood it, or rather as he had experienced it in the face of Jewish misunderstanding.

Paul was the chief architect of Christianity outside Palestine. He was by no means the only missionary, as the very existence of the Roman Christian community attested. He was himself ready to admit that others had laid foundations which he respected (15:18-21). But he had a conception of one gospel, one church, one empire (1:14-16). The saving righteousness of God which Paul saw at work in and since the passion of Christ includes all humanity.

Moreover the time was limited. The revelation of righteousness and the manifestation of spiritual power in the ministry of Christ signified the imminence of the end of history (see below on 11:26-27 and 15:18-21). The uniqueness of Christ meant the end of revelation, and this must be the prelude to the climax of God's purpose. To put this in more exclusively Jewish terms: if Jesus was the Messiah, the messianic age was present, the final act of the human drama was being played.

The full objective of the Messiah's coming was the gathering in of unbelieving Gentiles as well as recalcitrant Israel, and the triumph of the everlasting mercy of God (11:25-32). When this objective had been achieved that would be the glorious consummation divine wisdom had planned (11:33-36). The proclamation of this was the special responsibility of the churches—in fact their sole justification—and there was urgency about it. Paul saw his own divine commission as the apostle to the Gentiles (11:13; Galatians 1:16) in relation to this proclamation. It motivated his letter and put a cutting edge on his words.

The New Theology

Paul used the occasion of his anticipated visit to Rome to set forth his conception of what God is doing for humanity, in spite of the insensitivity of both Jews and Greeks (1:16). The mighty act inaugurated in the life of Christ is continuing in its effects. It is primarily a revelation of righteousness. The age-old need of righteousness was seen in the corruption of the pagan world and also in the failure of the favored Jews to recognize the presence of their Messiah.

Thus in the second place God's action has reference to human sin. Human beings are in the grip of sin and cannot free themselves. The moral sense—law, conscience, categorical imperative—convicts one of sin but does not liberate. But liberation is God's gracious gift, and it is available. One can be sure of that if one looks into the self-sacrificing love of Christ, which is the love of God. To respond to this love, to open one's mind to it, is what Paul calls faith. It is the essential preliminary step and it is open to all (10:8-12). Once this is done, new life begins. One makes a new start in the realization of that righteousness which God demands (8:1-4).

Thirdly, God's power deals with the death that accompanies sin. The new life that Christ makes possible is freed not only from sin but from death (5:12-21; 8:10-11, 37-39). There is inaugurated a new humanity, reconciled with God, emancipated from sin and death, morally empowered and spiritually privileged as no previous generation has been (8:1-39).

The era of law and the preeminence of Judaism are over. One cannot live on moral imperatives alone and no longer needs to try to (10:1-4). Judaism's position is unusual, and Paul feels obliged to discuss this at length (9–11). He holds to the conviction that the Jews will by divine mercy be delivered from their stubborn resistance. They will find their place with Gentiles in the final redeemed society (11:1-32).

These convictions were the result of Paul's mature reflection on his experiences as missionary and church builder during the period when Galatians, I and II Corinthians, and possibly other letters were written. His work had been done in the teeth of pagan opposition. Jewish opposition was equally real, and it demanded Paul's subtlest argument. The middle chapters of Romans reflect actual debates in the churches and synagogues concerning the Mosaic law and the priority of Jew to Gentile. Romans shows far deeper reflection on the Jewish problem than is mirrored in I Thessalonians 2:14-16.

The Church at Rome

Paul addressed a well-established Christian community that was already becoming famous in the Christian world (1:8). Its location in the metropolis would make it an important church. Its founder and the details of its origin are unknown. Converts from Palestine whose business took them to Rome must have sown the first seeds of the "good news of God."

Conceivably Claudius' expulsion of Jews from Rome (Acts 18:2) may have been caused by disputes in the synagogues over this new teaching about a Messiah. A reference to it by the Roman historian Suetonius can be understood in this sense. It is thus a good guess that the Roman church was formed before that time. It was Greek-speaking until the end of the second century and probably recruited its membership from Greek freedmen and slaves as well as Jews. Roman Catholic tradition assumes a visit of Peter, possibly in 42, to found the church in Rome.

Date and Place of Composition

The stage in his career at which Paul is writing and planning his missionary campaign west of Rome is clear from 15:19-28. He feels that his work in the eastern regions is complete. He still, however, must deliver at Jerusalem the financial contribution he has raised among his Gentile converts for the relief of the Jerusalem Christians, in fulfillment of the agreement made a few years previously at Jerusalem (Galatians 2:10). In that agreement Paul won recognition of his preaching to Gentiles without requiring circumcision as a condition of membership in the church. In return he admitted that Gentile converts should be made aware of obligation to the original Jewish members. Paul's understanding of the relationship of Jewish to Gentile Christians involved the responsibility of each for unity and mutual edification (15:27).

Paul attached much importance to this. II Corinthians 8–9

shows how much trouble he took to get the Corinthians to see the point. In addressing the Romans—a mixed church, in which Gentile members probably outnumbered Jewish—he expects to be understood when he explains that this task must be accomplished before he turns his face west.

For further details we may consult the narrative in Acts 20. There Paul's movements from the end of his Ephesian ministry to his departure from the Aegean area in his journey to Jerusalem are given. He is said to have traveled from Ephesus through Macedonia to Greece, where he spent three months. This stay is the most likely time for the writing of Romans, since he was originally planning to set sail from there directly to Syria and Jerusalem. The place was probably Corinth. Nearby Cenchreae is possible—in which case the reference to Phoebe in 16:1 has more point.

Changing his plans, Paul goes back through Macedonia, accompanied by several men, who may well be trustees of the money he is to deliver in Jerusalem. He spends Passover in Philippi and seven days in Troas. He then passes by Ephesus for a brief stop at Miletus in hope of reaching Jerusalem for Pentecost. Conceivably Paul could have dictated the letter at one of these places, or even on board a ship, though ancient sea travel did not provide much comfort.

For dating this period of Paul's career the only contact with outside historical sources is the statement of Acts 24:27 that after two years Felix was relieved by Festus as procurator of Judea. Unfortunately the sources are contradictory, so that the date of this event is uncertain. If we assume that it was 59 and that the two years are counted from Paul's arrest, the date of his three months' stay in Greece becomes the winter of 56-57. Other estimates have placed the date as early as 55 and as late as 59.

Romans thus belongs among the letters of Paul's middle period. These include I and II Corinthians and Galatians—also Philippians and possibly Colossians and Philemon if, as some believe, they were written from an imprisonment in Ephesus. Its greatest affinity is with Galatians, especially in relation to the meaning of faith and justification, the subordinate place of law in the divine dealing with human sin, and the antithesis of spirit and flesh.

Authenticity and Integrity

There has never been any doubt that Paul wrote Romans. Even the most radical criticism has accepted the authenticity of Romans, I and II Corinthians, and Galatians. However, some peculiarities in the transmission of Romans in the early church are revealed in the manuscripts. These raise questions about certain portions:

(1) The doxology, 16:25-27, is found in the majority of manuscripts at the end of chapter 14. In one manuscript the earliest written and therefore very important, it comes at the end of chapter 15. In some of the most trustworthy it appears at the end of chapter 16. This suggests that copies were in circulation which ended at these points.

It has been argued that the doxology is by a later hand than Paul's. That is reasonable on internal evidence, and would partly explain its various positions in the manuscripts. The point of adding it may have been to provide a conclusion for the whole collection of Pauline letters, as there is evidence that Romans was sometimes placed at the end of the Pauline section of the New Testament.

(2) The above considerations indicate that not all copies of Romans contained chapter 16. Though a very few scholars have viewed this chapter as an addition by another hand, the vast majority have seen no reason to doubt that it is Paul's work. The question is whether it was originally part of Romans or part of a letter to another church. The contents are more naturally explained on the latter view, and a plausible case can be made for Ephesus as its destination (see below on chapter 16).

(3) One manuscript lacks "in Rome" in 1:7, 15. This indicates attempts to remove traces of reference to a particular church and thus make the letter more obviously universal in its range. Such motives would also explain the removal of chapter 16—if it was removed rather than added to an original shorter form. It is not

impossible that Paul himself approved a longer and a shorter edition (see below on chapter 16).

I. Greeting and Thanksgiving (1:1-17)

1:1-7. *Salutation.* The opening salutation is different from those of the other letters of Paul. He had not founded this church and had not even visited it. Paul introduces himself as an emissary especially appointed to broadcast the good news of what God has done for humanity. A full explanation of what this means occupies the first eight chapters, and Paul begins this in earnest in verse 16. In his introductory words he contents himself with making three points.

(1) The content of the gospel is Jesus Christ, whom Christians call **Lord**. Christ is also recognized as God's **Son**, in virtue of his resurrection from the dead. This makes it clear that God's Spirit was operating through him to an unprecedented degree though he was also a real man, of Jewish descent (verse 3). Paul has no doubt about the real humanity of Christ.

(2) The career of Christ is not inexplicably new or strange, because it was part of the eternal plan of God. His Jewish descent means that he emerged in the life of the covenant people through whom God was revealing his good will. Jesus can be understood only within the framework of Judaism (verse 2; cf. 9:4-5 and John 4:22*b*).

(3) The gospel now made known in Christ has resulted in a new universal mission, which is the impulse behind Paul's activity. He calls it his **apostleship**.

1:1*a*. Paul is accustomed to think of himself as Christ's **servant**, literally "slave," as are all Christians. "Slave" is the proper antithesis of "Lord," or owner, and thus appropriate for the Christian relationship to Christ. When he is stressing the high privileges of Christians (e.g. 8:14-17 and Galatians 3:26–4:6) Paul uses other terms (see below on 6:15).

1:1*b*. The participle **called** may be understood as having the force of a noun—that is, a divinely summoned one (cf. verses

6-7; there is no word for **to be** in the Greek). An **apostle** is literally "one sent out," a missionary. But the New Testament usage refers not merely to traveling but to the responsibility of testifying to the gospel—the main point in this passage. Paul speaks of himself and his fellow apostle to Corinth, Apollos, as "stewards," imparting to the Corinthians what has been entrusted to them by God (I Corinthians 3:5-6; 4:1-2). The apostle is the custodian of the truth revealed in Christ. In Christian usage the term "apostle" became confined to the Twelve plus Paul; but there was an earlier, wider usage (see below on 16:7).

1:1c. The verb **set apart** is used again in Galatians 1:15 with reference to Paul's destiny to preach the gospel to the Gentiles. In Acts 13:2 it refers to his being commissioned with Barnabas at Antioch to the western campaign. The basic idea may come from the consecration of the Levites in ancient Israel (Numbers 8:5-22). Or possibly Paul may be thinking of his separation as a Pharisee from the ordinary, less scrupulous Jews. As a Christian he has come to regard the ideal of consecration, not negatively, as the avoidance of sinful contact, but positively, as the service of the good news of God's saving purpose in Christ.

1:2. The beneficent, divine activity which Paul is set apart to proclaim is not new. It was already envisaged in the Old Testament.

1:3-4. Christ was a son of **David** by physical descent, a reference which would mean that he was not merely a Jew but in the messianic succession. But there is something more important to assert, of an even higher order, **according to the spirit of holiness**. As a result of the **resurrection** which climaxed his earthly career Christ was **designated Son of God**. These two verses could conceivably be part of a rudimentary creed which Paul is quoting (cf. 4:25 and 10:9-10). On Christ's lordship, which expresses his relationship to human beings, see below on 10:9-11. His relationship to God is expressed by the affirmation of his sonship.

The phrase "Son of God" referring to Israel as a whole, or to the king considered as representative of the whole people, was familiar to Jews. It did not signify the Messiah except insofar as the Messiah was regarded as the king. But in reference to Jesus it was a part of the earliest Christian faith, because it went back to the thought of Jesus himself.

The matter has been much disputed, but in the light of Matthew 11:27 and Mark 12:1-11; 13:32 it cannot be denied that Jesus regarded himself as God's Son in the sense of having a unique mission and a unique relationship to God as his Father. This is the foundation stone of the church's estimate of him.

1:8-17. *Personal Address.* This paragraph begins in a more personal vein, complimenting the readers on their faith. Paul's intention to visit them has often been frustrated. He refers to this more in detail in 15:23-24. There we learn that the visit to Rome is part of a larger project, to preach his gospel as far west as Spain. His activity at Rome will be designed, not to make converts, but for the deepening of their spiritual experience and for their mutual encouragement.

1:13*b*-15. The last phrase of verse 13 implies that the Roman community is composed mainly of Gentiles. Whether the Jewish-Christian section among them was small or large, the Roman church as Paul now visualizes it symbolizes the turning of the pagan world to God. This is the special concern of his own apostleship. He feels an obligation to preach **to Greeks and to barbarians**, to all persons outside Judaism regardless of mental capacity, culture, or lack of culture.

"Barbarian" was the contemptuous term used by Greeks for people who lacked their culture and could not speak their language. This is parallel to Jewish contempt for Gentiles. The gospel knows no such distinctions (cf. Galatians 3:28 and Colossians 3:11).

1:16. What Paul has to offer is good news that makes him proud: divine **power** for human inability to achieve **salvation**. This is a gracious gift, but it is available wherever there is response, **to every one who has faith**. The logic here would seem to be that everyone needs salvation and that no one, not even the **Jew**, has any advantage. **First** is therefore surprising.

But Paul is too much of a Jew to forget that in fact Judaism has had great advantages in relation to God. Yet this power is also for Greeks whose previous experience has not been so markedly religious. It is for human beings of whatever history and culture who need salvation—it is for all. Paul will have to demonstrate the need of salvation, and 1:18–3:20 is devoted to this.

1:17. Paul mounts to a climax with this verse. It indicates why so much importance is to be attached to **faith** and introduces the other main key word of this letter, **righteousness**. The classic phrase "justification by faith," which has played such a part in Protestant theology, is based on this verse and on the argument of chapters 5–8. It is helpful to remember that the words "justification" and "justify" represent the same underlying Greek terms as underlie the noun "righteousness" and the verb "pronounce righteous."

The central affirmation of this letter is that a divine righteousness is **revealed** and in some sense communicated to those who have failed to achieve righteousness. This is implied in this verse. The negative assertion—that human life lacks righteousness—has to be proved in the detailed argument of 1:18–2:29.

The force of the present tense of the verb should be expressed more emphatically: **is** *being* **revealed**. Contrast 3:21, where Paul, using a different verb, looks back on the revelation as in one sense complete with the passion of Jesus Christ. Here, however, Paul is stressing the process of continuing revelation. In Christ's life and passion, and all that results from it in Christian experience, God's own righteousness is being made available. What has until now been regarded in Jewish thought about the end time as a feature of a future life is now, Paul affirms, a matter of present experience. This is the gospel of God, the achievement of Christ, and the new prospect for humanity. It is the continuation and the restatement in Paul's words of the teaching of Jesus himself about the realization, or inauguration, of the kingdom of God through his own ministry.

If the divine offer is to be accepted, the requirement for righteousness on the human side is what Paul calls faith. The curious combination of the words **through faith for faith** is probably nothing more than a form of emphasis. Human experience, whether of nation, race, family, or individual, nowhere exhibits perfection. But perfection is God's will. **The gospel of God . . . concerning his Son** (verses 1, 3) declares that God has taken the initiative in enabling all persons to attain it. The indispensable requirement on each individual human being is not moral effort but trust in God's purpose and a genuine response to his gracious offer.

This is supported by an Old Testament quotation, which would strengthen the argument in the eyes of a Jewish reader. Paul quotes, with an insignificant omission, the ambiguous Septuagint rendering of Habakkuk 2:4*b*, which is literally "The righteous out of faith shall live." This can mean either **He who through faith is righteous shall live** or "The righteous shall live as a result of faith." The original Hebrew probably means that the righteous shall live by faithfulness—that is, by faithful observance of God's commands. This is the very opposite of Paul's meaning.

But Paul gets support for his point from the Greek Septuagint translation. He will make clear what he understands by faith in chapter 4. We must define it briefly here as our initial receptiveness which allows God to begin his salvation within us. It precedes our doing good and even our renouncing sin. It sets up a right relationship with God out of which our service to him and to other persons naturally flows—righteousness *out of* faith.

Here **righteousness** does not have the abstract sense of moral rectitude usual in English and Greek usage, but a more dynamic sense which derives from the Hebrew. God's righteousness in the Old Testament is his concern that right shall be done, that the good person when wrongly accused shall be vindicated (e.g. Job), that Israel, striving to live as God's covenant people but oppressed by foreign powers, shall be set free. This last sense is prominent in Second Isaiah, where God's righteousness means his vindication or salvation of his people, for example:

> My deliverance [Septuagint "righteousness"] draws
>   near speedily,
> my salvation has gone forth.

. . . .
> but my salvation will be for ever,
>   and my deliverance will never be ended.
>> (Isaiah 51:5-6)

The process of spiritual liberation was set in motion by the impact of Jesus on Judaism. The prospect of final deliverance moved nearer. Paul's gospel is that the church is the sphere within which this experience continues to happen. He calls the experience the power of God for salvation and the revelation of God's righteousness. Later in the letter he refers to it as the fulfilling of the moral law (8:4; 13:10), the new life (5:17-21; 8:9-14), the final triumph (8:37-39), and mercy for all (11:32).

II. THE HUMAN SITUATION (1:18–3:20)

A. PAGANISM (1:18-32)

1:18-20a. *Natural Knowledge of God.* Paul now begins his demonstration of the desperate need for divine intervention referred to in verse 17.

1:18. The evil is described as **ungodliness** (i.e. lack of respect for religion) and the **wickedness** of those who **suppress the truth** (i.e. hostility to moral and intellectual endeavor). This does not go unnoticed by God. His reaction to it is described in parallel terms to the revelation of his righteousness in verse 17. In this case it is his **wrath** which **is revealed**.

The conception of the divine anger roots far back in Hebrew thought. It is primitive but not ignoble. It means, not the caprice of a vengeful deity, but the reaction of holy love to behavior which contradicts love. Israel experienced God as an active righteousness revealing itself and punishing unrighteousness.

1:19-20a. Sinful men may not claim the excuse of ignorance, for knowledge of God is available. They do not lack truth; they suppress it. Behind the visible world is an invisible Creator. The universe points beyond itself to an Author whom human observers, if they really think, will recognize and reverence. The New English Bible brings out in verse 20*a* a contrast between two Greek words: "His invisible attributes . . . have been visible . . . to the eye of reason."

Here Paul is not speaking of the full self-disclosure of the Father of our Lord Jesus Christ. He is referring to what is called natural religion. These two verses do not provide sufficient ground for a natural theology, nor are they typical of Paul's total thought about God. But at the present point of his argument he feels that there is a truth in natural theology which needs to be asserted (cf. I Corinthians 8:6 and Colossians 1:15-17).

1:20*b*-32.   *The Evils of Idolatry.* The terminology of this passage is considerably different from Paul's usual words. He allows himself to use language similar to that of the Stoics, which was current in Jewish writers outside Palestine. He is, after all, contemplating the pagan world. (For a typical piece of Jewish polemic against paganism see the Wisdom of Solomon 12:24-27; 13:7-9 and Isaiah 44:6-20.)

The wisdom which is the fear of the Lord knows instinctively that worship of the created world is a sin. Only the Creator must be worshiped. Both the everyday deification of specific objects (**the creature rather than the Creator**) and the philosophical absolutizing of the whole cosmos (Stoicism in Paul's day and immanentism and pantheism of all periods) are essentially idolatry.

All people are **without excuse** for involvement in idolatry and its degrading associations. Contemplation of the environment should warn one against this folly and make one sensitive to **truth about God**, which must not be given up in favor of lesser truths. This truth has consequences for philosophy and ethics as well as for religion. It is God's **decree**, or just demand.

1:21-23. These verses make it clear that idolatry is in Paul's mind. **They became futile** carries this implication (cf. 8:20). Paul refers first to its motivation in mental corruption (verse 21), then to the outward evidence in **images** of animal as well as human form.

1:24-31. Paul regards the accompanying moral degradation as caused by God. The thrice repeated **God gave them up**—that is, abandoned them to the consequences of their ungodliness—carries this meaning definitely. It is not enough to say that God simply permits it. In Paul's opinion, that would not relate God sufficiently closely to the human problem. It would dilute the conception of divine providence and give an insufficiently serious estimate of human degradation.

Paul surveys the evidence of moral delinquency. He describes it in terms of the working out of the divine wrath, which is in a continuous process of revelation (verse 18). Paul holds that God's attitude toward rapacity and debauchery may appropriately be described as anger. It is not enough to speak of a kind of impersonal process of retribution whereby men are involved in the consequences of their shameless conduct. That hardly does justice to the prominence of God as subject of the verb "gave them up" (cf. 3:5*b*).

The facts are frankly stated—perhaps influenced by conventional Jewish descriptons of the "abominations of the heathen." But they were true enough of that ancient Roman world, and they apply also to our modern culture. No reader today dare feel superior. Even those who have difficulty with the concept of divine anger must give Paul credit for facing the harsh realities of life in society. On the other hand he understands the function of Christ as being to deal with them and provide emancipation (cf. 8:3-4). The gospel of God is great enough to meet a situation as corrupt as that outlined here.

The three descriptions of social corruption considered here are:
  (1) the uncontrolled indulgence leading to sexual license that accompanied some idolatrous rites (verses 24-25);
  (2) sexual perversion (verses 26-27);
  (3) a **base mind** (New English Bible "depraved reason"), many specific consequences of which are listed.

1:28. The **base mind** is directly connected with failure to acknowledge God. This is subtly suggested by a play on words which might be freely translated: "As they *refused* the opportunity of attaining knowledge of God, God gave them over till their mind became like *refuse."*

1:32. The climax of the description of Gentile sinfulness is the remark that it is deliberate and self-congratulatory. Paul cannot believe that sinners act in utter ignorance of the divine sanction of morality and the divine condemnation of sin (cf. 6:23a). The connection between sin and death is developd more fully in 5:12-21.

B. JUDAISM (2:1–3:8)

Paul now turns his attention to Judaism. This is not mentioned explicitly until 2:17, though it is clearly implied in 2:12. But from the opening words of chapter 2 he is confronting people who are scandalized by the gross behavior referred to in 1:22-32 and are inclined to sit in judgment on it.

2:1-11. *Spiritual Arrogance.* This attitude of superiority is inexcusable. The sins of the refined and the religious are equally as blameworthy as the crude sins exposed in chapter 1. Hard-heartedness and impenitence may not express themelves in sexual vice, but they are no less deserving of God's anger.

This seems to be the main point, but other suggestions in these verses complicate the interpretation. The critical person Paul has in mind is twice said to be guilty of committing the crimes he condemns in others (verses 1 and 3; cf. verses 21-24). This is psychologically quite understandable. Jesus himself exposed this often in his condemnations of hypocrisy. Are we then to assume that **you, the judge, are doing the very same things** actually envisages Jews as guilty of the excesses detailed in chapter 1? This is a possible explanation when allowance is made for the corrupting influence of a pagan environment on Jews living outside Palestine.

An alternative explanation of the censorious attitude is that Gentiles are included in it. This is not so likely, however, because the terminology of this paragraph—God's **judgment . . . forbearance . . . wrath**—is Hebrew rather than Greek.

The presumption of verse 4*a* is not the *hubris* (insolence) which figures so largely in Greek tragedy. Rather it is one of the less happy consequences of the Jewish sense of privilege as recipients of divine favor (cf. 9:4-5).

The greatest teachers of Israel reminded their people that privilege implies responsibility (cf. Amos 3:2). The lax type of Jew who imagines he has a right to God's kind forbearance and ignores the opportunity of **repentance** will ultimately experience the stern judgment of God. Whatever priority the Jew has must include priority in requital for evil deeds (verse 9). God may have elected the Jews to special favor and responsibility, but he **shows no partiality**. In the new dispensation God's offer of righteousness is open to Gentiles as well as Jews, on the basis of faith, which is possible for all alike.

2:8 In this context **factious** is not so much the sense as "governed by selfish ambition" (New English Bible).

2:12-16. *Both Jews and Gentiles Sinners.* In verse 12 Paul speaks in terms of the Old Testament **law** to express the distinction between Jewish and Gentile ways of living. The Gentiles' sin cannot be defined as breaking the law, and their consequent perishing cannot be explained by reference to it. This is rather unprecise, but Paul does not say that Gentiles do not sin or that they do not suffer the consequences. Jews, on the other hand, sin in spite of the law and will be judged by its standards.

But Paul is moving on to a more positive statement in verses 14-15. Some Gentiles may be said to have the law **written on their hearts**, and in virtue of this their conduct does in fact conform to the law's demands. On the basis of this they may be reckoned to be **justified** (see below on 3:24).

Paul is here reasoning in line with the more generous Jewish attitude to the decent pagan. The use of the word **conscience** suggests that he is influenced by Stoic ideas, probably through Jewish Hellenistic thought. The recognition of this conformity of Gentile moral endeavor with the Jewish law is apparently not to be made known until the final judgment (verse 16). Again the thought lacks precision. It is an unusual line of argument for Paul. In fact verse 13 is contrary to his characteristic understanding of how one attains righteousness before God (cf. 1:17; 3:20-21; Galatians 2:16).

Some take verses 13-15 as a parenthesis and connect verse 16 directly with verse 12, thus lessening the confusion of the thought in the whole passage. We still have the ambiguity as to whether law means the Old Testament Mosaic law, as in verses 12-13, or moral sense generally, as in verses 14-15. In these latter verses Paul is more under the influence of Stoic ethics, with its innate moral sense, than of the rabbis who speak of the law **written on** the **hearts** only of Israelites. Some rabbis would not even allow the law to be taught to Gentiles.

2:17-24. *Jewish Profession and Practice.* Paul's exposure of Jewish guilt, following the exposure of the guilt of paganism in chapter 1, has got sidetracked into a comparison of Jew and Gentile. Now he calls attention to the gap between Jewish pretension and achievement. The law gives instruction not only in ordinary morality but in its finer points, so that the Jews can **approve what is excellent** ("are aware of moral distinctions," New English Bible). They thus have a missionary responsibility to be a **guide to the blind**—that is, the Gentiles. But instead of making the religion of Israel attractive to non-Israelites, Judaism does the opposite; it tends to monopolize **truth.**

The argument is somewhat rhetorical. It mounts to a climax in verse 24 with a quotation from the Septuagint of Isaiah 52:5, which adds the phrase **among the Gentiles** not found in the Hebrew.

2:25-29. *True Circumcision.* These verses take up again the contrast of Jew and Gentile, or rather the comparison between the best of Judaism and the best of Gentile moral conduct. This spiritualized conception of circumcision could well have been developed at greater length. Nowhere else does Paul touch on this theme.

Judaism, its rite of circumcision, and the whole conception of an elect people represent the primacy of unwavering devotion to God. Paul argues that it is possible for those who are not Jews to represent this ideal. If the Jews do not conform with the law's demand, their profession is meaningless. On the other hand a

Gentile may be the moral equal of a professing Jew, though a Jew might object that no Gentile does actually **keep the law**. Circumcision has significance if it is more than a physical mark. It is to be a symbol of consecration which is attested by good living.

Paul has gone further than most of his contemporaries in saying that possessing the law and circumcision do not by themselves mean obedience to the will of God. But he qualifies what he has said in the next paragraph (3:1-8) in attempting to point out the value of circumcision.

The notion of a spiritual circumcision is familiar to the Old Testament. For the later rabbis, however, any spiritualizing of it was intolerable. The outward mark was essential. It secured God's favor and entry into the age to come. It was God's ordinance, not simply a piece of symbolism.

3:1-8. Has the foregoing discussion left no distinctive place for Judaism? If all alike can know and do God's will, was the special revelation to which Jews appealed—**the oracles of God**—superfluous?

We have to wait until chapters 9–11 for Paul's full-length answer to these questions. But he realizes that he must say something in reply at this point. He has not given up the traditional belief that his people have a special place in the history of salvation. The Jews were the recipients of special revelation through Abraham, Moses, and the prophets. Israel's backsliding, which is what he is stressing here, does not erase history or alter its significance. It is part of the continuing problem for God the Lord of history, who has inaugurated a new saving action in Christ (cf. 3:21-26).

God's dealing with humanity also involves **wrath** and ultimate judgment. But he is Lord and Saviour, as the past history of Israel rightly understood testifies. Israel's present disloyalty to its glorious past does not nullify that past. The main factors in it were God's **faithfulness**, **justice**, and **truthfulness**.

We should translate "righteousness" rather than "justice" in verse 5 because it is the same word in Greek as in verse 21 and 1:17. God's faithfulness, righteousness, and truth mutually implied one another. All are implied in the main theme of Romans: the revelation of God's righteousness.

This whole paragraph appears to have been hastily put together, and it is wise not to interpret it too rigorously. The quotation of Psalm 51:4 in verse 4 is from a classic confession of sin. The point is that there can be no question of the divine justice which condemns human sin. Verse 7 is best taken as an imaginary objection, or one that Paul has met in debates elsewhere. This suggests to him a familiar slander on his preaching (verse 8).

C. THE UNIVERSALITY OF SIN (3:9-20)

Paul abruptly breaks off the foregoing development and proceeds to the logical inference from his argument in 1:18–2:29: the common sinfulness of Jews and Greeks. A series of quotations from Psalms and Isaiah assert the universal fact of sin, which he has demonstrated from ordinary experience. The appeal to scripture is necessary to make the argument convincing for Jewish readers. The point was admitted both in the Old Testament and in rabbinic writings.

3:9. *The Power of Sin.* Sin means the inability to carry out the will of God. **All men,** even the elect people who received special revelation, are under its **power.** It is assumed that **Greeks** as well as **Jews** have some conception of the will of God, a moral sense understood as divinely implanted (1:19).

Here then is Paul's diagnosis of the human problem: the whole world is **accountable to God** (verse 19*b*). What is a person to do? All claims to moral integrity must be given up. The basic problem for Paul is that stated by Job: "How then can man be righteous before God?" (Job 25:4).

Sin is a religious, not simply an ethical, term. For Paul the first man was the first sinner, and it is increasingly difficult for successive generations to avoid sin. Since Adam, in whom sin entered the world, sin is a condition of human existence. It has a stranglehold. It is in league with death (5:12-14). Humanity as sinner is in a hopeless plight. But God has broken the hold of sin. Through Christ God has inaugurated the possibility of a sinless humanity (3:21-25; 5:15-21).

3:10-20a. *Proof from Scripture.* The quotations in verses 10-18—some rather free—are from the Septuagint translation of Psalms 14:1-3 (or 53:1-3); 5:9; 140:3; 10:7; Isaiah 59:7-8; and Psalm 36:1. As words of the **law**—here used in the sense of scripture in general—they are final for **those . . . under the Law**, the Jews (cf, 2:12b). The guilt of the pagan world also is presupposed in the light of 1:18-32 and verse 9.

No human being can claim righteousness before God on the basis of moral conduct, **works of the law.** This is the premise from which Paul starts. Righteousness has to be attained on another basis, **apart from law** (verse 21).

3:20b. *The Function of the Law.* This clause, though parenthetical, is very important. It answers the implied question in the mind of a Jew: Why do you speak so derogatively about the law? Has it no function in the attainment of righteousness?

In Paul's understanding the function of the Mosaic law code—and of any moral code—was not to produce good conduct. It was to create awareness of sin. This departs from the normative rabbinic view but has solid prophetic teaching behind it. It is more fully stated later (5:20; 7:7-23; 8:3-4; 10:4; 13:8-10; also Galatians 2:19-21; 3:10-25).

The optimistic view that commandments and ideals simply have to be carried out—"We needs must love the highest when we see it," etc.—is radically challenged by this teaching of Paul's. He is too aware that ideals are not realized—and that when people saw the highest they crucified him.

III. The Divine Offer of Righteousness (3:21-26)

Paul affirms that, however serious the diagnosis of moral need as outlined in the previous two chapters, the situation is not hopeless. God has acted.

It seems probable that Paul is thinking of the reflection on the meaning of Christ's death which was already developing in the church, especially in relation to the observance of the Lord's Supper. It may be that the key words **redemption** and **expiation** belong to this earlier atonement theology. Such a pre-Pauline core might be: "The righteousness of God has been manifested for all who believe. They are justified by his grace as a gift, through the redemption which is in Christ Jesus, whom God put forward as an expiation by his blood."

3:21. *God's Saving Righteousness.* God has **manifested** his righteousness. Paul is now thinking of this as already complete in the passion of Christ. Hence the verb is in the past tense, not the present, as in 1:17, where he was stressing the continuing effects. There is no contradiction. The divine rescue operation, God's righteousness, is evidenced in the life, death, and resurrection of Christ. It can be seen in the transformation of lives as they respond to the proclamation of this by Christian preachers and grow in moral and spiritual stature in the expanding fellowship of the churches (cf. 6:1-14 and 12:1-2).

This happens quite apart from the function of the **law**, but is nevertheless foreseen in **the law and the prophets**—that is, in the Old Testament (cf. 1:2). The gospel is not an innovation in God's dealing with humanity. Nor can it be put in strict opposition to moral codes, though its effectiveness is positive while theirs is negative (cf. 8:3-4). It is rooted in God's **gift**, which is prior to God's demand, in the divine saving act rather than human moral endeavor (**works of the law**, verse 20).

3:22a. *The Response of Faith.* The benefits of God's saving act are open to any who have faith. This is not a human act or effort but a response, a reaching out of the hand to accept God's gracious offer (emphasized in verse 24).

It is important to grasp Paul's point here, for otherwise the whole argument of chapters 1–11 will be misunderstood. Faith is essentially a response to divine initiative. Sinfulness being universal, we can do nothing to secure our salvation other than fitting into the conditions created by divine grace made visible in Christ. It is not for us to set our goal and go after it in our own self-generated enthusiasm. The business of all humankind is to recognize our dependence on a gracious controller of our destiny, who is revealed in the self-sacrifice of Christ's death. Responding with gratitude, we can face our moral obligations with what Paul calls the "obedience" of faith (1:5; 6:16-17).

3:22b-24. *The Gift of Redemption.* Verses 22b-23 are really a parenthesis explaining **all** in verse 22a. **"Fall short of the glory"** reflects the creation of humanity in the image of God (Genesis 1:26) and the admission that the divine glory which should show in the way one bears oneself in fact is lacking. But it was expected to be restored in the age to come.

Justified is a verbal form from the same root as "righteousness." It means not so much "made righteous" in the sense of morally perfect as "pronounced righteous," that is "acquitted." The gift is thus freedom to leave court rather than go to prison, freedom to resume life with all its obligations, in grace (5:20-21), in the power of Christ (6:4-11; 8:10), in the Spirit (8:4).

Redemption strictly signifies the emancipation of a slave by the payment of money. There seems to be no thought here of the price. If that question is raised, the answer has to be: Christ's life, or **blood** (verse 25). This has been featured in some Christian theories of the atonement. But probably Paul is content with the simple sense of liberation. He uses the word again in 8:23 with reference to the final deliverance.

In I Corinthians 1:30 and Colossians 1:14 "redemption" means the present privilege of Christians, including forgiveness of sins. This blessing is here said to be "in" Christ. It is God's gracious gift, and its availability is due to what Christ was and did. Jews would point to its exemplification in their deliverance from Egypt and from Babylon. Christians point to the new life in Christ as the great example and to Gentiles, not Jews only, as the beneficiaries.

3:25a. *Expiation by Christ's Sacrifice.* The even more suggestive term **expiation** implies the efficacy of sacrifice. This was familiar to Paul and to Jews through the daily ritual of the Jerusalem temple. It was familiar also in the Gentile world. The blood of sacrificial animals was believed to have power for restoring a right relationship between God and humanity. Paul's affirmation is that Christ's **blood**—that is, his self-sacrifice—really does have this efficacy.

An alternative interpretation regards the word "expiation" as meaning the "mercy seat" (Exodus 25:17-22; Leviticus 16:13-15). This was the place where reconciliation was effected, according to Jewish ritual. In this view the mercy seat for Christians is Calvary.

In all this biblical language about expiation the thought is not that God has somehow to be coaxed into a forgiving mood. That is paganism. In the Bible God is always waiting to forgive sinners, even though he is said to be angry with them. God hates sin, and the basic problem is to get rid of sin and liquidate its power to cause hostility between a person and God (5:10*a*). This was the task to which Christ's life was directed (8:3-4). God was in Christ reconciling the world to himself (5:10-11; II Corinthians 5:19).

This passage has become classic in Christian theories of the atonement. Something necessary for the achievement of goodness was effected by Christ through his death. The word "expiation" draws a comparison with the death of sacrificial animals which was intelligible enough in Paul's day because this was a familiar feature of ancient religion. But it is difficult, if not meaningless, today.

This is only an analogy however. Christ was not an animal, and his death was not sacrifice but self-sacrifice. The point here is that as a result of the new insight into the method of divine grace which arises from contemplation of Christ's self-sacrifice a new beginning of moral experience becomes possible. A new spiritual outlook is generated—conversion, enlightenment, reorientation. Theological reflection on this experience sees behind it an initial act of God for salvation. That is the significance of the life and death and resurrection of Christ.

3:25*b*-26. Before Christ, God was tolerant, overlooking sins. Positively this is an aspect of his forgiveness. Negatively it might be taken to mean that he let sin go unpunished, thereby allowing doubt to arise concerning his justice. Paul seems to have some sensitivity to this. He asserts that what we now learn of God through Christ is all the demonstration and vindication God's justice needs. God deals with sinful humans by giving them a new start, and by exhibiting in Christ a creative love which will provide new motivation and rob sin of its power. In this way God's justice is seen at work. (On the objection that Paul's conception of God makes religion too easy cf. 6:1 and 15.)

IV. The Human Response: Faith (3:27–4:25)

3:27-31. *Faith Required of All.* Paul briefly draws two inferences from his announcement of the manifestation of God's righteousness. First, it leaves no place any more for human merit. The one who begins anew under the inspiration of what God offers in Christ will claim no moral progress as his own achievement. Self-congratulation is ruled out for Christians.

The word translated **boasting** in verse 27 is an aspect of the zeal characteristic of Judaism and seems to be a favorite word of Paul's. We see what he means by it in his autobiographical remarks in Galatians 1:13-14; Philippians 3:3-6; and II Corinthians 11:16–12:10. The basis of the Christian life is not moral striving but trust in God. Instead of "basis" Paul actually uses the word "law" (verse 27) because it was basic in Judaism. But in this context we must translate it **principle** or "authority."

3:29-30. The second inference is that faith is a great leveler. Jew and Greek alike are dependent on the one God who makes goodness arise out of faith. There is no distinction among those who live by faith, any more than there is in a common sinfulness. Even Jews owe their salvation, not to **works**, but to faith. This will be pointed out in the case of Abraham in chapter 4.

3:31. We expect Paul to sum up by saying that the Old Testament law, or moral obligation generally, no longer applies to Christians who take their stand on faith. The objection is anticipated from the Jewish side: You are setting up a rival principle to moral authority. What guarantee is there that people will behave morally? Paul is greatly concerned about this. He differs from his Jewish critic in his perception that what is needed is not exhortation but vision and impetus. These can come only out of what he calls faith.

Paul's answer to the objection is somewhat surprising. He claims that he does assign a proper place to the law. Verse 20 gives part of his meaning, but this needs to be developed more fully. Apart from 4:13-15, which subordinates the law to "promise," we have to wait for the arguments of 6:15–8:4. Paul is not yet ready to say Christ means the end of the law (10:4), or that he himself has died to the law (Galatians 2:19), though either of these statements would logically follow verses 9-26.

4:1-12. *Abraham as an Example of Faith.* At this point Paul finds it to his purpose to clearly illustrate what he means by faith. He therefore pauses to exemplify faith by reference to a man recognized by all Jews as of overriding significance in the human relationship with God.

Concerning the precise ground of Abraham's religious importance there was some divergence among Jewish theologians. Some of their thought must have been known to Paul. The majority view was that his acceptance with God was due to his **works**, that is, his good conduct. He could be regarded as having demonstrated perfect obedience to God's commands. Outstanding examples of this were his circumcision (Genesis 17) and his willingness to sacrifice his dear son Isaac (Genesis 22). Some rabbis held that he did in fact fulfill the law, even though it was not revealed until the time of Moses, centuries later.

Paul finds Abraham's significance elsewhere. It was not in his meritorious deeds or in his temptations, but in his trustful attitude to God, his faith. The main text in his interpretation is therefore Genesis 15:6 (cf. Galatians 3:6).

4:4-5. Paul's reasoning in these verses seems a little strained, but it would not appear so to those accustomed to the subtleties of rabbinic interpretation. "Believing" or "trusting" in Paul's mind implies the opposite of "doing" or "working." Working cannot be meant in the case of Abraham, Paul suggests (verse 4). In that case payment or **due** would be mentioned, not **gift**. It was not a matter of working at all but of trusting, of relating himself to God who pronounces righteous even the **ungodly** (see above on 3:24).

4:6-8. This idea is supported by a quotation from Psalm 32:1-2*a*. These verses were useful for Paul's argument because they refer to the blessing of forgiveness, thereby implying something other than meritorious obedience. They also use the same Greek verb that Paul has found in the Septuagint translation of Genesis 15:6 with the sense "credit to," "reckon as." The verb basically means "think," "count," "reckon," and in the metaphor of bookkeeping "enter to the credit of."

The bookkeeping metaphor is not adequate for the expression of our relationship with God. Our progress in goodness is never sufficient to establish a credit balance. God credits us by a divine gracious gift (verses 4-5; cf. 3:24).

4:9-12. Paul takes the idea of blessing from Psalm 32:1-2*a* and transfers this to the privilege of Abraham mentioned in Genesis 15:6. He then proceeds to point out that at that stage of Abraham's life he was still **uncircumcised.** From this he draws the inference that Abraham's real significance is as the forerunner of Gentiles, who are people of faith and on that basis recipients of God's offer of righteousness.

Abraham is also the ancestor of the Jews. But the relationship between him and them is to be understood as rooting in the faith which he had before he received the outward mark of Judaism, circumcision. This implies a distinction between Jews who have faith and those who are content with the badge of circumcision and strive to please God by their good works. This is not quite the same conception as in 2:25-29 between the merely outward circumcision and that which fulfills the law.

This method of using scripture strikes modern readers as arbitrary. But it conforms to rabbinic standards. Even if Paul's position might seem extreme to his Jewish readers, they could not object to his method of interpretation. We shall have further examples of it in chapters 9–11.

Paul's methodology, which goes against modern logic and biblical criticism, should not blind us to the force of his arguments in general. They are able to stand by their inherent logic. For example, the real weight of these verses is that Abraham's acceptance with God was not brought about by the ritual of circumcision. That rite was not the cause of God's approval but the **sign or seal** of it. Baptism, the Christian parallel to circumcision, was also called a "seal" from the second century onward. It confirmed what had been effected already by divine grace.

To Paul, Abraham was singled out by an awareness of God and sensitiveness to his call which was prior to his outward obedience. This was his "faith." This was what he "gained" (if this is the correct reading in verse 1; see the footnote to the Revised Standard Version). This idea stands out clearly enough, whatever interpretation of texts is used to support it.

We miss the reference to Genesis 12:3 which is quoted in Galatians 3:8-9. The argument of Galatians 3 supplements this chapter and brings out more clearly that the Christians are the true heirs of Abraham (Galatians 3:29).

4:13-25. *The Promise to Abraham.* Paul now picks out another episode from the Abraham narratives of Genesis. This is the promise that his destiny is to be a source of blessing for all nations (Genesis 12:1-3; 17:5; 18:18; 22:17-18). The logic is difficult to follow, because here, as elsewhere, the links of the thought are not all expressed.

The promise means God's guarantee of final salvation. For Christians this means all that they experience through Christ, who is the seed of Abraham (Galatians 3:16) and the authenticator of all God's promises (II Corinthians 1:20). The human side of the promise is trust in God. It is exemplified in Abraham, and is now called **righteousness of faith** and not living according to the law (**not . . . through the law,** a phrase which very emphatically begins the sentence in the Greek).

4:14-15. These verses are parenthetical. The principle of the law is utterly opposed to the principle of the promise, or of faith. Law demands obedience and, if that is not forthcoming, retribution (**wrath**). That is not the way of salvation. To imagine God's way of dealing with persons as confined to this method is to nullify both the promise and faith.

Verse 15*b* is obscure. It may mean that God's saving action lifts us to a level above the law. On this level transgression does not enter in—that is, moral failure does not mar the relationship between God and ourselves.

4:16-17. The alternative to the law is **faith, promise, grace,** and this marks the true succession from Abraham. **All his descendants** includes Gentiles as well as Jews (cf. 3:29-30). Rabbis could speak of Abraham as the first convert. Paul illustrates this from Genesis 17:5 (verse 17*a*).

Verse 17*b* memorably characterizes God as the object of faith: **gives life to the dead** gets point from verse 19. **Calls into existence the things that do not exist** includes the physical universe, the humanity made in God's image, and, finally, the perfected society in a perfected universe (8:18-23).

4:18-25. The root of faith is the conviction that God is as described in verses 17 and 21. God is **able** to put in the place of our nonexistent righteousness a righteousness of faith. God is able to overcome even death, as evidenced in the resurrection of Christ and foreshadowed in the birth of Isaac to parents who were near death. Curiously, Paul makes no use of the story of the sacrifice of Isaac, which might have served his purpose here.

In the total setting of chapters 1–8 the nonexistent thing which God causes to exist is the righteousness of sinners. This is his "new creation" (cf. II Corinthians 5:17). God is this kind of God. God creates righteousness where there is the receptiveness of faith (verse 22). The evidence for this is not only the example of Abraham and the words of promise but the death and resurrection of Jesus.

V. THE EFFECTS OF FAITH (5:1–8:39)

We are now ready to hear about the consequences of the divine offer of righteousness and our reception of it by faith. How does it actually work out in the new Christian experience? Chapter 5 explains this new life in terms of a general spiritual release and especially a release from death. The more ethical inferences will be drawn in chapters 6–7 and 12–14, though the distinction between religious and ethical is ours rather than Paul's. Christian ethics can be worked out only when obedience to God and gratitude for what God has given in Christ are seen as the preliminary to all moral endeavor and spiritual growth.

A. RECONCILIATION (5:1-11)

5:1a. *Justification by Faith.* This clause recalls 3:24 (see comment), with the difference that **are justified** is now in that characteristic Greek past tense which implies that the action is complete. The meaning is not that as soon as one has faith one is morally perfect; that would be a denial of plain facts. Nor do we have to interpret the verb as implying a legal fiction: you are not righteous, but God is prepared to treat you as if you were and be tolerant of any future sins.

Paul has indeed argued, in view of the evidence of human delinquency quoted in chapters 1–2, that everyone is guilty. No single individual, Jew or Gentile, deserves to be acquitted; everyone should be sent to prison (3:19-20). But his use of the verb "justify" presupposes not only the negative of our moral failure but the positive of Christ's perfect life and sacrificial death, which constitute a new factor in the moral situation.

We may compare this to a judge acquitting an accused person in view of fresh evidence brought before the court or a new counsel for the defense (cf. 8:33-34). Thus freed, the accused leaves the court to resume life among their fellow citizens. They are no more morally perfect than others, but they are not in prison and can make a new start with their life. In describing this new start we can dispense with the metaphor of the law court, as Paul does in verse 1b.

5:1b. *Peace with God.* Surprisingly, in the majority of manuscripts Paul seems to say "let us have" rather than **we have** peace in relation to God. This word "peace" expresses the new situation simply. It is synonymous with the more formal theological term **reconciliation** in verse 11.

The trouble with sinful living is that it is out of touch with God, which is one's rightful relationship. Worse still, it is a relation of enmity or hostility (verse 10a). The sinner refuses to acknowledge God's law and is, as it were, fighting against God. This is not merely a series of defiant acts but a settled disposition (cf. verse 10a and 8:7). The basic human problem was involvement in this broken relationship toward God, this state of cold war. God has taken the initiative to break the deadlock. The divine revelation through Christ makes a new relationship of peace possible.

5:2-5. *New Hope.* Christ has given believers **access to God's presence and a new experience of divine grace** (cf. 3:24), which means essentially God's willingness to have dealings with sinful humanity. In this sense it is the same as his **love**. This causes a new outlook on life and **hope**, or confidence, of ultimte salvation.

Paul does not speak of this new experience as being saved but keeps salvation for the future sense (verse 10b). This hope cannot be shaken by anything that may happen in life's hardships, which instead result in **character** that in turn strengthens hope. It is a product of the encounter with God which Paul describes by the vivid metaphor of the pouring out of **God's love.** The New English Bible phrase "flooded our inmost heart" sounds exaggerated but is not more so than Paul's Greek here. How different this metaphor from the legal one implied in "righteousness"! Paul connects God's love with the onrush of the **Holy Spirit** (cf. I Corinthians 13 and Galatians 5:22).

5:6-11. *Evidence of God's Love.* This talk about God's love is not pious fancy. There is concrete evidence of it in what Christ did, in his devotion to men and women without scrutinizing their merit. Human experience provides no parallel to what Christ has done even for the **ungodly**.

5:9. Reference to Christ's death suggests to Paul the thought of justification by **blood**. This has past and present reference. Paul now adds a future reference—the certainty of not having to experience the final **wrath**, that is, retribution, here thought of, not as in 1:18, but as connected with the ultimate judgment, as in 2:5.

5:10-11. To be **reconciled** is the same as to be justified. Paul's usage always implies our need to be reconciled to God, not God's need to be changed at all in the divine attitude toward us. Justification is not a judge's acquittal so much as a parent's welcome. Reconciliation brings in the idea of reunion with the life of the family.

B. FREEDOM FROM SIN AND DEATH (5:12–6:14)

5:12-21. *The New Humanity.* The new relationship of peace with God is also a new type of life for believers. They have been initiated into the great liberation from the power of sin, and this also means liberation from death. This is God's **free gift**, but it can be described as sharing the life of Christ (cf. **saved by**, literally "in," **his life**. Christians are pioneers of a new humanity "in Christ."

This is worked out in terms of a contrast between **Adam** and Christ. Adam is the representative figure of the old humanity, unable to attain righteousness because limited by sin and doomed to die. Christ is the dominant figure of the new humanity. He is the creator of the possibility of overcoming sin, of becoming righteous and continuing to **reign in life**, to **eternal life**—that is, life of a quality which is not affected by death.

This is Paul's doctrine of Christ as the second Adam. Though it occurs only here and in I Corinthians 15:45-57, it presents his main thought about how Christ is effective for human redemption. It is the theory of atonement to which he attaches the greatest value. It does not rest on the sacrificial analogy, but it recognizes the need of a humanity dominated by sin and mortality. It affirms that Christ introduces positive energies which are beyond the corrupting influence of sin and death. What Adam failed to achieve is achieved by Christ and made available to all who attach themselves to him by faith.

To follow this argument we must think corporately. Adam and Christ are both historic figures, but for Paul they are corporate entities and not isolated individuals. Adam stands for the whole of humanity, understood as in Genesis 3, yielding to temptation and involved in its consequences. Abraham similarly in chapter 4 stands for Israel depending on the great promise of its God. Christ is the conqueror of sin and death, not for his own release from earthly life, but vicariously for those who are to be incorporated in his body, the church, the new Israel.

This kind of thinking was natural enough for the ancient Hebrew. It is not so easy for the modern mind. The tendency now to absorb the individual into larger units like the state or the industrial corporation, dangerous as it may be to personal freedom, may make biblical modes of thought less strange.

5:12-14. The problem is stated in these verses. The **one man** is Adam. He was responsible for the entry of sin into human experience. But the real fact from which Paul starts is not the guilt of Adam but the universality of sin—**all men sinned**—and the universality of death, regarded as the inevitable result.

This is questionable to the modern mind, but it was a regular inference in Jewish interpretation. Death for Paul, as in the Old Testament, means more than the end of physical existence. It is a spiritual fact, connected with divine judgment on sin, and a part of the effects of sin. It exerts a sinister control (**reigned**). Sin and death are aspects of the kingdom of Satan, which is to be replaced through Christ by the kingdom of God. The metaphor of reigning is used again in verses 17 and 21.

Sin perverted human life from the very beginning. Paul thinks of it objectively, apart from whether it is deliberate or not, in fact apart from one's moral awareness. It is not synonymous with guilt, which is one's awareness of sin. This awareness depends on moral **law**. But sin is a wider term. It means all that prevents a person from realizing God's purpose and, in terms of Genesis 3, obeying the commandment.

The more individualized concept of guilt is included in the reference to sin as **counted**—an allusion to the Jewish picture of heavenly books which recorded all sins. The **transgression of Adam** was deliberate defiance of a divine command. **Type** is literally "stamp," hence "likeness" or "correspondence."

5:15-19. Verses 12-14 are really one long subordinate

sentence which is not finished. Instead Paul starts afresh in verse 15 and does not construct the clause anticipated by **as** in verse 12.

Where Adam failed Christ succeeded. Here begins a series of carefully balanced antitheses drawing out the parallelism between Adam and Christ. Something of precision is sacrificed, but the main thought is magnificently clear.

Trespass means a particular sinful act, an outcrop, so to speak, of the underlying sin which holds humanity in its grip. Christ makes possible justification, righteous living, and the triumph of grace over sin, thus reversing the process which produces their opposites. The old humanity was characterized by the **disobedience** exemplified in Adam. The redeemed humanity reproduces the **obedience** shown in Christ's perfect life.

Made righteous appears to mean complete moral perfection—a more developed state than is implied by justification (**acquittal and life**). This is why the verb is in the future tense.

5:20-21. This sentence goes beyond 3:20 in saying that the function of the **law** is not to solve the moral problem but to show it up in its true moral dimension. In a sense it aggravates it, **increase the trespass.** This paradox is explained in 7:7-13. It is divine **grace** which meets human need and is far more powerful than sin and all its effects, including death.

6:1-14. *New Life in Christ.* Christians are sure of salvation (chapter 5), but they have to develop in moral stature. Grace does not mean license but moral power. Moral obligation continues and should be gladly faced in the **newness of life** on which the Christian embarks.

6:1. The objection envisaged here (cf. verse 15) may be ironical only, assumed to come from a Jewish critic who felt that Paul's argument since 3:20 has been indifferent to moral issues. On the other hand there have been enthusiasts who from time to time in history have held that Christian freedom means freedom from all restraints. The term "antinomianism" is used to describe this aberration. It is most noticeable among groups—especially some in the second and sixteenth centuries and some modern sects—which claim control by the Spirit. Possibly there were groups of this sort among Paul's converts at Corinth, and also in the church at Rome. His language in chapters 5 and 7 exposes him to this objection, whether it was actually made by his critics or was simply rhetorical. He realizes he must make himself clear on the moral issue. His direct answer to it is verses 6 and 11.

6:2-4. Paul is still writing in terms of clear contrasts. Now it is not between Christ and Adam, nor even between Christ and sin, but between the believer's new life and the old life dominated by sin and death. The clean break from that old life is emphasized. It is compared to **death**, and this strong emphasis is part of the interpretation of **baptism** as a sharing of Christ's burial.

Baptism is no mere initiatory ceremony but points back to the passion and resurrection of Christ, which were the means under God of effecting the new life of freedom from sin. Entering the water is like Christ's entering the grave. Coming up out of the water is like Christ's coming out of the tomb. It may have been Paul who first thought of the comparison, though this is not certain. But it was a customary emphasis of his, as we see from its recurrence in Colossians 2:12. **Glory** is equivalent to "power"—possibly an echo of credal language.

6:5-11. The pre-Christian part of life is finished, even if not forgotten. Paul goes so far as to say it is **crucified**. He is sure that the life of the believer is utterly dependent on Christ, to such a degree that it can be thought of as a sharing of Christ's risen life after crucifixion.

Here is the basis of the idea of the church as the body of Christ, and of a life of faith as incorporation into Christ. This is the new solidarity in, or with, Christ, contrasted with the old solidarity in Adam. It is expressed in the word **united**, literally "grown together," found only here in the New Testament.

Sinful body does not mean body as opposed to soul or spirit. Paul can use the word "body" in the sense of "personality" or "self." The Greek here is literally "body of sin." The body or whole person is in the grip of sin, as explained in 5:12-21. "Sinful flesh," literally "flesh of sin," in 8:3 is not an accurate parallel because there it is implied that the flesh, the physical part of humanity, is the location of sin (cf. 7:18*a*).

That the sinful self is to be **destroyed**—literally "reduced to inactivity"—would seem to mean nothing less than inability to sin any more. But sinlessness probably goes beyond Paul's intention here. He does not say Christians *cannot* sin, as is said in I John 3:6-9. He has too shrewd a sense of the realities of experience to dogmatize on this point.

The moral struggle still goes on for redemption. Now, however, the scales are not hopelessly weighted against us, so that defeat is inevitable—as in the old conditions of existence before Christ introduced the prospect of victory. Being **freed from sin** means for Paul primarily being no longer subject to those conditions.

In spite of the importance Paul attached to baptism, he did not regard it as making moral endeavor meaningless. Then, as now, the notion that sacraments confer immunity from temptation and sin was familiar. Paul's teaching on righteousness is a safeguard against such unethical sacramentalism. The point he is making is that the baptized person has said goodby to their former existence; they are **dead to sin**.

6:12-13. These imperatives follow naturally. They seem unnecessary after the glorious indicatives of the freedom symbolized by baptism, of Christ's triumph in the resurrection made beneficial to all believers, of Christ's headship of a new humanity, and of the privilege of reconciliation with God. But Paul is too shrewd a man, and too faithful a shepherd of souls, not to know that even the redeemed person has to be exhorted to "become what you are." Watchfulness and moral endeavor are never superfluous.

6:14. The conclusion mounts to a peak of confidence. Sin's **dominion** is broken. The same word is used in verse 9 of death, and in 5:14, 17 we read of death's "reign." The reign of sin and death was the condition of humanity before Christ set up a new kingdom, drawing on himself all the attacking malice of evil and submitting in the end to death. But because he was the incarnate power of God, this was not the end but a new beginning. The kingdom, or supreme authority, is God's. The dominion, or lordship, is Christ's, acknowledged by believers in every mention of his name.

C. GOD'S HOLY SERVICE (6:15-23)

6:15-19. Verse 15 picks up verse 14*b* and also verse 1. It is unthinkable that the Christian's new status should be abused. Though no longer responsible to law, one is dependent on divine grace, which means the gift of righteousness (3:24) and life (5:21). This is developed under the metaphor of a change of ownership of **slaves**. Christian freedom is a new kind of allegiance. Sin is the old master who has no further claim. The figure is set out in terms of contrast between **law . . . sin . . . death . . . impurity . . . iniquity** on the one hand and **grace . . . obedience . . . righteousness . . . sanctification . . . God** on the other.

The comparison with slavery is somewhat humiliating—and Paul apologizes for it in verse 19*a*—but it makes the point clear. The difference about Christians as slaves is that theirs is a self-imposed slavery. Paul does not explicitly say this, and we must beware of attributing modern notions of free will to him. His discussion of divine control in chapters 9–11 shows that he allowed little or no place to it. Nevertheless we may venture to modify his metaphor in this way as we apply it to ourselves. Paul mainly thinks of the condition of humanity as being under the control of either sin or Christ. Modern individualism needs to take account of this. The other side of the picture is the Christian's freedom (8:15).

6:19. The meaning of **natural limitations**, literally "weakness of your flesh," is inability to understand what the new status involves if it is not explained. Paul therefore explains it by an analogy drawn from everyday experience—slavery. "Flesh" means our physical constitution as contrasted with mind or spirit (see below on 7:18).

Sanctification is the opposite of **impurity** (cf. I Thessalonians 4:3-8). Christians are part of a holy community, like Israel. They are incorporated by baptism into Christ. Sanctification is sometimes used in the sense of justification (cf. I Corinthians 6:11). Here it means the progressive moral growth stature which follows the initial justification or acceptance with God on the basis of faith.

6:20-23. Death as the **end**—that is, the result—of sin is comparable to **wages** due. This is in contrast to a new **life** that is **eternal**, which God bestows as an unearned gratuity. This life—which is not simply everlasting in duration but of higher quality—is for those who are **in Christ Jesus**, the holy community.

D. FREEDOM FROM LAW (7:1-25)

7:1-6. *Dying to the Law*. The thought of slavery to sin leads Paul to consider the tyranny of the moral law. The changeover of authority which is part of the believer's experience is now considered in terms of law. It is illustrated by reference to the subordination of wife to husband in the marriage relationship—a feature far less prominent in modern marriage than in ancient.

The point is that the death of a husband sets a woman free to marry again. Thus Gentile Christians are no longer bound to false gods or pagan customs, and Jewish Christians are freed from dependence on the law of Moses in order to serve Christ, who takes the place of the law.

7:4. Instead of saying the law is finished as far as Christians are concerned, Paul says they **have died** as far as the law is concerned. This is repeated with emphatic verbs in verse 6. The confusion is no doubt due to the thought of 6:4, 8 and to the wish to describe Christian experience in terms of death and resurrection.

Through the body of Christ is taken by some commentators to imply the thought of Christ's body as the sacrificial offering which atones for sin and creates freedom (see above on 3:25*a*). More probably it refers to the new community into which believers are incorporated. The New English Bible translation is "by becoming identified with the body of Christ."

Bear fruit for God suggests that the marriage metaphor is still in Paul's mind. The Christian's relation to Christ is not without results. Good works are produced. These are never the ground of our acceptance with God—as so strenuously argued in 3:20, 28—but they are the outcome of it (cf. 6:22).

7:5-6. On flesh see below on verses 18-20. **Aroused by the law** means "encouraged" or "occasioned" by it. This effect of the law is explained in verses 7-11. Verse 6 merges into the former analogy from slavery (6:16-20). **New life of the Spirit** parallels "newness of life" (6:4).

7:7-12. *The Law as the Stimulus of Sin.* The Christian has finished with law and now lives under new conditions. In what sense then can Paul speak of upholding the law (3:31)? He can no longer put off explaining what positive value he ascribes to it.

His imaginary Jewish objector is now pressing him to say definitely whether or not he equates law with sin. Paul cannot allow this objection to stand for a moment. His reply begins by reaffirming what he has said in 3:20: law makes us aware of what sin is. By the law we know our own actual sinfulness—our guilt.

In the objective sense in which Paul uses the term "sin" (i.e. in 5:12-14) a person may be sinful but not guilty. But here he is talking about guilt—that is, sin in its subjective and personal sense. This is not possible apart from the law, which confers moral awareness: **Apart from the law sin lies dead.** This connects with 5:20: "Law came in, to increase the trespass (cf. Galatians 3:19*a*).

Paul is clearly going much further than his previous statements. He has said that the law is not intended to be the means of attaining goodness (3:20*a*) or of effecting the promise (4:13). He now indicates that its function is to be a catalyst of moral struggle and inner tension.

There is acute discernment here, even if this cannot be everybody's experience, and even if the terminology is exaggerated—the references to death in verses 9-11, for example. Moral consciousness is not simply the incentive to good behavior. It may equally well produce a fascination with evil. Sin finds **opportunity in the commandment.** The Greek word underlying "opportunity" means "starting point" or "base of operations." This is not nonsense, but serious reckoning with the tragic facts of moral experience.

Some writers describe these facts in terms of Satan, or demonic action. Contemporary Jewish teachers sometimes used the notion of an evil impulse located within each human being. Paul ascribes these sinister facts to the operation of sin. This is his doctrine of sin at its most baneful level, making use of a divine gift—the law—to produce an inward conflict which may be spiritually fatal (cf. verses 22-24).

Verse 9 refers to childhood, before the dawn of knowledge of right and wrong. This period in the individual corresponds to the period from Adam to Moses in human history (5:13-14). Genesis 3 is at the back of Paul's mind here. He must also have been conscious of the Jewish custom by which a boy at thirteen became a "son of the commandment" *(bar mitzvah)*—that is, he assumed the responsibility of an adult Jew to live according to the law.

7:13-25. *Inner Tension.* It is not the law which causes the death described in verses 9-11. Law as a divine instrument serves the purpose of showing up sin in its blackest possible colors—**sinful beyond measure.** This is one of Paul's ways of referring to guilt, not sin in its objective sense. Sin makes use of the law. We cannot blame the law. Our guilt remains our own, except insofar as we are incapacitated by the power sin has over us.

7:14-17. This power is briefly illustrated by the metaphor of slave and owner—**sold under sin**, "the purchased slave of sin" (New English Bible; on **carnal** see below on verses 18-20). But this metaphor is overshadowed by the more sinister one of an indwelling evil influence which corrupts the nobler impulses and causes an intolerable inner conflict. This is the moral havoc wrought by **sin which dwells within me**. The picture is unmistakable and morally realistic. Rabbis sometimes explained this phenomenon by their doctrine of an evil "inclination," or an evil and a good inclination in tension within each person. Paul was probably influenced by that doctrine. But whereas the rabbis recommended the study of the law as the remedy, Paul is convinced that the "inclination," or indwelling sin uses the categorical imperative of the law to cause the inward conflict. Paul's Christian insight made him more aware of the dimension of that conflict.

7:18-20. The language here reveals another aspect of Paul's thought which he thought relevant to this matter of moral failure, but which is difficult for the modern reader: his view of the **flesh** (**carnal**, literally "fleshly," in verse 14 and **members** in verse 23 also mean flesh). Flesh for Paul starts with the sense usual in the Old Testament of the physical body as opposed to soul or mind or spirit. Hence it comes to mean what used to be called our lower nature. Flesh is not sinful in itself, but the apparent association with it of instinctive behavior and **passions** leads Paul to the view that it is the door through which the indwelling sin gains entry (cf. **sinful flesh**, 8:3).

The assumption of some scholars that this is evidence of Greek influence on Paul is not necessary. Hebrew ideas are a sufficient explanation. The absence of reference to Satan's activity in all this discussion is noteworthy.

7:21-25. Paul's use here of the word **law** in the sense of "principle" (cf. 3:27 and 8:2) is very confusing. The **law of God** is the Old Testament Mosaic law. **Another law** means the demand of his **members**—equivalent to **flesh** (verse 18) and **body** (verse 24). This goes against the law of God and therefore can be called outright the **law of sin**. Finally the **law of my mind** means either the Mosaic law or the moral law generally, with the addition that Paul's reason, his **inmost self**, approves of it. Nevertheless his "members" are a battleground and the winner in the conflict is **sin**, which leads him off as a **captive**.

Verse 25*b* appears to be out of place and to belong after verse 23. Here the military metaphor gives way to that of slavery. The meaning of **body of death** is given in verse 11 (cf. 6:6, 23). But

Paul knows of deliverance from his hopeless plight. The sublimity of verse 25*a* finds a parallel in the serene confidence of 8:37-39 (cf. Galatians 2:20 and Philippians 1:21).

How much are we to read into the first-person pronouns of this chapter? Some interpreters have inferred that it is autobiographical—that here we have a transcript of Paul's own experience of frustration and freedom. But there is no hint of reference to his conversion (Galatians 1:15; Philippians 3:6-9; Acts 9:1-22). Paul is certainly arguing from what he has himself gone through, but his object is something more than autobiography.

On the other hand, we have here no stylized composition or rhetorical exercise. Paul is really writing about the power of sin—not objectively, as in 5:12-21, or ethically, as in 6:15-23. Here he speaks in terms of inner conflict so threatening to the personality as to result in utter despair, apart from Christ. This is the true Christian experience interpreted by a man of supernormal intensity who had been disciplined in Judaism to the point of achieving the Jewish ideal ("blameless," Philippians 3:6) but in Christ was schooled to a complete transvaluation (Philippians 3:7-12).

A related question is whether Paul is dealing with the Christian life before or after conversion. This chapter by itself suggests preconversion experience, but the answer should consider other passages. In the light of chapter 6 it would seem necessary to say that the experience of the believer as well as that of the nonbeliever is under survey.

The paradox of Christian experience is that the power of sin is not broken after the first full response to the gospel (faith, conversion). The Christian is at the same time righteous and sinful, as Martin Luther said in a phrase both simple and profound. Righteousness, according to this letter, is real, not fictitious. But it does not amount to moral perfection or immunity from the downdrag of sin. Indwelling sin is not dislodged. There is internal tension so distressing as to be comparable to civil war, and on normal expectation this would be fatal. But the last word is with God, who is imparting his righteousness and will in the end reveal his mercy to all (cf. 11:32).

E. NEW SPIRITUAL ENDOWMENT (8:1-17)

Verse 1 of this chapter is parallel to 5:1. **There is . . . no condemnation** is the negative to the positive "since we are justified" in 5:1. We are now ready to move forward to a fuller understanding of the effects of what God has done in Christ for sin-ridden humanity.

We are in a better position for this move because the intervening chapters 5-7 have shown how Christ's power has dealt with our fundamental disharmony with God (5:1-11), the dominance of sin and death (5:12-21), and the continuing challenge of sin (chapters 6-7). The inadequacy of law has also been explained (5:20; 7:7-14). Now Paul can refer to it summarily as **the law of sin and death** (verse 2).

8:1-4. *Paul's Gospel.* These four verses might be said to contain the whole of Paul's triumphant theology. As in 7:21-23, **law** is used in verse 2 in the sense of "authority" or "principle." The new regime is inaugurated by the **Spirit** (see below on verses 5-11)—or alternatively by Christ as the second Adam (5:12-21)—which is, or creates, **life**. It cancels out the results of that other regime which spread **sin and death**.

8:3. The word **likeness** might seem to imply a limitation of Christ's real humanity. But the context and Paul's total view of Christ show that no such implication is intended. Christ was fully human and therefore **sinful** in the objective sense of sin (5:12-14), though not in the sense of being guilty. His life provided the complete antithesis to Adam's disobedience. Christ's mission on earth was **for sin**—that is, concerned with sin—or possibly "as a sin-offering," in the sense of 3:25. On **sinful flesh**, literally "flesh of sin," see above on 6:5-11; 7:18-20.

Condemned sin is a bold expression which stresses the reversal brought about by God's action in Christ. It is now sin, not the sinful person (verse 1), who is the prisoner being sentenced. Sin's dominance is broken. It is condemned **in the flesh** by Christ's becoming a human being. Apart from full identification with humanity Christ could not be its savior. He had to expose himself to sin and death without any immunity. By so doing he exhausted their power and robbed them of their rights (cf. Galatians 3:13).

8:4a. The reasoning behind the assertions of verses 3 and 4 has been given in the preceding chapters. The new point is the declaration that the **just requirement of the law** is to be met after all. That is what church experience involves. The righteousness of God, which is a divine gift, is not unrelated in its effects to the law's moral demands.

Paul has never denied that the Mosaic law, and all moral codes, have a just requirement. What Immanuel Kant called the categorical imperative, acting on principles which can become universal laws of nature, is a basic element in human experience, of which psychology and ethics have to take proper account. But this element does not inevitably produce good conduct. This is the plain fact of experience from which Paul's central argument in this letter starts.

Paul announces as his gospel that God offers resources over and above the human sense of moral obligation. This is the significance of the life of Christ and the life of the church motivated by the Spirit. This divine initiative in Christ and in the church involves the revealing of divine righteousness (1:17; 3:21), pouring out of divine love (5:5), incorporation into Christ (6:4-5; 8:29), and life in the Spirit (verses 5-17). It is the saving gift which makes all the difference between moral despair and moral perfection. Religion does what morality alone cannot do.

8:4b. The summary of verses 1-4 concludes with a characteristic Pauline contrast of **flesh** and **Spirit** (cf. Galatians 5:16-24). This states how the Christian is actually able to live up to the demand of the moral law and gives the final answer to the objection in 6:1, 15. Spirit has been mentioned in verse 2 and hinted at earlier in 7:6b. Paul now introduces it as the subject for development in the rest of the chapter.

8:5-17. *Life According to the Spirit.* Spirit means divinely provided equipment and moral power by which the Christian can withstand the downdrag of fleshly existence (cf. 7:14). It is the Spirit which gives power to **put to death the deeds of the body**—that is, to the old sinful way of life which Paul has enjoined his readers to finish with in 6:12-14.

8:9. The great difference between Christian and non-Christian ways of living is the Christian's endowment of divine guidance and power which Paul calls the **Spirit of God** or the **Spirit of Christ**. This verse is quite explicit about it. No sense of superiority is implied; this is excluded for Christians from the very beginning (3:27). It is simply that the Christian, having learned through Christ what God is like, is open to receive God's gift of righteousness and from then on is under God's control. In this chapter this is explained in terms of the Spirit.

8:10-11. Verse 10 lacks precision. It reads literally: "If Christ is in you, the body is dead because of sin but the Spirit is life because of righteousness." Some take this to mean that the readers have "died to sin" as in 6:2-11. But it seems more likely that Paul means that their bodies are subject to death because of sin which has all persons in its grip apart from Christ. On **because of righteousness** cf. verses 4; 5:21; and 6:11.

Verse 11 has sometimes been taken to refer to the life after death, but the context indicates that Paul means his readers' present situation. Their **mortal bodies**, even though Spirit-controlled, are still looking forward to final redemption (cf. verse 23).

8:12-15b. The Spirit is not only new moral energy by which Christians gain release from bondage to the flesh. It is a new relationship with God, a new high level of privilege. It is what some of the Greek religious groups called deification. Paul cannot use that terminology; but he goes so far as to affirm that Christians become **sons of God.**

His doctrine seems to be that though God is the Father of all persons, all persons are not his children until they enter on the experience of faith and are **led**, or motivated, **by the Spirit.** People need to be brought into this relationship. This is suggested by the metaphor in verse 15, not of birth, but of

sonship, literally "adoption" (cf. the same word in verse 23). This refers to a common practice of the Roman world in families where there was no heir to the property.

8:15c-17. Here is a glimpse into the prayers of the earliest churches, still using the original Aramaic **Abba** for **Father**. Prayer is connected with the activity of the Spirit again in verses 26-27.

It is the function of the Spirit to **witness**—to create consciousness of the new and unique privilege of relation to God. This has been described as peace and grace (5:1-2) and freedom from condemnation (verse 1), but the new metaphor is more warm and intimate. Those who are adopted into the family of God are **fellow heirs with Christ**, who alone could be called a "natural" son of the Father (cf. Galatians 4:4-7). The inheritance for Christians is a final share of the glory of God's presence. It has been implied in the use of "promise" in 4:13-25. One aspect of our present earthly life is that it lacks the divine glory (cf. 3:23).

Provided we suffer really means "if, as is actually true, we suffer." The suffering of Christians is not an option which they may refuse. The precise sense of suffering with Christ is not made clear, but it must signify that the Christian in this life is exposed not only to sin but to malice and misfortune as Christ was.

F. CERTAINTY OF FINAL REDEMPTION (8:18-39)

Paul proceeds to the theme of the consummation of God's purpose. The outpouring of the Spirit meant for him, as for all the early Christians, the beginning of the end of history—"the last days," as prophesied in Joel 2 and quoted in the first recorded Christian sermon (Acts 2:16-18).

It was a definite prophetic notion that when the Messiah appears, all who adhere to him will share the Spirit which he will impart. The Spirit is the life principle common to the Messiah and his people. Paul accepts this, and his own special emphasis is that the Spirit is inseparably connected with Christ. Others partake of it only by their union with him.

The Christian possession of the Spirit, however, is comparable to the **first fruits**, in contrast to the full harvest which is still in the future and the object of hope. It is described as the **glory that is to be revealed**, the full development of sonship (verses 19*b*, 23*b*) for which the present experience of the Spirit is the anticipation (verse 14).

Here Paul is touching on the basic paradox of Christian experience: The believer is saved, justified, even glorified, and yet is still to be finally redeemed. The kingdom came with Jesus and yet is to come completely at his final glorious appearing. The Christian is sure of victory over sin and death (5:12-21; 6:8-11) and yet the perishable has not yet put on immortality (I Corinthians 15:53-56). The Spirit is the guarantee of this final victory (II Corinthians 1:22; Ephesians 1:14). It is the first fruits of a harvesting already begun which will ultimately bring all humanity under the divine mercy (11:32).

8:18-25. *The Redemption of the Universe.* The imaginative and poetic quality of this passage warns us not to treat it as ordinary theological prose. How can **creation** share in the redemption of humanity or be said to long for it? What is the precise meaning of the term here?

Some interpreters take it to mean unredeemed humanity as contrasted with Christians. But almost certainly "creation" here means more than this. It includes animals and inanimate nature. Indeed we must assume that Paul is bold enough to conceive of the redeeming purpose of God as including the whole physical universe, considered as not yet perfect, whatever connection there may be between its imperfection and human sin. It is curious that there is no reference to sin and death as in 5:12-21.

8:20-21. The classic narrative of the Fall (Genesis 3) is presupposed here. Paul was probably also acquainted with contemporary Jewish speculation about the messianic age as destined to right all the wrongs and imperfections of human beings and the universe. The doctrine of the Fall is that the universe is not what God created it to be. Because of sin it **was**

subjected to futility, or "frustration" (New English Bible). This probably refers to the gods of the heathen, or to the elemental spirits of Galatians 4:8-9, or to the principalities and powers of verse 38. **Him who subjected it** must refer to God rather than Satan or Adam.

The thought of such subjection arose from reflection on the fact that the human environment is not ideal and will is not entirely free. But as soon as we become persuaded, by faith, that God has prepared redemption, we affirm that redemption must **set free** our whole environment—provided, of course, we think in biblical terms of the universe as God's creation. There have been Christians since the second century who do not think this and confine their idea of salvation to humanity alone. These Christians have never been in the mainstream of Christian thought. They tend to reject the Old Testament.

8:22-23. The strong and colorful verbs express the stress of life apart from Christ. Christians' full experience of **adoption** (cf. vs. 15) is future, but they have the **first fruits of the Spirit** to sustain them in their present existence.

For **bodies** the Greek has "body" in the singular, and it should be so translated. The meaning is not the physical body in contrast with the soul or spirit but the "person" or "self" (cf. 6:12; 12:1).

8:24-25. The replacement of faith by **hope** is understandable in this context, but they are not synonymous. In view of Paul's understanding of faith we cannot translate "saved by hope" (King James Version). The full meaning is that **we were saved**—that is, by Christ's achievement, regarded as complete and hence the past tense—so as to live now **in . . . hope.**

8:26-27. *Intercession of the Spirit.* That the Spirit **intercedes for us** distinguishes the Spirit from God. In verse 34 intercession is the work of Christ. **Sighs** is the same Greek root as "groan" in verses 22-23.

Too deep for words, literally "unutterable," possibly means "inarticulate" (New English Bible). Some have taken it to be an allusion to the practice of speaking in tongues discussed by Paul in I Corinthians 14, but this is hardly likely. Probably it means

152

an inward Spirit-motion, not audible, which is intelligible to God alone.

8:28-30. *The Divine Plan.* Verse 28 is often quoted in support of a vague optimism which can hardly be Paul's meaning. The precise sense cannot be certainly established, partly because not all manuscripts contain the word **God** as subject of **works.** Thus it is possible to take as subject **everything** (cf. the King James Version) or the Spirit, as in verses 26-27 (New English Bible). However, by the logic of the later choice the Spirit would also be the subject in verse 29, where it is out of the question.

Those who love him refers to the subjective aspect, and **called according to his purpose** to the objective which Paul is more concerned with, as verses 29-30 make clear.

8:29-30. Quite apart from human understanding or merit there stands the divine plan, in which Paul distinguishes:

(1) foreknowledge as the original conception (verse 29*a*);

(2) likeness to Christ as the object or pattern (verse 29*b*);

(3) the actual constituting of this new Christlike brotherhood (**called,** verse 30*a*) as the purpose taking shape in history;

(4) the divine activity within them, conferring the new status of justification (verse 30*b*);

(5) finally glorification (verse 30*c*), which is still future, though Paul can refer to it in the past tense of prophetic certainty. Our human distinction of past, present, and future is not applicable to the divine ordering of history. (On verse 29*b* cf. verse 17; 6:3-5; 12:5.)

The thought of divine predestination is an encouragement, not a solemn threat. It need not imply ultimate reprobation. These verses are the basis of Christian confidence, whatever difficulties life in this world may bring, whether inwardly in the continuing struggle with sin or outwardly from the mockery or malice of pagan neighbors.

8:31-39. *The Divine Love.* This is a hymn of triumphant faith rather than a logical argument. The Christian's confidence for the future in this world and the next is based on the Incarnation and the Cross. This great event is conceived as an act of God's grace (3:24) or as an act of Christ (verse 34) or as due to the love of God in Christ (verses 35-39).

8:33-36. The accuser of **God's elect** is thought of probably as Satan (cf. Job 1:6), possibly the law, or the critic behind 6:1, 15 and 7:7. But the question is rhetorical, as is the next question, and the answer to both is "no one." The metaphor is that of the law court. At the final trial the strength of the defense will far outweigh any arguments offered for the prosecution. The relative clauses in verse 34 suggest that a rudimentary creed is in mind.

On the heavenly intercession cf. Matthew 10:33; John 17; Hebrews 7:25; and I John 2:1. It is clear that this is not a peculiarly Pauline idea. **Persecution** was a real possibility; for Paul's own experience of it cf. Colossians 1:24 and II Corinthians 11:23-33. Verse 36 is quoted from Psalm 44:22.

8:37-39. But neither human evil nor evil influences from more mysterious sources can disturb the Christian's salvation, which is due to the **love** of God. **Angels . . . principalities . . . powers** refer to supernatural powers which were then widely believed to influence human life. **Height** and **depth** were astronomical terms referring to the position of planets in the sky and their power to affect what happened on earth.

This passage rises to an even higher level of confidence than verses 28-30, using not the theological language of election, but the personal language of love. Love for Paul is that which causes God to justify sinners. For its connection with the Spirit cf. 5:5 and I Corinthians 13.

VI. THE PROBLEM OF ISRAEL'S UNRESPONSIVENESS
(9:1-11:36)

Jewish recalcitrance has been at the back of Paul's mind since 3:1-8. He left this passage inconclusive because he wanted to get on to the statement of his main theme, the saving righteousness revealed in the Cross for the benefit of all the unrighteous (3:21-26). How poignantly he feels the rejection of the gospel by

Judaism is very clear from the opening verses of chapter 9. It raises the problem of whether God's purpose has been frustrated. This is unthinkable, and yet it has to be faced. To a loyal Jew it is a serious concern that his own people, privileged as they are in their experience of God's grace in revelation, have opposed the climax of revelation in the Messiah.

Paul eases the problem by making a distinction between the whole of Israel and the true Israel (9:6-13). He asserts that God's purpose to which the promises refer is a selective one. He moves on into a general argument concerning divine sovereignty, which is the main premise in the whole discussion in chapters 9–11. The extension of the church to Gentile members is brought in as an illustration of divine mercy. It means that the messianic age has begun and the new messianic people are in existence.

But what is the implication for Jews? How ultimate is the stern language about hardening, wrath, and stumbling applied to them? Predestinarian thought is difficult for us moderns. It is impossible to reconcile with freedom of the will, without which we cannot be held responsible for our wrong choices. Also its congruity with the Christ presented in the gospels is questionable.

Paul has evidently faced the possibility that Jewish failure to respond must be regarded as final. He certainly has not minimized the element of sheer disobedience and tried to pretend Israel was not really to blame. He is aware that it raises the question: Is God unfair?

God has been stern in dealing with Israel. But precisely because God, *their* God, is righteous, the Jews have to experience his wrath. For all ther profession to fulfill the law they have failed to do so. Nor have they responded to the prophetic announcement of God's continuing purposes, which for Paul includes the work of Christ. They have shown themselves to be lacking in that responsiveness to God which is the essential preliminary for a right relationship to him, namely faith.

By the end of chapter 9 the argument is getting dissipated. It has to be refocused in chapter 11, after the relationship of righteousness to faith has been examined in chapter 10. Paul's reasoning is strange by modern standards, but not by rabbinic standards. Its effectiveness must be measured by those standards and recognized as the substructure for the great affirmations of 11:22, 29-32 and the climax in 11:33-36.

A. GOD'S SOVEREIGN SELECTIVITY (9:1-29)

9:1-5. *Paul's Love for Israel.* Paul expresses **in Christ**—that is, as a Christian, with new insight into God's truth—his **anguish** over the unresponsiveness of his Jewish **brethren**. The vehement language in verse 3 is typical of Paul (cf. Galatians 1:7-9 and Philippians 3:2-7). The parallel with Moses in Exodus 32:32 is noteworthy.

On **sonship** see above on 8:12-15*b*. **Glory** means God's own reality, manifested to Israel in special revelations and supremely in the giving of the law through Moses. The **worship** is the ritual of the temple in Jerusalem (cf. I Kings 8:10-11). Climax of the list is **the Christ**, the Messiah, who **according to the flesh**—that is, by physical descent—was a Jew.

There has been much discussion about the interpretation of verse 5. The word order of the Greek is "the Christ according to the flesh who is over all God blessed for ever." Without punctuation, which was unknown in ancient times, this is quite ambiguous and could mean that Paul equated Christ with God. Since he does not make this equation elsewhere, however, it is likely that a period belongs after "flesh" and that what follows is a simple doxology.

9:6-13. *God's Choice of Israel.* God's **word** involves not only revelation but purpose, including the **promise** (cf. 4:13-25). According to Paul's concept of the reality of God's word the suggestion of failure is blasphemy. He believes in divine choice which is both apart from human merit and prior to human existence. The working out of God's purpose involves choosing some and rejecting others, even within the posterity of

156

Abraham, as shown by the quotations from Genesis 21:12; 18:10; 25:21, 23; and Malachi 1:2-3. **Jacob** is serviceable to the divine purpose simply because God decides to make use of him.

The argument is God-centered; it views history from God's point of view rather than from that of human beings (cf. verse 16). Jacob is not seen as representing obedience and Esau worldliness. It is simply that God made one an instrument and not the other. The verbs **love** and **hate** are here used in their Old Testament sense, quite objectively, for preference and rejection.

9:14-21. *God's Sovereign Power.* Is God unfair? Is God's justice called into question? God's action in choosing this one and not that one, and even "hardening" this man and not another, is really merciful in the light of Exodus 33:19 (verse 15) and the preceding episode about the worship of the golden calf. When sin has been committed, God's mercy will still be in evidence even though the sinners are punished. In the case of the non-Israelite **Pharaoh** (Exodus 9:16) God **hardens the heart**, that is, causes spiritual insensitivity, so that ultimately God's purpose with Israel may be carried out (cf. Exodus 7–11).

That Pharaoh actually opposed the Israelites' attempt to break free from their slavery is a fact of history. Its explanation is seen in this doctrine of divine hardening, of which Pharaoh personally was unaware. Something similar is said about Israel in 11:7-8. This certainly stresses the sovereign control of God over human destiny, but it is doubtful whether it safeguards the doctrine of God's righteousness as Paul professes to be doing (verse 14).

Absolute authority is terrifying if it is not righteous authority. This is the limitation of the analogy of the **potter** and the **clay** (cf. Isaiah 45:9). It expresses well the dominance of creator over creature, but it does not allow for the element of free will. A person is not simply pliant clay. People do in fact **answer back to God** by opposing the preaching of the advent of the Messiah.

9:22-29. *Mercy for Gentiles.* The potter metaphor is developed rather unexpectedly, but in a way to serve Paul's main argument. He is not interested in the contrast between beautiful vases and common pots. His concern is the contrast between what the potter reduces to mere lumps on his turning wheel, **vessels of wrath made for destruction**, and what he fashions with skillful fingers till they result in shapely pieces fit for a palace, **vessels of mercy which he has prepared beforehand for glory**. These phrases refer to those who resist and those who conform to God's will. Verse 24 drops the figure and in plain prose states that the redeemed are not to be identified with Israel but include Gentiles.

9:25-29. The inclusion of the Gentiles is supported by quotations from Hosea 2:23 and 1:10. These are not the most obvious passages in the Old Testament advocating God's favor to non-Israelites, and they were not passages which were taken by Jewish expositors to imply the rejection of Israel. Complementary to the Gentiles as "vessels of mercy" is the thought of Israel, or some from Israel, as "vessels of wrath." This in turn is confirmed by quotations from Isaiah 10:22-23 and 1:9.

The **remnant** idea has been anticipated in verses 6-7 and will be more positively treated in 11:2-6. The emphasis in this context is more on the punishing judgment of God on those who do not form the remnant.

The disobedience of Israel is not a new factor brought on by the advent of Christ. It has been in evidence from the beginning. God's sovereign wisdom has known it and even in some sense caused it (9:18, 22). His saving acts always divide humanity into those who believe and those who take offense (9:33). The new factor balancing Israel's unbelief is Gentile belief (9:30-31). This calls for a fresh consideration of faith in relation to righteousness in chapter 10.

B. GOD'S SELECTION OF THE GENTILES (9:30–11:36)

9:30-10:4. *Gentile Admission and Jewish Exclusion.* The reception of grace by Gentiles is described as **righteousness through faith** (cf. 1:17; 3:21-22; 4:13). Judaism, on the contrary, for all its pursuit of righteousness failed to attain it. This failure is

explained as stumbling, divinely caused in some degree, in the
light of two Old Testament passages, Isaiah 8:14 and 28:16. That
these same passages similarly conflated occur in I Peter 2:6-8
suggests that Paul is drawing on an early collection of proof texts.
Other reasons for Judaism's failure are given as ignorance and
hardening (11:7-8). The relevance of verse 33 becomes clearer in
10:5-8, where Paul explains **he who believes**. The **rock** means
Christ.

10:2-3. The Jews have **zeal**, but this leads astray unless
governed by knowledge of God's character and purpose. The
Jews fall short at this point. They also fall short in submission—a
serious lack in a religion like Judaism for which God is sovereign
and human duty is unquestioning obedience.

Zeal for God is characteristic of Hebrew religion. The Greek
word used here can have a bad sense—fanaticism, exemplified
in Paul himself before his conversion (Acts 9:1-2). But in
Hebrew the good sense predominates, and this is intended
here. For its exemplification in Paul cf. Galatians 1:13-14 and
Philippians 3:4-6.

The Greeks, who regarded excess even in goodness as
disproportionate, found this characteristic zeal laughable in
Jews. Why take religion so seriously? Why try to relate every
circumstance of life to the will of God? Paul experienced Jewish
zeal as opposition to the growing church and as a persecution
mania against himself (Acts 9:22-29; 18:12-17; 21:27-36). He
does not refer to this here, but analyzes the zeal of his fellow
Jews as deviation from God rather than loyalty. They have put
their own ideals in the place of what God has made known of the
divine will. Their very intensity has blinded them to new truth.
The Messiah has come and they have not recognized him. The
highest religion of the world is exposed as fighting against its
own highest development.

10:4. The tragedy of the Jews, Paul believes, is their inability
to see that the Messiah has come and that moral endeavor is no
longer a way of salvation. The **law** is no longer the highest
revelation of God; Christ is its **end**. This is a major affirmation
which requires careful interpretation. For Judaism the idea of

the law's being dispensed with, even by the Messiah, was intolerable. For Paul the light of Christ made possible a fresh beginning of thought about the law and salvation.

God's purpose in relation to human need is to reveal (that is, impart) righteousness (1:17). The law does not further this purpose, except negatively, for it reveals only lack of righteousness (3:20) and causes inner disharmony (7:7-20). According to the parallel argument of Galatians the law has only temporary usefulness for salvation. With the advent of Christ it becomes out of date (Galatians 2:19-20; 3:19-25). Christ, as it were, takes it over, so that for believers moral obligation can be described as the law of Christ (Galatians 6:2). Paul's logic then requires "end" here to be understood in the sense of termination rather than of fulfillment or perfection, as is urged by some commentators.

The Messiah's task was to be the instrument of God's redeeming righteousness. This has been achieved in the life, death, and resurrection of Jesus. Understanding and accepting this is what Paul means by faith, and it is the indispensable starting point for a right relationship to God.

Faith is not mere belief as opposed to action—as in James 2:14-26—but belief in the sense of a fundamental attitude which determines conduct. Christ has inaugurated this new possibility and therein replaced the Mosaic law as the basis of true religion. The law itself points forward to this; the true lordship, or authority, belongs to him.

10:5-13. *The Lordship of Christ.* Paul is aware that verse 4 will sound blasphemous to the Jews and absurd to the moralist. He proceeds to explain faith righteousness in terms of a contrast between it and legal righteousness. The latter puts the accent on human activity.

The same point is made in Galatians 3:11-12, and was perhaps a favorite argument of Paul's. This new, Christian righteousness is in a sense simpler. It does not begin with the demand for great moral effort. It is concerned first with the response of the heart and an inward conviction about something God has done in Christ. This discernment of divine action results in a confession of the lordship of Christ. On this basis one can proceed in the direction of good living. This is the new way of believing, rather than doing, as the approach to right conduct.

10:6-7. The references to bringing Christ down from heaven or up from the nether regions is unexpected. It is a Christian application of Deuteronomy 30:11-14, the point of which is that the law was God's gift and Israel did not have to make its own effort to fetch it from heaven. For Christians the supreme gift of God is not the law but Christ. No human effort to scale the heavens or to go to the uttermost bounds of the earth has brought him or made possible either his incarnation or his resurrection.

Paul's substitution of **abyss**—that is, Hades, the abode of the dead—for the Deuteronomic "beyond the sea" may show acquaintance with the myth of Christ's descent to Hades, which has found a place in I Peter 3:19.

10:9. Here is possibly a hint of an early creed which mentioned the lordship and resurrection of Christ. The public confession of Christ as Lord was no doubt a part of the earliest baptismal ceremony. The trinitarian confession (Matthew 28:19) must have evolved later. **Jesus is Lord** is the irreducible minimum of Christian faith. It distinguishes it from the monotheistic faith of Judaism and yet relates Jesus intimately with God by ascribing to him the title which in the Old Testament refers to God. Logically this implies bitheism, or two separate gods, and this is the standing objection to the Christian faith in the mind of a Jew.

The distinctive feature in the Christian understanding of God is the place of Christ. He is Lord. He is more than a human, and worship cannot be withheld from him, for in him the climax of God's saving acts has been reached. The Resurrection is the evidence of this. He is the emancipator from sin, the giver of righteousness, and the pioneer of a new humanity (5:12–6:11). He is the carrier of God's own love (8:39).

Converts from paganism would find this difficult, but the term "Lord" would be meaningful to them in the sense of a heavenly benefactor. Many cult deities were so addressed. What pagans had to learn was that worship of Christ excluded all other cults (I Corinthians 8:6).

10:11-13. The simplicity of faith righteousness is rooted in the mercy of God and knows no limits, as the quotation from Isaiah 28:16 in verse 11 assures. The old **distinction between Jew and Greek** is now outmoded. The "first" of 1:16 refers to the past only. Faith is the great leveler (cf. 3:28-30)! **Lord** in verse 12 refers to Christ, though in the quotation from Joel 2:32 in verse 13 it refers to God.

10:14-21. *The Need to Preach the Gospel.* There is urgent need for worldwide proclamation of the free mercy of God. This is recognized in the quotation from Isaiah 52:7 in verse 15*b*. It can now be identified with the Christian **gospel** or the **preaching of Christ**. Alternatively it can be called the **word of faith** (verse 8*b*). There is urgency because Israel's return to faith depends on the conversion of Gentiles (11:11-12, 25-26).

Verse 16, quoting Isaiah 53:1, seems misplaced. It reintroduces the main theme of chapters 9–11, Jewish obtuseness. Therefore it belongs with verses 18-21, which adduce further Old Testament quotations (Psalm 19:4; Deuteronomy 32:21; Isaiah 65:1-2) to prove that this opposition was experienced long before the advent of Christ. More positively, they prove that the Gentiles are included in God's purpose. The curious notion **make you jealous** is developed in 11:11-14.

11:1-6. *The Remnant Chosen by Grace.* The negative factor of Israel's disobedience (10:18-21) has been long evident and is not a result of Christian preaching alone. But it cannot be final or total. **God has not rejected his people whom he foreknew.** Their present recalcitrance is a case of stumbling rather than falling; it is not a complete collapse (verse 11).

Paul is now reminded of the doctrine of the **remnant** in reference to the experience of **Elijah** (I Kings 19:10, 18). This is an illustration of the divine **grace**. The argument of 10:5-8 is presupposed. What Paul there calls faith righteousness might equally well be called grace righteousness. Faith is the human response to God's grace—that is, his gift of righteousness (3:24).

The point Paul is making is the same as in 9:6-13. God's purpose is working out by concentration on a minority who respond to the call. Not all are responsive, but God can always discern some who are. There must be a **remnant** now, Paul believes; he calls them also the **elect** (verse 7). Is he thinking of Jewish Christians, or of a larger unit of Jews who are to be converted? The ultimate outcome is the saving of **all Israel** (verse 26), which apparently means both the elect and the **rest** (verse 7), and all humanity (verse 32).

11:7-12. *Israel's Temporary Obtuseness.* The problem remains concerning those who have not responded. Israel's stumbling is now examined on its more subjective side and described as due to moral insensibility. The **rest**, in contrast to the **elect** remnant, **were hardened**. This is not the same verb as in 9:18, with reference to Pharaoh, but the meaning is the same—made hard, insensitive. The variety of terms shows how much Paul has reflected on the problem. He explains the meaning by the quotations that follow, a conflation of Isaiah 29:10; Deuteronomy 29:4 (verse 8), and Psalm 69:22-23 (verses 9-10).

11:11. The contrast between stumbling and falling expresses the difference between Israel's present lack of cooperation with the divine plan and the conceivable loss of its ultimate salvation, which is part of that plan. It is a case of temporary failure rather than final disaster. A good thing has come out of it, the **salvation** of the Gentiles. This is not an afterthought on God's part, making a virtue of necessity—though verse 30*b* seems to suggest something like this. God has not been taken by surprise by Israel's defection, and mercy to the Gentiles has always been part of the divine plan.

Paul goes so far as to suggest that God will make a positive use of the Gentiles' response in the restoration of Israel. God will cause it to **make Israel jealous.** This is repeated in verse 14 and has been anticipated by the quotation from Deuteronomy 32:21 in 10:19. The meaning is a fresh stimulation of the Jews' zeal (10:2) so that it is directed again to the knowledge of God's will, which they have been ignoring. They need to be shocked into realizing the privilege of God's salvation by the sight of others entering upon it.

11:12. This is rhetorical rather than logical, like verse 15. But it shows that Paul is assuming the eventual restoration of Israel.

Failure and **full inclusion** ("falling off" and "coming to full strength," New English Bible) are somewhat unprecise, though they make a neat antithesis. "Failure" here might mean "reduction to a remnant." On the restoration of Israel cf. verses 23*b*, 24*b*, 26.

11:13-24. *God's Kindness to Gentiles.* The Gentiles must be warned not to be arrogant. The broken-off **branches**, whose place they have been allowed by God's election to take, are not discarded forever. God still has them in view; the consecration is not nullified (verse 16). That basic consecration now extends to Gentiles, and they should recognize their dependence (verse 18). They may be "vessels of mercy" in comparison with Jews who are "vessels of wrath" (9:22-23), but both Jews and Gentiles are in the hand of the divine potter. Therefore no boasting and no pride. Boasting is excluded where one's relation to God is concerned—that is, where faith is the decisive factor (verse 20*a;* cf. 3:27).

11:16. At the back of Paul's mind is the thought of the holiness of Israel. It is rooted in the "forefathers" (verse 28) but primarily rooted in the divine election, which passes from generation to generation and now from Jews to Gentiles.

11:21-24. The Gentiles have so far experienced God's **kindness**. But it is not inconceivable that they, like the Jews, could experience his **severity**, literally "cutting away." This rare word expresses God's judgment on those who defy God's will. Many Jews thought it applied only to God's attitude toward Gentiles.

No dualism in the character of God is implied. Kindness and severity are both included in God's love or mercy (verse 32), which means saving activity. Paul speaks in terms of mercy when he is dealing with the final outcome. He can also speak of God's wrath in this connection (2:4-9). But "kindness" and "severity" here refer to God's dealings with people during the course of history, and each may be experienced successively. For example, the Jews may be restored (verses 23-24) and the Gentiles rebuffed (verse 21; cf. verses 30-31).

11:25-32. *The Final Reconciliation.* This closing section deals with the consummation of God's plan in the restoration of Israel and the final salvation of all persons.

11:25. The word **mystery** refers to a secret concerning the events of the end which is now made known in Christian preaching. Israel's obtuseness is partial and temporary. The hint has already been offered in verse 11 that the place of the Gentiles in God's favor will make the Jews realize what they are missing. Paul now supplements this with the notion of the **full number of the Gentiles**.

Since the expression is not used elsewhere by Paul we must determine its meaning from the present context. The Greek word, literally "filling up," has many meanings—for example **full inclusion** in verse 12. In the light of the parallel expression **all Israel** in verse 26 we must take the fullness of the Gentiles to mean every living Gentile.

The verb **come in** is unprecise but presumably means entry into the final redeemed society. Nothing short of this does justice to verse 32*b*, or to the exalted outburst of verses 33-36.

11:26-27. The words **and so** must be understood as referring to the next step after all the Gentiles have entered. The quotations from Isaiah 59:20-21 and 27:9 refer to the salvation of Israel after the advent of the Messiah, the **Deliverer**.

Christian teaching was that the Messiah had already come. The final process had to that extent begun. The coming in of the Gentiles is being brought about by Paul's missionary activity. When it is complete, the full response of Israel will no longer be delayed. Such is the scheme which Paul has in his mind. **All Israel** must include not only the "elect" within Israel, but also the "rest"—that is, those who have thus far been unresponsive.

11:28-29. In verse 28 the neatness of a parallelism again leaves the meaning obscure. Opposition to the gospel reveals the Jews as **enemies of God**, opposing God's will, but the Gentiles gain by this (**for your sake**). The original election of Israel, however, means that they are still beloved. This is emphasized in verse 29.

11:30-32. Actions which have to be described as **disobedience** or even hostility to God testify to the reality of God's judgment.

But this is temporary. If we are thinking about the final outcome, we speak of God's **election** (verse 28), his **gifts** and **call** (verse 29), and his **mercy** (verse 32). And this means the ultimate elimination of human disobedience, compared to release from prison.

That Paul's thought climaxes in a conviction of the ultimate salvation of all persons is not accepted by all commentators. It has not been the majority view during the history of Christian theology. Nor is it suggested here without recognition of the complex issue of human freedom in relation to God's control. We must also recognize the baffling alternations of Paul's statements, both in chapters 9–11 and in his letters as a whole—for example, the contrast between triumphing mercy in 11:22-32 and judgment in 2:2-16; I Corinthians 6:9-11; and II Corinthians 5:10.

That he may have mercy upon all comes at the end of one of the longest considerations Paul gives to any single theme. It then immediately takes wings in the doxology of verses 33-36, because Paul realizes that he is in a realm beyond human logic. These words thus represent a considered climax and deserve to be given priority to other references to the theme of ultimate reward and punishment. The affirmation of mercy for all, therefore, should be given its full weight of meaning.

A widely held alternative interpretation is that Paul was thinking in terms of totalities rather than individuals—that both Israel and the Gentiles qualify for salvation but under each heading there may be individual exceptions.

VII. GOSPEL ETHICS (12:1–15:6)

This section of the letter is often referred to as ethics. The purely theological argument has been brought to a climax at the end of chapter 8, and chapters 9–11 are theological rather than ethical.

There is a point in this distinction, and in this regard Romans exhibits a similar structure to that of Galatians, Colossians, and

Ephesians. But it must be remembered that for Paul and the New Testament generally there is no separate and independent "ethic." Ethical ideal and demand are always related to what is known of God and God's purpose.

A. GENERAL PRINCIPLES (12:1-21)

12:1-2. *The Basis of Paul's Ethics.* The theological grounding of Paul's ethics is very clear in the opening verse. The basic principle is response to God, and this is expressed in terms of **worship**. This consisted mainly, according to customs, both Jewish and pagan, of animal sacrifice; and Paul again makes use of this analogy (cf. 3:25). His appeal is to **present your bodies as a living sacrifice**.

The basic meaning is that we are to make a total response to the grace of God, who has acted savingly in Christ. The sacrificial metaphor made this very meaningful for the first readers of the letter. Significant differences from the usual practice of sacrifice are implied, however:

(1) Paul is talking of living persons, not dead animals.

(2) Christians offer themselves to God. It is not a case of a priest performing ritual acts with the dead body of an animal. Worship is still corporate, and there is still a place for the guidance of priest or minister. But something is lacking without the personal participation of each individual.

(3) Whatever ritual acts may be performed, Christian worship is essentially **spiritual**. The Greek word is not that usually so rendered (e.g. 1:11; 7:14; cf. 8:5-15) but another which is difficult to translate here. "Rational" would be its most direct equivalent. Since it is related to "word," some take it to mean "in conformity with God's word," that is, the Christian revelation. But it suggests Greek rather than Hebrew background and in the main implies the opposite of "material." On the notion of spiritual sacrifices and all Christians as priests cf. I Peter 2:5, where "spiritual" is the usual word.

Worship in this sense is the whole of life. It is our adoring response to God, of whose mercies we are aware. We who would otherwise be unable to rise to our duty can do so because God has had compassion on us. A new humanity has been inaugurated.

12:2. For those who are incorporated into Christ life has a new quality (6:3-5). They have made the break from casual secular ways (6:6-14) and are no longer **conformed to this world.** The measure of this change is emphasized by the remarkable expression **renewal of your mind.** Paul is using formal language here to bring out the distinctive character of responsible Christian living, for which perfection is God's will, work is prayer, and duty is privilege. His conception of the Christian's growing likeness to Christ is also in the background here (cf. 8:29; II Corinthians 3:18; Philippians 3:21).

12:3-8. *Membership in the Body.* When it comes to particular aspects of Christian character Paul thinks first of sobriety and the need to avoid conceit. The natural tendency to take undue credit for spiritual and moral progress must be watched. Paul warns against it often (verse 16; Philippians 2:3; Galatians 6:3, 12-15) and expects the person of faith to realize the danger.

We note again the intimate relation of faith and morals. The Christian community provides the obvious opportunity of rendering "spiritual" service. All have faith, but not all have the same "measure of faith." Some are "weak in faith" (14:1).

12:4-5. Curbing one's pride has in view the relationship with one's fellows. This leads Paul to his conception of the church and each particular congregation as Christ's **body.** The essential idea was expressed in 6:3-11, but now the metaphor of the body is introduced—a living organism with many functions which, though different, work harmoniously together for the health and growth of the whole. This body is the instrument which Christ uses to carry out his purposes in the world.

In the more detailed application of the metaphor Christ is spoken of as the enlivening spirit (I Corinthians 12). Cf. also Christ as the head of the body (Colossians 1:15-18; 2:6-10; Ephesians 4:11-16).

12:6. In proportion to our faith means in right relationship with faith. One must observe the sobriety which faith requires (cf. verse 3) and avoid unrestrained utterance, to which a Christian prophet might be tempted.

12:9-21. *Instruction in Christian Virtues.* This section consists of more general exhortation, typical of what many regard as "catechumen virtues"—that is, the instruction given to new converts prior to baptism. It was based on the Psalms and wisdom literature. This material was already taking fixed form when Paul wrote.

This section, together with I Corinthians 13, may be called the Pauline equivalent to the Sermon on the Mount. Paul's familiarity with the legacy of Christ in this matter of ethical teaching is obvious.

The key word here, as in I Corinthians 13, is **love.** It is the comprehensive Christian term for obligation to one's fellow. It was exemplified in the Lord himself, and it is the highest fruit of the Spirit in the church. In the main it is the Christians' relations with one another that Paul has in view, but the broadening out of concern for non-Christians is clear in verses 17-21 and in 13:1-10.

12:9-16. The word **genuine,** literally "unhypocritical," refers to acting without the parade of insincerity which Jesus denounced unsparingly. In verse 11 **aglow with the Spirit** is similar to the phrase describing Apollos in Acts 18:25.

Serve the Lord seems to require the notion of some specific task done with **zeal** and spirit. Alternatively the point may be that all the Christian does for others is service of the Lord (cf. Matthew 25:34-40). An alternative reading, "serve the time," is found in some manuscripts. This would mean "use to the full your opportunities."

The Greek of **associate with the lowly** is ambiguous, for "lowly" can mean either persons or things (see the footnote to the Revised Standard Version). The gospel parallel in Mark 2:13-17 throws some light on this passage.

12:17-18. A word of Jesus (Matthew 5:38-39) provides a parallel to verse 17*a.* It is not likely, however, that Paul has this in mind, for in verse 17*b* he is writing in the manner of the best Jewish and pagan ethical writers of the time.

Verse 18 has in mind the difficulties Christians (and Jews) might have among unsympathetic pagan neighbors. Christians are not to cause trouble, either in the more personal contacts, as here, or in broader social and political involvement (cf. 13:1-7; on the social environment of the first Christian communities cf. I Corinthians 6–10).

12:19-21. "Getting even" is absolutely forbidden for Christians. Jesus' way of saying this is Matthew 5:43-48. Paul is more rabbinical and quotes scripture—apparently a free rendering of Leviticus 19:18; Deuteronomy 32:35 (verse 19) and Proverbs 25:21-22 (verse 20).

Burning coals has never been fully explained. There is some evidence that it signified not simply punishment but signs of repentance. Christian reaction to ill treatment should be not an equal return but the attempt to make the other person repent. This interpretation holds together the unity of verses 17-21. Verse 21 is very general in terms of the opposition of good and evil, which is fundamental for most moralists. This teaching is more concrete in 13:10 and more metaphorical, in terms of the light-darkness dualism, in 13:11-12.

B. THE CHRISTIAN'S CIVIC DUTY (13:1-10)

13:1-7. *Respect for Civil Authorities.* The keynote of Paul's advice is respectful submission on the ground that secular **authorities** would not exist at all apart from divine permission. They are real authorities, though subordinate to the overall sovereignty of God. What they do in promotion of good and restraint of evil is definitely the service of God.

13:1. A significant recent interpretation takes the **authorities** to mean supernatural powers using earthly rulers as their instruments. The idea was familiar to the Hellenistic world, and even Judaism could think of pagan nations as in subjection to angels, as Israel was to Yahweh (cf. Deuteronomy 32:8-9 and Daniel 10:13; 12:1). It is not certain whether Paul's use here presupposes that conception.

That he accepted the existence of these higher powers is clear in view of 8:38. But it is not so clear that he thought of them as controlling the life of nations through their civil rulers. It can be argued that in addressing Roman Christians on their duty to the state Paul had in mind the widespread notion that the state was part of the whole cosmic system, and the emperor himself, if not actually a god, was under divine control.

13:2. It follows that Christians should not be drawn into movements for the overthrow of properly constituted governments. Did Paul know of this tendency among the Roman Christians? Not necessarily; but he may have detected some official suspicion of the growing numbers of Christian groups, and he must have known of the precautions taken against secret societies.

Acts gives the impression that whenever Roman officials took notice of Christians they did not regard them as presenting a danger to the empire. Jews might be troublemakers, but not Christians! The official Jewish attitude toward the empire was similar to what Paul advocates here. But Jewish zeal did sometimes produce messianic claimants, who from the Roman point of view would be political agitators. Acts 5:34-39 is informative here. Paul may well have felt the need to warn the churches against allowing such ambitions to develop, and this had extra relevance for the church in Rome itself. Christianity is the agent of society's redemption, not its disruption.

For the similar Jewish attitude to secular authority cf. Daniel 2:20-23, 37-38; 4:28-37 and Wisdom of Solomon 6:1-11. For New Testament parallels with Paul's teaching cf. I Peter 2:13-17 and Titus 3:1. The very different attitude of Revelation is explained by the persecution situation which occasioned that writing and forced its author to the conviction that secular power—the Roman Empire—was in the control of Satan, a possibility not envisaged by Paul.

13:3-7. The Greek word **servant** was used in a broad sense, especially of household duties (cf. the New English Bible translation "agents" here). Acts 6:1-6 marks the beginning of the ecclesiastical development which applied this term—in this sense transliterated "deacon"—to a church officer subordinate to bishop and apostle. But Paul can use a form of this word of his own "ministry" (11:13).

The alternative term **minister** which Paul applies to tax officers in verse 6 originally signified donors of public benefactions to Greek city-states. The word picked up religious associations (cf. 15:16) and eventually settled down in Christian usage with reference to worship (liturgy).

Paul does not hesitate to describe the negative aspect of human justice in terms of the divine **wrath** at sin. He presupposes this as a conception familiar to Jews from the Old Testament. For his own understanding of God's wrath and its relation to the revelation of God in Christ, see 1:18-32 and 2:5-8. In executing the wrath magistrates are legally justified in doing what the individual Christian is forbidden to do (12:19).

The Christian's obedience to earthly rulers is motivated not only by fear of punishment, but also by **conscience**. This obedience is positive, prompted by desire to collaborate with the government in its task of achieving the good which overcomes evil (12:21). It is the will of God for human life (12:2*b*). On verse 7 cf. Mark 12:13-17.

13:8-10. *The Supremacy of Love.* This passage would naturally follow chapter 12, though there is no need to assume that 13:1-7 is an insertion. We may be inclined to distinguish "personal" and "social" ethics, but these distinctions would seem unnecessary to Paul. Moreover, there is a connection between verses 7 and 8. The Christian is to discharge all obligations, whether of public duty or of private relationships. Here the keynote is love. Paul's emphasis on the primacy of love for one's fellows accords perfectly with the teaching of Jesus (cf. Matthew 5:44 and Mark 12:28-34).

It should be noted here that Paul, in spite of his earlier statements about the tyranny of the **law**, can speak of its being fulfilled. There is no question of self-contradiction. Christians are equipped to fulfill the law's demands by their endowment with the Spirit.

172

C. IMMINENCE OF THE END TIME (13:11-14)

Here the keynote is watchfulness—the urgency of the Christian's existence underlying human relationships with public officials, fellow humans, and fellow Christians. The theme is not peculiar to Paul (cf. I Peter 4:7; 5:8 and James 5:7-8). It has its root in the teaching of the Lord himself (cf. e. g. Mark 13:33-37 and Matthew 25:1-13). Thus it was a regular feature of the earliest Christian ethical teaching.

Some scholars think it was part of the pattern of instruction given to new converts. The point of it was to encourage, not anxious calculation of the date of doomsday, but a moral seriousness which differentiated Christians from those around them.

The Christian has something better to live for than ease and sleep, self indulgence, sexual pleasure, or the common struggles and ambitions of the world. The life of faith and Christian engagement is like rising eagerly to meet a new day which is the new life Christ makes possible. The clothing, or **armor**, to be worn that day is Christ himself (verse 14*a*).

Life that shows something of the power and quality of Christ is not only secure against temptation. It is true living as contrasted with mere existence. It is the distinctively Christian understanding of success.

On the metaphor of "putting on" cf. Galatians 3:27 and Colossians 3:10, 12. The metaphor of **night** as the present life and **day** as the life to come has rabbinic parallels. But it was probably a Christian development, as part of baptismal catechism, to present Christian converts as children of light. The conception of their new life also as the putting on of a new garment may belong to the baptismal vocabulary.

D. PATIENCE WITH SCRUPLES (14:1–15:6)

The subject matter of this long section—abstinence from meat and observance of special days—appears somewhat trivial, even when allowance is made for the greater appeal of these things in the ancient world, especially among Jews. There seems to be considerable disproportion between the twenty-nine verses devoted to these matters and the meager seven verses devoted to the Christian and the state in chapter 13.

The interest here, however, lies in the way Paul, when giving judgment about a relatively unimportant issue, appeals to fundamental Christian principles. For example:

(1) the example of Christ (14:9; 15:3);

(2) charity (14:15), the attitude which regards a fellow Christian, not as weak and unprogressive, but as one for whom Christ died;

(3) the Christian church as a society for mutual service, not for the private cultivation of wisdom or holiness (15:1).

The key word is edification, in a corporate sense (14:19; 15:2). Christians should not criticize one another but labor together in God's work of building the perfect society (cf. I Corinthians 3:9-11).

14:1-4. *Scruples About Meat.* With **weak in faith** cf. the gospel expression "of little faith" (for example, Matthew 6:30). Here the emphasis is on "weak" in contrast with "strong" (15:1).

Welcome him is literally "take him to yourselves," that is, do not leave him on his own. In the relationships of the community the true Christian aim is **not for disputes** but rather **for peace and for mutual upbuilding** (verse 19).

14:2. Eating **only vegetables** is not our modern vegetarianism. The motive was not concern about killing animals but horror at eating the flesh of an animal slaughtered in a pagan ceremony. To a sensitive Christian, therefore, meat carried the taint of heathenism. The very place where it was bought might be a corner of a pagan temple.

Some have assumed that this problem was especially urgent at Rome, but it would arise in all towns in the Roman Empire. Embarrassment would arise if Christians were at dinner with pagan neighbors; one Christian might take the meat course and another refuse. Should Christians decline invitations to dinner, thus shutting themselves off from their pagan neighbors? Paul gives his advice on this in I Corinthians 10:25-31. Here he is dealing with the disputes among Christians themselves, between those who like Paul have no scruples (**we who are strong,** 15:1) and those who cannot set scruples aside.

14:3-4. Probably it was Jewish church members who had scruples against meat slaughtered under pagan auspices, as a result of their background of religious dietary restriction. Gentiles would be used to such meat and would be tempted to **despise**—that is, be scornful of their Jewish brethren for abstaining from it. On the other hand the abstainers **pass judgment** on those who eat.

But the welcome which God shows, and which is exemplified in Christ (15:7-9), must not be contradicted by such rivalry between broad-minded and scrupulous members of the church. A judging attitude is unthinkable among Christians. Only the **Master**—in Greek the same word as "Lord"—has a right to judge. Only he can say the behavior of any of his servants is not in accord with their relationship to him.

14:5-9. *Scruples About Special Days.* In Paul's view, the difference of opinion and practice about special days is in the same category as the meat question. Probably the reference is to Jewish Christians who continue to observe the sabbath and perhaps the feasts and fasts specified in the Old Testament, whereas Gentiles ignore them. But Paul sees the problem as whether there can be more than one expression of Christian faith in outward conduct and social habit. He is patient with both types and his argument moves toward general considerations which both will heed.

He is trying to get those on both sides to see that the others may be equally as right as they are. Each side may be acting in accord with Christ's guidance. The question is whether both sides are **fully convinced** that Christ's claim is paramount. Is their conduct, whether observing or ignoring, eating or abstaining, **in honor of the Lord**?

14:7-9. These verses imply a restraining principle. Christian liberty is never license but discharge of our responsibility **to the Lord**. In the whole of our experience, including death itself (and beyond), we are related to the Lord. Not everyone realizes this, but the believer does. One should let it determine one's attitude toward a fellow believer and not be harsh and critical.

14:10-23. *The True Standard.* Paul sounds the warning note of accountability at the judgment day (verses 10-12, quoting Isaiah 45:23). But patient pleading is the dominant tone of the whole discussion. The issue is serious, in Paul's judgment, because one person's liberty may become a **stumbling block** (cf. 9:32-33). This term appears to stand for whatever prevents or destroys faith. It may cause spiritual **ruin** to the scrupulous brother—that is, loss of faith to him personally (verse 23) and also disruption of a church (verse 20*a*).

The really deplorable thing about this mutual criticism is that it hinders the harmony and growth of the church. Food taboos are substituted for the true demands and privileges of the kingdom. If Paul had been addicted to quoting the sayings of Jesus he might have called this a preference for tithing "mint and dill and cummin" to the neglect of "weightier matters of the law" (Matthew 23:23). It comes down to a question of motivation—no Christian fruit except from a Christian root, **faith**. Conduct not thus motivated is **sin**.

15:1-6. *Christian Responsibility.* Verses 1 and 2 express the hallmark of the Christian community as contrasted with the whole of secular society. Being **strong** involves responsibility and self-subjection, not doing as you please. Individualism is suspect. Paul is perhaps thinking of the stress ancient Stoicism laid on the independence of the wise man, the Stoic ideal. Not independence but consideration for the weaker person is the Christian law (cf. Galatians 6:2). **Bear with the failings** makes the meaning more negative than the Greek intends. The New English Bible paraphrase "accept as our burden the tender scruples" expresses the sense better.

The example of Christ (verse 3, quoting Psalm 69:9) and scripture as a whole (verse 4) encourage the weak. Ultimately God will bring unanimity about these matters and rivalry will be dissolved in adoration of the God revealed in Christ. Then praise will take the place of argument. Verse 6 is the climax of the discussion.

E. WELCOME FOR BOTH JEW AND GENTILE (15:7-13)

The mutual relationships of Christians are to serve the glory of God. They cause one another—and the outside observer—to praise God. Antipathies must be overcome because Christ overcame the barrier that separated him from sinful humanity. Verses 8-9 make the point that Christ belongs to both Jews and Gentiles.

God's **truthfulness** is practically synonymous with his **mercy**. The Old Testament citations in verses 9b-12 are from the Septuagint of Psalm 18:49; Deuteronomy 32:43; Psalm 117:1; Isaiah 11:10). They might be called **promises** to the Gentiles, thus balancing verse 8b. Christ's coming is service of God and humanity in that it inaugurates a new order of righteousness based on faith which includes all people and dissolves inveterate divisions. Hence the prospect of **joy and peace** and of **hope**.

VIII. PAUL'S OWN MISSION (15:14-33)

15:14-17. *His Mission to Gentiles.* Paul's thought was beginning in verses 8-9 to move away from church dissensions to the ongoing divine purpose. He now develops this with reference to his own part in the mission to Gentiles. It is only by God's grace that he can carry it on and write letters to Christian communities as boldly as he does. He is Christ's **minister**—that is, "servant." This is not his usual term "slave" for his relationship to Christ, or yet the word transliterated "deacon," but the rarer word used in 13:6 of magistrates. He goes on to describe his funtion in terms of priesthood.

His use of this metaphor in verse 16 leaves his precise meaning a little ambiguous. Is he thinking of the the **gospel** itself, or rather of his proclamation of it, as the **offering**, comparable to the part of the sacrificial animal which the priests placed on the altar, while the Gentile converts are in the place of the worshipers watching the ritual performed? Or are the Gentile converts themselves conceived of as the offering? It would seem that the words **acceptable** and **sanctified**, which are used of the sacrificial victim in the Old Testament, make the second meaning the more probable.

In either case Paul is their ministrant, and his aim is to make people fit for the presence of God. This would include even the Gentiles, who according to Jewish ideas were separated from God by their polytheism and disgusting habits. He can even be **proud** of it, though pride is a dangerous emotion for Christians (cf. 3:27). But this is **in Christ Jesus**, (New English Bible), but arising out of all that he is, has done, and continues by the Spirit to do through the church.

Since Paul gives no hint that he is thinking of Calvary (as in 3:25), there is no need to follow those comentators who interpret the priestly metaphor to imply that the Cross is the altar. On the Spirit's sanctification cf. 6:19, 22 and I Corinthians 6:11.

15:18-21. *His Work Thus Far.* Notice two things:

(1) The wide area Paul's missionary activity has covered. In this the miraculous factor, the **power of the Holy Spirit**, must not be lost sight of. It was sheer miracle that the church took root in the Greco-Roman world. We know nothing either from the letters or from Acts of a visit to **Illyricum**, the province on the eastern coast of the Adriatic Sea. Some commentators suggest that Paul is not to be taken too literally here, and that preaching in this territory was done by Christians from Corinth or Thessalonica.

(2) Paul's principle of not building on **another man's foundation**. He has avoided spheres of work already opened up by others. This must be understood as not unwillingness to cooperate—I Corinthians 3:5-11 should rule out that interpretation. It is an expression of his sense of urgency. The time is too short to permit duplication of preachers!

The gospel is on the march west from its place of origin. Around the northeastern quarter of the Mediterranean Paul has **fully preached**, literally "filled up," **the gospel**. Apparently this means in the places where no other missionary has taught and others between them have covered the area.

The suggestion has been made that **as far round as** really means that Paul has in view the complete circle of the

Mediterranean from Jerusalem via Illyricum, Rome, Spain (verse 24), and back through Africa and Egypt. Evidently he thinks that it is God's will for the church to be planted in every region of the Roman Empire before the final day, which may be soon (13:11-12). Hence the urgency for the Christian missionary. This may be why he shows no concern for the extension of the church east from Jerusalem. If time is limited, the centers of civilization take priority. For Paul, the Roman citizen, civilization means the Roman Empire.

Prophetic visions of the conversion of the heathen are coming to fulfillment (verse 21, quoting Isaiah 52:15, the task of the servant of the Lord). Nothing less is meant by what Christ is effecting through Paul (verses 18-19). The saving righteousness of God is at work (cf. 1:16-17). Paul and his converts have the evidence plainly before them, and it indicates that human history has moved into its final phase (cf. Matthew 24:14).

15:22-23. *His Plans for Future Service.* Paul has had to put off visiting Rome till his responsibilities in the East have been discharged. Now he feels ready to move on to the West and tells of his plans.

15:24. With other Christian missionaries presumably covering Italy, Paul looks beyond to **Spain.** This land was an organized Roman province, connected by trade with the eastern Mediterranean. It had a number of Jewish synagogues where Paul could make contacts. But he would hardly have been able to use the Greek language, and so would have had to depend on interpreters.

Paul wants to be **sped** on his way by the Romans. The precise meaning of the verb remains uncertain, but it seems to have been a regular Christian practice (cf. I Corinthians 16:6, 11; II Corinthians 1:16; Acts 15:3; III John 6). Nevertheless he looks forward to enjoying the company of the Roman believers. That will be a spiritual tonic to him (verse 32*b*) and he will impart much to them. The **blessing of Christ** which he believes rests on his whole missionary project will fall on them if they welcome him for the sake of it (cf. 1:11-12).

15:25-29. Paul will be free to begin his western tour as soon as he has taken to Jerusalem a financial gift for the **saints**. This is his term not only for those at Jerusalem but for all church members (cf. 1:7; I Corinthians 1:2), the people of God as distinct from the rest of the world who are not yet aware of the gospel. He has raised the fund among his Gentile converts in **Macedonia and Achaia**—to which we must add Galatia and Asia (Acts 20:4; I Corinthians 16:1).

Paul attached much importance to this contribution. It was more than relief of poverty at Jerusalem; it was a bond between Jew and Gentile within the new Christian fellowship. It was a recognition of mutual indebtedness (verse 27). This view is different from that of Gentile-Jewish relations in 11:25-32, but this serves to show Paul's versatility. Paul the rabbinical theologian and Paul the practical pastor are the same man, who could do all things in Christ's strength (Philippians 4:13). His anxiety about the raising of the money shows in his extended appeal in II Corinthians 8–9.

Delivered is literally "sealed," a word implying confirmation. Perhaps Paul is thinking of how he will assure the Jewish Christian recipients that this contribution is a genuine act of Christian "sharing" (vs. 27).

15:30-33. We do not know what effect the gift had on the Jerusalem recipients, because Paul was arrested soon after arrival there (Acts 21:17-36). As a result, his visit to Rome took place in circumstances very different from those he envisages in this letter. That he sensed such sinister possibilities is clear from his request for **prayers**. But he was not delivered from the **unbelievers in Judea**. Even the greatest of God's servants do not have all their wishes granted.

IX. AN ADDENDUM (16:1-27)

This final chapter is not related to chapter 15. It contains personal messages, a warning against heresy, and a long ascription of praise.

How did Paul know so many people in a church which he had

never visited—more here than in any other letter? And with all
these individual names why no word of greeting to the officers of
the church at Rome, either personally or by title? It is not
impossible that Paul had met all these people in Asia and that
they had since moved to Rome. There was considerable travel in
the Mediterranean. For example, Prisca and Aquila, whom Paul
knew in Corinth and Ephesus, may well have returned to their
former home at Rome. But it would be more natural if the
people named belonged to a church familiar to Paul.

These questions about the content of the chapter, added to
certain variations in the manuscripts (see Introduction), have
inspired much discussion about whether it was an original part of
Romans. A good number of scholars today maintain that it was. On
the other hand a very few see it as the work of a later writer seeking
to give Pauline authority to the warning of verses 17-20. The
majority, however, view it as a short separate Pauline letter, or
part of a letter, which at some stage in the collection of Paul's
correspondence got attached to Romans. From the greetings in
verses 3-5 the most natural address for such a letter is Ephesus,
where Paul spent three years (Acts 20:31) and would have many
friends. This address also makes less surprising Paul's knowledge
of dangerous tendencies in the church.

A more recent modification of this theory suggests that Paul,
having expressed to the Romans his mature judgment on the
issue of Jew and Gentile, law and gospel, decided to publicize it
by sending a copy to Ephesus for dissemination in Asia, with
personal references appended. The omission of "in Rome" in
1:7, 15 in one manuscript supports the likelihood that one or
more copies were sent elsewhere than to Rome.

16:1-2. *Recommendation of Phoebe.* Phoebe is doubtless the
carrier of the letter—whether chapter 16 or all of Romans. She is
endorsed as a **sister**, a fellow Christian, and a **deaconess**,
presumably indicating that in the churches of Paul's day women
could be included among the deacons.

In chapters 1-15 **church** has been used in the inclusive sense;
here it occurs in the sense of a local congregation. **Cenchreae**
was the port across the isthmus from Corinth. **In the Lord**

means as a fellow Christian. The word translated **helper** may imply high social standing for Phoebe, enabling her to protect a suspected minority.

16:3-16. *Greetings to Friends.* Paul's first greeting is to **Prisca** and her husband **Aquila**, with whom he has worked at his trade of tentmaking (Acts 18:2-3; Prisca is called Priscilla in Acts). Possibly they were well-to-do, with a **house** large enough for Christians to meet in and enough wealth to be able to migrate from Rome to Corinth, then to Ephesus, and possibly back to Rome on the death of the Emperor Claudius in A.D. 54. We know nothing of the risk they took on Paul's behalf.

16:5*b*-15. The phrase **first convert** is literally "first fruits." The spread of Christianity is like harvesting. **Andronicus and Junias** are **kinsmen**—that is, Christians of Jewish origin like Paul. Another thing they have in common with Paul is that they have known imprisonment for the gospel, as preachers from place to place. We have no information about this, but we note that Paul includes them among the **apostles**, using that word in a sense not confined to the twelve but equivalent to missionary (cf. Barnabas, Acts 14:14).

It is even possible that the second name might be "Junia," a woman, in which case Andronicus and Junia would probably be man and wife. The contribution of women in those first days of the church's growth should be clear from this chapter (cf. I Corinthians 11:3-16; 14:34-35). There are still to be mentioned Tryphaena, Tryphosa, Persis, Rufus' mother, Julia, Nereus' sister. They are only names to us, but they hint at the liberating power of Christ's gospel. They, and the men too, may have been slaves or ex-slaves.

16:16. The **holy kiss** as a sign of fraternity is referred to by Paul elsewhere as if customary (I Corinthians 16:20; II Corinthians 13:12; I Thessalonians 5:26). I Peter 5:14 gives evidence for it outside Pauline circles. By the middle of the second century it had become a fixed part of the liturgy of the Lord's Supper.

16:17-20. *Warning Against Heresy.* The community has to be prepared to deal with persuasive teachers who propose deviations from the original preaching and cause **dissensions**.

Their motives are low and they are best avoided altogether. But the victory of God over **Satan** is not in doubt. This is something of a set piece (cf. Philippians 3:18-19 and Jude 17-25).

The short benediction of verse 20*b* is found in some manuscripts after verse 23 and in some after verse 27. This is part of the evidence that the ending of the letter was known in different forms to the early copyists.

16:21-23. *Greetings from Companions.* Paul's companions at the time of writing join in sending greetings. **Timothy** is well known from Acts 16:1-3 and references in Paul's other letters. **Gaius** is no doubt the Corinthian convert mentioned in I Corinthians 1:14. The identification of **Erastus** with the Erastus of Acts 19:22 and II Timothy 4:20 is less certain.

16:25-27. *Doxology.* The closing doxology has its own impressiveness. But the fact that it appears in the manuscripts at various places (see Introduction) raises questions not only about its place but also about its authorship. It may well be the work of a second century copyist making use of Pauline phraseology.

To declare that the **only wise God** commanded his saving purpose, which had been a **mystery**, to be revealed in Christ is the root of Pauline and Christian orthodoxy. But the stress on **through the prophetic writings** reads a little awkwardly, as if the phrase was deliberately inserted to meet heresy like that of Marcion (around A.D. 140), who rejected the Old Testament. On the whole it lacks the full Pauline impact.

THE FIRST LETTER OF PAUL TO THE CORINTHIANS

James L. Price

INTRODUCTION

Corinth

Leadership in resistance to the Roman domination of Greece brought disaster to the principal city in the Achaean League, and in 146 B.C. it was reduced to ruins. The Corinth which Paul knew was rebuilt on the site a century later, probably under orders from Julius Caesar. It quickly grew to be an important Roman colony.

From the dawn of Greek civilization the place seems to have been a major maritime center. Its strategic location at the meeting point for the shipping lanes of East and West assured the rebuilt Roman city a new era of prominence. Seamen persisted in the age-old practice of avoiding the dangerous voyage around the southern promontory of Greece, preferring to drag their smaller vessels on rollers across the four-mile-wide isthmus north of Corinth. Larger ships were unloaded at the Aegean port of Cenchreae and reloaded at the Western port on the Gulf of Corinth and vice versa. Accordingly by Paul's time Corinth had become a prosperous commercial center with a population estimated at around 600,000 and many transients.

There were other factors besides commerce which attracted people to Corinth. Near the city the Isthmian Games were held, second only in popularity to the Olympics. On the summit of Acrocorinth, a peak rising 1,800 feet above the city streets, was a famous temple to Aphrodite, the goddess of love. To this site were drawn many visitors, less interested perhaps in the magnificent view of the Peloponnesus Mountains than in the numerous sacred prostitutes attached to the temple. For Corinth had become a byword in the Greco-Roman world for vice. In the theater a Corinthian was the stereotype for a drunkard, and "live like a Corinthian" was a slang term for debauchery.

Paul's Mission to Corinth

Acts 18:1-18 provides a brief account of the founding of the church in Corinth. So far as we know, Paul was the first Christian missionary to Corinth. To many this city might seem a most unlikely place to preach the gospel, but Paul was challenged by the mighty metropolis. He stayed longer in Corinth than anywhere except Ephesus, and even there he kept in touch with the Corinthian community and guided its development.

One must draw largely on the Corinthian letters, as well as one's imagination, to expand the scanty information given in Acts on Paul's eighteen-month mission at Corinth. The author of Acts emphasizes the Jews' opposition to him and describes his arraignment before Gallio at their instigation (Acts 18:12-17).

An inscription about Gallio found at Delphi has provided an important point in determining Pauline chronology. Most scholars accept the date of Gallio's arrival at Corinth as the summer of 51, and he seems to have been proconsul there for only a year. Relating this clue to Acts, we may conclude that Paul's mission to Corinth began in the winter or spring of 50 and ended late in 51 or early in 52.

Aquila and Priscilla, whom Paul calls Prisca, are introduced in Acts 18:1-3. The note that they have recently come to Corinth because the Emperor Claudius expelled the Jews from Rome provides another point of reference to the general history of the time. This edict is mentioned by the Roman historian Suetonius and probably is to be dated about 49.

Of more interest to students of the Corinthian letters are the references to Apollos (Acts 18:24–19:7). In I Corinthians Paul speaks of Apollos with full respect for him and his labors (3:5-9; 4:6; 16:12), but it is apparent that some of his followers were troublemakers in the Corinthian church (1:11-12; 3:4).

After Paul's initial work at Corinth, Acts 18:18-22 reports that he made a trip to Judea and Syria, though some scholars question his visiting Jerusalem at this time. It is likely that his "third missionary journey" (Acts 18:23–20:37) began early in 53. His eventual destination was Ephesus, the capital and chief city of the province of Asia, which comprised western Asia Minor. He worked there for nearly three years (53-56). Both I and II Corinthians contain references to Paul's plans and movements following the Ephesian ministry. Acts reports only that he stayed in Achaia—probably at Corinth—for three months before leaving the region for Jerusalem (Acts 20:1-3). This last visit to Corinth probably occurred in 56.

Paul's Letters to Corinth

While at Ephesus, probably in 55, Paul heard of the distressing moral laxity in the Corinthian church. I Corinthians 5:9 refers to a letter by Paul in response to this report. This earlier letter no longer exists—unless the scholars are right who claim that a fragment is preserved in II Corinthians 6:14–7:1 (see comment).

Further reports of disorders at Corinth reached Paul at Ephesus. A delegation from the church came to him, and a letter sought his counsel on certain divisive issues (I Corinthians 7:1*a*; 8:1*a*; 12:1; 16:1*a*, 12*a*?). In answer to these disturbing reports, gleaned from several sources, Paul wrote I Corinthians. Some scholars have questioned the unity of this letter, pointing to seams in its fabric as evidence that it was made up of parts of several writings of Paul to the Corinthians. This evidence is not conclusive, however.

Paul sent Timothy to follow up the letter in the hope that some of the abuses in the church might be corrected. Reports from Timothy and perhaps other sources led Paul to conclude that the situation had become critical. Apparently he made a hasty visit to Corinth, altering his previous plans. Acts does not record this visit, but notes in II Corinthians 2:1; 12:14; 13:1-2, which cannot otherwise be explained satisfactorily, indicate that Paul paid a flying and "painful" visit to Corinth.

The crisis at Corinth had become worse by Paul's second visit. II Corinthians 2:4 refers to a sternly worded letter, composed by Paul "out of much affliction and anguish of heart and with many tears," and 7:8-12 speaks of its effect on the Corinthians. Scholars call this third letter to Corinth the "severe letter." Some have sought to show that these references must be to I Corinthians, but the description of it is ill suited to the content and mood of that letter.

Many scholars hold that II Corinthians 10–13 contains a substantial fragment of the severe letter. Observing the content and tone of the first nine chapters of this letter, they cannot believe that Paul could have experienced such a radical change of mood. He would not have put into the same letter the bitter, sarcastic remonstrance and self-defense found in chapters 10–13. Moreover they argue that several statements in chapters 1–9 presuppose or echo statements in chapters 10–13 (for example, cf. 1:23 with 13:2; 2:3 with 13:10; 2:9 with 10:6).

No notice is taken of II Corinthians by writers of the church before the middle of the second century, whereas I Corinthians is cited as early as the 90's. This lends force to the view that II Corinthians was compiled by an editor from several fragments of Paul's correspondence—including even perhaps some work of another author (see below on II Corinthians 6:14–7:1).

In contrast to those who find the severe letter in chapters 10–13, certain scholars have claimed that these chapters are a fragment of a letter written by Paul to the Corinthians later than the letter or letters preserved in chapters 1–9. Still others believe that chapters 8–9 should be separated from chapters 1–7 and assigned to one or more letters of Paul. Of these several theories, the case for identifying chapters 10–13 with the severe letter is the strongest.

The evidence for all such theories falls short of proof, however. There is no compelling reason why II Corinthians as it now stands could not have been dispatched by Paul as a single letter to the Corinthian church. Dictating a letter in ancient times was a slow process. For a letter of this length several interruptions would be quite probable. Such breaks may well explain the abrupt shifts of thought and mood found in II Corinthians.

Advocates of the theory that chapters 10–13 are the severe letter believe that Paul's last correspondence to the Corinthians survives in chapters 1–9. Most of them omit at the least 6:14–7:1 from these chapters. They have called the remaining Paul's "thankful letter." Unquestionably they are correct in holding that the dominant mood of chapters 1–9 is joyful confidence.

When Paul wrote his last word to the Corinthians he was hopeful that a basis had been established for a lasting reconciliation of the differences and distrust which had alienated the church from him. But he was not without misgivings and anxiety, and signs of this disquiet should not be overlooked. He was anticipating a third visit to Corinth in the near future. The situation in the church which confronted him when he wrote makes it reasonable to believe that he added chapters 10–13 before dispatching the letter and going for the last time to Corinth.

I. Epistolary Introduction (1:1-9)

1:1-3.*Salutation.* Paul's letters begin with conventional modes of address, but his introductions are never mere formalities. They provide clues to his self-understanding and conception of his mission. Sometimes they disclose his special purposes in writing. So in this letter the first sentence reveals a man emphatically defending his own authority and reminding his readers who they are.

It is a fitting beginning to a letter addressed to a congregation of rugged individualists. These people were at cross purposes, apparently eager to be independent of Paul and of traditional standards of personal conduct, and shirking their corporate responsibilities.

As we read on, it becomes evident why Paul writes as he does. If this young church is to mature, its members must recognize the legitimacy of his authority over them. They must also know themselves to be a congregation of God's people, sharing one Lord and a common life, and helping to shape the future of a community far wider than their own disorderly world.

Sosthenes (cf. Acts 18:17) may be Paul's secretary, or he may be introduced here as one esteeemed by the Corinthians. In any case his views do not intrude. Paul writes in the first person singular, as an apostle who is uniquely related to his readers as their "father in Christ Jesus" (4:15).

1:4-9. *Thanksgiving and Assurances.* Some have felt that here the polite conventions of letter writing momentarily led Paul to idealize the Christian community at Corinth. Presumably he could not have given thanks for actual conditions there. Others suppose that in view of the distressing reports he resorted to irony. Possessing **all knowledge** indeed! The Corinthians were **not lacking in any spiritual gift**, yet only in a proper regard for and use of these gifts would the church be **guiltless** in the day of judgment. Their present conduct in view of God's faithfulness was indefensible.

It is more probable that Paul continues to stress positively the true nature of Christian existence. A new historical situation and community exist as a consequence of the coming of Jesus as the Christ. If the Corinthians are to rise above their quarreling and callous independence they must acknowledge what God has done for them, what God now offers them, and what they ought to be—in Christ. Paul can sincerely be thankful that such **grace** has become available to the Corinthians though he knows that they have so little understood and appropriated the gift. He makes no reference to their progress or good reputation (cf. I Thessalonians 1:2-8).

II. SERIOUS DISORDERS REPORTED IN CORINTH (1:10–6:20)

A. DISSENSIONS (1:10–4:21)

1:10-12. *The Situation.* The unity of the church at Corinth is threatened by **dissensions**, literally "fissures," or "rifts." Perhaps it is too much to speak of opposing parties, or even of factions. Paul's words do not suggest that groups have separated and are meeting apart (cf. 11:17-22), but rather that cliques are forming within a single congregation. The **quarreling** has been reported to him **by Chloe's people**—presumably slaves of a woman known to the Corinthians. He condemns the spirit of the schismatics, not their opinions. He exposes their common errors, not their respective claims.

It is therefore not possible to infer the existence at Corinth of heresies, that is peculiar doctrines, or to identify the beliefs distinguishing those who say that they belong to Paul, Apollos, etc. The differing attitudes on moral issues which Paul discusses in chapters 7–9 have also sometimes been assigned to one or the other of the groups of verse 12, but such conjecture is unprofitable. The dissensions are here attributed to personal loyalties rather than to theological or ethical causes, and Paul does not refer to them in this way again.

1:12. The eloquent **Apollos**, a Hellenistic Jewish Christian from Alexandria, seems to have worked in Corinth after Paul's first labors there (cf. 3:6; Acts 18:24-28). The reference to **Cephas**—that is, Simon Peter—may imply a Corinthian ministry for this apostle, or it may indicate that the aura of Peter's authority remained with Jewish Christians baptized by him and now living in Corinth.

I belong to Christ is puzzling. Some take it, not as the slogan of a fourth party, but as a counter-slogan of Paul (cf. II Corinthians 10:7), or possibly as the marginal comment of a scribe which came to be copied in the text. But the indignant question **Is Christ divided?** (verse 13) suggests rather that some schismatics were exclusively claiming the name of Christ. Some

Christians at Corinth were asserting their freedom to the point of denying all restraints. They called themselves spiritual men and denied all authority apart from the Spirit of Christ and their private visions of him. It is not possible, however, to establish their identity as the "Christ party."

1:13-17. *The Primacy of Christ.* Eager to claim the loyalty of the Corinthian Christians, Paul nonetheless deplores the misguided sentiments of those enrolling themselves under his own name. Did some suppose that the authority of an apostle legitimized baptism? Whatever the answer to this question, Paul is glad to recall that he has **baptized** only a few. In this there is no pretext for hailing him as a potential party leader. Paul was not one to disparage baptism (cf. Galatians 3:27 and Romans 6), but he focused his energies on preaching. Doubtless he left baptism to his helpers, as Jesus may have done (cf. John 4:1-2).

His main concern is clear. No clique can own Christ or claim to be his favorite; no apostle's word or action can eclipse Christ's lordship. Ten times already in this letter Paul has named Christ. This name alone is the rallying point for Christian unity (cf. verse 10).

1:18-25. *Human Wisdom.* Many interpreters hold that Paul here gives special attention to those who unfavorably compare his own lack of sophistication and rhetorical skill with the learning and eloquence of Apollos. There is no reason to think that Apollos was at fault, or that Paul is critical of his fellow worker (cf. 16:12). It is a reasonable inference that the champions of Apollos were striving for **wisdom** in the way the **Greeks** sought it (verse 22*b*) and priding themselves in their intellectual prowess. But Paul's words in verses 18-31 seem to refer to an error common to all the schismatics at Corinth—namely, too exalted an estimate of the words or actions of particular leaders.

Lest the Corinthians conclude that the Christian message is after all a form of **wisdom** comparable to some popular Greek philosophy, or that Christian leaders as wisdom teachers are themselves wise, Paul emphasized two points:

(1) To human eyes the gospel itself—not the preaching of

it—is both offensive and absurd. To the **Jews** the idea of a crucified Messiah is self-contradictory and blasphemous, a **stumbling block**. Jesus' crucifixion leads **Greeks** to conclude that it is **folly** to make Jesus a clever teacher or a strong hero. The divine claims of one ignominiously executed cannot be taken seriously. Yet Paul reminds the Corinthians that **Christ crucified** has done something for them that all human wisdom and power could never accomplish.

(2) Paul asks his readers to consider their former lives and to recall the occasion of his first visit. Nothing in these human circumstances gives them any cause for boasting.

It would be wrong to conclude that Paul here idealizes simplemindedness and anti-intellectualism. He opposes misplaced confidence in autonomous reason and other powers to transcend ignorance and to save oneself. He is not condemning human wisdom, that is philosophy, in principle, nor is he scorning the powers of reason to discern truth (cf. Romans 1:19-20). But to him the pretensions of the Corinthians snobbishly following great teachers as though they alone have fathomed all mysteries, and parading their own sophistry in the grandiose rhetoric of Greek orators of the age, appear foolish indeed in comparison with that wisdom manifested in God's love in the cross of Christ, a wisdom powerful to save.

Some interpreters suppose that in verses 24 and 30 Paul identifies Christ with wisdom and that his thought is influenced by Jewish wisdom literature in which the wisdom of God is personified. The quotation in verse 19 is from Isaiah 29:14; that in verse 31 is from Jeremiah 9:24.

2:6–3:4. *God's Wisdom.* The chief difficulties in this passage are Paul's allusions to certain basic and commonplace features of his world view which are strangely archaic to modern ears. His main points are clear. Our comprehension of the purposes of God proclaimed in Christ depend on the Spirit's enlightenment. The quarreling Corinthians evidently do not fully possess this Spirit and therefore do not possess this wisdom—indeed have proved themselves unready to receive it.

2:7. Commentators do not agree about the reference to the

secret and hidden wisdom of God. It is unlikely that only the **word of the cross** (1:18) is implied, for Paul's proclamation of the cross was received by all his converts. Neither does Paul seem to be speaking here of some esoteric, revealed knowledge as he does in II Corinthians 12:1-5. On his own account such disclosures are not communicable. Rather this secret wisdom of God which Paul imparts and some are able to receive is probably the fullness of God's purpose of redemption in Christ, which includes the incorporation of both Jews and Greeks in the church and man's victory over death (cf. 15:51; Romans 11:25; Colossians 1:26-27).

Unlike initiation into the secrets of a pagan mystery religion, baptism does not confer saving knowledge in its gospels, one for "babes"—the word of the cross—and another for the **mature**. The preaching of Christ crucified, properly understood, is the wisdom of God for all people. But at least some of the Corinthians have not grasped its present meaning, to say nothing of its future promise.

2:8. The phrase **rulers of this age** has also been variously interpreted. Some limit it to Pilate and the Jewish rulers of Palestine. Paul probably has in mind the invisible powers of the spirit world behind these governing authorities, influencing their actions and blinding their eyes to the truth. Beliefs such as these were sacred by many writers of Paul's day, non-Jews as well as Jews. Paul believes that the power of these spirit-rulers, like the present age, is short-lived, doomed by the crucifixion of Christ. These rulers have unwittingly sealed their own fate, yet their final defeat awaits the coming of the **Lord of glory** and the resurrection. Christians are able to comprehend this wisdom only insofar as the Spirit of God reveals it to them. But since the Spirit has been given, what the future holds in store is in part present knowledge.

2:9-10a. The origin of the "scripture" which Paul cites here is not certain. Some detect a conflation of Isaiah 64:4; 65:17 and Jeremiah 3:16. Others see an allusion to Baruch 3:16, which which is dependent on Job 28, and find support in this text for the view that Paul identified Christ with the wisdom of God (cf. 1:24, 30).

2:10b-16. The meaning here is obscured by grammatical difficulties. The most important of these is the ambiguity in verse 13 reflected in the alternative readings of the Revised Standard Version footnote. Also Paul's varied use of the word **spirit** is at first sight confusing. He seems to have been influenced here by the Corinthians misappropriation of this and related terms. The word **spiritual** is otherwise infrequently used by Paul, and **spiritually** occurs only here.

Paul's argument seems to run as follows. There are certain things in a human being of which that person alone is conscious; so it is with God. There are **depths** of God's nature which, if known, must be disclosed by God alone. Yet not all people can receive this knowledge. Only the person who is **spiritual**, who is dominated by God's self-revealing Spirit, by being actively receptive and obedient can comprehend God's **gifts** (see above on 1:4-9). The person who is **unspiritual**, who is chiefly directed by the impulses and needs of merely physical existence, is insensitive to these gifts and to their value. Cf. 15:44-50, where the same contrasting terms are employed.

Only the spiritual person, therefore, **judges**, or investigates, **all things**—or persons, as the Greek can also mean—even the **depths of God**. Only the spiritual person is finally independent of all judgments other than God's. In these words Paul sets forth an ideal rather than an established fact. The quotation in verse 16 is from Isaiah 40:13.

3:1-4. The Corinthians, who are claiming to be truly **spiritual men**, are acting like **ordinary men**—at the most **babes in Christ**—as their **jealousy and strife** prove. Paul holds that the hallmark of the Spirit is love. The absence of love mocks the conceit and pretensions of the Corinthians.

3:5–4:5. *Cooperation Among the Apostles.* In referring again to the personality cults among the schismatics Paul emphasizes the nature of any apostle's work and its value in God's eyes. While it is possible to render verse 9a **we are God's fellow**

workers, the context seems to require "fellow workmen for God"—that is, in God's service.

3:10-17. The same idea is developed in the image of the **foundation** and superstructure of a building. It is just possible that this metaphor was suggested to Paul by those in Corinth who claimed Cephas as their leader, since he may have known of the tradition of Peter as the "rock" on which the church would be built (Matthew 16:18). But again Paul is not thinking of origins so much as of consequences. What matters most is not the primacy but the quality of anyone's **work**.

And the Corinthians are not warranted in making their comparative judgments. Only the coming **Day** of judgment, **will disclose** what sort of work each of the apostles has done. Good workmanship will endure, but the fires of judgment will destroy the worthless products of labor. Anyone's salvation depends, not on works—notice Paul's avoidance here of this plural—but on God's grace. Yet the master builder whose work stands the test will be rewarded in proportion to the work done.

3:16-17. Paul's architectural metaphors have a theological, not a logical, relation. **God's building** (verse 9) becomes **God's temple** because the work of God's Spirit is holy. Already Paul may be thinking ahead to those Christians who desecrate God's temple by the sexual immoralities he severely censures in chapters 5-6.

3:18-23. It is not obvious why Paul now resumes his attack on a particular type of **wisdom** which is **folly** with God. He supports this by quotations from Job 5:13 and Psalm 94:11. Does he have in mind some particular leader, perhaps claiming to belong to Apollos, who is threatening to destroy God's temple, the Corinthian church?

We can only conjecture, but it is clear from verse 21*a* that the quarreling at Corinth is still the subject for rebuke. The schismatics should not think of themselves as belonging to Apollos or one of the others. As servants of Christ and of his church the apostles belong to them all. Notice Paul's inversion of the slogans of 1:12.

4:1-5. Paul now brings his formal arguments against the

schismatics at Corinth to a conclusion. The apostles can be judged properly only in terms of their faithfulness **as servants of Christ**, entrusted with the **mysteries of God**. Instead of passing hasty judgments on the apostles the Corinthians had better give thought to themselves and to Christ, who will **judge** all people and their motives (cf. II Corinthians 5:10).

4:6-13. *The Humility of the Apostles.* Paul here makes explicit what the reader may have suspected earlier. In boasting of certain apostles the schismatics have been boasting of their own wisdom and superiority (3:18-23). Paul now says that he has taken himself and Apollos as illustrations of principles which might more obviously be applied to others.

In chapter 3 he has put forward the names of persons not really responsible for the divisions at Corinth. Those persons more directly to blame must now recognize that in one important respect their situation is precisely that of the apostles (verse 7a). All that they now possess as Christians has been given to them. Since all depends on grace, what cause does anyone have for boasting or for making invidious comparisons?

4:6-7. The meaning of Paul's rhetorical questions in verse 7 is somewhat obscured by the puzzling phrase in verse 6 **not beyond what is written**. An attractive theory is that these words should be omitted as a scribe's marginal comment later copied into the text. If the text as it stands comes from Paul, probably he is here opposing the self-styled "spiritual persons" who reject all traditions in favor of private revelations.

4:8-10. Having taken up the attack Paul now scorns the presumed superiority of the offenders. His sarcastic thrusts reveal the interrelatedness of his two major indictments:

(1) Contrary to their arrogant professions the Corinthians have not comprehended the wisdom of God.

(2) They are not "spiritual." Though they possess the gifts of the Spirit, they have wrongly supposed themselves fully instructed in a "secret and hidden wisdom of God" (2:7). They claim that they are now reigning with Christ, who has risen from the dead, and hence that they are able to stand in judgment on all others, including the apostles. Ironically Paul contrasts the

fanciful state of the Corinthians with the actual existence of Christ's apostles, who like gladiators condemned to death in the arena have sacrificed rather than glorified themselves.

4:11-13. Since Paul believed tribulations must be endured by all Christians before the consummation of Christ's kingdom, it is perhaps unwise to consider these verses merely autobiographical (cf. II Corinthians 4:7-11; 6:4-10; Romans 8:35-37). Only when the legitimacy of his apostleship was seriously questioned did Paul bring himself to record his unique experiences—and then with reluctance, as in II Corinthians 11:22-23 (cf. Galatians 1–2). In his sufferings Paul held in mind the teaching of Christ concerning nonretaliation, even though he was not always able to live up to it. Reviled and slandered at Corinth, Paul did not limit himself to blessing, but he did seek by every means to **conciliate**.

4:14-21. *A Personal Appeal.* Paul's disavowal in verse 14 is qualified by 6:5 and 15:34. He is moved by his feelings of special responsibility and affection to stress his paternal love for the Corinthians, but there is still irony in his words. They may have **countless guides**—literally "pedagogues," which in Paul's day meant, not teachers, but slaves who took small boys to school, so that the remark is no compliment—but they have but one **father**. Just as children may be expected to imitate their parents, so the Corinthians should see in Paul's humility a rebuke of their arrogant ways.

4:17-21. Because Paul is their father and is expected to exhort his children, **Timothy** is being sent for that purpose. He is evidently traveling by a roundabout route which will bring him to Corinth after arrival of the letter (cf. 16:10-11). But soon Paul will visit them himself.

These notes concerning his future plans reveal Paul's defensiveness. Was it being said that he was inconsistent in teaching, vacillating in decision, a big talker but a timid soul? His question in verse 21 anticipates events to come: a painful visit to Corinth, followed by his severe letter to the church. Indeed the hints contained in these verses are explicitly developed in II Corinthians 12:14–13:13, which provide the best commentary on this passage.

B. SEXUAL IMMORALITY AND LITIGATION (5:1–6:20)

A new subject is abruptly introduced with this section. Paul is still concerned with reports of the unruly conduct of Christians at Corinth—disorders symptomatic of the arrogant independence of this church's leadership—but it is probable that he has been presented new evidence. Perhaps the bearers of a letter from the Corinthians (cf. 7:1*a*; 16:17-18) have reported a case of incest in the church (5:1-5) and legal disputes among its members (6:1-6). Paul's concern may have led him to resume dictation of his letter with these subjects. Moreover since his visit to the Corinthians is to be delayed, their questions deserve an immediate reply.

It is noteworthy that from this point in the letter his instructions become quite concrete and specific. They are supported by theological principles which are sometimes only implicit.

5:1-5. *A Case of Incest.* Apparently a prominent man in the church has married his stepmother. His father must have died or been divorced, for this sexual union is not termed adultery. Such a marriage was forbidden by the Jewish law and also by a Roman statute.

But Paul does not appeal to law. The Jewish law was not binding for Christians, especially Gentile converts, and the offender was probably a non-Jew. Roman law may have been discounted by social customs at Corinth, as well as by the antinomianism—the belief in complete freedom from law—of some in the church. This would have provided further reason for the church's indifference to the matter (cf. 6:12).

Paul is certain that even pagan sensibilities are being offended, and in this he finds support for his condemnation of the man. Either the woman is not a Christian and therefore not subject to Paul's discipline, or he considers the man the principal offender.

5:2-4. Paul does not limit himself to demanding the severest punishment of this offender. He strongly condemns the complacency of all the church members. Instead of being undisturbed by the incident they should be grieving as though a death had occurred in their midst! A congregational meeting must be called at once and Paul's decision in the matter ratified as though he were **present**. Reference to the cooperation of Christ's **power** may suggest that the prayers of the congregation will confirm this action.

5:5. Most commentators believe that this verse commands excommunication and that it implies belief that the man will be left to the unlimited power of **Satan** (cf. Romans 1:24-32, where Paul speaks of the sexually immoral as given over to the wrath of God). Paul may intend that a curse of death be invoked on the man.

Elsewhere he writes that Satan's power causes unceasing pain (II Corinthians 12:7) and thwarts human purposes (I Thessalonians 2:18). But Satan's power is limited to the **destruction of the flesh**. Soon the **day of the Lord Jesus** will bring the resurrection, with a new spiritual body (cf. 15:42-50) and the possibilities of this corrupt man's salvation.

Christian love may seem to demand an unlimited forbearance of evil (cf. 13:7), but in Paul's judgment this situation requires the use of the **rod** instead of the **spirit of gentleness** (4:21). Failure to expel such an offender might encourage the sexual license shown in this church and seriously impair its witness to outsiders.

5:6-13. *The Purity of the Church.* Paul's repeated reference to the arrogance of the church's leaders (verse 6; cf. verse 2) emphasizes the gravity of the situation at Corinth. To condone the sexual immorality of a member is deplorable, but to boast of such freedom as a spiritual privilege is perverse. Moreover the lax attitude of these leaders is like **leaven**, infecting the life of the entire congregation.

In Paul's thought the leaven or yeast is associated with putrefaction and corruption. His allegory is based on the Jewish Passover, during which Jewish houses had to be cleansed of any trace of leavened bread, lest ceremonial impurity result. Christians, like loyal Jews, must keep the true Passover by making actual the ideal of moral purity symbolized by unleavened bread. Any impurity within the household of faith can only compromise this loyalty and ideal.

Paul's allegory is derived also from convictions associated with the Christian gospel. He recalls the tradition that Jesus was put to death just before the celebration of a Passover in Jerusalem, becoming for those who believed in him the **paschal lamb**, slain once and for all. This crucified and risen Lord, who himself purifies men from sin, demands of his church moral purity. Thus by their conduct the Corinthians are to become what they already are by virtue of Christ's sacrifice and their faith union with him.

5:9-13. In verse 9 Paul speaks of words he has written earlier which have been misunderstood at Corinth. He clearly is referring here to a previous **letter**. In this he warned against keeping company with **immoral men**—the translation of a more specific Greek word meaning those who indulge in extramarital sexual relations. Sex offenders stand at the top of Paul's list, here and in 6:9-20, because of their prevalence in the Corinthian church. The other offenders listed in verse 10 may have been suggested by the following progression of thought: the sexually **immoral** sin against themselves (cf. 6:18); the **greedy and robbers** sin against their fellows; **idolaters** sin against God.

5:11-13. Many scholars today maintain that II Corinthians 6:14–7:1 reproduces a part of the previous letter to which Paul refers in verse 9 (see Introduction), but this conjecture cannot be proven. We are not left to conjecture about the contents of the previous letter, however, for Paul now clarifies the points he made before. He has not urged the physical isolation of the church from non-Christians—which is indeed not possible. Rather he has written that the self-discipline of the church is necessary. The church must judge and expel from its membership the wicked person.

6:1-8. *Court Quarrels Among Christians.* The relation of the church to pagan society and Paul's conviction that the church must judge its own members lead naturally to a consideration of a third example of the disorderliness of the Corinthians. If church members are not allowed to judge outsiders, then neither should church members expect to be judged by them. Nevertheless this passage is a kind of digression. Paul returns shortly to the subject of the notorious sexual immoralities at Corinth.

6:1. Paul is indignant that Christians should be taking their trivial property disputes into pagan courts. **Unrighteous** simply identifies **unbelievers** (verse 6), non-Christians, and should not be taken as disparagement of the Roman tribunals. Paul believes that the state has received from God its mission to maintain peace and justice (cf. Roman 13:1-8). His letters disclose no disillusionment in this matter.

6:2-3. The rhetorical questions in these verses are parallel. Both have reference to the **world** of the **angels**—that is, to the domain of the "rulers of this age" (see above on 2:8). Elsewhere these are designated "principalities" (Romans 8:38) or "elemental spirits" (Galatians 4:3).

Some interpreters suppose that Paul speaks here of judgment of the human world as well as of angelic beings. Yet Paul consistently holds that the **saints**, that is Christians, have no authority in this age to **judge** unbelievers. And he nowhere writes of a resurrection of the unbelieving in the age to come which might provide opportunity for the saints to judge them. Always in speaking of the judgment to come Paul writes that it is God alone, through the agency of Jesus Christ, who judges (cf. Romans 2:11-16; II Thessalonians 1:7*b*-12).

6:4-6. The cause of Paul's outrage is that these legal squabbles among Christians are additional evidence of their immaturity. These acts threaten their Christian witness to outsiders. At the time the Corinthians are claiming wisdom there appears to be no one of them **wise enough to decide between members of the brotherhood.** Instead Christians are turning to **unbelievers,** pagans, who count for nothing in the church—the probable meaning of verse 4.

6:7-8. Do the Corinthians speak of sharing now in their Lord's messianic reign? (Cf. 4:8.) Their quarrelling reveals their actual **defeat,** not their victory. Indeed victory over all evil is not their destined lot in the present age. As their Lord suffered, they too must be ready to suffer wrong. Instead they are inflicting it—on their own **brethren**.

6:9-11. *Warning Against Immorality.* Paul sharply warns his readers that there are vices which disqualify one from inheriting the **kingdom of God**—that realm into which the Christian dead enter after their resurrection according to Paul's view (cf. 15:50; Galatians 5:19-21).

6:9*b*-10. The **greedy**, the **thieves**, and the **robbers** may refer to the Christians who are defrauding one another in their property disputes (verse 8). References to sex offenders recall Paul's outrage as he writes about the case of incest (6:1) and point forward to a continuation of attack on sexual immoralities at Corinth.

Homosexual renders two Greek terms, perhaps referring to potential and to actual homosexuals. In the Greco-Roman world homosexuality was not greatly condemned; but Paul, in company with Jewish teachers and other Jewish-Christians, attacks it as a grave evil (cf. Romans 1:26-27).

6:11 In Verse 11*a* Paul may refer only to the former lives of some of the Corinthians. More probably he is implying, on the basis of the reports he has received, the continued existence of all these vices within the church. If so, we may wonder how he can write of such Christians as in verse 11*b*.

Of course by **justified** he does not mean that they are already made righteous, or morally perfect. Rather they are at peace with God in their relation to Christ, even though they remain sinners (cf. Romans 5:1-11). **You were washed, you were sanctified** probably recalls that the Corinthians have received baptism and the gifts of the Spirit. Certainly Paul is not commending their moral qualities or their professed spirituality.

6:12-20. *Sanctity of the Body.* Some church members at Corinth evidently were claiming that sexual relations outside marriage were not immoral and that as Christians they were free to consort with prostitutes without blame. Probably **all things were lawful for me** was the slogan of these free-thinkers.

Paul agrees with them in principle, but he offers two serious qualifications. Some actions are definitely not **helpful** and some by their very nature are enslaving. Paul cannot agree that the sex act, like eating food, is only natural and therefore of no moral or spiritual significance.

Many scholars believe that the views against which Paul contends here spring from an ideology identified by second century Christian apologists as Gnosticism. Gnostics commonly believed that the human body, like all material things, was the creation of an inferior deity and thus destined for destruction. For this reason Christians influenced by Gnosticism were unable to believe in the resurrection of the body. For this reason also some of them believed that no bodily function possessed any importance for the spiritual life. Thus sexual acts could not really defile the human spirit, which alone could inherit the kingdom of God. These may be called Gnostic libertines.

Others, however, influenced by the same Gnostic view of the body as material and mortal, practiced asceticism. They denied the bodily functions their proper expression on the ground that one's immortal spirit had already been redeemed from the body. These may be called Gnostic ascetics.

The presence of this ideology in first-century Corinth is supported by Paul's letters to this church. Some historians prefer to label such views pre-Gnostic, lest they be confused with the complex Gnostic heresies of the second century.

6:13-14. Paul can agree with Gnostics that both the stomach and food are to be destroyed (cf. 15:50). But the Christian's body, Paul holds, being created **for the Lord**, is **not meant for immorality**. The mortal body, destined to be raised and freed from corruption, must not now be defiled. It goes without saying that Paul, contrary to the Gnostics, shares the Jewish belief that a person's whole being is a creation of God.

6:15-20. This passage touches on an important aspect of Paul's teaching. The present union of the believer with Christ is described as membership in his body (cf. 12:12-27). The extent to which Paul intends this figure to be taken realistically is a subject for debate. But it is obvious that this union is sufficiently real for him to exclude all other unions not compatible with it.

On the basis of Old Testament teaching (Genesis 2:24 is quoted in verse 16), reaffirmed by Jesus (Mark 10:2-12), he believes that sexual intercourse is not an inconsequential, isolated act but one uniting man and woman in an intimate, complete, and enduring bond. Consequently he is revolted by the thought that a member of Christ's body should ever be united with the body of a prostitute.

In Corinth most of the prostitutes were slave women attached to the service of a pagan temple. It was commonly thought that any man having sexual relations with these sacred prostitutes entered into communion with the god whom they served. This belief may explain Paul's emphasis in verse 15 and also his claim, otherwise questionable, in verse 18.

III. ANSWERS TO QUESTIONS FROM CORINTH
(7:1–16:12)

Paul's thoughts lead him directly to a matter about which the Corinthians have written. The appearance of the same formula, **now concerning**, in 8:1; 12:1; and 16:1 identifies other questions raised in their letter, delivered perhaps by Stephanas and his companions (16:17). Possibly the church also has raised a question concerning Apollos (16:12).

A. CELIBACY AND MARRIAGE (7:1-40)

7:1-7. *Marital Obligations.* Verse 1*b* probably cites a slogan of some Gnostic ascetics in Corinth (see above on 6:12-20). Possibly Paul's stern judgments on sexual immorality led some Christians to adopt the position that avoidance of all sexual relations provides the best preventive. Paul contends that this is a valid position for anyone to take provided he has received the **special gift from God** of celibacy—a gift given to Paul (verse 7). But since all do not have this gift, celibacy cannot become a general principle for Christians. Nor can it be considered a matter of merit.

Paul flatly rejects the view that the sexual relation in marriage should be denied to Christians. Indeed husbands and wives have no right to continence, and mutual consideration in the conjugal relationship is commended. That Paul should advocate this equality of rights for women in marriage is surprising in view of his Jewish heritage and other statements (cf. 11:3, 8-9), but his Christian faith was at cross purposes with his upbringing (cf. Galatians 3:26-28). The exceptive clause in verse 5 shows that he shared the current belief that sexual intercourse brought cultic impurity. But his main point is that prolonged continence constitutes a strong temptation and may be disastrous. He does not command continence, even temporarily, for those who do not have the gift.

7:8-9. *The Unmarried and Widows.* Since Paul repeats himself and returns to the special cases he has discussed in passing (cf. verses 8 and 25) the subdivisions of chapter 7 are inexact. Here Paul repeats his qualified acceptance of celibacy, perhaps for emphasis, and applies his view to two cases. The word translated **unmarried** may mean one separated from a former spouse as well as one never married.

7:8. Since Paul speaks of himself as unmarried, some have observed that this verse may indicate that Paul was a widower. This assumption is based on an inference drawn from Acts 26:10 that Paul was once a member of the Jewish Sanhedrin (council), to which only married men were eligible. Paul's testimony makes this assumption improbable. His unmarried state was the result of a gift of God, not an "act of God."

7:9. While Paul considers marriage to be proper for all Christians lacking the gift of continence, he only grudgingly approves of it as an antidote to sexual immoralities.

7:10-16. *Separation and Divorce.* Throughout this discussion Paul is careful to distinguish between the teaching of Jesus and his own opinions (verses 10, 12; cf. verse 25). Early Christian tradition had brought him commandments of **the Lord** and on the basis of these he charged his congregations (cf. 15:3*a*). He did not consider that his personal judgments had the same authority, but neither did he think of them as mere opinions. His judgments were responsibly determined under the Spirit's influence, and the word of an apostle was to be taken seriously.

Jesus condemned divorce and denied remarriage to husband or wife (Matthew 5:32; 19:3-9; Mark 10:2-12; Luke 16:18). Paul notes here only the commandment that the wife remain single, but he recognizes the common responsibility of Christian partners in marriage.

7:12-16. In referring to **the rest** Paul has in mind situations in which one marriage partner remains a pagan—cases of "mixed marriage." In this event the Christian convert must never initiate separation. But if the unbelieving partner desires separation, the Christian cannot insist on the continuation of a relationship which was begun before his conversion.

Paul's counsel is based on his belief that sexual union affects the whole personality, a view consistent with what he says in 6:16. In this case, however, Paul thinks of the positive potentialities for the unbeliever married to a member of Christ's body, and for the **children** of this marriage. Paul emphasizes only the possible effects of the marital relationship on the unbeliever; he cannot speak of certainties (verse 16).

7:17-35. *Maintaining the Status Quo.* When Paul wrote to the Corinthians he was dominated by a conviction that **the form of this world is passing away**, that the **time has grown very short** before the coming of the Lord in glory (cf. Mark 13:30). In view of this **present distress** he urges his readers to be single-minded. They should concentrate on the affairs of the Lord, on which their lasting well-being depends rather than on relations which are short-lived and full of tribulation.

7:25-35. Paul's advice to the **unmarried** in the Corinthian church is better understood in view of his conviction of the imminent end of the present age. He would **secure** for his converts their **undivided devotion to the Lord** and save them from those worldly tribulations which he associates with the last days.

One may suspect that Paul was rationalizing his personal

inclination when he wished that all Christians might follow his example in forgoing marriage. Undoubtedly he was idealizing the effectiveness of a celibate Christian's witness. But the interpreter should not overlook Paul's basic affirmation: **each has his own special gift from God** (verse 7). Most Christians, not having the gift of celibacy, find that the divided interests which attend marriage challenge and sustain a faithful obedience to Christ.

7:36-38. *A Special Case.* Interpreters have not been able to identify with certainty the situation Paul has in mind here. There are questions about the precise meaning some of the Greek words had in his day. **Betrothed** here is literally "virgin," and the verb translated **marries** in verse 38 apparently should mean "gives in marriage." Thus the advice has traditionally been assumed to be addressed to a father and to concern whether he should marry off his daughter. But it has always been difficult to make sense of this interpretation in view of Paul's other statements.

If the passage is addressed rather to the potential bridegroom—assuming that the verb could mean simply **marries** at the time the letter was written—two alternative interpretations are possible:

(1) The man may have taken the young woman under his protection to live with him, but agreed never to have sexual relations with her because of a common commitment to the ascetic ideal of continence. Later Christian writings describe "spiritual" marriages of this sort, and it is not impossible that this custom was known in the church at Corinth.

(2) More probably Paul is still speaking generally of the **unmarried** (verse 25), but especially here of those engaged couples who despite their belief that the end is imminent find it hard to refrain from sexual relations or to reject marriage in favor of the celibate life.

Whatever uncertainty must remain concerning the precise situation, Paul was consistent in his teaching. He expressed his preference for celibacy, recognized the rightness of marriage for persons lacking the gift of continence or self-control, and rejected the ascetic ideal as being impractical for everyone.

7:39-40. *Remarriage of Widows.* Apparently Paul did not believe that vows of celibacy were permanently binding. He may have recognized that special hardships were also being imposed on some widows in the church at Corinth. The freedom to remarry is not to be denied to them, Paul writes. But again he recommends the **happier** state. His word here echoes verses 28*b* and 35.

B. FOOD OFFERED TO IDOLS (8:1–11:1)

8:1-13. *Knowledge and Love.* In Corinth, as in other cities of Paul's day, the worship of many deities of the Greco-Roman world included animal sacrifices. Slaughterhouses were often located next to temples. Parts of these slain animals would be consumed by the altar fire, but the leftovers might either be given to priests or other worshipers or be sold in the market places. Some persons used portions of this consecrated food to give banquets at home or in the temples in honor of a god. People were invited to feast in the name of, or in communion with, the deity.

As a result of such practices a many-sided problem arose for converts to Christianity. Some Christians at Corinth had a simple solution. They held that the whole range of questions associated with the idol meats was of no consequence. If one ate or did not eat them one was none the **better** or the **worse**. Paul seems to be voicing his basic agreement with these persons when he quotes their sayings in verses 1*a* and 4. But he recognizes that this knowledge is being used by Gnostic libertines at Corinth to exalt themselves. Paul's counsel on this question is inconsistent with Acts 15:29.

8:1*b*-3. The brevity of the statements in verses 1*b*-2 may obscure the force of Paul's indictment. As in the case of wisdom he recognizes two kinds of knowledge:

(1) that which some Corinthians imagine they possess fully;

(2) the true knowledge which the Christian does not now

possess but will eventually gain as a result of having been known by God.

Perhaps one may contrast the attitude of those who know that they are enlightened, and who proudly defend their actions as justified by this knowledge, with the attitude of others who acknowledge God as revealed in Christ, and who therefore recognize that they do not yet know as they ought. For since a Christian's knowledge is that God is **love**, the criterion that one's knowledge is true is that one is likewise loving (cf. 13:1).

It is probable that verse 3 should read: "But if one loves [i.e. loves others] one is known [i.e. acknowledged] by God." This meaning is supported by the earliest papyrus manuscript and by the context.

8:4-6. These verses present a more difficult problem for the interpreter. Paul seems both to deny and to concede the existence of many gods. The influence of contemporary theology on Paul explains this apparent paradox. Of course to the Jewish monotheist the gods of the pagans—Artemis, Hermes, and the rest—were idols. Yet a real existence was not denied to certain invisible powers and authorities. These affected the lives of men and women and people were tempted to worship them.

Numerous passages support the view that Paul acknowledged the existence of these angelic beings. Indeed on one occasion he writes of the "god of this world" (II Corinthians 4:4), evidently not referring, as he does here, to **one God, the Father from whom are all things.** It is against this background that Paul's somewhat equivocal teaching concerning idol meats must be viewed. .

8:7-13. Paul's counsel here is an elaboration of his warning **take care lest this liberty of yours somehow become a stumbling block to the weak.** It is clear that the "weak" to whom Paul refers is the Christian with an uneasy **conscience** about anything associated with idol worship. To the **man of knowledge** this person appears only to be overscrupulous. Adequate knowledge should dispel these absurd fears once and for all.

But Paul knows that the emotions of some persons are more deeply affected by the popular beliefs which they have so recently renounced. They are not easily emancipated. In principle it is not evil for anyone to purchase this idol meat and eat it in one's home or another's. But in practice some persons by doing so will be led to relapse into paganism. Such a disastrous result cannot be lightly dismissed. To prevent the fall of the weak, those who have no doubt about the rightness of their views should be willing to forgo their rights. While Paul is sure that their basic position cannot be denied in this matter of Christian liberty, he certainly does not share their spirit. One may ignore the pagan gods. They do not exist. But one cannot ignore a **brother** and the existence of his tender conscience.

9:1-27. *Renunciation of an Apostle's Privilege.* The sudden defensiveness which appears at the beginning of this chapter seems unsuited to the context. Some interpreters assign the entire passage to another, perhaps later, letter to the Corinthians. But there is no need to resort to such a hypothesis. In speaking of forgoing his rights (8:13) perhaps Paul became conscious that some readers might consider him uncertain of his authority as an apostle. They might view his readiness to pattern his actions according to the judgments of the weak as a telltale sign of self-doubt.

In a series of short rhetorical questions he reveals the ground for his self-assurance, echoing other apologetic passages in his letters. He rests his defense on an appeal to the motives which have prompted him to renounce the legitimate rights of an apostle. Surely the Corinthians know that he might have claimed their financial support. Other apostles have exercised this right, fully justified by custom (verse 7), scripture (verses 8-12), cultic practice (verse 13), and a commandment of the Lord (verse 14).

9:19-23. Though Paul may have digressed somewhat in self-defense, it now becomes evident that he has not lost sight of the main thread of his argument. The Christian is indeed **free** of the judgments of others, free to do what Christian knowledge dictates. But like a **slave** the Christian is bound to do those things which further the gospel and build up the Christian community.

Paul may have acted differently as particular circumstances demanded, but he cannot be fairly charged with personal insecurity or aimless vacillations. Since the church's mission is directed to both Jews and Greeks he has adopted different strategies. And since members of the church hold conscientiously different opinions in matters of conduct, as the idol-meat controversy illustrates, the apostle of Christian unity needs to be flexible in his attitudes. The action must be suited to each situation as it arises (cf. 10:31–11:1).

9:24-27. The illustration of a foot **race** is suggested perhaps by the Isthmian games held at Corinth. The thought of these various athletic contests may have led him to mix the metaphors of racing and boxing. At any rate these figures of speech reinforce his warning in chapter 8. The "man of knowledge" must recognize his need for self-examination and hard discipline—as Paul has in the course of his work—lest at the end, having taught others to run, he find himself **disqualified**.

10:1–11:1. *Additional Guiding Principles.* Traditions of Israel's exodus from Egypt are now recalled. The purpose is to warn the proud libertines who believe themselves secure in their knowledge and exempt from temptations to idolatry. In drawing this lesson from history Paul assumes that his Gentile readers share the conviction, common in the early church, that as Christians they are the spiritual descendants of the Israelites. By this he means not merely that they hold many beliefs in common but that the Christian church, being the community of the Messiah, is the new Israel of God (cf. Galatians 6:16). Christians at Corinth are a part of the congregation of God's people at the end time, experiencing the fulfillment of his purpose of redemption which was partially accomplished by his mighty acts at the time of Israel's exodus.

This seems to be the meaning of Paul's curious expression **upon whom the end of the ages has come.** The Christian community has come into existence at the point of intersection between two ages—the present age and the age to come—so that the end of the old age coincides with the beginning of the new. Thus Paul can view the Christian's life on the one hand as

211

existing in the last days of the age that is passing. On the other hand it is entering the new and final age soon to be manifest to all, since the kingdom of Christ is a present reality.

10:1-4. From this perspective Paul views the important events in Israel's history associated with God's purpose of redemption. He uses a mode of scriptural interpretation, known as "typology," which was familiar in his day. This method sees events described in the Old Testament as "types" or foreshadowings of contemporary experiences which, though generally different, have some suggestive similarity. Thus for Paul each redemptive event in Israel's history foreshadows the final victory of God's righteousness now manifested in Jesus Christ.

The crossing of the **sea** (cf. Exodus 14:21-31) and the enveloping **cloud** which protected the Israelites on their wilderness journey (cf. Exodus 13:21-22; 14:19) are types of Christian baptism. The miraculous **food** (cf. Exodus 16) and **drink** (cf. Exodus 17:1-7; Numbers 20:2-13) supplied Israel in the desert are types of the Lord's Supper. The **Rock** from which the water sprang is a type of Christ himself.

Comment on the exodus traditions in Jewish wisdom literature may have provided patterns of thought for Paul here. Or perhaps he and his Hellenistic readers were acquainted with such interpretations as are found in the writings of his older contemporary, Philo of Alexandria, who sought to reconcile Judaism with Greek philosophy. For example, Philo identified the rock with the wisdom of God. Rabbis, noting its location at two different places (Exodus 17:6; Numbers 20:1), explained that it **followed** the Israelites in their trek through the wilderness. But Paul's Christian view of the coming new age makes his reading of the exodus traditions unique.

10:5-13. These considerations enable us to appreciate the force of Paul's warning. The libertines in the church at Corinth have neither perished nor disqualified themselves (cf. 9:27). But the Old Testament types warn them of the possibility of such disasters. They must recognize the threatening, seductive nature of the influences surrounding them (verse 12).

Participation in the Christian sacraments provides no final security. All those redeemed by God from Egypt's bondage had undergone a baptism, had partaken of sacramental food and drink. Yet **with most of them God was not pleased.** Many succumbed to evil desires (cf. Numbers 11:4-34), idolatry (cf. Exodus 32:1-6), immorality (cf. Numbers 25:1-9), testing God (cf. Numbers 21:4-9), and grumbling (cf. Numbers 16:41-50), which led them to apostasy.

10:14-22. Paul now makes clear the potentially dangerous situation at Corinth. Once again he applies his premise that a Christian's faith prohibits any kind of relationship incompatible with one's union with Christ (cf. 6:15-16). But this time he links the reality of this union with the **table of the Lord**. If a Christian partakes of a ceremonial feast in a pagan temple, he severs himself from **participation in the blood of Christ** and the **body of Christ**.

Paul recognizes that his readers may draw the false conclusion that despite his previous disclaimer he believes in the existence of the pagan deities after all. And so he appeals to Jewish practice and to scripture. One would not find here support for polytheism, but Paul has found support for his view that pagan sacrifices are offered **to demons and not to God.**

At first sight it might seem that Paul's argument is highly artificial. Yet earlier statements in this letter have clearly revealed his belief that angelic powers lay behind the pagan world order. It was a short step to conclude that these powers were active at pagan temples. In tempting Christians to partake of idol meats in these places the "elemental spirits" became, in Paul's thought, demonic powers. And so he writes that the table in an idol's temple is a **table of demons**.

10:23-30. Reinforcing his argument, Paul cites again the slogan of the Corinthian libertines (verse 23; cf. 6:12). He reiterates also his major principle that concern for others affects the exercise of Christian liberty (verse 24; cf. 8:9; Romans 14:13, 15, 19; 15:1-2). Christians may continue to buy their meat in the **market** and serve it in their homes. They need raise no **question** which their consciences do not raise, for scripture declares that all on earth belongs to God (Psalm 24:1). Moreover Paul sees no objection to their being dinner guests in the homes of **unbelievers**. Parenthetically (verses 28-29*a*) he thinks of one occasion at such meals when tactful consideration for someone's conscience would impose a voluntary limitation on one's freedom of action. But Paul is chiefly concerned here to defend the right of Christians to eat anything set before them in pagan homes and to express their sincere **thanks** to God for such benefits.

10:31–11:1. At this point did Paul have what he had just dictated read back to him? In appealing to his own example he now gives testimony in words reminiscent of those in 9:19-23. It could be argued that his advice has effectively put an end to a Christian liberty. The people of God now seem to have a new legalism determined by the scruples of the weaker members of the church. But his last words on the subject show that he has always acted freely, in matters of food and drink as in all things, **to the glory of God**. He has sought, as any Christian must seek, to pattern his actions after the example of Christ.

C. CONDUCT AT CONGREGATIONAL MEETINGS
(11:2–14:40)

Paul's attention turns to reports of various disorders in the worship services at Corinth. He can **commend** the church for not forgetting him and the **traditions** he has taught. Yet recent local practices exhibit a practical misunderstanding of these traditions and offend Paul's sensibilities.

11:3-16. *The Scandal of Unveiled Women.* First to be noted is the fact that some women are taking part in the worship services with their heads uncovered. Paul's protest is vigorous and emotional, based on theological considerations, social convention, and an argument from nature. From the biblical account of creation he adduces the belief common to the Jews that woman is inferior to man (Genesis 2:8-9). This conviction underlies the whole discussion.

11:3. Paul's statement of the hierarchical orders is somewhat obscure. Perhaps it may be paraphrased: "While every male has Christ for his head [Christ being the agent in his creation; cf. 8:6; Colossians 1:16], woman's head is man as Christ's head is God [that is, one is clearly subordinate to the other; cf. 3:23; 15:28]."

11:4-9. In verses 4-6 Paul uses **head** in both figurative and literal senses. His meaning is clarified in verses 7-9 by words which echo Genesis 1:26-27. Man's uncovered head symbolizes his acceptance of the authority given to one created in the **image . . . of God.** To cover his head with a symbol of inferiority would be dishonorable. But woman was created for subjection. She **dishonors her head**, which is man, in uncovering her head, for by so doing she asserts her will to be his equal. For Paul this challenge to authority is as much a public disgrace as the unnatural act of cropping or shaving a woman's head.

11:10. Paul sums up his theological argument in this verse. Since woman is created for man she **ought to have a veil** (literally "authority") **on her head.** The meaning is further obscured for us by the continuation, **because of the angels.**

It is perhaps a modernization to say that Paul conceives the veil to be a sign of woman's authority in the sense that it protects her against assault or molestation. Yet this understanding finds support in the ancient interpretation of the passage as an allusion to the "sons of God" who were seduced by the beauty of the "daughters of men" (Genesis 6:1-4). The idea of veiled women exercising authority over angelic powers is found in some Jewish writings, but it seems foreign to this context and to Paul's thought generally.

Other passages in the letter provide more probable clues. Paul has affirmed that Christians live at the intersection of two ages. The present age is passing. For the short time remaining, human affairs are partially dominated by invisible powers (cf. 2:6). Moreover in 6:3 angels are explicitly mentioned as beings not yet judged by men or subjugated to Christ (cf. 15:24). For Paul the subordination of woman to man is inherent in the social structure of the present age. Therefore he argues that out of deference to the angelic rulers and guardians of this world order

Christian women ought not to appear in public assemblies without a veil—the symbol of the authority which men hold over them within this age. Again Paul's expectation of an early end to the present age determines his social conservatism (cf. 7:17-40).

11:11-12. The other side of Paul's belief—that with Christ's present lordship over the church the new and final age has been anticipated—struggles for expression. **In the Lord**, Paul observes, man and woman are not **independent** of each other (cf. 7:4). Nevertheless in this matter Paul's prejudices resist the more important implications of his own revolutionary faith that in Christ there is "neither male nor female" (Galatians 3:28).

11:13. There is a defensiveness in the rest of the argument. Yet Paul's appeal to his readers' sense of propriety is not without force in view of the prevailing social conventions. Respectable, modest women did not appear in public with their heads uncovered. Only women with no proper self respect, or cult prostitutes, went without veils. The libertines in the church may have argued that the Christian is freed from the unwritten laws of society and certainly can express this freedom in church. Paul reasons that women ought not to come before God in a manner considered indecent elsewhere. Perhaps he is thinking of the public suspicions caused by indecorous dress (cf. 5:1; 6:6; 10:27-29).

11:14-16. Possibly Paul's argument from **nature** appeared as weak to his first readers as to later ones. If a woman's **hair** provides a natural **covering**, then why should an artificial one be thought necessary?

Throughout this discussion it is obvious that Paul is rationalizing a social custom of which he approves and that in conclusion he resigned himself to the fact that none of his arguments are fully convincing. He falls back on the **practice** of the **churches of God** and will not concede that the Corinthian congregation has any freedom in this matter.

11:17-34. *Abuses of the Lord's Supper.* This passage is especially important. It contains not only the oldest account of the institution of the Lord's Supper—written as much as ten years before Mark's—but also Paul's understanding of its significance.

216

11:17. This statement is set in contrast to verse 2, but its precise meaning is uncertain because of the ambiguity of the opening phrase in the Greek. It reads literally "But in instructing this"—which could refer either to the advice about women's veils or to that **following**. The latter meaning seems more likely, and on this assumption we can take the sentence as an important transition.

Paul is now ready to discuss at some length two disorderly situations affecting the worship services at Corinth far more seriously than the scandal of unveiled women. These were abuse of the Lord's Supper (verses 18-34) and contentions over "spiritual gifts" (chapters 12–14). It is because of these problems that Paul seems to be saying: "I certainly cannot commend you, since your gatherings as a church are more harmful than helpful to you."

11:18-19. Some scholars have viewed the **divisions** here as another reference to the parties of Apollos, Cephas, etc. (cf. 1:10-12). But the following verses suggest differences of social or economic status among members of the church rather than leadership rivalries. Verse 19 should be understood in this context as meaning that in the last days **factions** must come to test the genuineness of the Christian's life and work (cf. 3:12-15; Matthew 24:10-14; II Peter 2:1-3).

11:20-22. Some doubt exists concerning the exact nature of the meetings which have brought about the abuses implied by Paul's words (cf. verses 33-34). Evidently the Corinthians gather as a church from time to time to share a common meal which is, or which includes, a celebration of the **Lord's supper**. The more prosperous members of the church arrive first, generously supplied with food and drink. The poorer members come later, after longer work hours, with their meager provisions. Unwilling to delay their meal, the early comers eat and drink, some of them to excess, without waiting to partake of the Lord's Supper with their brethren. Rumors of such selfish gluttony and drunkenness have convinced Paul that some of his Corinthian converts seriously misunderstand the meaning of the sacrament and of the **church** as the body of Christ.

11:23a. The Corinthians are maintaining the traditional observance (cf. verse 2) which Paul **received from the Lord**—that is, through the testimony of Jesus' disciples—and passed on to them. But this very fact turns an otherwise disgraceful church supper into a highly dangerous event. To drive home the fearful consequence of their profanation of the Lord's Supper Paul recalls the solemn circumstances of the original meal.

11:23b-25. Great interest has centered on comparison of Paul's account with the other New Testament records of the Last Supper—Mark 14:22-26 (cf. Matthew 26:26-29) and Luke 22:14-20. The most striking differences between Paul's account and that in Mark and Matthew are the words **do this in remembrance of me** and the reference to Jesus' **blood** as establishing a **new covenant** (cf. Mark 14:24).

Though this account provides documentary evidence earlier than that in the gospels, most scholars consider Mark's the most primitive. They think that Paul's tradition reflects the liturgical usage and perhaps the sacramental associations of the Hellenistic churches.

On the other hand some have argued for the greater antiquity of Paul's tradition. They point to the lack of parallelism in the bread and cup sayings in comparison with those of Mark's version, which they judge to be an intermediate step toward the exactly parallel formulas of the second century church. The longer version of Luke's narrative found in most manuscripts includes a passage which many scholars consider an interpolation (Luke 22:19b-20), but which may be based on an early independent source reflecting the tradition known to Paul.

Some light on Paul's understanding of the tradition is shed by his rhetorical questions in 10:16. There he refers first to the **cup**, associating it with a genuine **participation in the blood of Christ**—that is, in the benefits of his death (cf. Romans 3:25; 5:9)—and then to the broken **bread**, which he associates with a real sharing in the life of the risen Lord of the church.

Here the bread saying in verse 24 may have the same signification: **This is my body which is for you**—that is, for your salvation now and in the future (cf. Romans 5:6-11). The cup saying in verse 25 is tied with the benefits of Christ's passion, as in 10:16, but specifically now with the establishment of the **new covenant**. In Christ's death God sealed with his people a new covenant (cf. Jeremiah 31:31-34)—once again a covenant ratified by the blood of a sacrifice, as in the days of Moses (cf. Exodus 24:8).

Paul's reference to the Lord's Supper here is too fleeting to provide evidence for a developed theology of the sacrament. Interpreters have persisted in asking what he understood by **This is my body.** In what sense was Christ present, symbolically or realistically, in the bread and the wine? Moreover questions have persisted concerning the nature of the sacramental union of the believer with the Lord. Should one speak of this relationship as mystical or ethical? All efforts to restrict Paul's meaning to one or the other of these may do violence to his comprehension of the relation of Christ to persons of faith, a union renewed with each faithful "participation" in the body and blood of Christ.

11:26-32. Paul draws only two corollary deductions in his instruction to the Corinthians:

(1) They are reminded that the Lord's Supper is a memorial of the betrayal and **death** of Christ. They are to **proclaim** this solemn event—and not with incongruous levity—until his coming, i.e. his final advent.

(2) They are warned that to partake of the supper in the unworthy manner exhibited by some of them outrages the meaning of Christ's death and incurs his **judgment**. Indeed Paul supposes that God's judgment is already being manifested in cases of sickness and death in the Corinthian church. It is clear from other passages (for example, Romans 1:18; 2:5-9) that Paul believed that God's judgments fall in the present as well as the future. But he seems to attribute these disasters at Corinth to a quasi-physical infection resulting from desecration of the Lord's Supper.

The Corinthians must therefore **examine** themselves and take an attitude exactly opposite to that which they are displaying at their suppers. The death they memorialize is at once God's sentence of death on sin and the surrendering of Christ's life for salvation. Thus whenever Christians receive the bread and cup properly they judge themselves guilty before God, accept afresh God's verdict on sin, and in faith receive the divine forgiveness.

Discerning the body has been variously understood as having reference to Christ's body present in some sense in the bread and wine, or else to Christ's body the church. In this context both meanings may be implied.

11:33-34. If Christ's broken body were truly being remembered at the Corinthian church suppers, no one would act greedily or in ways which humiliated fellow members. Paul's conclusion is tantalizing to the reader wishing more light on this subject: further instruction will be given during his visit (cf. 16:5-7).

12:1-11. *Spiritual Gifts.* Chapters 12–14 reveal that there were Christians in Corinth who claimed to speak under the spontaneous inspiration of the Spirit of God. Those who possessed such **spiritual gifts** were provoking rivalries and disorder in meetings of the congregation. It was not altogether clear to the church what were the legitimate claims of these **prophets** (verse 28) or **spirituals** (14:37), or what their respective roles in worship should be. Apparently some members were making extravagant estimates of the importance of speaking in **tongues**, and perhaps also of **prophecy.** As a consequence some leaders lacking these gifts were being lightly esteemed.

The nature of prophecy in the early church is uncertain, and the testimony of the New Testament concerning the phenomenon of speaking in tongues, or glossolalia, is equivocal (cf. verse 28; chapter 14; Mark 16:17; Acts 2:4; 10:46). Some light is shed on glossolalia from the comparative studies of historians of religion and from modern recurrences. In general it may be defined as the ecstatic utterance of emotionally agitated religious persons, consisting of a jumble of disjointed and largely unintelligible sounds. Those who speak in this way believe that they are moved directly by a divine spirit. Their utterance is therefore quite spontaneous and unpremeditated.

12:2-3. Paul reminds his readers that some of the evidences of inspiration in the church at Corinth resemble the religious ecstasy of pagans. The mere fact of ecstatics in their worship is insufficient evidence of the presence of the Spirit of God. It is necessary to test the spirits, and a rule of thumb, so to speak, is given (verse 3; cf. I Thessalonians 5:17-21; I John 4:1).

The cry **Jesus be cursed** must allude to an actual occurrence. Various possibilities have been suggested—for example, a Jewish visitor in the Corinthian congregation cursing the Christian Savior above the din of ecstatic speaking, an apostate renouncing the Lord amid noisy worshipers, or an emotional partisan muttering contempt for those whom he supposes to be preaching "another Jesus" (cf. 16:22; II Corinthians 11:4; Galatians 1:6-9). Paul's positive criterion is that any person who exalts Jesus as Lord speaks by the Holy Spirit.

It is easy to see that this standard does not eliminate all difficulties, as Paul recognizes elsewhere (cf. Philippians 1:15-18). Moreover in this passage Paul acknowledges that only some persons have the capacity to **distinguish between spirits** and that this capacity is itself a gift inspired by the Spirit of God (verses 4-6).

12:4-7. In beginning his discussion of God's **gifts** to the church Paul emphasizes three things:

(1) their variety;

(2) their single source despite the wide differences in their outward manifestations;

(3) their common purpose—the good of the entire community rather than of isolated individuals.

Perhaps he stresses variety to teach the Corinthians the error of looking for leadership to a few persons whose inspiration is manifested in spectacular behavior. Inspiration within the church cannot be so narrowly defined. The common good is served by the contribution of many different types of persons inspired by the Spirit, each possessing a special gift essential to the life of the church.

12:8-9. It is not surprising in this letter to find that Paul gives pride of place to **wisdom** and **knowledge**, for those gifts were conspicuously absent at Corinth, the claims of the church to the contrary notwithstanding.

By **faith** he is evidently not referring to faithful acceptance of the gospel, which is essential for any Christian. Instead he means that intensity of faith which some manifest in the church. Occasionally this intense faith is seen in performances of **healing** and other mighty works, explained as the outpouring of God's Spirit in the last days (cf. Galatians 3:5).

12:10-11. It is certainly no accident that Paul ends this list with those gifts of the Spirit most highly prized by his readers. Of course he shows a greater sensitivity than they to the problem of differentiating between genuine and false **prophecy** and **tongues**. He admits that God endows some persons with these gifts, but he insists that God provides the church with persons gifted to **distinguish between spirits** and others to make some sense of the utterance of the ecstatics. Paul intends to discuss the mutual dependence of persons possessing these last four gifts (chapter 14), but for the moment he is moved to take up the essentially complementary relationship of the entire membership of the church.

12:12-31a. *The Members of Christ's Body.* Cf. Romans 12:4-5. Students of antiquity have found parallels to Paul's figure of the body and its members in Greek and in Jewish literature, and there has been much speculation concerning the specific source or sources of his ideas. But in any case the practical application in this context is unique. Just as a living organism depends on the proper functioning of all of its parts, so does the church. It cannot thrive if it considers some members—the prophets and the "spiritual"—all-important to its well-being and the rest nonessential.

12:22-27. The meaning of Paul's idea that the inferior **parts**, or members, are more honorable is not clear. Perhaps his words in 1:26-31 are instructive. What is honored by God and in the church seems foolish to the world, which commonly honors spectacular gifts. In any case Paul's metaphor should not be pressed to the wall; his main idea is evident. In any church, as in the natural body, all parts are necessarily interrelated and function for the common good. If any part should attempt to be the whole, or to exist independently, the life of the organism would be threatened. The many parts together constitute a living whole (verse 27). Whatever mystical overtones one may discern in Paul's figure of the church as Christ's body, his explicit emphasis in this passage is on the church as a cooperative, working body of Christ.

12:28-31a. Paul's second list of **gifts** differs from his first (verses 8-10). Special significance is assigned to the services of **apostles . . . prophets . . . teachers** (cf. Ephesians 4:11). It is unlikely, however, that he enumerates the three to signify established orders—that is, offices with a universal status—distinguishing them from the sporadic ministries of individuals such as **healers, helpers,** etc. Again glossolalia appears last. The differences in the two lists support the view that there were no fixed patterns for the church's government and ministry in Paul's congregations.

12:31b–13:13. *The Way of Love.* Since love has not been mentioned as a gift in chapter 12 and since prophecy as a **higher** gift (12:28-31a) comes up for consideration at the beginning of chapter 14, some scholars think that this famous hymn extolling love is an interpolation. Few doubt that Paul wrote it, but several point to the abrupt transitions at its beginning and end as enforcing their judgment that it did not originally occupy its present position.

That Paul's thought should have taken this turn is not unreasonable, however. He has been emphasizing the special services rendered by many different persons for the common good. He has touched on the idea of the church as a community of persons whose fellow feeling leads them to care for and share fully with each other. For him love is the supreme gift of the Spirit which marks the church as the body of Christ. No one person in the church possesses all the gifts earlier noted, but every person can receive this particular gift. Indeed everyone should seek it (14:1), else the special gifts fail their purpose.

13:1-3. Chapter 13 does not stand as an odd block in its present context, for glossolalia and prophecy remain in the foreground. Paul likens Christians who **speak in . . . tongues** yet lack love to a noisy combination of instruments used during pagan festivals. He does not disparage prophecy, any more than intense **faith** and self-sacrifice, but he considers each of these excellent gifts quite valueless without love.

The variant reading "that I may boast" instead of **to be burned** is well attested in the manuscripts. It may be understood as follows: "If I give away all my goods piece by piece and finally give my body [divesting myself of all security and freedom for the sake of others] so that I may boast, and yet lack love, I gain nothing."

13:4-6. Paul finds it easier to write about the attitudes and actions which love avoids than to define its qualities. But beginning positively he joins two fruits of the Spirit—patience and kindness—as elsewhere in his letters. Possibly he conceives of kindness as the active counterpart of patience. Here he must be thinking of a Christian's typical actions as reflecting God's actions toward all people (cf. Romans 2:4; 9:22; Matthew 5:43-48).

It is unlikely that in these verses Paul draws an abstract or composite picture of the person possessing love. Many commentators have suggested that the traditions concerning Jesus inspired Paul's portraiture, but this is only a guess. Rather we may be sure that the disorderly situation in the church at Corinth has influenced Paul. He has chosen his terms with a view to rebuking the arrogant and self-important persons in the church who are behaving so shamefully toward others.

13:7. The precise connotation of this series is uncertain. The verb translated **bears** has been used earlier in 9:12*b*, where it is translated "endure." But its primary meaning is "cover," and Paul's thought may be that love keeps confidential the faults or mistakes of others, not wishing to make a public issue of them.

In the Greek **believes** is the verbal form of "faith," and **endures** has the sense of standing one's ground. The repetitious **all things** can also mean "always." Perhaps, therefore, Paul's meaning is: "Love keeps under wraps shameful deeds [so long as there are possibilities for repentance and forgiveness]; love always possesses faith, always hopes, always remains steadfast."

13:8-11. After his description of love's qualities Paul fixes his thought on the lasting power of love in contrast to the ephemeral forces of **prophecy** and **tongues** and **knowledge**. His first analogy contrasting **imperfect** with **perfect** knowledge, childish with adult behavior, may obscure the meaning of the passage for the modern reader, suggesting a natural development toward maturity. Paul's idea is influenced by his expectation of a new age. Appropriate to the age that is passing away are the ecstatic phenomena, as well as the inspired but partial knowledge through which Christians perceive imperfectly the ways of God. But in the coming age these things will be abolished; the need for them will vanish.

13:12. Paul's view that this expectation is already partially fulfilled is seen in his second figure. It is uncertain what kind of **mirror** he has in mind—the ordinary polished metal one or the magician's distorting mirror. But the greater value of a **face to face** encounter over the reflected image is obvious. That our knowledge—that is, acknowledgment—of God results from God's knowledge of us is a common biblical belief altogether congenial to Paul's way of thinking.

13:13. The words **So faith, hope, love abide,** or last forever, should rather be rendered: "Now [for the present] faith, hope, love remain"—that is, they are important. When sight replaces faith and hope is consummated, what need will there be for them? Paul appeals to the Corinthians to turn from their too exclusive, too acquisitive interest in the spectacular gifts to value the **higher gifts** (12:31a) and above all else to make their aim **the greatest of these . . . love.**

14:1-33a. *Prophecy and Glossolalia.* Paul now gives his judgment that the gift of prophecy is **greater** than that of glossolalia. The prophet speaks intelligibly to the congregation, benefiting all, whereas the speaker in tongues **utters mysteries** without being understood—in the absence of an interpreter—and benefits only himself in his conversation with God. The content of Christian prophecy is not defined. It is simply described as an instruction which encourages and consoles the church (cf. verses 24-25, 29-32).

14:6-12. Paul illustrates in simple analogies the importance of understandable language in the worship of the church. When music and the spoken word are employed for communication, they must convey clear meanings.

14:13. This counsel may be understood in two ways. Either the ecstatic **should pray for the power to interpret** his experience to the congregation himself, or he should recognize that his utterance is of no value to others unless an interpreter is present. The second understanding seems preferable, since Paul elsewhere separates the gifts of glossolalia and interpretation (verses 26-28; cf. 12:10).

14:14-19. The reference to **my spirit** and **my mind** are intriguing, both as an analysis of glossolalia and as a contribution to our understanding of Paul's conception of human nature. He does not use psychological terms in a consistent way.

Spirit sometimes connotes self-awareness or, as we might say, consciousness (cf. 2:11; Romans 8:16). At other times, especially in rhetorical or liturgical passages, Paul writes "my spirit" or "your spirit" simply as a personal designation (cf. 16:18; Romans 1:9; Galatians 6:18; Philippians 4:23). But Paul also writes of a special spirit animating a person's activity and orienting the will. In this sense the human spirit is susceptible to the influence of the divine Spirit (cf. 2:12-13; Romans 8:4-27; Galatians 5:16-18).

Mind likewise has a complex range of meanings in Paul's letters. Usually it connotes one's capacity for judgment or planning—the intelligent grasp of experience, which under various influences leads either to good or to evil actions (cf. 2:15-16; Romans 8:5-8; 12:2). But in relation to such terms as "heart" or "conscience" Paul uses "mind" with other nuances of meaning, and again one must note the lack of precision in rhetorical passages. In this passage **my mind** clearly refers to Paul's intelligent comprehension of experience, an understanding which makes possible the articulation of its meaning.

14:20-33a. When inspired by the gift of glossolalia Paul's spirit is affected by a power which suspends, or at least seriously diminishes, this capacity for understanding. He is not able—or not willing—to quench the impulse of the divine Spirit in his life or in the lives of others. Nor does he wish to deny that glossolalia is a gift, given on occasions to himself as well as to others in the church. But Paul does not seek this particular gift. His decided preference is that he and his converts may have experiences of divine grace which can be understood and interpreted to others in a rational way.

14:20-25. Such an attitude seems to Paul **mature**, in contrast to the attitude of the Corinthians, which is that of **children.** He therefore undertakes to instruct them by arguing from scripture (verse 21, a free rendering of Isaiah 28:11-12). **Tongues are a sign** given **for unbelievers**, and in comparison with prophecy the phenomenon holds little value for the corporate life of the church. Even its value for these **outsiders** is dubious when its practical effects are compared with those of prophetic preaching.

In verses 24-25 (cf. verses 29-32) Paul adds somewhat to our limited knowledge of early Christian prophecy. He suggests that an unbeliever may be **convicted** by the prophet's inspired proclamation of the will of God. While calling the unbeliever to account the prophet is able to read the **secrets of his heart**, apparently by clairvoyant power (cf. Acts 11:27-28; 21:9-11).

14:26-33a. Paul imposes a pragmatic curb on the **confusion** at Corinth by demanding that in public worship glossolalia be limited to **two or . . . three** ecstatics, one at a time. Even these are to be permitted only if an interpreter is present to explain the meaning of the experience to the whole congregation. Otherwise glossolalia should be a private matter. In public worship the emphasis should rather be on prophecy, and even this should be disciplined.

It is interesting to note that Paul believes that the prophet can consciously control the spirit of inspiration and that his revelations are **subject to prophets**—probably meaning that the prophets in the congregation are to evaluate one another's utterances.

14:33b-40. *Women at Worship.* This passage may seem to be an afterthought. Some have conjectured that it is a later insertion. It is logical, however, that in summing up his

227

instruction on spiritual gifts, with his insistence on decency and order in public worship, Paul should be reminded of the reports of the indecorous behavior of the unveiled Corinthian women who have been praying and prophesying in the church (11:2-16).

He has just written of the discussions and questionings to be expected in response to the prophets' utterances. He now assumes that public discussions during the services are the ordinary practice at Corinth, and he counsels that women **keep silence** at such times. **Let them ask their husbands at home.** Doubtless Paul does not mean to deny women all opportunities for speaking under the impulses of inspiration (cf. 11:5, 13) or to imply that any speech by women in the church is **shameful**.

14:36. Once again (cf. 11:16) Paul's words reflect his acute sensitivity to the Corinthian opposition to his views of women.

14:37-40. By way of protest Paul provides another rule of thumb for distinguishing genuine from false ecstasy. Those refusing to heed his instruction cannot be truly inspired. Paul's command silencing women has for us historical interest only. But his principle that all things having to do with the church's worship **should be done decently and in order** transcends the local situation at Corinth.

D. RESURRECTION OF THE DEAD (15:1-58)

15:1-2. *The Gospel Paul Preached.* It cannot be accidental that Paul left until last his teaching concerning the resurrection. This formal introduction of the subject supports the view that he considered the resurrection incomparably important. His awkward style, more evident in the Greek, reflects a heightened consciousness both of his responsibility and of that of the Corinthians in giving careful thought to this matter.

Paul usually employs the future tense about God's deliverance rather than the present tense **are saved**. But the qualification **if you hold it** [the gospel] **fast** preserves his conception of salvation as both conditionally future and presently experienced.

15:3-11. *The Resurrection Tradition.* On Paul's having **received** the first and most important truths of the gospel and **delivered** them to the Corinthians cf. 11:2, 23.

The Christian tradition was older than Paul's preaching which disseminated it. Where in this passage does one locate the division between the tradition Paul received and his own commentary? Probably verse 5 marks the beginning of Paul's comment, though this also was based on traditional reports.

15:3b-4. The formula **in accordance with the scriptures** expresses an important aspect of earliest Christian proclamation, but one which was by no means always self-evident (cf. 1:18; II Corinthians 3:4-18). One cannot be sure whether or not Paul knew a particular story of the finding of the empty tomb, such as those in the gospels. He reports as fact: **he was buried, . . . he was raised on the third day.**

15:5-7. Paul considers the postresurrection appearances of Jesus to be the primary—indeed the indispensable—evidence. It is not possible to harmonize satisfactorily his list of these appearances with the other Easter narratives of the New Testament. Some consider the reference to **more than five hundred brethren** a variant of the Pentecost tradition (Acts 2). Others believe it reports a Galilean appearance otherwise unknown. The appearance to **James** is also generally believed to have occurred in Galilee.

15:8. Paul is convinced that the last of these appearances, the one to him (cf. Acts 9:3-6; 22:6-10; 26:13-18), was not unlike the others (cf. 9:1; Galatians 1:1). **As to one untimely born**—literally "as to the abortion"—refers, not to the lateness of this event, but to Paul's sudden appearance among the company of witnesses, which could be likened to a premature birth. Whether "the abortion" was being applied to Paul as a coarse insult by those who opposed his apostleship cannot be known, but Paul thinks of it as a disparaging term.

15:9-11. In view of his origin Paul considers himself **unfit to be called an apostle**, for he **persecuted the church of God** (cf. Galatians 1:13; Acts 8:3; 9:1-2). But God's **grace** converted him and, supported by this grace, he has persevered. Since his credentials are extraordinary, in self-defense he stresses his energetic labors (cf. II Corinthians 3:1*a*-3; 11:21*b*-29).

15:12-19. *The Resurrection of Christ and of Others.* An important question is raised by the argument here, and throughout this chapter. What are the particular persons and beliefs Paul is opposing? Are members of the church at Corinth, who have accepted the incredible mystery of the risen Christ, finding it impossible to believe in the resurrection of others? Paul assumes that there are some persons who are saying that the resurrection of Christians is an impossibility, for in these verses he explicitly counters this denial.

But are there still others in the church who are misunderstanding Paul's proclamation that believers in Christ are risen with him, who are saying that the Christian's resurrection is a past event? Are some of the self-styled spiritual men claiming that they are already reigning with Christ? Probably so, but there are elements of conjecture in this conclusion.

The popular mystery religions were claiming that their initiates had already overcome death and were living the life of the gods. But one cannot be sure to what extent these ideas influenced Christian conceptions of baptism and the Spirit.

Unquestionably there was enormous resistance among the Greeks to the idea that the body should survive death to become the instrument of the immortal spirit or soul. Paul's letter has shown that there were some in the church at Corinth who shared this commonplace contempt for the body (see above on 6:12-20). They believed that the body was unaffected in salvation. This view was a defense on the one hand for libertine behavior and on the other for asceticism. Of special importance in this connection is Paul's earlier reference in the letter to the Christian's resurrection (6:13*b*-14).

In this reply to Christians who deny that the dead are raised it is important to note the form of Paul's argument. It is a circular one, designed to reduce to logical absurdity the position of his opponents. If the **resurrection of the dead**—that is, of human beings—is impossible, then the reports of the resurrection of Christ, who was truly human, must be false, and belief in these reports vain. But without the reality of Christ's resurrection the Christian faith—the whole of it—is without foundation. Sad conclusions follow: believers are still **in your sins**; those who have died believing **have perished**; and the deluded Christians, who hope for that which cannot be, **are to be pitied**.

15:20-28. *Christ's Resurrection and the End.* Paul appeals to two Old Testament motifs in elaborating the consequence of Christ's resurrection. First this event can be described as the **first fruits**. The first sheaf of the harvest, brought to the temple on the first day following the Passover celebration, represented the entire harvest, given by God and consecrated to him. Just so the raising of Christ by God's power portends the resurrection of all persons belonging to him.

15:21-22. The result of the Easter event leads Paul also to introduce the motif of Adam as a "type" of Christ (see above on 10:1-4; cf. Romans 5:12-14). Those who are **in Christ**—who belong to Christ—will share in his victory over death. In contrast, those who are only **in Adam** are like Adam destined to die as a consequence of sin.

15:24-28. This "little apocalypse" should be placed alongside I Thessalonians 5:1-11. Both passages stress the "already fulfilled" aspects of God's purpose in Christ as well as the "not yet completed." Neither should be separated from other passages which emphasize the same idea.

Again we observe Paul's assumption that the world lies under the dominion of angelic or demonic rulers (see above on 2:8)—probably as a result of the sin of Adam, or of humanity (cf. Romans 8:19-23). Christ's rule will defeat these powers, who are already "doomed" (2:6), and will vanquish **death**—perhaps personified as Satan.

In verse 27 the language of Psalm 8:6 introduces the thought of the final subordination of all things to God. Paul is not qualifying the divinity of Christ. His thought may be that as the representative of redeemed humanity Christ, the Son of man, acknowledges the sole sovereignty of God. The denial of this supremacy of the Creator constituted Adam's fall.

15:29-34. *The Need for Belief in the Resurrection.* After sketching briefly the drama of the end, Paul resumes his attack on those who deny the possibility of resurrection. Many interpreters have tried to avoid the Revised Standard Version translation of verse 29, since it is difficult to think that Paul would approve of baptism by proxy. But at this place he is throwing up questions to expose the illogical nature of the beliefs and practices of those denying the resurrection. He withholds his personal judgment of baptism **on behalf of the dead**.

15:30-32. If death had the last word, Paul argues, his own courage and that of other Christians would be foolish bravado. **Die every day** is not merely rhetorical. Paul thinks of the sacrificial pattern of his life as a crucifixion (cf. II Corinthians 4:8-12; Galatians 6:14, 17).

The reference to having **fought with beasts at Ephesus** has provoked speculation. Were there gladiatorial contests at Ephesus? If so, was Paul thrown into the arena? Then how did he escape? Was Paul only threatened with this possibility? The reference seems to be a specific crisis. But Acts 19 and Paul's catalog of personal crises in II Corinthians 11:23-29 do not support the hypothesis that Paul actually fought against wild animals at Ephesus, and most scholars take the allusion to be figurative. The quotation in verse 32*b* is from Isaiah 22:13.

15:33-34. Who provide the **bad company** Paul warns against in his quotation from the Greek dramatist Menander (fourth century B.C.)? Those denying the resurrection? More probably those persons having **no knowledge of God**—as we might say, the materialists in Corinthian society. The attitudes of the libertines in the church already reflect such ruinous influences.

Come to your right mind may be rendered: "Become sober [that is awake from your drunken sleep] as is fitting." By the use of a common figure of speech Paul appeals once again to the expectation of the Lord's coming at any moment (cf. 16:13; Romans 13:11-14; I Thessalonians 5:2-11).

Some commentators have protested that Paul's argument in this passage is not strong. Denial of the resurrection does not result in cutting the nerve of moral effort, encouraging profligacy, and rendering all **good morals** profitless. But Paul cannot view any life which is separated from faith and hope in Christ as other than meaningless.

15:35-50. *The Resurrected Body.* The burden of Paul's argument in this important passage is that there is both a radical difference and a real continuity between the body that dies and the body that is raised by God's power. He turns here from the fact of the resurrection to a description, insofar as he can give one, of the **kind of body** which survives death.

15:36-41. To those **foolish** persons who can conceive of no body for the human spirit other than a grossly material one Paul recalls the miracles of creation. He speaks of the transformation of bare seeds into plants and the great variety of **bodies**, each possessing a **glory** of its own and appropriate to its function and environment. So by analogy one can reflect on the miracles of God's new creation.

15:42-44a. The point of these antitheses is that the **spiritual body** that is raised, while linked to the **physical body** as seed to plant, has a unique glory which is superior to the weak body which dies.

15:44b-49. Paul realizes that arguments based on logical deductions from natural processes are insufficient. Recalling the only adequate basis of the Christian hope, he affirms that the paradoxical term **spiritual body** derives its meaning from Christ's own resurrection. Christians themselves hope to possess such a spiritual body because of their faith in him who as **man**—the Son of man—became for all people a **life-giving spirit**.

Christ as the **last Adam** (see above on verses 21-22) marks for Paul the beginning of the new creation. Christians who have borne—and continue to bear—the image of the **man of dust** (cf. Genesis 2:7) **shall also bear the image of the man of heaven.** This hope has its present counterpart in Paul's conviction that those in Christ already bear this image, though not visibly.

Note the textual variant in verse 49 (see the footnote to the Revised Standard Version). Either reading is compatible with Paul's thought, but the context seems to require the future tense.

15:50. This emphatic statement shows Paul's agreement with a conclusion commonly held among Greeks. Christian belief in the resurrection is not to be confused with the revivification of the body that is buried.

15:51-58. *The Assurance of Immortality.* Unlike the esoteric truths of the mystery cults Paul's **mystery** is the dominant idea in this summation of his teaching about the coming day. Not only will the dead undergo transformation in the resurrection, but with the final coming of Christ the living will also be **changed** (cf. I Thessalonians 4:13-18). His belief in the imminence of the end is further manifested. On the **trumpet** cf. Isaiah 27:13.

15:53. Paul's use of the term translated **immortality** must not become a basis for confusing his hope with the immortality of the soul, the survival beyond death of the disembodied spirit. The whole of Paul's teaching runs counter to this speculation in Greek philosophy. The expression **put on immortality** superficially resembles the language of the mystery religions, but Paul's teaching opposes the ideas of rebirth and deification set forth in the pagan cults.

15:54-57. The exultant cry in verses 54-55 echoes Old Testament passages (Isaiah 25:8; Hosea 13:14) but not the conclusions reached in them. Apart from Christ's **victory** no such conclusion is possible. Paul views **sin** as death's weapon to destroy humanity and the **law** as increasing the power of sin rather than correcting it (verse 56). This epigrammatic sentence becomes intelligible in the light of Romans 7:7-25.

15:58. Some of Paul's contemporaries, and later interpreters, distorted his expectation of the new age into a passive, otherworldly hope. But this statement stresses the ethical implications which he drew directly from his belief.

E.   Final Exhortations and Personal Notes (16:1-18)

16:1-4. *The Offering.* Paul's instructions are concluded on a practical note. The **contribution for the saints** was prompted by the needs of the poor among the Christians in Jerusalem (cf. Romans 15:26), but also by Paul's desire to manifest the unity of the church. The apostle to the Gentiles was asked by the Jerusalem Jewish Christians to raise money for their needy (cf. Galatians 2:10). He accepted this mission with enthusiasm, believing that his converts would benefit from it (cf. II Corinthians 8:1-5).

Paul's advice that the money be gathered **every week** may reflect something more than his concern for regular giving. He may remember some embarrassment, at Corinth or elsewhere, caused by a single hasty solicitation. Be that as it may, the situation at Corinth warrants his careful plans for the handling of the money.

16:5-9. *Paul's Travel Plans.* Paul's itinerary outlined here corresponds to the travel notes in Acts 19:21 and 20:1-2. He wishes to explain why he is not able to come directly to Corinth. At a later time (II Corinthians 1:16) he defends himself against the charge that at **Ephesus** he has been "vacillating." At this time, however, an overland trip through **Macedonia** seems necessary.

Paul's movements are directed by God's Spirit and not merely by his personal inclinations (verse 7*b*). His plans were changed at a later time, according to the implications of II Corinthians 2:1. An emergency situation arose which occasioned a "painful" visit sometime between the writing of this passage and II Corinthians.

16:10-18. *Requests Concerning Colleagues.* This letter is to arrive at Corinth before **Timothy** (cf. 4:17). Perhaps Timothy already has left for Macedonia enroute to Corinth—possibly with Erastus (cf. Acts 19:22; Romans 16:23). Paul is not certain what sort of reception his emissary will receive. Does he suppose that Timothy's shyness (cf. II Timothy 1:7) may prevent him from carrying out his mission? The Corinthians must not discourage Paul's youthful colleague, but **speed him** on his **return**.

16:12. Apparently **Apollos** has come back to Ephesus after his work at Corinth (cf. Acts 18:24–19:1). Paul writes as he does concerning Apollos to rid his readers of all suspicion that he opposes Apollos or is jealous of his influence.

16:13-14. Several ethical commands are inserted here. The watchwords of verse 13 give expression to keep expectation of the end. In view of its imminence these attitudes or responses are enjoined. But in view of chapter 13 there stands fittingly as Paul's "last word": **Let all that you do** (literally "let all that comes from you") **be done in love.**

16:15-18. The phrase **first converts** is literally "first fruits" (cf. 15:20). Perhaps the **household of Stephanas** assisted with the offering of verses 1-4; the Greek word translated **service** here is used to refer to it in II Corinthians 8:4 and 9:1, 12, 13. Paul does not write of Stephanas and his companions as holding an official status in the Corinthian church. But he urges an unruly congregation to give deference to **such men,** who are qualified by their services to receive its respect.

F. The Conclusion (16:19-24)

6:19-21. *Closing Greetings.* Paul thinks of all the **churches** as forming one church (cf. 1:2, 13; 12:27). It is therefore fitting for congregations in the province of **Asia**—western Asia Minor—to send greetings to the Corinthians from **Aquila and Prisca,** who with Paul founded the church in Corinth (cf. Acts 18:2, 18). Apparently this couple established house churches wherever they lived (cf. Romans 16:5).

The custom of a **holy kiss** arose spontaneously in the early church. Later it was a part of the ritual of Christian worship, but it came into disfavor with changing social attitudes.

Paul sometimes wished to authenticate his letters by a signature **with my own hand** (cf. Colossians 4:18; II Thessalonians 3:17; Philemon 19).

16:22-24. *Imprecation and Benediction.* Did the thought of sending this letter on its way bring a fleeting premonition of impending crisis? The curse in verse 22 has been compared with the anxious note at the end of the other letters—for example, Galatians 6:11-17.

Some commentators have sought to recover an ancient liturgy from this letter's concluding passage. **Our Lord, come!** translates an old Aramaic phrase, **maranatha**, which most versions of the New Testament have left untranslated. It could be the indicative form—"The Lord is coming"—thus reflecting a creedal formula of the early church. But the imperative form, as a prayer, is more probable (cf. Revelation 22:20). According to an early book of church order, the Didache, *maranatha* stood at the ending of the Lord's Supper prayers. After the usual benediction invoking the Lord's **grace**, Paul assures his readers that in spite of their many faults he loves them all.

THE SECOND LETTER OF PAUL
TO THE CORINTHIANS

James L. Price

INTRODUCTION

See the Introduction to I Corinthians.

I. EPISTOLARY INTRODUCTION (1:1-11)

1:1-2. *Salutation.* In resuming his correspondence with the
Corinthians Paul associates himself with **Timothy**, his emissary
to them (cf. I Corinthians 4:17; 16:10-11). But the personal
nature of the things he is now moved to write excludes any
contribution to the letter by Timothy.

The Roman province of **Achaia**, of which Corinth was the
capital, included all of Greece south of Macedonia. Paul's
greeting joins the blessings of **grace** and **peace from God**, terms
which for him mean a condition of life, not merely subjective
feelings. It also affirms the earliest Christian confessional
statement: **Jesus Christ** is the **Lord** of the church.

1:3-7. *Thanksgiving for God's Comfort.* Paul's thanksgivings—which regularly follow his salutations, as was customary in
personal letters of the period—are always directed toward God.

But it is noteworthy that here he addresses God as **Father of our Lord Jesus Christ** (cf. Colossians 1:3; Ephesians 1:3, 17).

God's **mercies** and **comfort** have been made known to Paul through his sharing in the sufferings of Christ. This could mean simply that his own sufferings resemble those which his Lord endured. But Paul is convinced that faith establishes a vital union between the believer and the Lord—a union which he describes elsewhere as a crucifixion with Christ (Romans 6:6; Galatians 2:20). This suggests that he is identifying his sufferings with the historical suffering and death of Jesus in a realistic way, that he believes they are in some way a continuation of Jesus' passion. Of course he does not think his sufferings as an apostle have redemptive value, nor does he believe that the cross of Jesus was somehow an incomplete action of God (cf. I Corinthians 1:13). But as the founder and father of this church he has been called to bear special affliction on its behalf and also to receive special assurance.

From this paradoxical experience of suffering and comfort the church derives special benefit. Also as fellow members of Christ's body the Corinthians are themselves liable to share in the sufferings of Christ. In the midst of these they can also share abundantly his comfort. The union of all believers in Christ's crucifixion and resurrection carries with it the inference that those who are Christ's are fully sharing his comfort as they participate in his suffering.

1:8-11. *Deliverance from a Deadly Peril.* Turning from the general to the specific, Paul recalls a particular **affliction** suffered **in Asia**—that is, the Roman province comprising western Asia Minor, of which Ephesus was the capital. Evidently his Corinthian readers already knew of the incident, since he gives no details. Modern readers may recall his allusion to having "fought with beasts at Ephesus" (I Corinthians 15:32; cf. I Corinthians 16:9) but still are left in the dark. Acts 19:23-41 reports a riot caused by Paul's preaching at Ephesus but mentions nothing which would cause Paul to feel he **had received the sentence of death.**

This is the first of several dark allusions in this letter to specific events and situations which cannot be recovered. It is evident, however, that deliverance from this crushing experience has imprinted itself vividly in Paul's memory. It affords him a ground for **hope** and confidence which cannot be shaken by subsequent disasters. The Corinthians can be expected to share, and to support, Paul's assurance through their **prayers**.

II. REVIEW OF RECENT RELATIONS
WITH THE CORINTHIANS (1:12–2:4)

A. PAUL'S DEFENSE OF HIS INTEGRITY (1:12–2:4)

1:12-14. *Sincerity in Act and Word.* Paul is convinced that he has been forthright and consistent in his dealings with the Corinthians. His term **boast** and its cognates appear twenty-nine times in II Corinthians—always with an apology, for he believes that the Christian has but one case for boasting, his Lord (cf. I Corinthians 1:28-31; Romans 3:27-28). Yet he feels compelled to specify his legitimate claims when they are disputed, and he cannot fail to commend specific actions he has taken when they are being distorted so as to appear vicious.

He has written in the same straightforward manner exhibited in his actions. His speech has not been adorned with sophistical rhetoric, so typical of popular teachers of wisdom (cf. I Corinthians 2:1-5). Awareness of the **grace of God** has inhibited such conceit. With the coming of the Lord Jesus the Corinthians will justly be proud of Paul, as he will be of them, though now they allow him to be maligned. At least their partial understanding gives him confidence that progress may be expected.

1:15–2:4. *Explanation of Changed Plans.* Evidently some persons at Corinth have been seriously doubting Paul's integrity. They have accused him of **vacillating** in decisions and saying **Yes and No at once**. Paul feels these charges so keenly that in setting the record straight he twice takes an oath to the truth of his statements.

1:15-17. Paul felt a need for as many visits to this church as possible while he was in the area. To afford a **double pleasure**, he says, he **wanted** to visit Corinth before going to **Macedonia** and then to return there from Macedonia before leaving for Jerusalem. The Corinthians were evidently informed of this desire. They took it as a promise of an additional early visit not included in the itinerary announced to them in I Corinthians 16:5-9. But when the time came to leave Ephesus, Paul reverted to his original plan. Instead of making the promised visit he set off for Macedonia by another route. This changing back and forth is what Paul is now defending.

1:18-22. Paul's first oath, **As surely as God is faithful**, leads him to write of Christ as the fulfillment of God's **promises** to his people. At first sight one may suppose that Paul digresses aimlessly. But perhaps he wishes to make explicit certain theological motives for his own faithfulness since some in Corinth have their doubts. His fidelity to his calling is grounded in his grateful response to God's work revealed in the gospel of God's Son, and in his awareness of his commission as an apostle, which has been sealed by the Spirit. All of his plans and actions relating to the Corinthians must be viewed in this perspective. On **Silvanus** (Silas) **and Timothy** cf. Acts 18:5.

The legal figure of a **guarantee** (cf. 5:5)—that is, the first installment of a payment to be made in full—parallels closely the cultic figure of "first fruits" in Romans 8:23 (cf. I Corinthians 15:20). The gift of the Holy Spirit following Christ's resurrection provides a promise and a pledge of the new age that is to come.

1:23–2:2. Returning to his self-defense, Paul takes a second oath. It was to **spare** the Corinthians that he abandoned his plan of going to Corinth on his way to Macedonia. He was determined not to make **another painful visit** to them. The visit alluded to, Paul's second to Corinth (cf. 12:14; 13:1-2), is not mentioned in Acts. Evidently it occurred after the writing of I Corinthians, though a few scholars have tried to locate it beforehand (see below on 2:3-4).

When Timothy returned to Ephesus after his follow-up visit to Corinth (I Corinthians 4:17; 16:10-11), bringing a report that I

Corinthians had effected little or no improvement in the situation there, Paul no doubt decided that an immediate personal visit was called for. Accordingly we may suppose that he went directly to Corinth by sea and after the painful encounter returned at once to his work in Ephesus. Such a quick trip might well be omitted by the author of Acts.

2:3-4. After the painful visit Paul wrote a letter to the Corinthians **out of much affliction and anguish of heart.** It was a stern letter, yet intended not to **cause** more **pain** but to relieve it. A few scholars interpret this as a reference to I Corinthians. But the description of the stern letter and of Paul's mood while composing it does not suit the contents of I Corinthians, and the circumstnces of its writing seem to call for a later time (see above on 1:23–2:2). On the other hand, many scholars believe instead that a substantial part of this severe letter is preserved in chapters 10–13 (see Introduction to I Corinthians).

B. A Plea to Let Bygones Be Bygones (2:5-17)

2:5-11. *Forgiveness of the Offender.* Once again Paul alludes to a particular event. The action of some person in the congregation at Corinth **caused pain.** The reference seems to be to a public rather than a private incident. The whole church was pained by someone's defiance of Paul.

Those scholars who identify the letter of verses 3-4 with I Corinthians equate this offender with the incestuous man of I Corinthians 5:1-5. But that offender was to be handed over to Satan, and it is unlikely that that injunction was later revoked, for incest was more serious than personal defiance. Rather Paul must refer here to someone who flouted his authority in the presence of the congregation during his painful visit (verse 1). In his letter (verse 9) he demanded that this offender be punished. Now he acknowledges that punitive action has been taken by the church and asks that the offender be forgiven.

2:6-8. The term **majority** might suggest that a stubborn minority are still rejecting Paul's authority, but 7:14-15 refers to the church's total obedience. Perhaps the minority are wishing to inflict a more severe punishment and this instruction to forgive is directed especially to them.

2:9-11. In verse 10 Paul wishes to play down the personal affront, yet in the words which follow it is evident that he does not make light of the offense. When he writes of **Satan** as **gaining the advantage** it is not a mere dramatic figure of speech. The thought that any believer in Christ might be severed from him and delivered to Satan's power for destruction makes Paul tremble (cf. I Corinthians 5:4*b*-5). No doubt it was fear that the Corinthian congregation as a whole might succumb to this fate that so unsettled him in this crisis.

In his severe letter he probably laid down an ultimatum, subjecting his church to this final **test**. Unless its members repented, he would be driven to deliver them all to Satan's power. With an almost inexpressible sense of relief he puts this dreadful crisis behind him. The church has met the test. Hopefully its members will continue to do so. Yet the possibility that they may fail cannot be completely dispelled (cf. 13:5-10).

2:12-13. *Anxiety in Troas.* When dispatching his severe letter Paul evidently informed its bearer, **Titus** (cf. Galatians 2:1-3), of his own itinerary in detail, with instructions to meet him and report on the letter's reception as soon as possible. Then Paul himself set out north from Ephesus, probably overland, to **Troas** at the northwestern tip of Asia Minor near the site of ancient Troy. Now he tells the Corinthians of his great distress of mind as he vainly hoped that Titus would meet him at this seaport. He found opportunities there for preaching the gospel, but his traumatized emotions kept him from entering this open **door.** Therefore he crossed the Aegean to **Macedonia**, probably to Philippi (cf. Acts 16:11-12).

2:14-17. *Triumph in Christ.* Without actually reporting that Titus had finally met him in Macedonia with good news (cf. 7:5-16) Paul implies it. He interrupts his story with an outburst of thankfulness toward God, thankfulness for the triumphs of Christ in which his apostle shares.

Certain scholars find the break so abrupt that they believe a part of a different letter, extending through 7:4, has been inserted here (see Introduction). Paul is moved to drive home to his readers the true significance of his ministry as an apostle, taking advantage of the reestablishment of his authority at Corinth. His journey to Corinth now becomes a victory march. In imagination he sees Christ marching **in triumph**, leading his apostles in his train. He surveys now his ministry as a whole, not just his work in Achaia. Everywhere **Christ always leads us in triumph.** The good word from Corinth makes Paul confidently expect this comprehensive victory.

2:14b-16. The gospel of Christ is depicted as the **fragrance** of God's **knowledge.** The apostle is a person deputized to spread the **aroma of Christ.** The precise reference of this latter detail is not certain. Perhaps Paul likens the influence of his ministry to an incense sometimes used in the processions of royalty, or perhaps he thinks of his own life as an aroma of sacrifice. In either case Paul thinks of an apostle of Christ as the messenger both of **life** and of **death**, of salvation and of judgment. Rabbinical scholars have held that the metaphors used by Paul in verse 15 were common among Jewish writers, who spoke of the law of Moses as the aroma of life to the good but of death to the evil.

2:17. Before launching on a long digression concerning the source and nature of his ministry Paul again defends himself. In this letter he is unable to forget for long those in Corinth who are questioning his integrity as an apostle. The phrase **like so many** gives the first hint that they include not only recalcitrant members of the Corinthian church. There are also visiting **peddlers of God's word** who have sought to undermine his influence and draw the congregation into their own orbit (see below on 3:1-3, 7-18; 11:4-6).

III. The Apostle's Ministry (3:1–6:10)

This section is a long digression contrasting the ministries of the Mosaic law and of the Spirit given with the Christian proclamation.

A. LETTERS OF RECOMMENDATION (3:1-3)

The implication of a question he has just written (2:16*b*) holds Paul's attention momentarily. Surely he has been made **sufficient** for his ministry, yet he finds it necessary to **commend** himself to the Corinthians. **Again** may refer simply to the earlier self-commendation in this letter (1:12), but it is likely that boasting in the severe letter (cf. 2:3-4) provoked criticism. **Some**, meaning the rival teachers (see above on 2:17), have brought **letters of recommendation**—from another church or possibly from the apostles in Jerusalem (see below on 11:22-23). But the only such letter Paul should need is the church members themselves. This letter is written on his own heart—"our" is better attested in the manuscripts than **your** (verse 2; see the Revised Standard Version footnote).

Paul passes up no opportunity to reassure the Corinthians of his affection. Moreover the Christians at Corinth are a **letter from Christ**—that is, through their thriving, though far from perfect, community they commend the gospel to the world. **Delivered**, literally "ministered," here probably means "written from dictation." The Corinthian Christians are a letter of which Christ is the author and Paul is the scribe. This letter has been written, **not on tablets of stone**, like the law in the days of Moses, but on **human hearts**.

B. THE MINISTRY OF THE NEW COVENANT (3:4—4:18)

3:4-6. *Sufficiency from God.* Paul's authority and his **confidence** as an apostle are grounded in the fact that God has made him **competent** as the minister of a **new covenant in the Spirit** (cf. Jeremiah 31:31). This contrasts with the old covenant **in a written code**, literally "in the letter"—that is, the Mosaic law.

3:7-18. *The Splendor of This Ministry.* Some interpreters consider that this passage is directed against the visiting teachers alluded to in 2:17 and 3:1. They identify these teachers as Judaizers, Jewish Christians seeking to impose on the Corinthians the demands of the law (see below on 11:4-6 and the Introduction to Galatians). But the thrust of Paul's commentary is not that the gospel abrogates the demands of the law—for example, circumcision and the food restrictions. Rather he emphasizes here the **permanent** (new-age) splendor manifested in Christ and in his church, as contrasted with the **fading** (present-age) splendor of the revelation to Moses.

3:7-11. The word translated **dispensation** in these verses is literally "ministry," which is the theme of this section. The rabbis used the narrative of Moses' transfiguration (Exodus 34:29-35) to magnify the lawgiver's lasting glory. Paul uses it to exhibit the limited significance of Moses' ministry of **death** and **condemnation** in contrast with the ministry of the Spirit. Of course he does not wish to deny the glory of Israel's law (cf. Romans 3:2-3; 7:12; 9:4-5). He is intent only on showing that the transient glory and historical role of the old covenant has been surpassed by the glory of Christ (verse 10; cf. 4:6).

3:12-13. Paul treats Moses as a "type" (see comment on I Corinthians 10:1-4) not of Christ but of the apostles and their ministry, which is his main interest in this passage. Their ministry is a manifestation of God's glory and so can be compared with the ministry of Moses. But the apostles' **hope** in the permanent makes them **very bold**. This is in contrast to Moses, who according to Paul's interpretation used a **veil** to hide the transiency of his ministry.

3:14-16. Paul's conception of the gospel as the fulfillment of Judaism is often linked with his consciousness of its rejection by his "kinsmen by race" (Romans 9:3). In this passage the **veil** of Moses symbolizes for him the blindness of Jews to the divine glory that is Christ's. If only they would turn to **the Lord**, this **veil . . . over their minds** would be lifted.

Paul's phrase **old covenant** is the source of the Christian name "Old Testament" for the Hebrew Scriptures. The Greek word meant both "covenant" and "testament." The Latin translators who chose the latter sense in this passage were no doubt influenced by Paul's argument from that meaning of the word in Galatians 3:15-17 (cf. Hebrews 9:15-17).

3:17-18. The statement **Now the Lord is the Spirit** provides explicit evidence that Paul equated the risen Lord Jesus and the Holy Spirit. He is able to use "Christ" and "Spirit" interchangeably in his letters. But it is not correct to say that Paul intends to draw a simple identity between the two, any more than a sharp distinction. Though in this context **we** means the apostles, it is probable that in verse 18 Paul intends **we all** to apply to all Christians.

4:1-18. *Hope Despite Affliction.* Paul again becomes polemical. The defensiveness which is never far beneath the surface of his comforting reassurances in this letter now erupts vigorously. There is nothing **underhanded**, literally "hidden," about his ministry!

4:3-6. The imminence of the end, as Paul understands it, explains both the blindness of unbelievers and the hope of the apostles. In the coming of the Christ the divine glory has been finally manifested. His coming can be likened to a new creation. Yet in Paul's view the end of the present age coincides with the beginning of the age to come (see comment on I Corinthians 10:1–11:1).

In the final time of the age that is passing angelic world rulers influence for ill the decisions and actions of men (cf. 2:6; 6:3; 11:10; 15:24). Among these invisible powers is Satan, called here the **god of this world**, literally "of this age," who has **blinded the minds of unbelievers** to prevent them from perceiving God's **light** in Christ.

4:7-12. The apostles of Christ also contend with Satan, who works to gain an advantage over them and over their converts (cf. 2:11). Besides this they face all sorts of affliction, carrying **in the body the death of Jesus.** For the present the **treasure** of their apostolic ministry is held in **earthen vessels**—that is, fragile pots and jars—so that it may be recognized that the **transcendent power belongs to God.**

4:13-18. Paul quotes Psalm 116:10 to confirm that it is **faith** that sustains his preaching. In this faith in a coming salvation he joins with himself his Corinthian readers, as fellow members of the body of Christ. Paul does not conceive of his own salvation apart from that of his converts, just as he cannot consider the benefit of his own suffering and consolation apart from them (cf. 1:6-7). With the coming of the end the god of this world and all other powers will be subjugated, and God will raise from the dead all those persons who belong to the Lord Jesus. The thought of God's **grace** abounding for many leads him to be confident of victory in the face of all destructive forces (cf. Romans 5:19-21).

C. The Hope of an Eternal Home (5:1-10)

5:1-5. *Longing for the Inheritance.* This section has attracted much attention. Not only does Paul's hope of life after death possess an intrinsic interest, but also some interpreters see differences between the hope expressed here and that in I Corinthians 15:42-53 and I Thessalonians 4:14-17.

Paul writes here, not of the immortality of the soul, but of the spiritual body of the resurrection, conceived first as a heavenly **house**, then as a heavenly garment. His figures are drawn from rabbinical and apocalyptic interpretations of the biblical traditions. The **tent** life of the Israelites during their wilderness sojourn—commemorated in the annual feast of Tabernacles—provides a meaningful context for his gospel of fulfillment to his Greek as well as Jewish readers.

Paul is contrasting the Christian's present existence with a future mode of existence **prepared** by God. This inheritance can now be possessed by those who have received the Spirit in baptism as a **guarantee**, a down payment (see above on 1:18-22). Therefore Paul can write that we **have** it (cf. Romans 8:19-25).

Believing that the end will come soon, Paul hopes to inherit his **heavenly dwelling** before having to experience death. Changing his figure, he expresses his longing that a new garment may be **put on** over the old one—that is, that his present body before its dissolution at death may be changed into a spiritual body. The idea of having to exist after death without any body, of being **found naked** at the last day, is abhorrent to him. He is therefore unable to speculate about an intermediate state. We do not find here material for a doctrine on the nature of a Christian's existence between death and the general resurrection at the last day.

5:6-10. *The Coming Judgment.* Paul is able to persist with **good courage** in the knowledge that he is supported by the Spirit. It may seem surprising that he can write of being **away from the Lord**, since he feels so keenly the reality of Christ's presence. A parenthetical clause in verse 7 provides a clarification: to be **in the body** does not imply separation from Christ, but union with Christ through **faith** is imperfect in comparison with the vision of Christ when hope is fulfilled. Consequently Paul longs for the consummation of Christ's kingdom, and indeed for his own death, if by this means he may be **at home with the Lord**. But this outlook does not lead him to otherworldly contemplation. Rather he seeks by every means to **please** his Lord here and now.

5:10. Prospect of the full exposure of one's life **before the judgment seat of Christ** is an essential element in Paul's expectation. It is not a threat but an encouragement. His conception of salvation includes a belief in the moral accountability of the person of faith. No one is saved by works, but only by a faithful response to God's grace revealed in Christ. Nevertheless **what he has done in the body** must be submitted to Christ's judgment.

D. THE MINISTRY OF RECONCILIATION (5:11–6:10)

5:11-13. *Serving God and the Corinthians.* While Paul is confident that his aims and motives are known to God, the situation at Corinth is not fully predictable. Perhaps his readers will suppose that he is **commending** himself **again** (see above on 3:1-3). The vagueness of the statements in verses 12-13 suggests that he intends to say more about those in the church who pride

themselves **on a man's position and not on his heart** as well as to
deal more directly with the charge of being **beside ourselves** (cf.
chapters 12–13). His concern for the moment is that the
Corinthians recognize the sober, straightforward way he has
dealt with the misunderstandings which arose between them.
His actions have sought not personal advantage but the church's
good.

5:14-17. *The Love of Christ.* The primary reason Paul cannot
live for himself is his keen apprehension of the love of Christ,
revealed in his death **for all.** The verb translated **we are
convinced** recalls a conviction formed in the past. Possibly
Paul's first experience of the risen Christ led to the
acknowledgment that if Jesus as Messiah brought divine
forgiveness to those he gathered around him, then the benefits
of his death are for all persons.

5:14b-15. The meaning of Paul's conclusion **therefore all have
died** is not obvious. Does he mean that, since Christ died the
death which sinners deserve to die, he died in their stead, in
their behalf? Cf. I Corinthians 11:25; Romans 5:21; Galatians
3:13-14.

Or does he refer here to the death—the crucifixion—which
one undergoes in giving a faith response to the cross and in the
act of receiving baptism? Cf. Romans 6:6-11; Galatians 6:14;
Colossians 3:3.

Interpreters are sharply divided. The context is not decisive,
for Paul's concern is not to set forth a doctrine of the Atonement.
Rather he is insisting that the consequence of Christ's death and
resurrection is that Christians are bound to **live no longer for
themselves but for him.**

5:16-17. As a result of this redirection of his own life Paul
affirms that he is now unable to judge anyone from a **human
point of view,** literally "according to the flesh." Before his
conversion he so **regarded** all persons, even Jesus. He viewed
the traditions of Jesus' teaching and claims as blasphemous, and
the cross as a shameful thing, God's curse (cf. Galatians 1:13-14;
3:13b). But since becoming a man **in Christ** he has been
convinced that God's **new creation** has begun. As he writes

elsewhere, those who are in Christ Jesus no longer think or act according to the flesh, but according to the Spirit (Romans 8:1-8).

5:18–6:2. *The Urgency of Reconciliation.* In the new creation, as in the beginning, all things are the work of God. **In Christ God was reconciling the world to himself,** i.e. overcoming the rebellious creatures, **not counting their trespasses against them.** God's initiative in the coming of Christ is viewed by Paul against the background of human revolt. God is the reconciler even though God is the one against whom humanity has set itself.

The gospel of the crucified Christ has revealed to Paul the gravity of the human situation—our hopeless complicity in Adam's sin, banishment from God's presence, subjection to God's wrath, as well as the wonder of God's reconciling work in Jesus Christ.

This imagery of enmity and reconciliation, i.e. peace, runs parallel in Paul's thought to his imagery of guilt and justification, i.e. acquittal. This is shown explicitly in Romans 5:1-11. In his application of the legal figure of justification by grace Paul emphasizes the wonder of divine forgiveness. In the development of this image of personal relations, the reconciliation of those who are estranged, Paul emphasizes the gracious quality of divine love. The event which made these complementary metaphors appropriate is for Paul the death of Christ. God's unconditioned forgiveness and gracious act of reconciliation, were thereby shown to involve great cost.

In referring to the **world** Paul probably has in mind the restoration of all things, the whole of creation. He conceives this to be "in bondage to corruption"—an opposition to God transcending the rebellion of all people "in Adam" (Romans 5:12-14; 8:19-25). But again we should note that Paul is offering the Corinthians no theory of the Atonement. Rather he is proclaiming the way of reconciliation and the imperative need that we accept the way which God has provided.

5:20. God makes his appeal through those who are **ambassadors for Christ.** This term, like "apostle," emphasizes both the representative and the authoritative nature of the work of those so designated to act **for Christ**.

5:21–6:2. Paul returns to the reality which gives content and power to the Christian's proclamation. Verse 21 is epigrammatic. Paul shares the belief of other New Testament writers that Jesus **knew no sin**—that is, never sinned by his own decision or action (cf. Hebrews 4:15; I Peter 2:22; I John 3:5). Yet in some sense God in Christ took on himself the sin of the world (cf. John 1:29-34).

This conception lies at the root of all "substitutionary" theories of the Atonement. Christ, though not himself a sinner, identified himself with us in our sin, becoming so involved in it that he shared our fate and dealt effectively with our predicament. This conviction is often held to be basic to Christian faith and hope, and it is certainly not unreasonable. Paul resists in principle all claims to rational explanation of it (cf. I Corinthians 1:21-25, 30; 2:1-5; Romans 8:3). Rather, conscious of the imminence of the end, he quotes Isaiah 49:8 to underscore the urgency of immediate acceptance of God's **grace**.

6:3-10. *Authentication of Apostleship.* Under pressure of deep emotion Paul catalogs the hazardous experiences he has endured. There is poetry in the pathos of these torrential words. He has employed no **weapons** in this struggle except those which, under the Spirit's inspiration, support his integrity as an apostle. The paradoxes of his career in verses 8-10 doubtless refer to abuses suffered at Corinth and elsewhere. But they may also reflect Paul's conviction that in his own life some of Christ's sufferings were renewed (with verse 10*b* cf. 8:9).

E. An Appeal for Personal Reconciliation
(6:11–7:4)

6:11-13. *Openheartedness.* Paul longs for a more comfortable relation with his **children**, a relation in which both parties can feel and speak freely toward each other. He knows that his "severe letter" has restored authority over this church (see above on 2:3-4, 12-13, 14-17). The impasse in the church has been overcome. But the reconciliation of Christ calls for a more open relation than exists at the moment of writing. Apparently he senses that the relation is still strained by the inhibited **affections** of the Corinthians.

6:14–7:1. *Avoidance of Unbelievers.* This passage appears as an abrupt change of subject, an interruption in the train of thought. Paul's appeal in 7:2-4 can be read as a logical sequel to 6:11-13.

Some scholars, observing in this section a number of words not used by Paul elsewhere, conclude that it was written by someone else and for some unknown reason was later inserted into II Corinthians. Studies of the Dead Sea scrolls have shown striking affinity between ideas expressed in this passage and ideas taught by the Essenes, the sectarian Jews at Qumran. **Belial** is a common designation of Satan in their writings. Possibly, therefore, some Christian teacher with a background of Essene ideals called for this radical separation of the church from unbelievers.

Another hypothesis affirms that Paul wrote the passage but claims that it is a fragment of the previous letter mentioned in I Corinthians 5:9 which was inserted here by a later editor of the Corinthian correspondence. Paul's fleeting description of this earlier letter, which was misunderstood by the Corinthians, corresponds with the content of this passage. This hypothesis is a popular and not implausible one.

Yet this passage may well be an integral part of II Corinthians. There are numerous digressions and seemingly irrelevant asides in Paul's letters, especially in this one. It must be recalled that he dictated his letters. Often he relies on the knowledge of his readers to supply the missing links in his progression of ideas. Having stressed openheartedness, perhaps he realized its possible misappropriation by the Corinthians as a careless tolerance of the beliefs and conduct of unbelievers.

The quotation in 6:16c-18 is a conflation of several Old Testament passages: Leviticus 26:11-12 (cf. Ezekiel 37:27); Isaiah 52:11 (cf. Ezekiel 20:34); II Samuel 7:14; and Isaiah 43:6.

7:2-4. *Mutual Confidence.* As long as the Corinthians harbor suspicions that Paul has **wronged** some of them, they are restricted in their affections toward him. Paul wishes, not to condemn, but to seek reconciliation. He writes out of love rather than bitterness. As he has said before, his heart is wide open toward the Corinthians. He wishes now to enfold them in his heart, where he would hold them until death. He is therefore able to express his **great confidence** in them. In the midst of affliction—the mark of Paul's apostleship—he experiences **comfort** and joy (see comment on I Corinthians 1:4-9).

F. THE MEETING WITH TITUS (7:5-16)

7:5-7. *Dejection Turned to Joy.* Paul now resumes the account of his travels and of his moods before writing this letter—an account interrupted in 2:14. When he reached Macedonia he was **afflicted** with anxiety about the reaction of the Corinthians to his severe letter (see above on 2:12-13). Then the news which Titus brought and the contagion of this colleague's assurance brought God's **comfort** to him in the midst of affliction (cf. 1:3-7). Both Paul and Titus were greatly relieved. They experienced a shared joy as they discussed the church's longing to see Paul and remorse in remembering how he had been treated during his last visit (cf. 2:1). The Christians at Corinth were now zealous to do as Paul commanded, to defend and satisfy him.

7:8-13*a*. *Effect of the Severe Letter.* There was a time when Paul felt **regret** over the tone of the stern letter he had sent to the Corinthians by Titus. He did not wish to grieve those whom he loved. But in view of the outcome Paul confesses that he no longer has this feeling. He draws distinction between **godly grief**—"pain God is allowed to guide" (Moffatt translation)—and **worldly grief**, a despair which produces spiritual **death**. He can see no reason to regret the letter since the pain it caused has promoted healing.

It is noteworthy that Paul does not absolve the Corinthians of all blame. He only absolves the guilt of the church's members who supported the individual wronging him. This situation has been a severe test of the relation between him and his church (cf. 2:9).

7:13b-16. *The Joy of Titus.* The recent crisis has had a salutary effect on Paul's colleague. Titus now realizes that Paul's pride in the Corinthian church was justified in spite of earlier misgivings. It is unlikely that Titus expected the **fear and trembling with which** the Corinthians **received him.** Does Paul find some satisfaction in reflecting that their mood resembled his own mood when he first came among them (I Corinthians 2:1-5)? In neither situation can the outcome be explained as the consequence of any person's "plausible words of wisdom," but only as a demonstration of God's Spirit and power.

IV. THE OFFERING FOR THE POOR
IN JERUSALEM (8:1–9:15)

In I Corinthians 16:1-4 (see comment) Paul directed the Corinthians to put aside some money on the first day of every week for the relief of the impoverished Christians in Jerusalem. Similar instructions, he told them, had been given to the churches in Galatia, and on his arrival at Corinth he would make the proper arrangements for delivery of their contribution.

Apparently the crisis in the church's relation to Paul frustrated the initial plans for a systematic collection. But now that a reconciliation has been accomplished this project, dear to Paul's heart, receives his attention. The resumption of the offering will do more than substantiate the Corinthians' loyalty to him. The satisfactory growth of the church, as of all the Gentile congregations, depends on their rendering this service to the Jewish Christians in Jerusalem (cf. Romans 15:25-29).

More than likely Paul hopes that the demonstration of good will by his Gentile converts will help to reinforce the unity of the body of Christ and allay the deep-seated prejudice of Jewish Christians against the converts' rejection of the Mosaic law.

Paul approaches the subject of this collection with such tact and deliberate restraint that the style of his writing is altered. Observing this, some scholars have concluded that chapters 8–9 were originally part of another letter or that they were formed from the fragments of two letters. This doubt about the integrity of the passage lacks firm justification. Possibly the change in mood is due to nothing more than a lapse in the time of dictation.

A. EXCELLING IN GENEROSITY (8:1-15)

8:1-5. *The Example of the Macedonians.* Paul is not drawing invidious comparisons in calling attention to the **liberality** of the Macedonians in the midst of their **extreme poverty**—though he probably remembers that some Corinthians pride themselves on their so-called riches (cf. I Corinthians 4:8). It is the **grace of God**, not some superior virtue of the Macedonians, which is responsible for their self-dedication and joy in giving. Nevertheless the generosity of the Macedonians is exemplary.

8:6-15. *Motives for Completing the Collection.* The Corinthians, who **excel** in so many ways, are urged to take the lead in this also. Paul emphasizes that he is neither commanding that they be generous nor prescribing the amount of their gifts. He calls on them to respond to the **grace of our Lord Jesus Christ**, revealed in the gospel of God's self-giving, as the authentic motive for Christian generosity.

It is unlikely, as some have held, that he refers in verse 9 to the humility of the man of Nazareth. Rather, as in Philippians 2:6-11, he is thinking of the voluntary abasement of the preexistent Christ, who became man, bringing to the poor the riches of heaven (cf. 5:18-19). It is this divine love in action which provides the believer with the supreme motive for sacrificial giving. Paul sees the proof of genuine love in a Christian's **readiness** to give, not in the amount of the gift. What is important is the intention to offer the gift one desires, without reservations. To support the ideal of equality in Christian sharing Paul cites the experience of Israel with manna in the wilderness (Exodus 16:18).

B. COMMENDATION OF THE EMISSARIES (8:16–9:5)

8:16-24. *Their Character.* Paul is scrupulously tactful in introducing the delegation which is to precede him. These men are coming to Corinth to collect money, and so he assures his readers that they are honorable men of excellent reputation, men of good will who share his confidence in the church. The two brothers who are unnamed (verses 18-19, 22) have provoked unending speculation. It is not possible to identify them certainly with persons known from other New Testament sources. Paul declares that they are **messengers**, literally "apostles," **of the churches**, suggesting that both have been formally **appointed**—which perhaps means "elected." For the moment Paul seems chiefly concerned that his role as administrator of the collection be properly understood (verses 20-21).

9:1-5. *A Plea to Cooperate with Them.* Here it rather appears that Paul is merely repeating himself. Some, noting this, have conjectured that this is a fragment of another letter addressed to all the churches of **Achaia** (see above on 1:1-2), but this hypothesis has received little attention. It is likely that Paul experienced another interruption. Resuming his dictation, he wished to say more about the discussions in Macedonia concerning the **offering**, literally "ministry," **for the saints**. He wants the Corinthians to know that he has spoken confidently to the Macedonians about them.

Apparently he wishes also to labor the point made earlier (8:10-11), that the Corinthians' "readiness in desiring" should now be matched by a readiness to complete their undertaking. Finally Paul wants to make explicit his decision not to come to Corinth until the mission of the **brethren** has been accomplished. No doubt he is made cautious by the recollection of the humiliation suffered during his last visit (cf. 2:1-11). His presence might make the collection seem a sort of peace offering to him. In this situation he is eager that the church feel no duress but be given every opportunity to respond voluntarily.

C. The Benfits of Generosity (9:6-15)

9:6-11. *An Abundant Harvest.* From the proverbial wisdom of his people Paul draws the conviction that a truly generous person receives in return gifts from God and other people out of proportion to one's own giving. He quotes **God loves a cheerful giver** from a line appearing in the Latin Septuagint of Proverbs 22:8 but not in the Hebrew. Verse 9 is quoted from Psalm 112:9.

The prudential motive may seem unworthy to some readers. The biblical writers, however, do not hesitate to employ the sanctions of reward and punishment in moral exhortations. A recognition of their proper force is inseparable from faith in God's sovereignty in a moral universe. Nevertheless Paul insists that true generosity arises from a free heart that forgets prudential calculations. In his judgment the realization that **every blessing**, literally "all grace," of God in Christ is undeserved provides the essential motive for Christian generosity.

9:12-15. *A Bond of Thanksgiving.* In conclusion Paul stresses two results of liberal giving:

(1) the needs of worthy persons are met;

(2) the recipients are led through the gifts to praise God.

The collection is now designated as a **service**, literally "liturgy"—a term which could refer to any voluntary patriotic, charitable, or religious act but was used especially of worship. Paul envisages here the Jerusalem Christians in their worship remembering the Gentile Christians in the western provinces and celebrating the **surpassing grace of God** manifested through their giving. In this thought Paul himself is led to pray (verse 15).

V. DEFENSE OF PAUL'S APOSTLESHIP (10:1–13:10)

At the beginning of chapter 10 there is again an abrupt change of mood, a difference in approach and style. The break is more marked here than elsewhere—for example between 2:13 and 2:14 or chapters 7 and 8. Especially evident is the author's rising emotion of hurt and anger. For this and other reasons many scholars are convinced that 10:1–13:10 is not a continuation of the "thankful letter," as they commonly call it, preserved in chapters 1–9 (see the Introduction to I Corinthians). We are introduced here, they say, to a quite different letter, of which the original beginning and perhaps also the ending have been lost.

Some of these scholars hold that this is the substantial fragment of a later Corinthian letter, written possibly as late as Paul's Roman imprisonment but more probably following the most recent of the letters preserved in chapters 1–9. During this short interval Paul received a disturbing new report from Corinth. On the other hand an impressive number of scholars have concluded that this is part of the earlier severe letter mentioned in 2:4 and 7:8.

The second of these hypotheses has stronger support but falls short of being fully convincing. Rather we can reasonably assume that Paul has resumed dictating his letter after a short delay. His mind is no doubt so preoccupied with his imminent visit to Corinth that he has become tense and jittery. How deep and lasting is the reconciliation brought about by his ultimatum and the assistance of Titus? How influential are the opponents who are disparaging his integrity, impugning his motives, and even casting doubt on his sanity?

An undercurrent of anxiety has been evident earlier in the letter (cf. 1:12-14, 17-18, 23-24; 2:17; 3:1, 5; 4:2-3, 5; 5:11-13, 16; 6:3, 8-13; 7:2-3). Paul can never completely suppress the anxiety, even though he devoutly wishes to be rid of it. Now, as he anticipates confronting his detractors, this anxiety and hurt erupt in a torrent of feeling.

259

A. REFUTATIONS OF SLANDERS (10:1-11)

10:1-8. *Worldly and Spiritual Weapons.* Though clearly provoked, Paul makes an earnest entreaty, prompted by the example of Christ. His detractors accuse him of **boldness**—at a safe distance. Let them wait and see how a man of authority exhibits boldness when faced with false accusers and unfounded charges.

Those who maintain that 10:1–13:10 was written before chapters 1–9 cite Paul's sarcastic use of **confidence** as evidence, saying that it could not have followed 7:16 and 8:22. Both of those passages, however, express confidence in the loyalty of the Corinthian church, whereas now Paul refers to self-confidence.

10:2. Certain persons at Corinth accuse Paul of **acting in a worldly fashion,** literally "walking according to the flesh" (cf. 1:17*b*). According to one influential view, Paul's principal opposition at Corinth arose from a group of Gnostic libertines whose lawless attitudes and ecstatic behavior reflected their beliefs that they were truly "spiritual" and that they had risen and were reigning with Christ (see comment on I Corinthians 6:12-20). These, it is said, constituted a schismatic group in the church claiming to belong exclusively to Christ (verse 7*b*; cf. I Corinthians 1:12).

Some obscure passages in II Corinthians may support this theory. In 4:5 Paul refers to the accusation that he is preaching himself. In 11:4 he casts aspersions on those who have received a "different spirit." In 12:1-4 he may be meeting the objection that he has had few if any experiences of the "visions and revelations" vouchsafed to spiritual people, whose ecstasy attests their spirituality (cf. I Corinthians 14, especially verses 6-12, 18-19, 37-38).

Perhaps these self-styled "spiritual" people were contending that Paul walked according to the flesh and thus was an ineffectual, worldly-minded man. He must scheme and seek his own advantage, whereas they themselves walked "according to the Spirit" in their freedom from law, in their knowledge and wisdom inspired by their private visionary experiences, and in their possession of spectacular spiritual gifts, especially "speaking in tongues." This theory is not without merit but it may describe only one group of Paul's opponents at Corinth (see below on 11:4).

10:3-6. Unlike some of the Gnostics, Paul knows that he does **live in the world**. But he does not contend against its forces "according to the flesh." His **weapons** were designed by God and he is enlisted in Christ's service.

It is argued that the reference to the church's **obedience** as not yet given (verse 6) must have preceded 2:9 and 7:15, which say this obedience has been demonstrated. But Paul seems to mean rather that he is **ready to punish every disobedience** caused by his detractors. At the time of his visit the chance will be given for a further concrete demonstration of obedience.

10:7-8. Some have taken these verses to indicate that Paul's opponents have created a "Christ party" as a faction in the Corinthian church (cf. I Corinthians 1:12), but this is not clear. Possibly some persons claimed a special relation to Christ through their knowledge of him or of certain traditions from his ministry. But this inference must draw support from other passages, where allusions to this special advantage are only implicit (5:16; 11:4-6; 12:11*b*). It has been said also that Paul's own slogan has been "I belong to Christ." Against this is the plain fact that he nowhere else boasts of an exclusive attachment to his Lord. Paul's **authority** is derived from Christ, but he does not boast of being Christ's favorite (cf. 11:23–12:13; I Corinthians 3:5-9; 4:1-5).

10:9-11. *Letters and Actions.* The specific nature of the indictment against Paul in verse 10 is clear though the Greek contains several grammatical difficulties. There are persons in the Corinthian church who are making fun of Paul's puny physique and inelegant speech and contrasting his appearance with his presumptuous threats and foolish boasts set forth in **weighty** letters. Paul meets this attack, here as elsewhere, by admitting that he is no superman, no clever rhetorician in the Greek tradition. But the charge that he has been unreliable, inconsistent, indecisive, and vacillating is wholly unfounded. It must be acknowledged, however, that Paul's strategy in mission and his changes in plans have given his opponents a wedge to further their aim in creating distrust (see comment on I Corinthians 9:19-23).

B. CLAIMS TO AUTHORITY AT CORINTH (10:12–11:21*a*)

10:12-18. *His Pioneer Work.* Paul is furious that his opponents should take pride in the church at Corinth while daring to revile its founder and true spiritual leader. He can boast justifiably of the Christian mission in Achaia, for he pioneered in this province, a field **apportioned** for his labor (cf. Romans 1:5: Galatians 2:9; Acts 9:15). While he has imposed a **limit** on his own activity, not wishing to claim credit for **other men's labors**, the conceit of his opponents knows no bounds. They **commend themselves** and are **boasting of work already done in another's field.**

It is evident that this reference is not to rebellious members of the Corinthian church but to rival missionaries (cf. 2:17; 3:1; see comments on 3:7-18; 11:4). Those persons no doubt used their success in Corinth as an argument to convert other churches to their version of Christianity.

10:13-16. In contrast to his rivals Paul does not wish to extend his field of work until the harvest he has sown has been reaped. But of course his pioneering missions among the nations are not yet completed. From Romans 15:24-29 we learn that his plans for **lands beyond you** include a visit to Rome and work in Spain after delivery of the offering in Jerusalem.

It has been argued that this must have been written from Ephesus as part of the severe letter rather than from Macedonia, where chapters 1-9 were written. But Paul is thinking here of his mission field, of which Corinth marks the present western limit. Neither he nor his readers would concern themselves with whether at the moment he is east or north of them.

10:17-18. Paul cites Jeremiah 9:24 to insist that he is not seeking self-glorification in recalling his foundation of the church at Corinth. This work among the Gentiles was commissioned by the Lord, and Paul hopes that the last judgment will bring to him the only commendation that matters.

11:1-6. *His Concern for the Corinthians.* This section combines biting sarcasm with moving tenderness. So Paul is a fool, is he? Then concede that he is a fool in his love for his converts.

11:2-3. Just as God was jealous of Israel, so Paul is jealous of those whom he has begotten (cf. I Corinthians 4:15; 9:1c). As the father of a daughter, i.e. the church at Corinth, he has **betrothed . . . a pure bride to her one husband**, Christ. Is it surprising that he should long for this bride's single devotion to her betrothed and be alarmed when signs of her corruption appear? In extending this metaphor by an allusion to **Eve** he may be drawing on a Jewish interpretation of Genesis 3 which held that Cain was begotten through her seduction by the **serpent**.

11:4. Some interpreters hold that this verse suggests simply a hypothetical possibility. Paul knows of the Corinthians' susceptibility to corrupting influences and warns in advance against them. His words here, however, as well as his invective in verses 12-15 and the hints in 2:17; 3:1; and 10:12, 15-16, imply an existing danger. Visitors preaching a **different gospel** have come to Corinth. That they were Jewish Christians is clear from verse 22.

Beyond this the question of their identity and the content of their teaching is not precisely known. The popular assumption, which some scholars share, is that they were Judaizers such as came to Galatia (see above on 3:7-18). Against this view is the fact that Paul, though ready only a short time later to argue at length against the Judaizers' teachings in Rome, nowhere makes any effort to refute them in his correspondence with the Corinthians.

Other scholars believe that the visitors to Corinth were a group who also invaded the church at Philippi and that Paul's attack on them in Philippians 3 shows they were Jewish Christians who had Gnostic libertine ideas. Such visitors would of course be warmly welcomed by sympathetic members of the Corinthian church (see above on 10:2).

11:5-6. Since in the Greek **these** is simply "the," the traditional interpretation has been that **superlative apostles** (cf. 12:11) refers to the original Twelve, or to the leaders among them. This possibility is defended by a few scholars today (see below on verses 22-23). Most, however, have taken the phrase to be a sarcastic term for the visitors stirring up trouble in the Corinthian church. Further support for the view that they were Gnostics is found in verse 6, in the shift to an idea reminiscent of the opening lines of I Corinthians: God's foolishness is wiser than human wisdom.

Since the Corinthians inordinately admire preachers who are clever and elegant in speech and yearn for **knowledge** other than that revealed in the gospel, they have been easily seduced and exploited.

11:7-21a. *His Self-Support.* Paul's love for the Corinthians is expressed in not wishing to **burden** them financially. It is ironic that this verse has been perverted into evidence that he does not care about them (verse 11). Moreover, he has not followed the Lord's commandment that "those who proclaim the gospel should get their living by the gospel" (I Corinthians 9:14). This too is being used to deny the genuineness of his apostleship. Paul has allowed **other churches**, those in **Macedonia**, to support his work in Corinth (cf. 8:2; Philippians 4:14-18).

11:12-21a. This has become a matter of principle and Paul is determined to adhere to it (cf. 12:13-15). Indeed he will use it to rebut the **false apostles** who boast deceitfully that they work **on the same terms**. His countercharge is that his accusers are preying on the Corinthians, taking scandalous advantage of them. His judgment of them is most explicit in verses 13-15, but he does not define their dangerous doctrines. Probably their attacks were concentrated on his person.

C. Bases for Boasting (11:21*b*-12:13)

11:21*b*-33. *His Sufferings.* With withering sarcasm Paul has taunted his readers over their willingness to **bear with fools**

(verse 19). Surely they can give heed to another **fool** when he **dares to boast.**

11:22-23. Verse 22 makes it explicit that some of Paul's opponents—evidently the visiting preachers rather than the rebellious members of the Corinthian congregation—were Jewish Christians. Were they also emissaries sent from Jerusalem by the original apostles? If so, possibly in these verses Paul is comparing himself with the senders as well as those sent (see above on verse 5).

It has been forcefully argued that the visiting preachers were at least claiming to represent the Twelve. The fact that Paul was bound to concede the apostles' authority and could only declare himself their equal made this thrust the more insidious. Whether or not Paul's opponents were thus exploiting for their own advantage the unimpeachable authority of the Twelve, it is obvious that the apostles were not themselves responsible for the situation at Corinth. Paul harbored no such suspicions (cf. I Corinthians 15:8-11 and Galatians 2:6-10). Moreover, though it is probable that the visitors brought to Corinth letters of recommendation from some Jewish Christian community (cf. 3:1), we cannot be sure that this community was Jerusalem.

11:23-33. Whatever his opponents' credentials, Paul does not permit them to be normative. Actions speak louder than words. No person can equal his own ministry—in the hardships, humiliations, and personal indignities he has suffered as a servant of Christ (cf. 6:4-10; I Corinthians 15:9-10; Romans 15:18-19).

Acts 16:22-23 reports that in Philippi Paul was imprisoned after a beating "with rods"—the Roman practice—whereas the Jewish punishment was thirty-nine **lashes.** Acts 14:19 tells of his being stoned at Lystra, and Acts 9:23-25 gives another version of the humiliating escape from **Damascus.** Otherwise Paul's list here shows up the gaps in the Acts narrative of his career.

12:1-10. *His Strength in Weakness.* Paul's statement in 11:30 stands as the theme of this section. **There is nothing to be gained** by boasting, Paul protests. Yet he feels forced by his accusers to write of the experiences of ecstasy which have been granted to him, and especially to mention one extraordinary vision and audition of the **third**, i.e. highest, **heaven**. His recollection of the specific time, **fourteen years ago**, shows how indelibly this unutterable experience was impressed on his consciousness.

It also prevents our equating this vision with his conversion experience, which must have taken place more than twenty years earlier, and which he describes rather as an appearance to him of the risen Lord (I Corinthians 9:1; 15:8; Galatians 1:15-16; cf. the fourteen-year interval of Galatians 2:1, which seems to be an unrelated coincidence).

12:5-10. Paul does not wish to offer incommunicable experiences, however important to his own inner life, as evidence of his divine commission. His **thorn . . . in the flesh** has been to him a constant reminder that he is not to capitalize on spectacular gifts. His testimony is to be the self-evidently meaningful word and deed. To many persons his speech and labor have seemed **weakness** itself. In such weakness, however, Christ's grace and power are made perfect.

Speculation has persisted about the specific nature of the thorn in the flesh—for example, malaria, an eye disease, stammering, epilepsy. It was probably some physical malady, chronic and painful (cf. Galatians 4:13-15). Yet many ancient fathers of the church, as well as the Protestant Reformers, held that it was a spiritual affliction, that he was never able to feel himself secure from Satan's wiles and was subject to all the temptations of the flesh in their acute forms (cf. 2:11; I Corinthians 9:26-27).

12:11-12. *His Signs and Wonders.* Though the opponents picture Paul as a nonentity, he contends that the standard marks of a **true apostle** accompanied his ministry among the Corinthians. Patiently he went about his work, and God wrought through him—through his weakness—**signs and wonders and mighty works** (cf. Romans 15:18-19; Galatians 3:1-5; Acts 14:3). His enemies may distort the facts but they cannot deny them.

D. PLANS FOR A THIRD VISIT (12:13–13:10)

The grammatical forms of Paul's references to a **third time** (12:14; 13:1) are ambiguous. They can mean either that he is coming to Corinth the third time or that he is making preparations the third time—that is, he has planned this visit twice before but postponed it (cf. 1:15-17, 23).

According to the latter interpretation Paul might be writing of preparations for only a second visit to Corinth. A few scholars have defended this view, largely on the basis that Acts records only two visits (Acts 18:1-18; 20:2-3). That the Acts narrative is incomplete, however, is evident from Paul's statement elsewhere (see above on 11:23-33), and efforts to deny that a second "painful" visit (2:1) took place have been unsuccessful. Both the context here and other passages in the Corinthian correspondence indicate that Paul is now promising the Corinthians a third visit.

12:13-18. *Continued Self-Support.* Some have supposed that **Forgive me this wrong** is Paul's admission that he has wronged the Corinthians in accepting no help from them (cf. 11:7-12). Thus there is room for suspicion that he doubts their willingness to support him. It is more probable that the apology is ironical.

12:14-15. His refusal to live at the expense of the congregation has been subject to misunderstanding. But Paul does not intend to abandon this principle on the occasion of his third visit to the church. He desires the love of its members, not their possessions. And it is his prerogative as their father to assume the burden of financial responsibility (verse 14*b*).

It is not possible to know certainly whether the rhetorical question in verse 15*b* is a plaintive or a barbed appeal. Even if we infer the latter, however, Paul's affection for the Corinthians shines through the sternness of his rebuke (cf. 11:1-3, 11). This passage should not be overlooked when contrasts are drawn between the attitudes reflected in chapters 1–7 and 10–13.

12:16-17. Paul here shows his sensitivity to a tactic which his opponents may have been using against him. It is perhaps being hinted that though he has not openly accepted the church's support, he is craftily pocketing the money ostensibly collected for the saints at Jerusalem. Paul answers this absurd charge by asking simply whether anyone can produce a shred of evidence that he or Titus has defrauded them.

12:18. There has been much discussion of this statement about the sending of **Titus** and an unnamed **brother**. How can it be related to the recommendation in 8:6, 16-23 and 9:3-5 of Titus and two "brothers," one perhaps subordinate to the other, who are being sent to complete the collection?

The tense of **urged** and **sent** here seems to imply an earlier mission, and the scholars who view chapters 10–13 as part of a letter written at an interval after chapters 1–9 cite this as evidence. On the other hand those who view chapters 10–13 as part of the severe letter preceding chapters 1–9 must assume that Paul sent Titus and a companion on a similar mission once before, presumably when the collection was begun (cf. 8:10; I Corinthians 16:1). This is of course possible, but the only basis for the interpretation is that the theory requires it.

If this passage and chapter 8 are part of the same letter, this is naturally understood as a second reference to the same mission. The tense here is the same as in 8:6 and may properly be rendered: "I have urged Titus to go, and have sent the brother with him." The meaning is probably that Paul has already dispatched them on their journey, which involves collections in one or more other churches on the way. Thus they will reach Corinth after the letter commending them has arrived. But it may be that he has simply commissioned them, and they will bear the letter when he finishes it.

Since only **Titus** is cited in the following question, the unnamed **brother** is evidently not yet known to the Corinthians. His commissioning is mentioned to show that Paul delegates the fund raising to others and never touches the contributions himself.

12:19-21. *A Plea for Complete Repentance.* Although the crisis has passed, the apprehension expressed here suggests Paul's painful recollection of his previous visit and its aftermath. The church members must surely understand by this time that he seeks only their **upbuilding**, their welfare, and that it is God's judgment with respect to their relations with Paul that really matters.

The contrast between the acknowledgment here of the moral failures of Christians at Corinth and the praise for them in such passages as 1:24; 3:3; 7:4, 11, 15-16; 8:7 has been used as an argument against the unity of II Corinthians and for the theory that this passage is a part of the severe letter. But the references to that letter in chapter 2 would lead us to expect fuller criticism than this, including clear reference to the church member whose punishment Paul is commanding and to the church meeting which pained him so. In view of the situation at Corinth a shift of Paul's mood from confidence to **fear** as he looks forward to his imminent visit is understandable.

13:1-4. *A Warning to the Unrepentant.* Possibly at this point Paul had read back to him what he had said since resuming dictation. He may have concluded that he had made large concessions to those who were claiming that his ministry was unimpressive, that he was weak and ineffectual. At any rate he must have realized that he had placed great emphasis on evidences of his apostleship which many would view as weakness and defeat. He had not wished to be overbearing in the exercise of his authority at Corinth. He had not wished to use means other than those which love dictated, which the example of Christ prompted. The Corinthians, however, must know that he would not hesitate to act with authority if the situation demanded it. If the visiting preachers had persuaded the membership of the church to ask for a sign of his authority, the **power of God** must be manifested in judgment.

As he looks forward to the coming visit Paul repeats his ardent desire to avoid another painful scene. Yet he feels it imperative to make clear that he will not come seeking peace at any price. Justice must prevail. Nevertheless he will not act with haste. He will examine **any charge** judiciously, **requiring the evidence of two or three witnesses.** This procedure is to be used with **those who sinned** and are still unrepentant (cf. 12:21). It would scarcely apply, as some have proposed, to the offender whose punishment was demanded in the severe letter (see above on 2:5-11) since his attack on Paul was witnessed by the whole congregation.

Some who consider this passage part of the severe letter view 1:23 as an "echo" of **I will not spare them** (verse 2), but the reverse seems more reasonable. That is, Paul postponed his visit to spare them for a time, so that they might repent, but now when he actually comes he will not spare those who have failed to take advantage of the postponement.

13:5-10. *A Plea for Self-Examination.* Because of the subtle influences of his opponents Paul considers that the Corinthians may be thinking of examining him when he comes before them. Emphatically he commands them to **examine** and **test** themselves. Like him they live the life of **faith**. Surely there is reason to hope that self-knowledge and final victory will be theirs. If indeed they correct themselves he will have no occasion to provide **proof** (verse 3) of his apostleship and doubts may never be dispelled. He hopes that he may be vindicated in the eyes of all. But what is more important is that the church **do what is right**.

13:8-10. Assuming, with most commentators, that by the **truth** Paul means the gospel, the implication is that he is determined to assert his personal authority only in order to vindicate the gospel. If the gospel is made effective in Corinth through the power of the indwelling Christ, he will do nothing to show his authority, even though by inaction he may appear **weak** and **may seem to have failed** (verse 7).

Like Jeremiah this man of God much prefers to take constructive rather than destructive action (verse 10*b*; cf. Jeremiah 1:9-10), but either means is intended for the upbuilding of God's people. Stern words of reproof and correction are far preferable to **severe . . . use of . . . authority**, however subject to misunderstanding and distortion a letter may be. The severe letter was effective; Paul doubtless hopes this one will be also.

VI. CONCLUSION (13:11-14)

13:11-13. *Final Appeal and Greetings.* Some who divide II Corinthians into two or more letters hold that this ending originally followed 9:15. Others keep it as the conclusion to 10:1–13:10. The postscript is too brief to identify related themes or to establish the specific mood of its writer. It is, however, a fitting ending to the letter viewed as a whole. Paul makes a final appeal for self-correction, for loyal submission to his rightful authority, for the members of a divided church to work together for the common good. The Christians with Paul in Macedonia send their greeting. Paul has spoken to them of the Corinthian brethren (cf. 9:2). On **holy kiss** see comment on I Corinthians 16:19-21.

13:14. *Benediction.* This closing prayer is probably Paul's best known benediction, no doubt because it mentions Jesus Christ, God, and the Holy Spirit, an association that later found expression in the doctrine of the trinity. It is in keeping with Paul's character for him to think first of the **grace** of Christ, or of the grace of God revealed through Christ. Thereby God's **love** has been apprehended, and therefrom the **fellowship** of the Holy Spirit has become a continuing reality.

THE LETTER OF PAUL
TO THE GALATIANS

Victor Paul Furnish

Character and Significance

In Galatians, as in Romans, we meet many of the weightiest themes of Paul's preaching: justification by faith, life in Christ, the responsibilities of love, the meaning of the Cross, the function of the Mosaic law, and life in the Spirit. In Galatians, however, Paul is not as free to develop and comment on these ideas in his own way as he is in Romans. For he is caught up in the heat of controversy—as even the frequently broken syntax of his sentences indicates. He must defend not only the chief points of his gospel but also his apostolic credentials.

This is a fervent letter, written with vigor and feeling. But it is also erratic, its argument often hard to follow, its tone frequently harsh, its meaning sometimes obscure, its substantive issues sometimes overshadowed by personal feelings. Yet precisely because Paul here throws himself without reserve into the proclamation of the gospel, the letter has a power unique among his writings. It has exerted an influence out of all proportion to its modest size.

The occasion for writing this letter is indicated most

succinctly in 1:6-7: Paul's astonishment that the Galatians are turning to a false "gospel," being "bewitched" (3:1) by troublemakers who seek to pervert the gospel of Christ. The specific issue is whether Gentile converts to Christianity must undergo circumcision (6:12-13), but Paul is convinced that this particular question has broader implications. He understands it to involve the very core and substance of the gospel, and to raise the fundamental issue of the Christian's relation to the Old Testament law. Because the gospel is in danger of perversion, and because his opponents in Galatia have spared nothing in attacking him personally, Paul in responding is edgy and defensive, frequently to the point of anger.

But it would be wrong to overemphasize the belligerent aspects of this letter. Its power derives primarily from the magnitude of the themes discussed and the vividness with which the crucial points of Paul's preaching are expressed. Its chief importance is theological. It became the scriptural anvil on which the key emphases of Protestantism were hammered out. For this reason it has been called the "Magna Charta of the Reformation." It also affords an intimate and candid view of Paul's own theological concerns, presuppositions, and methods.

Galatians is important also for what it reveals about the organization and structure of the church in Paul's day. Cephas (i.e. Peter; see below on 1:18-20), James the Lord's brother, and John are named as Jerusalem apostles (1:18-19; 2:9). We read here of a church council (2:1-10), of an agreement to divide the mission field along ethnic lines (2:9), and of a dispute between Peter and Paul (2:11-14).

Finally, Galatians provides certain valuable data about Paul's own life and ministry. He refers to his past life as a Jew and his persecution of the church (1:13-14), his conversion and call to preach (1:15-16), his visits to Jerusalem (1:18; 2:1), his activity in Antioch (2:11-14), and a bodily ailment suffered in Galatia itself (4:13). Yet it is not part of Paul's purpose to convey autobiographical information as such. It is only in the course of his total argument that these facts emerge.

However important it is for reconstructing the earliest history of the church and the events in Paul's life, the chief significance of Galatians now, as when it was first written and read, is what it declares about the meaning of the gospel for life.

The Address

Galatians was written, not for a single congregation, but for several. The salutation is "To the churches of Galatia" (1:2). Though it is thus a circular letter, intended for more than just local reading, its form and substance indicate that the churches were facing the same problems and being threatened by the same troublemakers (see below). But where were these churches located?

The problem arises because "Galatia" is ambiguous. The name was first used of an area in the central plateau region of Asia Minor inhabited from around 275 B.C. by a people known as "Galatians." However, after the death of its king, Amyntas, in 25 B.C., the kingdom of Galatia, with its chief cities of Ancyra, Tavium, and Pessinus, was incorporated into a Roman province to which the older territory gave its name. The province included not only certain territorial additions made about 25 years earlier but also new extensions, especially to the south, including such cities as Iconium, Lystra, Derbe, and Pisidian Antioch.

By Paul's day the province had been further extended to embrace areas in Paphlagonia and Pontus. Hence the question: When Paul addresses himself to the "churches of Galatia," is he using the term to designate congregations in the old kingdom of Galatia or anywhere within the whole Roman province of Galatia? The question is not easily answered. It has led to the "North Galatia" and "South Galatia" hypotheses.

There is no possibility that Paul addresses churches in the whole province, for the congregations he writes to were obviously established about the same time and under similar circumstances (cf. 1:6; 3:1-5; 4:12-15, 20). This could not be true if he were writing to churches in the entire provincial territory, North and South. In favor of the northern view is the fact that when the cities in the southern part of the province are named in

Acts 13:1–14:28 they are never described as Galatian. Thus when Acts does speak of Paul in Galatia (16:6; 18:23) the reference is probably to the North, the old Galatian kingdom. Moreover, it is argued, the residents of southern Galatia would not be likely to think of themselves as Galatians. Hence Paul's reference to "foolish Galatians" (3:1) would have no force if addressed to them.

On the other hand nothing is said explicitly in Acts about Paul's founding churches in the northern part of the province; he only "went through" (16:6). And in that area his work is described, not as "strengthening the churches," as Syria, Cilicia, and southern Galatia (Acts 15:41; 16:5), but as "strengthening the disciples" (Acts 18:23). This perhaps means scattered Christians as yet not organized into congregations. Proponents of the South Galatia hypothesis also point out that Paul normally refers to his churches by using the provincial term. "Galatian" would be the only single word he could use when addressing the churches of Iconium, Lystra, Derbe, etc.

The arguments pro and con are many and complex, and it is doubtful whether a clear consensus can ever be achieved. But this does not lessen the importance of the question, because a decision on the area to which the letter was sent has a direct bearing on its date.

Date and Place of Composition

If Paul is writing to South Galatia, he is addressing congregations founded on his "first missionary journey" (Acts 13, 14). Therefore the earliest possible date is sometime after this first period of his apostolic activity. If on the other hand he is writing to the northern areas, he is addressing churches founded on the "second missionary journey" (Acts 15:36–18:21), and his letter must be assigned to a later phase in his ministry.

But even if a decision on this point were possible, we would still have to determine how soon after his "founding visit" Paul wrote the letter. Does the remark that the readers are "quickly" deserting God (1:6) imply that not much time has elapsed since the Galatian Christians were converted? Ought the phrase "at first" (4:13) be interpreted to mean the first of two former visits, thus indicating that Galatians postdates not just the founding visit but also a second one? Such questions are not easily answered.

Other approaches to the problem of dating Galatians are also inconclusive. The parallels in content between Galatians and Romans are striking. But while many commentators agree with J. B. Lightfoot that Galatians stands to Romans "as the rough model to the finished statue," others are not so sure. Nor is there agreement on whether Galatians was written before or after the "Jerusalem council" (Acts 15), whether it reflects the concerns with which Paul was preoccupied during the period of the Corinthian crisis, or whether Paul's writing a letter rather than going in person to Galatia indicates that this belongs among the "imprisonment letters." There is, then, perhaps a wider range of possibilities for the dating of Galatians than for any other authentically Pauline letter.

Determination of the place of composition is dependent on the letter's date. Those who believe it was the earliest of Paul's extant letters (A.D. 48 or 49), written before the council of Acts 15, locate it at Syrian Antioch (cf. Acts 14:26-28). The majority, however, prefer the years when Paul was working in the Aegean area (50-56), and many associate Galatians with the time of the Corinthian correspondence (55-56). Corinth is most often named as the place, but many favor Ephesus, and some have suggested Macedonia. The hypothesis that Galatians was written from prison opens the possibility that it dates from the end of Paul's ministry (57-62) during his imprisonment at Caesarea or at Rome.

The Galatian Troublemakers

The letter is occasioned by a threatened, if not actual, apostasy among the Galatians, prompted by men to whom Paul refers as "some who trouble you" (1:7). Therefore the question of who they are and what they are teaching and doing is crucial. It is commonly held that they are Judaizers—Jewish-Christian legalists perhaps sent by leaders of the Jewish wing of the church to institute among Gentile converts such Jewish rites as circumcision. Those who hold this view regard the warnings about the misuse of freedom in chapter 5 as directed, not at the troublemakers themselves, but at those who might, on the basis of Paul's anti-legalistic emphasis on justification by faith apart from works (3:5-29), fall into the opposite error of libertinism.

To a few commentators it has seemed more plausible that Paul's problem is with two different groups: legalists on the one hand and libertinists on the other. Thus he is compelled to fight on two opposite fronts at once. This dilemma explains his own perplexity (4:20) and the apparent shift in emphasis from the dangers of legalism (chapters 1–4) to the dangers of libertinism (chapters 5–6).

A more complicated analysis identifies the troublemakers as Gnostics—Christians who practice some of the Jewish rites like circumcision but interpret them in mystic, non-Jewish ways and are not legalists in the usual sense (see comment on Philippians 3:1–4:1). This would explain, it is held, the otherwise puzzling comment in 6:13 that "even those who receive circumcision do not themselves keep the law." It would also explain other problems which the usual view—that the opponents were Jewish-Christian legalists—leaves unresolved.

There is finally the possibility that Paul himself is not fully informed about the identity of his opponents, their teaching, or even the effectiveness of their mission among the Galatians. In 1:6 and 3:1 he seems to presume that they have already met with some success. But in 1:7 his saying that they "want to pervert the gospel of Christ" implies that he regards them only as an imminent threat. Because he himself does not have all the details, he is forced to launch his counteroffensive in a way which covers various possible dangers.

I. Salutation (1:1-5)

Here Paul identifies himself, indicates to whom his letter is sent, and bestows on them an apostolic blessing. One senses immediately his concern to defend his apostolic status in the declaration that his authority derives from no ecclesiastical body and has been mediated to him by no human agent. Rather its source and ground is God revealed through the resurrected Lord (cf. verses 15-17). Why the emphasis on this point? Is Paul's apostolic authority doubted because it derives from men only, thus requiring a denial? More likely he has been criticized as not having apostolic credentials certified by the church's leaders. He himself here confirms this point (cf. verses 16c-24) and yet later partially corrects it (2:1-10).

1:2. This is the only salutation in which Paul speaks of **all the brethren who are with me.** It is impossible to know who are in Paul's mind—perhaps the whole congregation from which he is writing, or a small group of companions with whom he is traveling, or possibly those associated with him during a period of imprisonment (cf. Philippians 4:21; see the Introduction).

1:3-5. When Paul speaks of Christ's self-giving, he has in mind his death (cf. 2:20; Philippians 2:7-8). There is a certain parallelism here between **our sins** and **the present evil age.** To be rescued from "this age" is to be freed from sin, for sin means bondage to this-worldly values. It is Christ's death which makes possible this freedom, as Paul emphasizes in chapters 5–6, especially 6:14.

II. The Occasion for Writing (1:6-10)

The most striking feature of the opening of this letter is the absence of Paul's customary "thanksgiving"—a formal paragraph giving thanks to God for the faith and love of his readers. The reason for the omission is not difficult to ascertain. Paul is upset not only with his opponents but with his readers. Hence the thanksgiving is replaced with the blunt words of verses 6-9. Paul's amazement has a twofold cause: that the Galatians would desert God and turn to a **different gospel** and that this would happen **so quickly.**

To what interval of time does Paul refer—since his readers'

conversion, or since his last visit, or since the arrival of the troublemakers in Galatia? In any case the whole matter has come as a shock to him.

1:6-7. The care to distinguish between a **different gospel** (meaning the content) and **another gospel** (meaning more than one) is significant in the light of the agreement reported in 2:1-10. As far as Paul is concerned there is only one true gospel—though it may be preached to the circumcised on the one hand, the uncircumcised on the other.

Paul's remarks here clarify I Corinthians 9:20-23, where he speaks about missionary strategy. Strategic adaptations should not involve theological adaptations, for in that case, as in Galatia, the one true gospel would be perverted.

1:8-9. In contrast with Philippians 1:15-18, where he rejoices that his opponents are preaching Christ, Paul here shows not the least willingness to be tolerant. Twice he invokes divine censure on the preachers of any false gospel. The difference in attitude is due to the difference in the situation. The Philippian opponents preach the true gospel even though they are insincere. These opponents, however, do not preach the true gospel and—whether they are sincere or not, no matter what their personal status and credentials—should be accorded no hearing.

Thus the issue Paul addresses in Galatians is the truth of the gospel. The rest of the letter is an attempt to define what this is and to exhort the Galatians to hold it fast without compromise.

1:10. The emphasis falls on the word **now.** Surely the strict words of verses 8-9 do not support the charge made by Paul's opponents that he has been ingratiating himself to his congregations. Ultimately he is accountable only to the God from whom his apostleship derives.

III. Paul's Defense of His Apostolic Authority (1:11–2:10)

1:11-16b. *The Circumstances of His Call.* Again (cf. verse 1) Paul emphasizes the divine origin of his gospel and call. These were received, he says, not from human beings, but through **revelation.**

1:13-14. Paul's reference to his former attainments in Judaism and his persecution of the church is probably in answer to opponents who have been citing his past to support their charges against him (cf. Acts 8:3; 22:3-5 and Philippians 3:5-6). They would find there grounds for doubting Paul's present sincerity. But Paul himself regards the fact of his call from the law to Christ as evidence of its divine origin.

1:15-16b. Paul stresses God's initiative in calling him. Like the Old Testament prophets he regards his call as prenatal (cf. Jeremiah 1:5; Isaiah 49:1) and makes no distinction between his conversion and his commissioning. He was called for a specific task and purpose, to preach the gospel to the Gentiles.

It is significant that Paul is not preoccupied with the historical circumstances of his conversion and call. Though in these verses we have the most explicit reference to the event to be found in his letters, none of the details recounted in Acts (9:1-19; 22:4-16; 26:9-18) are present except, indirectly, in the indication that it occurred near **Damascus** (verse 17).

1:16c-24. *His Independence of the Jerusalem Apostles.* Grammatically verses 15-17 constitute just one sentence. But substantively Paul moves on to a second argument for the validity of his apostleship when he says: **I did not confer with flesh and blood.** It is useless to speculate on what he did in **Arabia,** for his point is only what he did not do after his conversion. He did not **go up to Jerusalem** for instruction, but **went away** without consulting those who were apostles before him. This remark is intended to corroborate the strictly divine origin or his apostleship and his gospel.

1:18-20. Paul further emphasizes his independence. Only after an interval of **three years** did he go to Jerusalem. He remained only a short time, conferred with only one of the apostles, and **saw** only one other.

Cephas is Aramaic, as Peter (2:7-8) is Greek, for "rock," the nickname Jesus gave Simon, the leader of the Twelve (cf. John

1:42). **James the Lord's brother** is now the leader of the Jerusalem church.

It is impossible to know the reason for Paul's visit with Peter—whether to obtain information, to make an accounting of his ministry, or simply to get acquainted. The last is the most probable, for Paul's main concern is to demonstrate his independence of Jerusalem. He mentions the visit only to show its insignificance so far as the impetus for and content of his ministry were concerned. The added oath in verse 20 indicates Paul's defensiveness and perhaps also his knowledge of counterarguments already or likely to be presented.

1:21-24. Leaving Jerusalem, Paul went **preaching the faith** in the regions of **Syria and Cilicia.** Little else is known of this period of his ministry, which Acts appears to skip over (cf. Acts 9:30 and 11:25-26). It has been suggested that Paul means here only that he started out in Syria and Cilicia, and that before revisiting Jerusalem (2:1) he went on from there to Asia, Macedonia, and Greece. These are travels assigned to a later period in the Acts narrative.

Paul's comment that he was **not known by sight** to the Christians of Judea raises some question about the reference in Acts 22:3 to Paul's having studied with Rabbi Gamaliel in Jerusalem. Verses 23-24 underscore the point already made, that Paul's past life as a persecutor of the church authenticates rather than casts doubt on the divine origin of his apostleship. Verse 24 adds the new point that opposition to Paul is something recent.

2:1-10. *His Approval by the Jerusalem Apostles.* Paul's second visit to Jerusalem was different in several respects:

(1) Paul was accompanied this time by **Barnabas,** an apostolic associate (cf. I Corinthians 9:6; Colossians 4:10, and many passages in Acts) and **Titus** to whom Paul elsewhere refers as his "brother" and "partner" (II Corinthians 2:13; 8:23).

(2) The meeting was not with Cephas only, but with the other **reputed . . . pillars** of the Jerusalem church, James (cf. 1:19) and John (verses 2, 6, 9).

(3) Paul specifically refers to both the purpose and outcome of

this visit. Its purpose was to lay before the pillar apostles the gospel which he had for seventeen years been preaching to the Gentiles (verse 2). Its outcome was an agreement to divide the mission field into work with Jews and work with Gentiles (verse 9).

Most commentators have regarded Acts 15:1-29 as a parallel, complementary account of the Jerusalem consultation Paul describes here. But there are important differences in the two passages. These differences have led some to believe that this letter must have been written before the meeting of Acts 15 (see the Introduction). Accordingly, the consultation Paul tells about here is to be identified with his visit to Jerusalem mentioned in Acts 11:27-30.

2:1-2. Paul is intent on correcting the mistaken notion that he or his gospel was in any sense on trial in Jerusalem. He was not summoned for a public hearing. He **went up by revelation** for a private consultation only after a long, uninterrupted period of preaching. This emphasis conforms to the point he has already made about his independence of Jerusalem. Conceivably **fourteen years** is reckoned from his conversion (1:16), but more likely it is reckoned from his first visit to Jerusalem (1:18).

2:3-5. The critical issue for Paul's gospel and ministry concerns the Christian's freedom from the law (verse 4). This has been raised in concrete fashion by the dispute over the need for Gentile converts to be circumcised. For this special reason Paul mentions **taking Titus along with me** (verse 1). Though Titus was an uncircumcised Gentile, not even the Jerusalem apostles **compelled** him **to be circumcised.**

Some interpreters hold that the emphasis here is on the word "compelled" and that Titus did in fact voluntarily agree to circumcision out of consideration for Paul's total relationship with Jerusalem. According to this view the jumbled syntax of verses 4-5 reflects Paul's embarrassment about having made such a concession and his eagerness to maintain that it was no essential surrender of his position.

On the other hand it is hardly conceivable that the "no compromise" position of 5:2-4 could be so radically stated by one who earlier in the same letter has admitted any kind of concession respecting circumcision, for whatever reason. It is more probable that Titus left the Jerusalem meeting just as he had come to it—an uncircumcised Gentile Christian. Therefore, Paul means in the strictest sense what he says about not having yielded submission **even for a moment.** Titus has become a living witness to the approval accorded Paul's gospel by the pillar apostles themselves.

Because those to whom Paul refers as having **slipped in to spy out** the Gentiles' **freedom . . . in Christ Jesus** are called **false brethren,** they are obviously within the church.

2:6-8. Though Paul stresses the recognition accorded his ministry by the Jerusalem apostles, he still guards against the impression that his gospel has been in any detail corrected or supplemented by them. He made no concessions. His preaching after the consultation was different in no respect from what it had been previously (verse 6). Paul's ministry had its own integrity and authenticity, grounded in a divine call through which he, like Peter, had been **entrusted with the gospel** and endowed with apostolic **grace.**

Nothing is said here about two gospels (see above on 1:6-7); there are only two ministries of the one true gospel. Yet the significance of the agreement lies, not just in the missionary agreement in verse 9, but in Jerusalem's recognition of Paul's mission to the Gentiles, which confirms his preaching of freedom in Christ.

2:9-10. Two symbols of the agreement at Jerusalem are mentioned. One is **the right hand of fellowship** which is formal and fleeting. The other is an offering from Paul's Gentile churches for Jerusalem (verse 10), which is material and continuing. Paul's stress on his own eagerness to raise such an offering may indicate that his opponents use this agreement too in order to prove Paul's subordination to those who were apostles before him. References to the Gentile offering in his other letters (Romans 15:25-32; I Corinthians 16:1-4; II Corinthians 8–9) indicate the importance he attached to it as a symbol of the unity of the church, the ecumenical scope of the gospel, and the oneness in Christ of both Jew and Gentile.

IV. PAUL'S DEFENSE OF HIS APOSTOLIC MESSAGE (2:11–3:18)

A. LIFE BY FAITH APART FROM WORKS (2:11-21)

2:11-14. *Peter's Vacillation.* Little else than what these verses tell us can be known about the confrontation of Paul and Peter (Cephas) at **Antioch,** a center of Gentile Christian activity. Neither the occasion of Peter's visit—whether to inspect, to preach, or to confer with Paul—nor the time of it is definitely ascertainable. In 1:18–2:10 events are reported in historical sequence—note **Then** in 1:18, 21; 2:1—but the expression which opens verse 11 seems to break the sequence. It is conceivable that the Antioch affair actually preceded the Jerusalem consultation (verses 1-10). It is mentioned after it in the letter only because it is Paul's best evidence for the validity of his mission.

2:12. On his arrival in Antioch, Paul reports, Peter found a Christian congregation already integrated. Jewish and Gentile Christians were participating fully together even at the points counter to Jewish law, and Peter willingly joined their fellowship. But presently **certain men** came to Antioch representing **James.** Paul does not name them, either because nothing requires it or because he does not wish to accord them even that minimal dignity. Whether he means to identify them with the **false brethren** of verse 4 is doubtful.

In any case their coming caused Peter to withdraw from table fellowship with the Gentile Christians, **fearing the circumcision party**—that is, those who argued for the necessity of such Jewish requirements as circumcision and the kosher table as conditions for full participation in the gospel and the church. It may be that James and his representatives sought to mediate between these extremists and Paul. But Paul himself gives no clue as to the specific dynamics of this internal struggle.

2:13. Peter and others—**even Barnabas**—were lured into forsaking their own principles in the matter. Paul accuses them, not of a fundamental change of mind about the nature and implications of the gospel, but of acting **insincerely,** hypocritically, in respect to their own best judgment. And he does not say that Barnabas was persuaded of anything. Rather he, like the others, was **carried away** and deserted his own convictions.

2:14. Discerning that the **truth of the gospel** was endangered by Peter's tactic of retreat and compromise, Paul faced the issue head-on, charging him with hypocrisy. The reference to Peter's living **like a Gentile** must relate to his prior willingness to eat with the Gentile Christians, which had been an affirmation of the truth of the gospel of freedom. It is important for the argument that Peter's subsequent withdrawal from the integrated table be blamed, not on his doubts about the validity of that gospel, but on his acceding hypocritically to the representations of **certain men . . . from James.** It is also important that Paul's readers know Peter was brought to public account for his actions.

Paul's intention in Galatians is not historical but hortatory. He is writing not simply to chronicle the events at Antioch but to address the Galatian Christians with words of warning and instruction. Hence it is impossible to reconstruct those events in detail or to analyze the subtleties of Paul's dispute with Peter.

The words Paul says he spoke to Peter are actually directed to the Galatians. Paul exhorts them not to forsake the truth of the gospel by acting hypocritically with respect to the freedom Christ bestows on Jew and Gentile alike. This hortatory motive in verses 11-14 is reflected in the omission of any report about Peter's response to Paul's challenge. It is also seen in the way the words addressed specifically to Peter merge into a discussion which far transcends, yet never quite loses sight of, the particularity of the events at Antioch (verses 15-21).

2:15-21. *Justification by Faith.* Paul states without qualification his absolutely fundamental thesis that being **justified**—that is, man's right relationship with God—is not won by **works of the law** but comes only **through faith in Jesus Christ.** It is this truth he warns the Galatians they dare not compromise. Paul describes himself as a Jew **by birth** and then proceeds to affirm that this Jewish heritage is not of itself the way to justification (cf. Philippians 3:3-11). To Jews, Gentiles were **sinners** because they did not share in the Jewish national heritage of law and covenant. But for Paul all men—Jews as well as Gentiles—are sinners (cf. Romans 3:22*b*-23). Therefore all are equally dependent on God's grace, received through faith (cf. Romans 3:24-25).

The posing of faith and works in this antithetical way is a distinctively Pauline contribution to Christian theology. It not only permitted and prompted the church's Gentile mission but also led in due course to its irreconcilable break with the synagogue.

2:17. The Antioch situation is still in Paul's mind. He acknowledges and then dismisses an argument of his opponents against the integrated table. If their doctrine of freedom in Christ leads Jews to break the dietary regulations of the law by eating with Gentiles, then **Christ** has become an **agent of sin!** Paul's response to such logic is emphatic. The objection has no more validity than the prejudicial formula "Gentile sinners" because both identify sin with breaking particular injunctions of the law. For Paul, sin in its most radical dimension is pride and boasting, to which both Jews (cf. Romans 2:17, 23) and Gentiles (cf. I Corinthians 1:19-31) are in bondage.

2:18. Paul seems to ponder the terrible consequences if he were to change his tactics and lay on Gentile converts the formalities of the law. These are the **things** that by preaching the gospel he has torn down. Were he now to enjoin them, he himself would become a **transgressor** of the true gospel of freedom in Christ.

2:19. Now Paul moves far beyond the previous criticism of works of the law to a criticism of the law itself. He says, not that the law is dead, but that he—his "ego"—is dead to the law, that the law no longer has dominion over him. Paul speaks here of the meaning of the Christian's life, and the passage should not be interpreted in a narrowly autobiographical sense. He stresses the Christian's relationship to God, by which alone one has true life and true freedom. For in dying to that which enslaves—the law—one is authentically free to live in God.

Parallel ideas are present in Romans 7:4, 6, where it is said that one dies to the law "through the body of Christ," not **through the law.** Verse 20*a* shows that these statements involve no essential contradiction, because the law itself plays a role in the death of Christ, through whom freedom is bestowed. Cf. 3:10-14.

2:20. Three essential aspects of the new life are expressed in this verse:

(1) It is bestowed in the twofold event of crucifixion-resurrection (cf. Romans 6:5). By participation in Christ's death one dies to the old self and is freed from the tyranny of the past, the world, and one's own ego. And by participation in Christ's resurrection one lives to God and is freed for a life of responsible and grateful obedience. The Christian's life is so invested by the power and grace of God that Paul may say it is not the Christian who lives but Christ who lives in the Christian (cf. 4:19).

(2) The new life is lived **in the flesh,** i.e. in the world. Paul nowhere suggests that the Christian life requires withdrawal from the world. But it is **by faith,** for thus one participates in Christ's crucifixion-resurrection, dies to the old self, and lives to God in Christ. Faith is response to God's saving initiative taken in the cross, openness to the gift of grace, and obedience to the demands of love.

(3) Paul defines the object and content of this faith as the **Son of God who loved me and gave himself for me.** The phrase is parallel with the declaration of John 3:16: "For God so *loved* the world that he *gave* his only Son, that whoever *believes* in him should not perish but have eternal life." In each passage it is the whole event of the incarnation, but especially the crucifixion, which is in the author's mind as the decisive act of self-giving love (cf. 1:4). And in each passage the benefits of Christ's passion are said to be received by faith, which each writer understands as grateful obedience to the commandment of love (cf. 5:6, 13-25; John 15:9-13).

Love is total, unconditional surrender to God's will, the complete giving of oneself to others, as the instance of God's own sacrificial love in the cross effectively reveals. Hence the appropriation and implementation of this self-giving love is set sharply over against works of law, which require formal and conditional obedience but not the radical and unconditional obedience seen in the cross.

2:21. This recapitulates the whole preceding argument. Compelling the Gentiles to live like Jews (verse 14) would in effect reinstitute the statutes of the law as the way of righteousness (verse 18). But the Christian dies to the law (verse 19) as he shares in Christ's crucifixion-resurrection (verse 20), by which the law has been stripped of its power. The affirmation of verse 21*a* is an exhortation not to **nullify** God's **grace** by compelling the Gentiles to live like Jews. That would presuppose that righteousness is through law. If that is true, Christ's death was a magnificent but meaningless tragedy.

B. The Authenticity of the Gospel (3:1-18)

3:1-5. *Demonstration from Experience.* Fearing that the Galatians no less than Peter and his group (2:11-14) are in danger of falling away from the truth of the gospel, Paul addresses them with sharp words. He implies that they have been distracted from the crucial center of that gospel, **Jesus Christ . . . crucified.** He seeks to demonstrate the authenticity of this gospel first from their own experience. He reminds them that they received the Spirit **by hearing with faith**—literally "by [the] hearing of faith," which probably means "by the hearing which faith is"—and not **by works of the law.** Faith is "hearing" in the extended sense of surrender, commitment, and obedience (cf. Romans 10:14-17).

The antithesis of faith and works momentarily becomes the corresponding **Spirit** and **flesh,** as Paul contrasts worldly "guarantees" of salvation—for example, circumcision and the kosher table—with the gift of God's Spirit, to which faith alone is the appropriate response. But then in verse 5 attention is shifted from those who have received the Spirit to the one who supplies it, and to the mighty deeds (**miracles**) which are wrought thereby (cf. I Corinthians 12:10, 28-29).

3:6-18. *Demonstration from Scripture.* Scripture itself bears witness to the authenticity of Paul's gospel. The Galatian opponents have evidently argued, on the basis of Genesis 17:10-14, that only those who are circumcised are truly Abraham's **sons** and heirs of the promise of salvation. In response the apostle appeals to two other parts of the Abraham story (cf. Romans 4):

(1) He cites Genesis 15:6 (verse 6) and assumes his readers will recognize that the key words are **believed**, i.e. "had faith," and **was reckoned**, as opposed to "earned." Righteousness is not achieved by works of law, but is bestowed as a gift on those who live by faith.

(2) He quotes Genesis 18:18 (verse 8) as support for the further claim that, since Abraham's true sons are those who live by faith, Gentiles as well as Jews may share in the promises.

3:10-12. Still more scriptural attestation to the truth of the gospel is available. The law itself (Deuteronomy 27:26) testifies that those who seek to do it are **under a curse.** From Paul's standpoint this is so because the law demands doing, in a formal, legalistic sense, while Abraham's example and Christ's death both demonstrate that righteousness and true life come through believing.

Paul's chief criticism of the law is not that its demands are impossible, but that they are superficial and that conformity to them is ineffectual. Faith, in fact, asks far more than conformity to rules of conduct. It asks for the surrender of the whole person, nothing withheld. The law is a curse because it asks for doing and presupposes that righteousness is earned thereby, whereas in reality doing leads to pride in accomplishment, which is the essence of sin. Habakkuk 2:4, cited in verse 11, is another favorite Pauline text (cf. Romans 1:17). Verse 12 quotes Leviticus 18:5.

3:13-14. Redemption **from the curse of the law** comes

through Christ in whom the **blessing of Abraham** has been fulfilled. This blessing is identified with the Spirit's coming **through faith**, as in verses 1-5. The statement that Christ has **become a curse for us** is prompted more by the words of Deuteronomy 21:23, interpreted as a reference to the crucifixion, than it is by the logic of Paul's own argument in this passage. He probably has in mind the general idea that Christ bore man's sins "in his body on the tree" (I Peter 2:24; cf. Romans 8:3).

3:15-16. Here is Paul's chief explanation of how Christ redeems human beings from the curse of the law. He uses the illustration of a legal testament or **will.** His argument is based on the coincidence that the Greek word used in the Septuagint for God's covenant with Abraham also had this meaning. That covenant remains valid, he claims, because a will can be neither nullified nor supplemented.

In Genesis 12:7, as in Deuteronomy 21:23 cited earlier, Paul finds a reference to Christ. This time he takes advantage of the noun **offspring,** which though plural in meaning is singular in form. The offspring is Christ, in whom is the fulfillment of God's covenant with Abraham, and by whom one is redeemed from the curse of the law.

3:17-18. Paul's use of Old Testament proofs is continued as he points out that chronologically the **covenant** and its **promise** preceded the giving of the law. The law in no way suspends or supplements the prior arrangement. God's covenant is embodied, not in the law, but in the promise fulfilled in Christ. Therefore when the prophet Habakkuk says, "He who through faith is righteous shall live" (verse 11), he bears witness to the necessity of believing in Christ as opposed to doing works of the law.

V. THE FUNCTION OF THE LAW (3:19–4:7)

3:19-22. *The Definer of Sin.* The question opening this section has been raised by the course of Paul's own argument, which has so far suggested a purely negative evaluation of the law and its works (cf. Romans 7:7-25). Some proper role for the law in God's plan is presupposed, but Paul's first response—**because of transgressions**—is too compact to suffice without the clarification supplied by Romans 3:20; 4:15; 5:20. These show that the phrase here means the law's function is to cause sin to come into being. It was given "for the purpose of producing transgressions" (Moffatt translation) and thereby presumably of laying persons open to receive the benefits of God's grace.

Paul rejects the notion that the law is contrary to God's **promises.** He holds, rather, that its function is to define a person's legal standing before God. Therefore it is incapable of effecting righteousness and transforming one's relationship to God. Righteousness is **given to those who believe** in Jesus Christ. Even as he defines the law's place in salvation, Paul presumes its inferiority to the promises and to the faith. The law is secondary and temporary. **It was added . . . till the offspring should come.** It is not a gift of God himself, but **ordained by angels** and offered through an **intermediary,** i.e. Moses.

3:23-29. *The Restrainer of the Immature.* The crucial word in this passage is **custodian,** the translation of the Greek word for a household assistant—usually a slave—to whom the superintendence of a minor child was entrusted. By applying this term to the law Paul stresses two points:

(1) The law's function is to impede and hold down, in sin! (cf. Romans 7:7-25).

(2) Its tenure as an effective instrument of God's plan is limited—until **faith should be revealed** and **Christ came.**

Paul may also be thinking of another limitation of the law—that it had its jurisdiction only within Judaism—for he emphasizes that **in Christ Jesus . . . all** are **sons of God, through faith** (cf. verses 7-9). One's relation to God is defined by humble and obedient openness to receive, not by prideful eagerness to achieve.

3:27-29. The inclusiveness of the gospel is illustrated by reference to baptism. It is the sign and seal of one's crucifixion and new life with Christ (cf. 2:20) and can thus be spoken of as having **put on Christ** (cf. Romans 13:14; Ephesians 4:24). Since baptism unites all persons with Christ (cf. I Corinthians 12:13) it unites them with one another, for all are brethren "for whom Christ died" (I Corinthians 8:11; cf. Romans 14:15). All who believe, without distinction, have one Lord (Romans 10:12-13; cf. Ephesians 2:11-22; Colossians 3:11).

The description of Christians as **Abraham's offspring** reflects the argument of verses 6-18 but also introduces a new element into Paul's development of the custodial function of the law. When sons and daughters come of age and pass from life under the law to life in Christ, they become full **heirs** of the promises of God (cf. 4:1-7).

4:1-7. *Slavery Under the Law.* This concluding passage on the law has an instructive parallel in Romans 8:1-17. A person apart from Christ, living under the law, is like a minor **child** for whom the inheritance is only prospective. Such a person is **no better than a slave,** not free to inherit what has been promised. Paul avoids saying that people without Christ are slaves to the law; rather they are **slaves to the elemental spirits** (literally "elements") **of the universe** (cf. verse 9; Colossians 2:20).

Commentators interpret this reference in different ways—for example, as basic religious teachings shared by all, or as demonic powers which played a role in many ancient religions. In either case Paul is contrasting life in Christ (in freedom) with life under the law (in bondage).

4:4-7. The "fullness of time" (so literally verse 4*a*) is parallel with the **date set by the father**. It expresses the purposefulness of God's sending the Son in fulfillment of the promise made to Abraham (3:14). This is the strongest statement of the incarnation in Paul's letters, made so by the added phrases **born of woman, born under the law.** But the emphasis here is on the twofold purpose of Christ's coming: first, to **redeem** persons from bondage; second, to make possible their **adoption as sons.** Redemption is the freedom which God's act in Christ makes possible: freedom from the self-defeating struggle for status before God, from enslaving preoccupation with one's own worthiness; and freedom for the full attainment of one's true maturity as an heir of God's promises (cf. 3:13; Romans 3:24; 8:23; I Corinthians 6:20; 7:23).

When Paul speaks of **adoption as sons** he is mindful of a second aspect of salvation: the bestowal of full rights as heirs and full access to the Father. Here and in Romans 8:14-17, 23 he connects adoption with the gift of the **Spirit**, by which one is enabled to place full confidence in and pledge total commitment to God the Father. As symbolic of this relationship Paul cites the words by which God is addressed in prayer: **Abba! Father!**

That God is thus addressed in both Aramaic and Greek suggests a fixed liturgical form, perhaps the introductory words of a prayer offered by the newly baptized convert expressing the new access to God found in Christ. In conclusion Paul stresses that salvation is from God. By God's initiative the **Son** was **sent** and the Spirit given. The ultimate reference of all preaching and the fundamental object of all faith is God (cf. I Corinthians 3:23).

VI. FREEDOM IN CHRIST (4:8–6:10)

A. THE IMPORTANCE OF FREEDOM (4:8–5:1)

4:8-20. *Another Appeal to Experience.* Paul's concern in this letter is that the Galatians hold to the truth of what the gospel declares about Christian freedom. The "contrary gospel" (1:9) to which the Galatians are being attracted would in fact lead them back into their preconversion bondage. Slavery to the law (verses 1-3) is essentially the same as their pagan slavery to **beings that by nature are no gods.**

4:9. There is special significance in Paul's preference for the phrase **be known by God** as a description of the Christian life. The knowledge of God about which Paul speaks is love of God, a response to God's knowledge, i.e. love, of us (cf. I Corinthians 8:2-3). Paul is perhaps seeking to correct the false idea that there is some special mystic knowledge available to the Christian which would be a mark of spiritual superiority. On **elemental spirits** see above on verses 1-7.

4:10-11. It is possible that Paul intended verse 10, like verses 8-9, as a question. The effect would then be: "What will you come to next? If you desert the central truth that righteousness is a gift to those who live by faith, and are bewitched by the notion that performance of good works or religious rites (c.f. circumcision) allows you to make a claim on God, the end can only be a total loss of freedom to become the person God created you to be." This possibility leads Paul to the momentary pessimism of verse 11 (cf. verses 15-20; contrast 5:10).

4:12-20. *Paul's Relations with the Galatians.* The basis of Paul's entreaty here is neither scriptural nor theological but personal. First he would have the Galatians follow his example and forsake bondage to the law for a new freedom in Christ. As Paul renounced the supposed advantages of Judaism to preach the gospel to the Gentiles, so now he asks them to renounce the supposed advantages of the false teaching to become as he is—in Christ.

Beyond this is Paul's appeal "for old times' sake." The Galatians gave him warm welcome under very trying conditions (verses 12b-14) and found his message worthy of their fullest commitment (verse 15). What the **bodily ailment** was which detained Paul in Galatia and whether that was his "thorn in the flesh" (II Corinthians 12:7) is uncertain. His testimony that the Galatians would have given him their own **eyes** indicates the depth of their former affection for him and the extent of their initial commitment to his gospel.

4:16-19. The relationship between Paul and the Galatians is changed now, because of something he has either said or done (verse 16; see the Revised Standard Version footnote). The original readers undoubtedly were better able to discern Paul's reference than we are. This is also true of verses 17-18, the precise meaning of which is now obscure.

The motives of the false teachers are here criticized, just as Paul's motives have been called into question by them (see above on 1:10). There is special poignancy in the appeal of verse 19, though the metaphors are mixed. Paul's mention of his **travail** suggests he is like a mother to them, even though finally he speaks of Christ's being **formed** in them. The thought is that the new birth effects such a radical transformation of one's whole being that it is no longer that person who lives but Christ who lives in them (cf. 2:20).

4:20. Finally Paul frankly admits his perplexity over the Galatians. Throughout this letter, as throughout II Corinthians 10–13 (cf. especially 11:4-13), Paul is anxious and upset. He is worried about his congregation, agitated by troublemakers, and frustrated about his inability to rectify the situation. He is aware of the need to use strong words of rebuke, yet reluctant to use them. He wishes a personal visit were possible, that somehow a mutual understanding could be reached which would allow him to change his tone.

4:21-30. *Another Demonstration from Scripture.* Paul returns to the story of Abraham (cf. 3:6-29) for scriptural evidence concerning the importance of freedom. In rabbinical fashion he makes the account of Abraham's two wives an **allegory** (Genesis 16:15; 21:1-21). Sarah was a **free woman** and her son **Isaac** was born **through promise**—a word used earlier to refer to the gospel (cf. 3:8, 14, 16-18). But **Hagar** was a **slave** and her son Ishmael was born **according to the flesh.**

4:24-27. Paul extends the allegory by identifying the two women with two different **covenants,** presumably an "old" and a "new," and with two different Jerusalems—one **present,** earthly, another **above,** heavenly. In verse 27 the passage quoted from Isaiah 54:1 speaks of Jerusalem before and after the Exile. With her people gone into captivity Jerusalem (the **barren** woman) has more cause for rejoicing than before, since after the ordeal her prosperity will exceed that of former times. The **children of the desolate one** will outnumber those of **her that is married.** Thus Paul insists that the new Jerusalem offers far more than the old. Freedom offers far more than slavery, and the gospel far more than the law.

4:28-30. The **children of promise** are Abraham's heirs by virtue of belonging to Christ (cf. 3:29). The reference to Ishmael's persecution of Isaac (verse 29) probably derives from rabbinic elaborations of Genesis 21:9. **So it is now** perhaps alludes to the harassment of the Galatians by the troublemakers.

The description of Christians as **born according to the Spirit** recalls 3:2-5, 14; 4:6 and anticipates 5:16–6:10. Paul means the admonition of Genesis 21:10, quoted in verse 30, to be applied by the Galatians to their own case. They ought to dissociate themselves from the false teachers who seek to lead them back into bondage (cf. 1:8-9).

4:31–5:1. *Exhortation to Remain Free.* The meaning of scripture is plain: to be in Christ is to be free from legalistic constraints of all kinds. Any compromise stains the integrity of the gospel. To give away one point is to give away all and return to the **yoke of slavery** (cf. 4:8-11).

The succinctness of this conclusion accentuates two paradoxes which go to the very center of Paul's thought:

(1) The paradox of indicative and imperative, the event and its demand. **We are . . . children . . . of the free woman;** we have been **set . . . free.** Therefore **stand fast** and **do not submit** (see below on 5:25-26).

(2) The paradox of freedom itself. Christ has freed us **for freedom!** The meaning of this Christian freedom is explored in the following section.

B. The Meaning of True Freedom (5:2–6:10)

5:2-15. *Faith Rendered Active in Love.* The occasion for this letter is the dispute about **circumcision** (see above on 1:6-10) and it is in this connection that Paul writes of freedom. Christians who view circumcision as a necessary requirement are denying the truth of the gospel. Security cannot be attained by the performance of religious or moral duties but only by faith—surrendering all attempts to win one's own way with God.

5:3-4. One's decision about circumcision has broad implications. To accept circumcision means, in principle, to place oneself under the jurisdiction of the **whole law.** When Paul speaks of being **severed from Christ** he uses the same verb used in Romans 7:2-6 of the Christian's "discharge" from the law. To be in Christ is to be discharged from the law, and to be under the law is to be severed from Christ. The same thought is implicit in **fallen away from grace,** for grace and law are also antithetical concepts (cf. Romans 6:14).

5:5-6. Justification comes, not by law, but **through the Spirit, by faith.** It is not an event on which Christians may look back with pride but a goal to which they look forward in **hope.** The Christian life permits no complacent contemplation of past attainments but involves ever new commitments (cf. Philippians 3:7-14). This is what Paul means by **wait**—not the purposeless passivity of loitering, but alertness, expectancy, and obedience.

The kind of waiting and hoping to which the Christian is called is clarified in verse 6, one of three instances where Paul declares that it is a matter of indifference whether one is circumcised. In I Corinthians 7:19 he says what does matter is "keeping the commandments of God," which for him are summarized in the single commandment to love one's neighbor (cf. verse 14). That comment is parallel with the statement here that what really matters is **faith working through love.** These two illumine the third passage (6:15), which refers to a "new creation."

It is possible that here Paul has in mind both God's love and human love. Faith is made active by God's love, to which it is a response, and finds expression in our obedience to the commandment of love.

5:7-12. Obedience in love is also described as obedience to the **truth** of the gospel, from which Paul fears his readers are being distracted. The proverbial saying of verse 9 is used, as in I Corinthians 5:6, to describe the corrupting influence of boastfulness. Presumably the false teachers of Galatia are in mind.

The mood of verse 10 is more optimistic than that of 4:11, 16-20, but the words are of course intended as an admonition to cast out the troublemakers. The persecution to which Paul refers in verse 11 is probably the sharp criticism of his opponents (cf. 4:29). He cites it as evidence to refute the claim that he himself has been preaching circumcision for Gentiles. That would contradict the gospel (cf. verse 2) and thus remove the **stumbling block of the cross.** The partiality of all good works stands under the divine judgment of the totality of God's demand, which the cross demonstrates. That is why it is a stumbling block to the Jews especially (cf. I Corinthians 1:23). The invective of verse 12 is comparable to that of Philippians 3:2.

5:13-15. Freedom is not to be confused with libertinism. Freedom from the legalism of life under the law does not mean release from responsibility. Instead it constitutes a summons to the greater responsibilities of life under grace. The gospel asks more, not less; for though it prescribes only one requirement—love of the neighbor—that one is unqualified and its implications cannot be specified in advance.

The Christian is not deluded by the alleged security of legalism, recognizing that authentic freedom is attained only as one lives in radical dependence on God's grace and in radical obedience to God's will. That will is summarized in the commandment of Leviticus 19:18*b*. Where freedom is not exercised in love, it leads to mutual destruction, the tragedy and violence of which are graphically portrayed in verse 15.

5:16-26. *Life in the Spirit.* Just as love is the proper content of freedom, so the Spirit is its proper context, that which gives power and guidance. In verse 16, as in Romans 8:4, Paul uses the phrase **walk by the Spirit.**

Verses 16 and 18 express complementary truths about life in Christ. Taken together they form another instance of the indicative-imperative motif in Paul's thought (cf. verse 1; see below on verses 25-26). The reference to being **led by the Spirit** emphasizes God's gift by which one lives; the exhortation to **walk by the Spirit** stresses the attendant demand.

The opposite of walking by the Spirit is "walking according to the flesh" (Romans 8:4), an idea alternately expressed in verses 16*b*-17. In the competition for a person's life the **desires of the Spirit** are opposed by the **desires of the flesh.** These latter may be identified with the demands of legalism (cf. 3:2-5) just as surely as with the promiscuities of libertinism. But it is the problem of libertinism which engages Paul's attention here, as the listing of a miscellaneous group of typical pagan vices makes clear.

5:22-24. Over against the **works of the flesh** is placed the **fruit of the Spirit.** This fruit (singular) is the "full harvest of righteousness" (Philippians 1:11, New English Bible). It is bestowed on those who live by faith.

It is significant that **love** stands first in the list which describes the content of that life. **Love, joy, peace,** etc. are not to be regarded as separable Christian virtues in the ordinary sense. One does not achieve them by one's own heroic effort, but receives them by faith. By God's grace, in the power of the Spirit, one's whole life is transformed, and these are the marks of that transformation—not to be confused with the "gifts of the Spirit" (I Corinthians 12:4-11; cf. 3:5). Life by faith, in the Spirit, is also life in and with Christ, to whom the Christian belongs as the old self is **crucified.**

5:25-26. The discussion here is explicitly hortatory. As in verse 1, the imperative of Christian responsibility issues from the indicative of God's action. This twofold aspect of the gospel finds its classical formulation in verse 25, which may be paraphrased: "Since we are utterly dependent on the power and prompting of God's Spirit, let us live in relation to his purpose."

God is known both, and at once, through what God gives and demands, through what God bestows and claims. God has given life and made it good by endowing it with freedom and purpose, directing and empowering it by the Spirit and constantly renewing it in love. God claims the life given, for the gift is only fulfilled as the demand is met and as that freedom is used in the service of God who bestows it. But there is no service of God without service of one's fellow humans, in which the **whole law is fulfilled** (verse 14).

6:1-10. *Specific Examples.* Paul applies the phrase **law of Christ** to the central truth of the gospel, for which his letter has been a plea: that righteousness is given to those who live by faith. Faith becomes active in love (5:6), in bondage to which one becomes authentically free. Love seeks to reclaim and set right the trespasser by taking unto itself the **burdens** of sin and guilt. This is the law of Christ, the kind of love revealed in the cross (cf. I Corinthians 9:21-23).

6:3-5. Verses 3-4 are characteristically Pauline warnings about pride (cf. Philippians 2:3-4). The Christian ought never use the failings of another as an occasion for self-congratulation. All have sinned and fall short of God's glory (Romans 3:23). In relation to God's wisdom all are fools, and in relation to his power all are weak (I Corinthians 1:25; 3:19), really **nothing**.

Verse 5 does not contradict verse 2, for the new word **load** refers to one's individual responsibility before God, from which one can never flee. It does not mean sin and guilt, from which, in the sharing of love, a person may be redeemed.

6:6-10. These admonitions are loosely connected with, but not unrelated to, the discussion of life in the Spirit. Though these traditional sayings ought not to be interpreted too specifically with reference to the Galatian situation, each has a certain indirect applicability. Those who receive the gospel become joint shareholders with those by whom it is preached (verse 6). They are accountable to God for the responsible use of their freedom (verses 7-8). Its misuse leads to destruction but its proper use to eternal life.

There is a play on words in verse 9 which cannot be reproduced in English, but its effect is suggested by a paraphrase: "Let us not 'go to seed' in our sowing!" In time the harvest shall come, for it is wrought by the Spirit's power (cf. 5:22-23).

The admonition to **do good** is synonymous with the command to love. Paul's emphasis on the **household of faith** is of course not meant to restrict love to those within the community of the church.

VII. CONCLUSION (6:11-18)

6:11-16. *A New Creation.* This final paragraph was not dictated to a stenographer but written in Paul's own hand (cf.

I Corinthians 16:21). It is a summary of the appeal which he has been making throughout: that compromise in the matter of Gentile circumcision would empty the cross of its power and invalidate the truth of the gospel. The Galatian troublemakers are charged with preaching circumcision only in order to avoid the censure and persecution which might otherwise result (cf. 5:11).

Those who are turned away from the true gospel, then, are hypocrites not only with respect to their Christianity but also with respect to the law. The false teachers are not any better Jews than they are Christians (verse 13). They apparently regard circumcision as a symbol of religious prestige; and here, as in 4:17, that is cause for reproof.

6:14-16. The Christian's **glory,** i.e. boast, is in the **cross of . . . Christ.** To be in Christ is to be completely reoriented in terms of ultimate values and objectives. So total is this reorientation that it may be spoken of as crucifixion of the self—or of the **world.** Justification comes, not through works of the law, but through the cross, the **law of Christ** (verse 2), which is the law of love (cf. 5:14). For through the total self-giving of love one's own "ego" dies and Christ lives in the person (cf. 2:19-21). Faith is thus active in love, and this is a **new creation** (note the parallelism with 5:6). This total inner transformation is the **rule,** the cardinal principle, of true religion.

In form verse 16 is a benediction. In function it is an exhortation to **walk,** i.e. order one's life, according to the guidance of the Spirit. Those who so walk constitute the authentic **Israel of God,** the true sons of Abraham.

6:17-18. *Final Plea and Benediction.* Before concluding with his usual benediction Paul refers to the **marks of Jesus** which he bears. The reference is probably to the scars of his apostolic sufferings (cf. II Corinthians 6:4-10; 11:23-29). These mark him as a slave of Christ, just as the identification on Roman slaves and soldiers designated whose they were and to whom they owed allegiance.

What Paul describes as "the daily pressure . . . of my anxiety for all the churches" (II Corinthians 11:28) is nowhere better demonstrated than here in Galatians. Nowhere is there a more poignant appeal for release from it than in his hope that henceforth **no man** will **trouble** him by wandering from the truth of the gospel to which they have once been converted.

THE LETTER OF PAUL
TO THE EPHESIANS

Victor Paul Furnish

INTRODUCTION

Character and Purpose

Ephesians is not a letter in the strict sense, though its opening
and closing have been designed to make it appear so. Its tone is
cool and distant. It nowhere deals with local problems, and its
author nowhere has in mind a particular group of readers. It is
rich with the rhetoric of worship and doctrine, and it deals with a
single theme. Moreover manuscript evidence makes it probable
that the words "at Ephesus" (1:1; see the Revised Standard
Version footnote) did not stand in the original document. As late
as the middle of the second century the heretic Marcion was
identifying this writing as the Letter to the Laodiceans (see
comment on Colossians 4:15-17).

Various theories have been advanced about the purpose of
Ephesians. One views it as a circular letter to a group of
churches, but since it is not precisely comparable with the other
circular letters in the New Testament (Galatians and I Peter) this
hypothesis has not commended itself to many. Another, widely
accepted in the English-speaking world, regards Ephesians as a

compilation of Pauline texts designed specifically to introduce the central themes of Paul's theology. According to this view the author was not Paul himself but an admiring disciple who composed Ephesians as a covering letter to be circulated with Paul's collected letters as a kind of foreword.

But this view is purely hypothetical. There is no evidence that Ephesians ever stood as the opening letter of the Pauline group. There is nothing within the letter itself to indicate that it was intended to introduce Paul's thought. Many of the alleged citations of Paul's letters can better be explained by reliance on common liturgical and ethical traditions (see below) rather than by literary borrowing. And the content of Ephesians is influenced by a single dominant concern—namely, the unity of the church under the headship of Christ. The purpose of Ephesians must therefore be defined in relation to this central theme.

The author's clearest indications of his purpose in writing occur in 2:1–4:16. In this central section he is concerned to emphasize the unity of Jews and Gentiles within the Christian community. His readers are Gentile Christians (cf. for example 2:11). They apparently need to be reminded that the history of Israel and the inheritance of Jewish Christianity is an essential part of the tradition in which they stand. The development of this theme proceeds on the basis of several significant theological concepts which have given Ephesians a place of theological prominence not only within the New Testament but also within the history of Christian doctrine.

Though the author's originality should not be downplayed, his indebtedness to various theological, liturgical, and ethical traditions is substantial. Citation from a hymn in 5:14 is the most obvious instance of this, but there are others as well—perhaps 1:5-8, 9-12*a*, 20-23; 2:4-10, 14-17. The author's exhortations—especially the "household table" (5:21–6:9) and the "armor of God" passage (6:10-17)—reveal a similar use of traditional ethical forms and ideas. There are numerous and striking points of similarity to the Dead Sea scrolls.

Authorship

The letter claims to be from Paul (1:1; 3:1-13; 6:21-22) writing from prison (3:1, 13; 4:1; 6:20). Accordingly it is traditionally grouped with Philippians, Colossians, and Philemon as written from Rome shortly before Paul's death. At a relatively early date the church at Ephesus was regarded as the recipient, though the original text of the letter probably did not indicate this (see above).

Several considerations, however, weigh decisively against Pauline authorship:

(1) Not only is the literary style and vocabulary different from Paul's, but certain key concepts are stated and developed in a non-Pauline way (for example, "mystery"; see below on 1:9-10).

(2) The author accords the apostles a status and role never given them by Paul (see below on 2:20*a*; 3:5-6).

(3) The author always uses the term "church" in a universal sense, while Paul applied it to local congregations.

(4) Many of the distinctively Pauline theological emphases are reinterpreted, modified, or subordinated to the author's own special interests.

One further characteristic of Ephesians also raises difficulties for the hypothesis of Pauline authorship—its close relationship, in form and content, to Colossians (see Introduction to Colossians). Parallels in subject matter are numerous. About a third of the words in Colossians are in Ephesians; about a fourth of the words in Ephesians are in Colossians. Seventy-three of the 155 verses in Ephesians have verbal connections with Colossians. Thus defenders of Pauline authorship are required to hold that Ephesians and Colossians were written one after the other while certain thoughts were still fresh in Paul's mind.

But such a hypothesis raises further difficulties:

(1) Why are there crucial differences between Colossians and Ephesians in the handling of important topics and ideas? For example, see below on 1:9-10, 23*b*; 3:5-6; 4:14-16; 5:15-20; 6:18-20.

(2) Why in a relatively unimportant passage would Paul slavishly copy two sentences from a letter he had written

earlier? The similarity of 6:21-22 to Colossians 4:7-8 is too precise to be attributed to anything but literary dependence.

(3) Why would Paul follow the same pattern and use so many of the same thoughts and phrases in composing two writings with decidedly different purposes? Colossians is a letter to a specific congregation about a local problem of false teachers. Ephesians is a general essay on the nature of the church.

Many New Testament scholars today believe, therefore, that the author of Ephesians was not Paul but a devoted admirer of Paul who wrote in his name. His literary style, his place in the religious tradition known also from the Dead Sea scrolls, and his concern to remind the church of its Jewish heritage suggest that he was a Jewish Christian. It is not possible to determine the place from which he wrote. He addressed himself to no particular congregation or area but to Christendom at large.

Date

Ephesians is to be dated in the period after the apostles, when the church had become predominantly Gentile and was in danger of losing a sense of its continuity with Israel, when it was looking back on its apostolic heroes and according them special honors, when it had available richly developed liturgical and theological traditions, and when it was conceiving of itself and its mission in boldly universalistic terms. Since Ephesians was known to Ignatius (35-115) and perhaps also to the authors of I Peter and I Clement (about 96), a date before about 95 is probable.

Theological Perspectives

The central theme of Paul's preaching, "Jesus Christ and him crucified" (I Corinthians 2:2), still survives in Ephesians (2:13-16; cf. 1:7; 6:2, 25). But it is by no means the determinative element in the author's theological perspective. Rather the exaltation and enthronement of Christ by and with God "in the heavenly places" is given special prominence (e.g. 1:20; 2:4-6).

In the preexistent Christ the will of God has been revealed and accomplished: the unity of all things (1:3-10; 3:11) and their subjection to the cosmic Lord (1:19-23). Salvation, then, is understood as that cosmic peace which is established when all things and all persons are reconciled to God and hence to one another through the redemptive deed of Christ (2:11-21).

Salvation is effected for the individual believer as one dies to the old life and is raised to new life through baptism into the church, Christ's body (1:22-23; 2:4-7). The church itself, "the fulness" of Christ, was in God's purpose from the beginning of creation and therefore has a cosmic status. It is the place where:

Christ actually reigns (1:22-23; 4:15-16; 5:23-24);

where God is praised (3:21);

where the Spirit dwells (2:22);

where the "mystery" of God's will is revealed to the apostles and prophets (2:20; 3:4-5);

where that will is made known to the "principalities and powers in the heavenly places" (3:10);

where the gifts of God's grace are received and expressed in the transformed lives of the members of the one body (4:1-16).

For this author, then, the cosmic reign of Christ and the status of the church as existing in God's purpose from the beginning of creation are definitive and inseparable concepts. The significance of Christ's person and the nature of the church are closely identified. In this he differs from Paul, to whom, however, he is deeply indebted for many of the basic elements of his theology.

Yet at other points, as well, Pauline concepts are significantly altered. One example is the concept of salvation by grace apart from works. Though this is emphatically stated in Ephesians (2:5, 8-10), here it presupposes that the believer looks back on salvation as a past accomplished event. In Paul's own letters, on the other hand, salvation is regarded as a present and future event. The dimensions of faith and salvation related to an imminent second coming of Christ are almost totally lacking in Ephesians. The traces of the earlier Christian expectation which remain are due largely to the author's use of traditional formulas and phrases.

It is primarily because of the original and systematic

development of the idea of the church that this anonymous author has a place of special prominence among the theologians of the New Testament. His influence in the subsequent history of Christian doctrine has been considerable. In the twentieth century, because of the treatment of such questions as tradition, the ministry, the nature of Christian unity, and the role of the church in God's plan of salvation, Ephesians has been one of the basic documents in the ecumenical discussion.

Whether this is justified, whether the attempt to formulate the Christian message and tradition in terms of the nature of the church can ever be successful, and whether a doctrine of the church is properly central in the preaching of the gospel are questions with which the interpreter of Ephesians is inescapably confronted.

I. Salutation (1:1-2)

The letter opens in a typically Pauline way. It is probable that the original manuscript contained no reference to Ephesus (see Introduction) and was therefore addressed to Christians in general. Here, as in Paul's own salutations, **saints** describes Christians as people called of God and set aside for his service. They are also **faithful**, i.e. believers, **in Christ Jesus**. It is one of the author's concerns throughout this whole treatise to specify what true belief in Christ, the head of the church, requires.

II. Liturgical Preface (1:3-23)

The Pauline letters normally include, following the salutation, a section of thanksgiving to God, though in one instance (II Corinthians) this section takes the form of a liturgical blessing of God's name. Here both blessing (verses 3-14) and thanksgiving (verses 15-19) are used, and the whole section is rich in the language of Jewish and Christian worship. It is in fact very likely that the author has taken over and adapted some lines from the

Christian hymnody with which he was familiar. These opening paragraphs sing of God's electing purpose accomplished through Christ, God's gracious gifts of redemption and forgiveness, God's call to praise, and God's bestowal of the Holy Spirit as a guarantee of a future inheritance.

A. HYMN (1:3-14)

1:3-8. *God's Purpose to Bless.* God's blessedness is here described as a gracious bestowal of a **spiritual blessing** on humanity, not as an abstract quality of God's existence. The phrase **heavenly places** occurs nowhere in the New Testament except in Ephesians. Here it is used five times, as a description of that cosmic sphere where Christ rules and to which the Christian has been raised to new life in him (verse 20; 2:6). But it is also a realm where the powers of darkness and evil are still active (3:10; 6:12).

1:4-6. The meaning of **spiritual blessing** in verse 3 now becomes clearer. It refers, first, to God's eternal **purpose**. In love God has willed that all persons should be **holy and blameless before him** and should attain to their full stature as children of the heavenly Father. In this context holiness and blamelessness, while not excluding the idea of moral purity, are associated primarily with the believer's election to sonship (verse 5).

The Greek word translated **be . . . sons** literally means "adoption as sons" and occurs in several significant passages in Paul's letters (Romans 8:15, 23; 9:4; Galatians 4:5; see comment on Romans 8:12-15*b*). It emphasizes both God's initiative in establishing a relationship with persons and the character of that relationship—God's paternal love and judgment, a person's responsibility to obey. In verses 6, 12, and 14 the purpose of this divine election and adoption is formulated in related ways: **to live for the praise of** God's **grace** and God's **glory.** Thus according to this hymn humanity was created and destined for the service and the praise of the creator.

Throughout the hymn there is emphasis on the sovereign freedom of God, the eternality of God's redemptive purpose, and Christ's role as the revealer and mediator of God's grace. Christ is the one in whom God's purposes have been set forth and realized. He is the **Beloved**, preexistent Son through whom God has **freely bestowed** his **glorious grace, riches . . . which he lavished upon us**. There is a certain baroque quality to these words, crowded as they are one on another in an attempt to express the superlative blessing of God.

1:7-8. The meaning of this blessing and the function of Christ as its agent are further exhibited in the reference to **redemption through his blood**—that is, through Christ's life-giving death. The effect of this is the **forgiveness of our trespasses** (cf. Colossians 1:14).

By the time Ephesians was written these phrases had already become a fixed part of the Christian vocabulary, probably associated especially with the baptismal liturgy. Therefore the author feels no need to elaborate them here or to define the precise way in which Christ's death frees the believer from sin. For Paul "redemption" meant more than pardon for past offenses. It meant freedom from the power of sin. For him grace itself was a gift of power capable of bringing about a total inner transformation. Elsewhere in Ephesians Christ's death is mentioned (2:13-16; 5:2, 25), but it does not play the same pivotal role here as in the authentic Pauline letters (see Introduction).

1:9-10. *All Things United in Christ.* Again God's sovereign freedom and divine initiative in redemption are stressed. And again Christ's role as the agent and means of God's will is prominent. The **mystery of his will** has been revealed in Christ.

In this hymn, as elsewhere in the New Testament, it is not the hiddenness of a mystery but its manifestation which is emphasized. The idea has special importance in Ephesians where Christian preaching in general can be described as proclamation of a "mystery" (6:19). The term is also employed in Colossians, where it refers to Christ himself as the mystery (Colossians 1:26-29; 2:2-3).

But in Ephesians as nowhere else in the New Testament, this mystery is interpreted specifically as God's purpose, revealed in Christ, that Gentiles as well as Jews should be members of the one body (3:3-6), gathered into one church under one Lord for the common praise of God and a united witness to God's word (3:9-13).

1:10. Two related ideas are present here:

(1) the eternality of God's plan for the church, a **plan for the fulness of time**;

(2) the oneness in Christ of **all things . . . in heaven and . . . on earth**.

There is repeated stress on the unity of God's creative and redemptive activity. In Ephesians these two are inseparably related. Therefore the church itself, viewed as the earthly instrument of God's salvation, is accorded a fundamental place in the divine creation.

The reference to God's **plan for the fulness of time** recalls the words of Paul in Galatians 4:4-5, but the basic theological perspective is rather different. Paul speaks of the redemptive event of Christ's incarnation—especially his death and resurrection—which represents God's intervention in history on humanity's behalf. But here the idea is more of a **plan** for the whole course of human history, culminating in a cosmic unification of **all things** under the sovereign rule of Christ.

1:11-14. *All Things Created for God's Praise.* God's **purpose** for creation, God's will for human beings, is that they should **live for the praise of his glory**. This phrase is probably another of those fixed liturgical and doctrinal expressions which abound in these opening paragraphs. It is characteristic for this author that the church is the place where God is praised—"to him be glory in the church" (3:21). Humanity was created for the praise of God, and this is fulfilled in the community of those who are united in obedience to the one Lord who is above all.

1:12. Some commentators have interpreted **we who first hoped in Christ** as a reference to Jewish Christians, among whom the author apparently includes himself (cf. 2:11), in distinction from those of Gentile background—**you also** (verse

13). Since the arguments for such an interpretation are not conclusive, it is better to regard **we** as including the whole Christian community, as elsewhere in the passage. This writer uses "hope" as a comprehensive term for Christian faith in general (cf. verse 18; 2:12; 4:4).

That Christians have been **destined and appointed** for the service of God does not imply a doctrine of mechanical predestination. Rather it emphasizes the initiative of God in calling persons to their proper role as believers in Christ and obedient members of Christ's church.

1:13-14. In contrast to Colossians, where the Spirit is mentioned only once (Colossians 1:8), the **Holy Spirit** holds an important place in the theology of Ephesians. Here, as in 4:30, **sealed** probably points to Christian baptism as that time when the Christian is inwardly consecrated to the service of God and sacramentally incorporated into the body of Christ, the church. The words are derived from Paul (II Corinthians 1:22), for whom God's presence in the Holy Spirit is regarded as a down payment of the promised inheritance. **Inheritance** is for this author a general term which expresses the totality of future blessings to which the obedient Christian may look forward when the "kingdom of Christ and of God" (5:5) is fully present.

B. Thanksgiving (1:15-23)

The liturgical blessing of God's name in verses 3-14 is followed now by a section of thanksgiving to God for the faith and obedience of the readers. This is climaxed by a doxological affirmation of the working of God's power in Christ (verses 20-23). This juxtaposition of blessing and thanksgiving paragraphs never occurs in the other Pauline letters. Its presence here is probably another indication that the author of Ephesians is not Paul himself.

1:15-19. *Thanksgiving Proper.* The author acknowledges the Christian loyalty of his readers. He finds this expressed both by their profession of **faith in the Lord Jesus** and by their relationships within the church, **toward all the saints**. As in the Pauline letters the opening words of thanksgiving to God become at once a prayer of petition for the continuing and increasing faith of those addressed. It thereby becomes an indirect exhortation to the readers to discipline themselves in that direction. The author prays that the readers may be given an openness to apprehend the glory of God, who is the **Father of glory**, and to receive what God's goodness continually offers.

The content of this **wisdom** and **revelation** is the **knowledge** of God, understood by this author—as by Paul (I Corinthians 13:12)—as a transforming encounter with God. Elsewhere in Ephesians it is described as attaining "to mature manhood, to the measure of the stature of the fulness of Christ" (4:13), regarded as a gift of God's grace. The thought of 3:16 is similar.

1:18-19. *Eyes of Your Hearts.* The metaphor recalls references to the "eyes of the soul," by which God is "known," which appear frequently in Greek and Hellenistic religious philosophy. But mention of the heart as the seat and center of deepest knowledge and experience is particularly characteristic of Hebraic thought, as attested by the many Old Testament occurrences of the metaphor. It refers, not just to some mystic communion of the inner self with God, or to some private display of divine truth. It means an actual transformation of the whole person, accomplished as one is opened to receive the grace of God bestowed in Christ.

The author may regard this also as the content of the **hope** and the **inheritance** to which God has called people. In the next phrase he speaks of that divine **power** by which authentic knowledge has been produced, the glorious hope of redemption has been fulfilled, and the riches of the final inheritance have been bestowed.

1:20-23. *Hymnic Conclusion.* The doxological character of Ephesians is especially evident here where the language of petition in verses 15-19 yields to the rhetoric of praise. God's power has been effectively **accomplished, in Christ**—in his resurrection **from the dead** (cf. 2:5-6), his exaltation to the **right**

hand of God **in the heavenly places** (see above on 1:3-8), and his lordship over all things.

These descriptions of Christ's work, common to many parts of the New Testament, have been influenced by the wording of Psalms 8:6 and 110:1. Here the author goes further than Paul in ascribing ultimate authority to Christ. Paul applies the words of Psalm 8:6 to God and specifically says that even Christ is one day to be subjected to the Father (I Corinthians 15:25-28; cf. I Corinthians 3:23).

1:21. The first readers of Ephesians would understand the words translated **rule . . . authority . . . power . . . dominion** as referring to supernatural beings. Enthroned in a cosmic hierarchy, these beings played a great part in certain ancient religions and were often mentioned in late Jewish apocalyptic literature. Here it is affirmed that Christ's universal rule renders impotent every such false pretender to cosmic power. Christ alone, installed by God and endowed with power, has dominion over all created things. There can be no other claimants to his title, for Christ is **above every name that is named**.

1:22-23. Verse 22*a* is quoted with only slight variations from the Septuagint translation of Psalm 8:6. But verses 22*b*-23 move far beyond the psalmist's perspective and set forth the overall theme of Ephesians: God has enthroned Christ as the **head over all things for the church, which is his body, the fulness of him who fills all in all**. This particular statement about Christ's relationship to the church has been framed in a way which leads to profound results for an understanding of the nature of the church.

1:22*b***.** It is significant that the same Christ in whom God purposed to unite all things in heaven and on earth (verse 10), and to whom all claimants to cosmic power have been subjected, has been made **head** over all these things **for the church**. The church is in a sense the locus of Christ's cosmic reign, the focus of his power, the place of his sovereign rule.

For this author the church is vastly more than a phenomenon of world history or the result of particular social needs and forces. For him the church was in God's purpose from the beginning of creation and has a cosmic status in the eternal order of things. It is not just a consequence of the gospel, an organization to fulfill the institutional requirements of the Christian mission. It is rooted in the original purposes of God and is part of the **plan for the fulness of time** (verse 10). This conviction is basic to the whole theological outlook and plan of Ephesians.

1:23a. It is important to note here a further development of the **body** metaphor as applied to the church. Paul speaks of the church as Christ's body insofar as Christians are members of one another "in Christ" (Romans 12:5). He develops this idea especially in I Corinthians 12:12-31, but even there he does not call Christ the "head" of the body. This identification is made, however, in Colossians 1:18 and 2:19, and now becomes a key concept in Ephesians (cf. 4:15; 5:23).

Whereas in the Pauline letters, including Colossians, the term "body" is used not only of the church but in other ways as well, in Ephesians it is employed exclusively of the church. And here, as in Colossians, the members of the body are understood to bear an organic relationship not only to one another but also to Christ, their head (cf. 4:15-16).

1:23b. Finally to be noted is the striking assertion that the church is the **fulness of him who fills all in all**. Commentators differ in their interpretation of these words. Some hold that Christ is regarded as the fullness of the church, others that the church is regarded as the fullness of Christ. In the latter case one would better translate the phrase "the fulness of him who is being fulfilled," meaning that the church's existence is necessary to Christ's functioning as Lord.

It seems more likely, however, that the phrase is simply a shorthand expression of the author's later contention that it is Christ's presence and power as head which "fills" the church, builds it up (4:12), makes it one, and nourishes it for growth (4:15-16). In Ephesians, then, Christ's relationship to the church, its fullness, is described in the terms Colossians uses to indicate God's relation to Christ: "in him all the fulness of God was pleased to dwell" (Colossians 1:19); "in him the whole fulness of deity dwells bodily" (Colossians 2:9).

In Ephesians the accent falls heavily on the role of the Christian community in God's plan of salvation. For this author the church is one of the basic parts of God's creation. Its organic integrity is assured by Christ as its head, and its life and growth are sustained by the presence and power of Christ, who is the fullness of its being.

III. THE UNITY OF THE CHURCH (2:1–3:21)

Chapters 2–3 are the central theological section of Ephesians and emphasize the unity of the church. This unity comes as each believer is united with Christ and becomes one with all who share in the new life God has given (chapter 2). The author interprets Paul's ministry as directed primarily toward the concrete, historical realization of that unity, by which the church truly becomes the church and is enabled to make an effective witness in the world (chapter 3).

A. RESURRECTION WITH CHRIST (2:1-10)

2:1-3. *Spiritual Death.* Apart from Christ one is **dead** in one's **trespasses and sins**. This spiritual death involves one's alienation from God, estrangement from fellow human beings, perversion of the divinely bestowed freedom to make responsible choices and the disintegration of every faculty for wise judgment and moral behavior.

2:2. The metaphor **walked** is used, as by Paul himself, to depict the style and direction of one's life. Religious mythology current in the author's day spoke of a demonic ruler of the earth whose function was satanic—though the name is not used here for the ruler. Instead, the ruler is called the **course**, literally "eon," **of this world** and the **prince of the power of the air**. Formerly the readers were spiritually dead, governed by false pretenders to universal dominion—those powers of this world over whom, in reality, God rules in Christ (cf. 1:20-23).

2:3. Some interpreters believe that **we all** contrasts with **you** (verses 1-2) and that the Jewish Christian author thus associates himself with his Gentile readers (but see above on 1:12).

The moral decadence of life without Christ is further described. It is ruled by human **passions**, guided by nothing surer than the transient **desires of body and mind** and controlled exclusively by worldly goals and values. But human beings, because of their humanity, because they are creatures of a just and righteous God, stand ever subject to God's judgment. **Wrath** therefore means, not capricious or vindictive anger, but God's righteous, aggressive judgment of evil wherever found (cf. Romans 3:21-23).

2:4-7. *God's Saving Love.* In Ephesians, as throughout the New Testament, God's righteous judgment presupposes God's loving compassion. The two are not separable. The prologue of this letter has already praised God's love and mercy (1:5-8). That theme now reappears with the heavy rhetorical ornamentation so favored by this author—**rich in mercy . . . great love**.

Verses 4-5 resume the thought of verse 1*a*. Even at the very moment when we were most helplessly and hopelessly under the dominion of evil powers and pressures God in his love entered into history to save and redeem us. God's grace and love bestowed in Christ have not only brought forgiveness but **made us alive together with Christ**. The parenthetical comment in verse 5 is the chief topic of verses 8-10 (see comment).

The believer's new life is **in** and **with** Christ. Three times in rapid succession the author employs words which have the Greek prefix "with": **alive . . . with Christ; raised . . . up with him** to **sit with him** (on **in the heavenly places** see above on 1:3-8). The first readers of this letter would remember their baptism as the event in which this experience of being in and with Christ was most effectively real. Being in and with Christ is a corporate, not just a private, matter. All believers are **together** in and with Christ. It is Christ's work not only to reconcile persons to God but also to reconcile them to one another (cf. verses 13-22).

2:8-10. *Salvation by Grace.* These verses develop the thought contained in the parenthesis in verse 5. The idea of salvation by grace through faith is thoroughly Pauline. But the presupposition that such has already taken place for believers at some time in the past is not to be found in Paul's own letters (cf. Romans 6:1-23, where resurrection and life with Christ are conceived as still future). Paul's theology has here been distilled into a formula, but in the distillation something important is endangered. Paul understood that the decision of faith by which God's grace is appropriated must be ever newly actualized in the life of the believer. For this reason salvation can be sure and complete only in God's own future.

2:8b-9. Here also is a reflection of Paul's theological emphases, but again there is a difference—in this instance due to a different historical context. Paul's doctrine of grace was developed in opposition to the Jewish conviction that salvation came by doing "works of the law" (cf. Galatians 2:16). Here that problem is no longer in sight and the reference is only to **works** in general. This represents a quite proper broadening of Paul's point to apply to all human efforts designed to earn salvation.

2:10. But this author by no means minimizes the importance of good works. They are a necessary part of the Christian life, even though they are not the way to salvation. This point is made in a unique way. Christians are God's **workmanship**, i.e. production, **created in Christ Jesus for good works**. This is part of what their sonship involves (1:5), part of that for which they have been called (cf. 4:1-6). The idea that these good works have in fact been **prepared beforehand** by God has no New Testament parallel.

B. Reconciliation in Christ (2:11-22)

The salvation God has effected for believers through Christ involves the oneness of Christ's church. In him Jews and

Gentiles have been reconciled to God and therefore to one another. The key word in verses 11-18 is thus **peace**, which describes this twofold reconciliation in Christ. Verses 19-22 conclude the section with a statement on the nature of the church.

2:11-12. *Grace for the Heathen.* The author here addresses converts from the heathen world, asking them to consider what God's grace (see above on verses 8-10) has meant to them. The reference to **circumcision** is very Pauline, for Paul repeatedly insists that true circumcision is inward, not outward (cf. Romans 2:25-29). Nevertheless the Gentiles did lack certain real advantages enjoyed by the Jews.

Separated from Christ is used to describe the Gentiles' previous situation generally. Its meaning is defined by the phrases which follow. They were separated from God's people, from God's promises, from the hope of redemption in Christ, and from God. The central purpose of Ephesians is to admonish the Gentile Christian readers that now, within the church, this Jewish heritage may and must be made their own (see Introduction).

2:13-18. *Christ Our Peace.* The glorious and surprising fact of the Gentiles' redemption is expressed in the two simple words which open verse 13: **But now . . .** These words are set over against **at one time** in verse 11 and **at that time** in verse 12.

Through Christ's death the Gentiles have been included in the people of God. Their estrangement has been overcome, and they have been **brought near** (cf. Colossians 1:20-23). In Judaism the terms "far" and "near" were frequently used of the non-Israelites and Israelites respectively. Here the author seems to have in mind the words of Isaiah 57:19, for in verse 14*a* he identifies Christ himself as **our peace, who has made us**, Jew and Gentile, **both one** in the church.

2:14*b*. Moreover Christ **has broken down the dividing wall** between Jew and Gentile. Some commentators believe the metaphor refers to the wall which was erected in the temple in Jerusalem to separate the Jewish and Gentile areas. This interpretation, however, is highly conjectural and does not take into account that such an allusion would be lost on the original readers.

Others propose a Gnostic background for the metaphor (see comment on Philippians 3:1–4:1), citing the Gnostic myth of the redeemer's descent which broke down the wall of separation between the heavenly and earthly realms. Thus the intention here would be to identify that redeemer as Christ and to underscore the cosmic significance of his atoning work (cf. 1:10).

In any case the author says that reconciliation with God means reconciliation with one's fellows, that within the community of believers there can be no dividing walls. The church is one because those within it are joint recipients of the saving grace of God in Christ. It is not said that incorporation into Christ somehow erases the differences among people. It is affirmed, however—and this is more important—that for those in Christ such differences no longer alienate them from one another.

2:15-18. The word **flesh** refers to the whole redemptive event of Christ's coming. It especially refers to his death (verse 13), by which the power of the Jewish law, with its divisive and hostility-producing **commandments and ordinances**, has been decisively broken.

The unity of God's people in the church is further stressed in the vivid picture of the church as a new humanity, **one new man**. Reconciliation does not require the capitulation of one side or the other; it involves the transformation of both. Reconciliation among persons always has as its primary dimension their joint reconciliation with God (verse 16). This is accomplished **in one body**, perhaps a reference both to the crucified Christ, through whose death on the cross reconciliation occurs, and to the church itself as Christ's body, whose life has come through his death. Unity in the church is further supported in verse 18 with mention of the **one Spirit** (cf. I Corinthians 12:4-27) through whom all **have access** to their common Father (cf. 3:11-12).

2:19-22. *The Church, God's Temple.* The Gentiles are no longer alienated from God's commonwealth (cf. verse 12) but are now **fellow citizens with the saints**. Whether "saints" refers to the Christian community in general, as in 1:1, or to Jewish

Christians in particular depends on whether the phrase **members of the household of God** is strictly parallel in meaning. It probably is, and thus "saints" would refer to all Christians. The word "household" depicts God's church as the family, bound together as one under God's paternal care.

2:20a. A second metaphor describes the church as a building founded on the **apostles and prophets**. The author regards these as the certified recipients of God's revelation and official bearers of the Christian tradition (cf. 3:5, which along with 4:11 also shows that Christian prophets are in mind). The contrast with Paul's metaphor in I Corinthians 3:10-15 is significant. For Paul, Christ himself is the foundation and the apostles and prophets are only builders on it.

2:20b. This metaphor is expanded by a reference to Christ as one of the vital components of the church's structure. The Greek word used may mean either **cornerstone** (cf. "foundation-stone," New English Bible) or "capstone." The first meaning refers to the stone situated at the corner of a foundation from which the builders take their bearings for all the other walls. Thus Christ would be presented as the one who by his presence defines the shape and scope of the church, points it in the way it is to go, and enables its sturdy construction.

A capstone, on the other hand, is the topmost stone of a wall, the last to be put in place. If this is what the author has in mind—as most recent commentators hold—then Christ is described as both effecting and symbolizing the completion and wholeness of the church, the crowning element under which the structure is united and strong.

This latter interpretation accords with the other metaphor of Christ as head of the church. The former is more in keeping with the immediate context, which speaks of the church's foundation and of its continuing construction.

2:21-22. Whichever interpretation is followed, Christ is here regarded as the one **in whom the whole structure is joined together** (cf. 1:10). Moreover the church is conceived, not as a static mass, but as dynamic and living. The building **grows into a holy temple in the Lord.** The church's true being is a becoming.

This author by no means regards the church as still incomplete, for that would contradict his view of the church's eternal status in God's creation (see above on 1:10).

Rather he seems to connect the church's growth with the idea of verse 22 that the believers are together being constantly **built into it for a dwelling place of God in the Spirit**. The **one Spirit** through whom the believer has **access** to God (verse 18) is thus resident in the church, the all-inclusive body of Christ, the place where God is praised.

C. PAUL'S MINISTRY OF UNITY (3:1-21)

In this section the author (see Introduction) reveals the high regard in which he holds the apostle under whose name he writes. **Paul** is represented as one of the **holy apostles** to whom the **mystery of Christ** has been revealed, and whose mission has been especially to the Gentile world. His is thus a ministry of unity, calling all people unto Christ and into the one church.

3:1-6. *A Steward of God's Grace.* Now the author self-consciously assumes the role of Paul. He considers Paul a missionary of the first rank, one whose imprisonment was specifically for the **Gentiles**. Moreover the grace of God given to Paul involved a special **stewardship**, which was fulfilled in his Gentile mission. This mission was to proclaim the **mystery of Christ**, which was revealed to Paul and the other apostles and Christian prophets as it had been made known in previous generations.

3:5-6. God's **Spirit** (cf. 1:13; 2:18, 22) is named as the means of revelation. In contrast to Colossians 1:26 the circle which receives the revelation is narrowed down from the "saints," i.e. all Christians, to the **holy apostles and prophets**. In verse 6 the content of the "mystery" is specified. In the church the Gentiles are "co-heirs, companions, and co-partners" (Moffatt translation) with the Jews—a compact summary of the longer discussion in 2:11-22.

3:7-9. *A Minister to the Gentiles.* Here Paul's role as an apostle to the Gentiles is reemphasized. Verse 7 doubtless has his conversion in mind (cf. Galatians 1:15-17). **Though I am the very least of all the saints** is true to Paul's spirit but betrays the hand of a later author. Here even Paul's modesty is intensified, as shown by a comparison with I Corinthians 15:9, where he refers to himself as "least of the apostles." **Unsearchable riches of Christ** is simply an alternative designation for the gospel, though like the word "mystery" it suggests that Christian wisdom has depths and dimensions unmatched by any other (cf. **manifold wisdom**, verse 10).

3:9. Several points made previously are here repeated:

(1) The gospel is a declaration of God's **plan** for salvation (see above on 1:10).

(2) This plan was once **hidden** but is now revealed. In Christ God's eternal purposes have been set forth and made known through apostles and prophets in a way hitherto impossible (cf. verse 5; 1:9).

(3) The same God who created the world is its redeemer. Since "before the foundation of the world" (1:4) God's purpose has been to save.

3:10-13. *The Role of the Church.* The church is the means by which the **wisdom of God** is cosmically proclaimed and therefore plays a crucial role in God's plan for salvation. That plan involves the proclamation of the riches of God's grace, the revealing of the mystery of Christ, and the subsequent subjection of all people and all powers to God. The church, through the preaching of its apostles and prophets, and through its very being, bears witness to the power of God expressed in God's sovereign rule and redeeming grace.

The **principalities and powers** are those cosmic deities which, according to the ancient world view shared also by the early Christians, inhabited and ruled the spheres between earth and heaven (on **in the heavenly places** see above on 1:3-8). Colossians insists that such authorities are not to be worshiped and are themselves subject to the lordship of Christ. Here there is an additional emphasis on the church as the means by which this cosmic dimension of Christ's rule is demonstrated.

3:11-13. Whereas it is the church which makes known God's purposes—God's **manifold wisdom**—it is Christ himself through whom they are **realized**, i.e. accomplished. More specifically, it is in Christ that the believer has **access** into the presence of God (cf. 2:18). Because of God's forgiving, renewing grace bestowed in Christ, the person of faith can stand before God's glorious presence as one "holy and blameless" (1:4), with **boldness and confidence**.

The precise meaning of verse 13 and its relation to what has preceded is not certain. It bids the readers not to be discouraged over Paul's afflictions but to know that they serve the cause of the gospel and are especially efficacious for them.

3:14-19. *Prayer for the Inner Man.* After an interruption (verses 2-13) the author now resumes the introduction to a prayer for his readers begun in verse 1. He prays that they may be **strengthened with might through his Spirit in the inner man**. "Inner man" here translates the same words rendered "inmost self" in Romans 7:22. Both instances refer to one's essential personhood, which when yielded to the powerful working of God's Spirit can become thoroughly new.

The next phrase of the prayer (verse 17*a*) elucidates the first. One's inmost self is made new by the Spirit as Christ is received therein, and the life which is opened to Christ's presence is **rooted and grounded in love**. This is the widest, longest, highest, and deepest **knowledge** of all, the very **fulness of God**.

3:20-21. *Doxology.* This stately doxology brings to a close the most specifically doctrinal section of Ephesians. The phrase **glory in the church and in Christ Jesus** echoes the author's emphasis on the church as the body of Christ, who is its head. The church is the place where God is praised, and to this service of praise humankind has been appointed since creation (cf. 1:5, 6, 12, 14).

IV. THE IMPERATIVES OF THE CHRISTIAN LIFE (4:1–6:20)

The second half of Ephesians (chapters 4–6) is primarily a series of ethical admonitions. It differs from the first half in style and content. Yet the two sections are closely related, for this author believes that the imperatives of the Christian life are grounded in what God has accomplished in Christ and in what was intended through the unity of all things in Christ and in the church.

A. THE BASIS FOR CHRISTIAN ETHICS (4:1-16)

Paul's authority is again invoked in verse 1 (cf. 3:1) as the author begins his exhortations. These are introduced by an appeal to the true basis for Christian ethics: God's call to unity, peace, and love (verses 1-6) and the bestowal of spiritual gifts for the common good (verses 7-16).

4:1-6. *God's Call.* Christians have been "destined" as God's sons (1:5), "sealed" by his Spirit (1:13), and "called" to hope (1:18). They have been made "alive" in Christ (2:5) and reconciled to God and to all of God's people in Christ's body (2:11-22). **Therefore** they are to show themselves worthy of these riches of grace and manifest them within the life of the Christian community. **Unity**, the hallmark of the church and of all creation, is to be maintained by **love**, expressing itself in **lowliness . . . meekness . . . patience . . . forbearing**.

4:4-6. The slogans in these verses recapitulate the argument of chapters 1–3. They suggest that the unity of the Spirit is already present, as a gift, in the church. On **one body** cf. 2:16; on **one Spirit** cf. 2:18; on **one hope** cf. 1:18; 2:12; on **one Lord** cf. 2:4-7, 13-22; on **one baptism** cf. 1:13-14; on **one God and Father of us all** cf. 1:5; 3:14-15. **Faith** here, as in verse 13, refers to the totality of Christian doctrines and practices.

4:7-10. *The Gifts of Christ.* Christian unity is not to be confused wth uniformity, for the members of Christ's body have been variously endowed. Whereas Paul speaks of gifts of the Spirit (I Corinthians 12:4-11) this author refers to them as gifts of Christ (verse 7). In verse 8 he endeavors to prove this with a citation from Psalm 68:18.

Rabbinic commentators regularly applied these words to

Moses, who ascended Mt. Sinai to receive the law from God and then gave it as a gift to Israel. Influenced by this rabbinical interpretation, the author of Ephesians changes the original verb from "receive" to "give" and then applies the psalm to Christ rather than to Moses. He then seeks to justify this in verses 9-10. An ascent, he argues, presupposes a previous descent. The psalm must therefore refer to Christ, who was sent from the Father and returned to God (a prominent theme in John, e.g. 3:13). It is probable that the **lower parts of the earth** is a reference not only to Christ's earthly incarnation but to his further descent into Hades to preach to the dead (cf. I Peter 3:18-22). On Christ as the Lord and fullness of **all things** see above on 1:10, 22-23.

4:11-16. *Specific Gifts.* The author resumes his original point that Christ has bestowed various gifts on the members of his body (verse 7). Mentioned first are **apostles** and **prophets**, as in Paul's own list (I Corinthians 12:28). But in Ephesians these offices are regarded as closed, for the apostles and prophets belong to that select group which formed the foundation of the church (2:20) and were the original guarantors of revelation (3:5). The collective goal of the church's ministries is indicated in verses 12-16. All these various phrases and figures pertain to the life of the Christian community, not just to the faith of individual Christians.

4:12-13. Christ's **body** is built up as its members attain **unity** in Christ, founded on a common **faith** in him. It is the church, then, which as a whole—**we all**—attains to **mature manhood, to the measure of the stature of the fulness of Christ**.

4:14-16. The goal of these varied ministries is negatively stated in verse 14. The ministries are to prevent the disintegration of the church which occurs when its members are childishly attracted to false **doctrine**. Instead the church should manifest throughout the **love** of Christ, by which it lives.

As in 2:21-22 the author implies that there is no life without **growth**, and he reaffirms that this growth comes from Christ, **who is the head** of the **body** (cf. Colossians 2:19, where, however, the body is not the church but the whole cosmic order).

B. EXHORTATIONS ON PERSONAL MORALITY (4:17–5:20)

The ethical exhortations of this section are not closely tied to a single theme, but they all bear generally on the importance of personal morality. Christians are **children of light**. They should **put on the new nature** appropriate to their new status.

4:17-24. *Putting Off the Old Nature.* The term **Gentiles** is applied no longer to the Gentile Christian readers of Ephesians but to non-Christians in general. A series of phrases describes their moral plight (verses 17-19; cf. Romans 1:21-32). Conversion to Christianity ought to mean a radical separation from pagan immorality (cf. 2:1-7).

Only in verse 21 does this author use the term **Jesus** alone, and it may constitute an appeal to the ethical teaching of the historical Jesus as the church formulated these traditions. It may also be directed against Gnostic denials of the reality of the Incarnation. The radical newness of life in Christ is emphasized with the metaphor **put off** and **put on**, which would recall the total transformation of character symbolized and inaugurated at the time of one's baptism. On the other hand the tense of **be renewed in the spirit of your minds** refers to a continuing experience.

4:25–5:2. *The New Life of Love.* All the counsels of this section concern one's life within the community and those social responsibilities which community life involves: truthfulness, forgiveness, honesty and philanthropy, and edifying speech. Even more significant is the basis on which these exhortations are founded: the character of God and what has been done for us. **For we are members one of another** alludes to the doctrine of the church as Christ's body. In 4:32*b*–5:2 the reality of God's love, bestowed in Christ, forgiving persons and caring for them as a Father, is reaffirmed.

The new life, then, is a life of love, modeled after God's love revealed in Christ's sacrificial death **for us**. There is no full doctrine of atonement in Ephesians and Christ's death is not a central theological concept for this author (see above on 1:7-8). It is enough for him to know that Christ's death has somehow made the church one (2:14-16), and that the love thus revealed and bestowed should form the substance of the church's interior life.

5:3-14. *Walking as Children of Light.* Here the appeal for responsible ethical action is continued. The readers are exhorted to behave in ways appropriate for **saints**, a term which thus begins to take on specifically moral connotations. The vices listed in verse 4 (cf. Colossians 3:8) were also condemned by non-Christian moralists in the ancient world. But the alternative, **instead let there be thanksgiving**, is specifically Christian and conforms to a view of the new life as one lived in the continuous praise of God. Further support for the exhortations comes in verses 5-6, where disobedience is said to result in exclusion from the future **inheritance** and subjection to God's **wrath**.

Only here in the New Testament does one find the **kingdom** described as belonging to **Christ and . . . God**, and the contrast with Paul's thought is noteworthy (cf. I Corinthians 15:23-28). The admonitions of verses 6-7 echo Colossians 2:4, 8, but here no specific group of false teachers is in mind.

5:8-14. The use of **light** and **darkness** to represent morality and immorality is familiar not only from other New Testament occurrences but also from the Dead Sea scrolls and other late Jewish literature. Verse 10 is an appeal to seek out God's will as revealed in Christ, while the words of verses 11-13 refer to the presumed immorality camouflaged by the cultic rites of secret religious groups. In verse 14 the author quotes apparently from an early Christian hymn (see Introduction).

5:15-20. *Prudent Living.* The readers are admonished to **understand what the will of the Lord is** and to live as **wise**, i.e. prudent, men in the midst of a perverse world. The striking expression **making the most of**, literally "buying up," **the time** is borrowed from Colossians 4:5, where it is used in an exhortation to pass up no opportunity in bearing witness to those outside the church. Here it is applied in a general way to the whole Christian life.

The words against drunkenness are cited from a Greek

version of Proverbs 23:31. The exhortation to a Spirit-led life of praise and thanksgiving is simply an alteration of Colossians 3:16-17. Again (cf. verse 16*a*) the words are disengaged from a specific reference in Colossians, namely Christian worship, and extended to cover the whole Christian life.

C. THE CHRISTIAN HOUSEHOLD (5:21–6:9)

This section discusses relationships among members of a household. In both form and content it has many parallels in early Christian literature, especially Colossians 3:18–4:6 (see comment). It is possible to read 5:21 as an introduction to the whole section, for in each relationship the necessity of loyal obedience is emphasized. At no point, however, is servile capitulation in mind. The principle of reciprocal responsibility is always observed (5:25; 6:4, 9).

5:21-33. *Husbands and Wives.* These counsels are greatly expanded in Ephesians (contrast Colossians 3:18-19), doubtless because of this author's overarching concern to define the nature of the church, to which he finds a parallel in the institution of marriage. Thus while this passage is primarily hortatory (verses 22, 33) it also further expounds the central theme of Ephesians.

With regard to the marriage relationship itself the author has two basic convictions:

(1) As declared in scripture (Genesis 2:24) husband and wife **become one.** "One flesh," which is found in many manuscripts, seems likely here because it is equated with the author's own theological idea of one body (verses 28-29).

(2) The husband is regarded as the **head** of this body (cf. I Corinthians 11:3).

The exhortations to each partner are issued in the light of these convictions: the wife is to be obedient and respectful to her husband, and the husband is to love, nourish, and cherish his wife, with whom his own life is completely identified. The analogy drawn between marriage and the relation of Christ to his church provides the exhortations with even deeper dimensions. Christ is both **head** and **Savior** of the church, and his was a self-sacrificing, sanctifying love (verses 28, 33). Those who hold that Paul is the author of Ephesians must explain the significantly different orientation which characterizes the discussion of marriage in I Corinthians 7.

This passage is chiefly important, however, because of what it further reveals about the author's view of the church. The head-body metaphor (cf. e.g. 1:22-23) is repeated. But now it is said also that Christ is the church's **Savior**—a title used only once by Paul (Philippians 3:20)—the significance of which is not immediately explored. What is stressed is the church's duty of unconditional obedience to Christ (verse 24). This author, in contrast to Paul (I Corinthians 3:23; 15:20-28), identifies the authority of Christ with that of God (cf. 1:20-23).

Christ's lordship over the church is closely related to his love for it, exhibited and bestowed in his death. The church is thought of as the "bride" of Christ, to whom she is **presented** properly washed and clothed in matrimonial attire. The **washing of water** is baptism, a sacramental act which is given special prominence through Ephesians (cf. 1:13; 2:5-6; 4:5). The attendant **word** is probably the baptismal formula ("in the name of . . ."; cf. I Corinthians 6:11). By water and the word Christians individually and in their corporate life as the church are called to the service of God, the "praise of his glory" (1:12, 14; cf. 1:6). It is in this sense that the church is **holy and without blemish**. Reference to Christ's nurture of the church in verse 29 recalls the figures of 2:20-22 and 4:15-16.

Verse 32*a* should be translated "This mystery is great," meaning "of great significance." **Mystery** is not used here as it is elsewhere in the letter (1:9; 3:3, 9; 6:19), where it refers specifically to the unity of Jews and Gentiles within the church. Rather it is applied to the figure of the church as Christ's bride, which this author finds presented already in scripture (Genesis 2:24, cited in verse 30). The emphatic **I am saying** indicates that he is offering his interpretation of the Old Testament passage in conscious opposition to others.

6:1-4. *Parents and Children.* These verses expand the parallel section in Colossians 3:20-21 in two respects:

(1) The exhortation to children to obey their parents is grounded in the commandment of Exodus 20:12 and Deuteronomy 5:16. It is reinforced by reference to the **promise** of a long life **on the earth** (adapted from Deuteronomy 5:16).

(2) To the admonition to fathers is added the counsel to bring up their children **in the discipline and instruction of the Lord**. Not only are fathers to be reasonable in what they expect of children. They are also to be constructively concerned for their proper nurture. It is perhaps too much to find reference here to Christian education in the home. But it is noteworthy that the same Greek verb used of Christ's relation to the church, and husband's to his wife ("nourishes," 5:29), is used of a father's responsibility to his children (**bring . . . up**).

6:5-9. *Slaves and Masters.* As in the instances above, the author seeks a religious basis for the obedience and respect which is to characterize the relationship. He neither condemns nor condones the institution of slavery as such (on the question of Christianity and slavery see Introduction to Philemon). Slaves are reminded that they are also **servants**, literally "slaves," **of Christ** and thereby bound to do the will of God, who rewards all good work regardless of who does it (verse 8).

The relatively inconspicuous phrase **whether he is a slave or free** is of extreme significance. The slave is told that before God there is no distinction. Thus the slave's present earthly servitude has been transcended at the point which matters most. Therefore the slave is to obey **in singleness of heart**—that is, **from the heart** and **with fear and trembling**. This latter is a favorite Pauline phrase and has reference to one's consciousness that one's real **Master . . . is in heaven**. Hence the masters too have a responsibility, for they have that same Master in heaven. Their responsibility, also, is to do the **will of God from the heart**. In their case this means to be patient and forbearing with their slaves.

D. STRENGTH IN THE LORD (6:10-20)

The exhortations of Ephesians conclude with words about spiritual strength. Christians are to arm themselves with the strength God supplies and to maintain their vigil of prayer both for their own fight against evil and for the apostolic ministry.

6:10-17. *The Armor of God.* These verses have no parallel in Colossians, but the imagery of a holy war and spiritual armament is found in many ancient religious texts, including the Old Testament, where God is portrayed in armor (Isaiah 59:17). The Christian is now admonished to **put on** the Lord's armor, God's strength, to battle various moral and spiritual foes. The battle is serious, for it is not against human agencies but against the supernatural powers who inhabit the cosmos. The Christian's confidence is made firm in the knowledge that all these are subject to Christ, but the need for moral strength and vigilance is not thereby diminished.

6:13-16. Christians put on God's might as they put on a new nature (4:24), and the various items of spiritual armor are described (cf. I Thessalonians 5:8). **Righteousness** and **truth** are also linked together in Isaiah 11:5. It is paradoxical that the feet of the Christian soldier are to be shod with the **gospel of peace**. But **above all** one must be equipped with the covering **shield** of a protecting **faith**.

6:17. The verb **take** means literally "accept." The **helmet** and **sword** are to be received as the last and decisive pieces of equipment. The helmet symbolizes **salvation**, here regarded, with faith, as providing the Christian protection. This concept of faith and salvation and the presumption that salvation is an accomplished fact distinguish this writer from Paul. Cf. I Thessalonians 5:8, where Paul alters the phrase from Isaiah 59:17 to read the "hope of salvation."

6:18-20. *The Importance of Prayer.* Strength for the Christian's war against wickedness comes, finally, from prayer (cf. Colossians 4:2-4). The call to stay **alert** and persevere is parallel to the Pauline exhortations to sobriety and wakefulness (Romans 13:11; I Thessalonians 5:6), which were directly related to Paul's lively sense that the end of all things was at hand. Here that sense is considerably diminished.

The open door of Colossians 4:3 is interpreted by this author as Paul's **mouth**. Hence the request that there be prayers for the apostle's boldness in proclaiming the **mystery of the gospel** (on the meaning of "mystery" see above on 1:9-10). The **saints** are all other Christians.

V. EPISTOLARY CLOSE (6:21-24)

6:21-22. *The Mission of Tychicus.* These verses follow closely Colossians 4:7-8 and are strong evidence against the hypothesis of common authorship. This author is dependent on Colossians. By the inclusion of this commendation of Tychicus he seeks really to commend his own letter as authentically Pauline. On Tychicus see the comment on Colossians 4:7-8.

6:23-24. *Apostolic Benediction.* Never does Paul cast his benedictions in the third person as the author does here. **Peace** has been one of the fundamental points of this treatise (cf. 2:14). **Love with faith** is almost an echo of Galatians 5:6, but for Paul himself "hope" is a closely related idea (Galatians 5:5; cf. I Corinthians 13:13; I Thessalonians 1:3). **Grace** is at once the beginning and end of an apostolic letter (cf. 1:2).

THE LETTER OF PAUL
TO THE PHILIPPIANS

Leander E. Keck

INTRODUCTION

To the church at Philippi goes the honor of being the first known Christian congregation in what is now Europe. The occasion of its beginning is related in Acts 16:6-40. This account, however, gives no clues for understanding the Letter to the Philippians, since it deals with persons and issues never mentioned in the letter and ignores those which the letter does mention. The interest of the Acts narrative is in Paul. The founding of a church in the city, though implied (Acts 16:40*b*), is never described.

Philippi, a Macedonian city located some ten miles from the Aegean Sea, had been made a Roman colony. The church there appears to have been almost entirely Gentile—note that Jewish sabbath worship took place outside the city and apparently only women attended (Acts 16:13).

Despite the unhappy circumstances in which Paul had to cut short his first visit (Acts 16:39*b*-40) the church took root and became the only congregation that supported his work financially (4:14-16; cf. II Corinthians 11:9). This is another key fact that Acts ignores. Paul stayed in touch with these friends through their gifts, brought by members such as Epaphroditus (2:25-30), and presumably visited them again (cf. Acts 19:21; 20:1-3). All this took place in the decade beginning around A.D. 50.

Place and Date of Composition

It is not clear where and when Paul wrote Philippians. The traditional view is that he did so at Rome near the end of his life, three or more years after his last visit to the church. The author was a prisoner (1:12-13, 17; 2:17, 23), and Paul is known to have been in prison for at least two years at Caesarea (Acts 24:27) and then under house arrest for two years at Rome (Acts 28:16, 30-31). Although Caesarea has been advocated by a few scholars, more have preferred Rome.

The case for Rome rests largely on the references to the "praetorian guard" (1:13) and to "Caesar's household" (4:22). The praetorian guard was an elite military unit established by Augustus as the emperor's bodyguard. The Greek word elsewhere in the New Testament is translated "praetorium" (Mark 15:16; Acts 23:35), meaning a government headquarters building such as existed in many cities of the Roman Empire. "Caesar's household" refers to the official staff—a term used of those in the service of the imperial government both in Rome and throughout the empire. These phrases, then, favor but do not require Rome as the place of writing.

Against both Rome and Caesarea is their remoteness from Macedonia. The references to frequent travel between Philippi and Paul's place of imprisonment in 2:25-30 (see comment) all but exclude Caesarea and cast serious doubt on Rome. Also against both these cities is Paul's promise to visit Philippi on his release (1:26; 2:24).

Shortly before the trip to Jerusalem that resulted in his arrest and imprisonment in Caesarea and Rome, Paul declared that his work in the Aegean area was completed. He planned to go through Rome and open up a new mission field in Spain (Romans 15:22-32; cf. Acts 19:21). Dating the letter after that statement requires assuming that Paul not only abandoned his plans for Spain but decided to go back where he had considered his work was no longer needed.

These comments in the letter point rather to a place near enough to Philippi so that continual contact could be easily maintained and to a time when Paul was actively working in that region. During this period Paul stayed longest in Ephesus (Acts 19) and this city seems the most likely place.

It is true that Acts says nothing of an imprisonment in Ephesus. A riot in the amphitheater is reported (Acts 19:23-41) but no arrest. The silence of Acts, however, should not be taken to mean that what is not reported did not happen. That the Acts account is incomplete can be seen from Paul's own mention of many imprisonments and of having received three times the Roman punishment of beating by rods (II Corinthians 11:23-29).

Paul's statement that he "fought with wild beasts at Ephesus" (I Corinthians 15:32) is doubtless metaphorical—though some have seen it as referring to an actual narrow escape in the arena. Even so it points to serious difficulties in the city. Further probable evidence of trouble in Ephesus is found in Paul's reference to Prisca and Aquila as having "risked their necks for my life" (Romans 16:4). This couple met Paul in Corinth and moved with him to Ephesus (Acts 18:1-2, 18-19, 26). Romans 16 (see comment) is generally regarded as not an original part of Romans and is probably addressed to the church at Ephesus.

Not to be overlooked is the fact that Colossae was near Ephesus. Since both Colossians and Philemon were written in a prison from which Paul was in contact with the Colossian church (which he had not founded), the same imprisonment in Ephesus may be involved. These two letters have likewise been traditionally assigned to the imprisonment at Rome. The question of whether they were written there or at Ephesus is parallel to that regarding Philippians (see Introduction to Philemon).

In sum, then, the case for Rome rests on what we know about Paul's imprisonment from Acts but is undercut by what we may rightly infer from Philippians itself. The case for Ephesus, on the other hand, rests on what we infer from Philippians and other letters but is undercut by the lack of explicit mention in Acts of an imprisonment there. Scholars are therefore divided in their views on this question. The present writer holds the Ephesian theory.

If Philippians was written from Rome, it dates from the end of Paul's career, around 60-62. If it was written from Ephesus, it comes from the midst of Paul's most active period, around 54-56, when he also wrote I and II Corinthians and Galatians (and probably Colossians and Philemon). Relating Philippians to these letters, especially Corinthians, helps explain the content of all the letters. Applying the description of the local situation in 1:12-18 to the church at Ephesus sheds light on Paul's work during this period in his life.

Unity

Though no one today questions seriously whether Paul wrote Philippians there is renewed debate about the composition of the letter. Every careful reader is startled by the sudden change in tone and topic in 3:1-2. Here the flow of thought is ruptured completely, but is apparently resumed at 4:10. Why should Paul interrupt his expression of gratitude with a sarcastic polemic? To this question two kinds of answers have been given.

Those convinced of the unity of Philippians offer psychological theories to explain Paul's abrupt change of mood. For example, there may have been an interval between dictating 3:1 and 3:2 during which he spent a sleepless night or received an unexpected report of difficulty in Philippi which he felt must be treated immediately. Some have minimized the break by stressing the underlying theological continuity—a line of reasoning that would prove the same man wrote chapters 2 and 3 but does not prove that he wrote them in the same letter.

The second type of answer comes from those who seek a literary solution and therefore see here an editorial joining of two or three separate letters or parts of letters. On this hypothesis various attempts have been made recently to divide Philippians into its constituent parts.

All these agree that a second letter begins with 3:2 (or 3:1*b*) but do not agree on where it ends or on whether it is the only other letter. Most who see a third letter find it in 4:10-20, which they view as Paul's thank-you note written immediately after Epaphroditus' arrival with a gift of money from the Philippian church (2:25-26). But 4:10-20 follows naturally after 2:25-30 and before 4:21-23.

Probably there were only two letters, reconstructed as follows:

Letter A, 1:1–2:30; 4:10-23;

Letter B, 3:2–4:9. (3:1 may be an editorial splice; no one really knows what to make of it, including those who believe there is only one letter).

Letter A is virtually complete. It was occasioned by the return of Epaphroditus to Philippi following recovery from his illness. It contains Paul's interpretation of the partnership symbolized by the gift he had brought.

We have only the latter part of Letter B. It was occasioned by an invasion of Paul's churches by Christian teachers who were undermining his interpretation of the gospel (see below on 3:2–4:1). Because this problem grew much more serious in Corinth, what Paul wrote in II Corinthians 11–12 helps to explain letter B, which was evidently written during the same period from Ephesus (or Corinth?). Letter A probably came from Ephesus.

I. GREETING (1:1-2)

In accord with current style the letter identifies first its writers, then those addressed, whom it greets with a wish of **grace** and **peace**.

1:1a. The writers call themselves **servants** (literally "slaves") of Christ, for this is the status implied in having a **Lord** (literally "master"). Usually Paul introduces himself with the more authoritative title "apostle" (cf. I and II Corinthians, Galatians, Colossians). **Timothy**, an associate of Paul's who was with him when the Philippian church was founded (Acts 16), is named as a courtesy, but Paul is obviously the sole author of the letter (cf. verse 3).

1:1*b.* Paul designates his readers as residents of **Philippi** and **saints** (literally "holy") **in Christ Jesus**. In the New Testament "saint" refers, not to the elite Christian, but to the church member. All Christians are saints, not because they are especially good, but because the Holy Spirit, whose work is to make life holy, is with them.

Bishops (literally "overseers") **and deacons** (literally "servers") has long caused difficulty, for this is the only uncontested letter from Paul which mentions these offices in church administration. Romans 12 and I Corinthians 12 assume that one's role of leadership is determined by one's gifts, understood as gifts of the Spirit, not by the office one may hold. Some have therefore portrayed early Christianity as having almost no structured order. The Dead Sea Scrolls have caused the evidence to be reexamined, however, because the community described in them had an "overseer." On the other hand Paul's use of the words hardly proves an early Christian hierarchy. They must be taken simply in the sense of "overseers and helpers." (Or is this detail added by the compiler to update the letter?) Precisely what the deacons did is not clear in any case.

II. PARTNERSHIP IN THE GOSPEL (1:3–2:30)

In this section, the bulk of the letter, Paul thanks his friends for their support and uses the opportunity to illumine what such partnership in the gospel means. After the customary thanksgiving paragraph he interprets his own current experience. He asks the readers to live worthily of the gospel, as he himself has, and suggests the standards of this mode of life which are appropriate to their partnership.

He then takes up the immediate situation facing them, which is the work of his associates (2:19-30). If Philippians is a single letter, then at 2:30 the thought is interrupted by chapter 3 and is continued at 4:10. If, on the other hand, Philippians is composite, mentioning Epaphroditus' work at 2:30 prompts Paul to speak explicitly of the readers' generosity (4:10-20), after which he bids them farewell.

A. The Thanksgiving (1:3-11)

A standard item in all of Paul's letters—and in those written in his name—is the paragraph of thanksgiving. This sets the direction and tone of the letter as a whole by speaking of both readers and authors in ways that are appropriate to the immediate occasion. This thanksgiving quickly moves to a discussion of the basis for Paul's attitude and ends with a prayer for the life of the church. Throughout, the double emphasis on Paul and the readers is maintained.

1:3-5. *Gratitude for Partnership.* The thanksgiving begins by emphasizing the constancy of Paul's gratitude. **All** and **always** should not be pressed, since they are stylistic elements in a stylized paragraph and are found regularly in statements of prayer. It is not a matter of style, however, for Paul to mention **joy**, for this is a frequent note in the letter.

More problematical is **your partnership in the gospel**, which is perfectly ambiguous. In Greek as in English it connotes both fellowship and financial sharing in a business enterprise. Scholarly opinion has been divided on whether Paul alludes here to the money brought from Philippi by Epaphroditus. He may be speaking of a whole series of gifts from the Philippian church—at least four if we read 4:15-16 together with 2:25-30 and II Corinthians 11:7-9. He interprets these gifts, not as deeds of charity for a needy apostle, but as tokens of participation in the gospel enterprise.

In this light the question arises whether verse 3 should also be translated to reveal the same train of thought. The second **my** here is not found in the Greek, which again is perfectly ambiguous. It can mean either **I thank my God in all . . . remembrance of you** or "I thank my God for all your remembrance." This latter sense gives the whole paragraph—and the whole of Letter A (see

Introduction)—a coherence grounded in a concrete historical situation. This was the Philippian's partnership reaching from the beginning of Paul's European mission until the present.

1:6-8. *Reasons for Gratitude.* Paul shifts to the rationale behind his thankfulness. He mentions first his confidence that God will finish his work. This is a clear expression of the early Christian tension between, on the one hand, the Christian life as inaugurated by Christ's resurrection and appropriated by faith and, on the other hand, the consummation of this salvation. This tension between the "already" and the "not yet" is expressed by the phrases **the first day**—the day the Philippians first believed in Christ—and **the day of Jesus Christ**—that is, the day of consummation (see comment on II Thessalonians 2:2).

Verse 7 gives another reason for Paul's gratitude. The readers remain in his **heart** (another ambiguity, which can mean that he remains in their hearts) and are **partakers** (literally "co-partners"; see above on verses 3-5) throughout his recent experience of **imprisonment** and **defense and confirmation of the gospel**. Precisely what Paul has been undergoing is not clear (cf. verses 12-14). Verse 8 expresses Paul's deep desire to be with the Philippian church again.

1:9-11. *A Prayer for the Readers.* Paul prays that his readers may have increased **love** disciplined by **knowledge** and **discernment**, so that they can **approve what is excellent**—better translated "find out what is important." Their moral achievement will be vindicated at the end. All this is for God's **glory**.

This paragraph of thanksgiving has opened up themes basic to the whole letter: Paul's situation, the support of the Philippian church, the need for righteousness among Christians—all set against the horizon of the **day of Christ**, which keeps things in perspective.

B. PAUL'S EXPERIENCE INTERPRETED (1:12-26)

Having emphasized partnership in the gospel, Paul now shares with his readers the meaning of his recent life. The section is framed by the key term translated **advance** at the beginning and **progress** at the end. The first speaks of the advance of the **gospel** by means of Paul's experience. The second refers to the readers' progress and is a transition to the next topic.

The passage asks how the gospel can advance when its representatives are in prison or divided. Has not the end of Paul's freedom ended the advance of the gospel and arrested the progress of his converts? To deal with this Paul speaks first of his own bondage (verses 12-17; here **my imprisonment**, literally "bonds," appears three times). Then, after a transitional comment in verse 18, he speaks of his response to the imprisonment.

1:12-17. *The Effect of Paul's Imprisonment.* Paul's bondage, he says, has not bound the gospel. In fact it has advanced it on two fronts: government personnel understand his imprisonment and other Christians have more boldness now.

1:13. On **praetorian guard** see the Introduction. This verse does not mean simply that the civil servants and military persons have information about Paul the prisoner. Rather it means that they learn how Paul regards his situation—literally that his "bonds become manifest in Christ." They have come to know that he is Christ's captive whether he is Rome's prisoner or not.

1:14-17. The impact of Paul's fate on the **brethren**—the local Christians—is even more fascinating, for his phrases here imply more than they say. The usual interpretation of verse 14 is that the example of Paul's fortitude has kindled the courage of the members of the church in the city. Such may have occurred. But this meaning does not fit what Paul goes on to say in verses 15-17, which should be part of the same paragraph.

In these verses we are plunged into the middle of a discussion of preachers' motives. Paul is not opposing a teaching but is commenting on teachers—not what they say but why, and the fact that they preach at all. The situation described has arisen **because of my imprisonment.** Wherever he was imprisoned, Paul's arrest suddenly has thrown the full responsibility of leadership on others who respond in differing ways. In some of them **envy and rivalry** have developed.

The most intriguing detail is verse 17*b*. Is Paul accusing ambitious church members of being **bold** in their preaching with the aim of goading the police into keeping him out of circulation while they seize places of leadership? Whatever the precise circumstances, it is clear that Paul is discussing motives, not as a general problem of Christian ethics, but as part of a power struggle in the church (cf. 2:21) which goes on behind the preaching of the gospel.

1:18. *The One Important Consideration.* Paul's attitude toward all this surprises those whose image of him is based largely on Galatians and II Corinthians. Instead of a torrent of invectives he expresses a "concerned indifference." His sole concern is that Christ be made known, whatever the motive might be.

Does Paul speak this way because his magnanimity enables him to rise above personal hurt, or because he has learned patience through being in prison, or because he has mellowed with the passing years, or because imprisonment has clarified for him what is important, or because he believes that the nearness of the Day of Christ demands concentration on spreading the gospel? All of these possibilities have been suggested. Whatever the reason, the fact that Christ is proclaimed causes Paul to rejoice in the midst of personal bondage and disappointment. God's word is not dependent on his own freedom any more than it is dependent on the motives of the preachers. Still, a deeper reason for Paul's surprising tolerance appears in the next paragraph.

1:19-26. *Paul's Response in His Imprisonment.* Quoting Job 13:16*a* Paul says he is confident of his **deliverance**—a word which can mean either "release" or "salvation." Though some commentators prefer a purely religious meaning, it is probable that Paul is saying he expects to be released from prison (cf. verses 25-26). Yet he implies by the ambiguity what he states explicitly in verses 20-24. His confidence is based on his faith in intercessory prayer. He hopes, however, that both his **life** and his **death** will have integrity so that **Christ will be honored** through him regardless of what happens.

1:21-24. How seriously Paul means this is shown here. When Paul says **to live in Christ** he affirms that his whole existence is determined and controlled by Christ. In this light **to die** can only bring gain, not loss. Death does not destroy this relationship but leads to its consummation. Therefore he does not know whether he prefers life with **labor** or death with gain. His duty, however, is to live for the sake of the church. Hence he will not try merely to stay alive, nor will he try to die as a glorious martyr in order to secure his reputation. This passage discloses the mind of Paul as few do. It reveals a man so dominated by his labor and his Lord that in a life-and-death situation he scarcely knows which alternative is to be preferred.

1:23*b*-24. The chief problem with the passage lies between the lines. Paul assumes his death will result in his departure from the **flesh** and his entry into the presence of the Lord. The problem arises from the fact that in I Corinthians 15 and I Thessalonians 4 Paul insists on a resurrection of the dead. If at death one goes immediately to the Lord, why is a future resurrection necessary?

No completely satisfactory solution has been found in Paul's writings. Many have speculated about his thinking on an "intermediate stage" between death and resurrection. Others have seen Paul's thought developing in another direction: immediate entry to full salvation. Probably we should recognize that there were two streams of thought on the subject of life after death. How Paul related them (if indeed he did) is simply not clear (see comment on I Thessalonians 4:13-18).

1:25-26. Paul restates his confidence that he will not only be released but see the Philippians again. He views his future relation to the church dialectically: because of **his** return they should **glory** (literally "boast") **in Christ**. This attitude is consistent with that of I Corinthians 1:10-31 and II Corinthians 11:16–12:10. In this way Paul's whole existence will have integrity appropriate to the gospel, for whether he is released or imprisoned, whether he lives or dies, what happens to him will promote the gospel (cf. verse 12). The entire passage is a commentary on **for me to live is Christ**.

C. The Readers' Partnership Interpreted
(1:27–2:18)

Paul now turns to the other side of the partnership in the gospel and interprets the life of the Philippians. The passage is carefully structured. 1:27-30 states the theme, a way of life worthy of the gospel. 2:1-16 develops this with particular emphasis on humility and harmony in the church. 2:17-18 returns to the theme of Paul's possible death.

1:27-30. *Life Worthy of the Gospel.* This is an appeal for a life of integrity in time of difficulty. Having expressed his hope of seeing the Philippian church again, Paul insists that its members develop a **worthy** life, whether or not he comes. He pleads for integrity based on the **gospel**, not on his presence. He asks them to maintain their unified stability and exertion for the gospel.

Faith of the gospel probably means faith which the gospel elicits. Paul recognizes that this faith, this trust, is not to be taken for granted, especially in duress, but must be worked for, struggled for.

1:28. If the Philippians unite in such a struggle they will not be **frightened** by **opponents**. Who these may have been is unknown. This is not yet a martyr situation, for the suffering has not led to death. If the Philippians achieve the sort of stance Paul counsels, it will be an **omen** of the situation of the Christian in the world—**salvation** for the Christian, **destruction** for the opposition. Paul does not develop the idea of destruction (see comment on II Thessalonians 1:7*b*-10). He is quick to add that this ultimate working out of things is not the achievement of the Philippians but the work of God.

1:29-30. One underlying rationale for Paul's attitude is the necessity and the nature of suffering. It does not undermine faith, he holds, nor is it an absurdity that defies theological insight. Instead it is a natural ingredient of Christian life itself. It

345

is in fact **granted**—bestowed as a gift or a privilege. **For the sake of Christ**, however, is an absolutely necessary qualification. Not every pain Christians endure falls within the scope of Paul's remarks, but only suffering in which Christ's cause is involved. Paul is not glorifying suffering as if he were a masochist, but is interpreting the daily meaning of being made participants in the grace of Christ, which centers in the cross.

The second underlying point is that Paul and the Philippians are involved in precisely the **same conflict**, though they are not in the same place or going through the same experiences. Theologically speaking, all Christians who stand for the gospel against those forces that oppose it are in the same struggle. This unity of the church transcends regional and theological differences, just as it runs deeper than organizational unifications.

2:1-18. *Christian Unity.* Paul takes up in detail the kind of unity he has called for. Verses 1-4 spell out the attitudes he sees as appropriate to the gospel. Verses 5-11 highlight this gospel, using an early Christian hymn, while verses 12-13 draw the basic mandate from it. Verses 14-18 return to the situation of the readers and of Paul, and end with the summons to rejoice in the midst of difficulty. A proper understanding of 2:1-18 requires seeing it as a whole and in its setting, as well as its details.

2:1-4. *A Shared Mind-Set.* Carrying forward the concern for unity (1:27) Paul writes a striking sentence. In the Greek the rhetorical effect of the fourfold conditional clause of verse 1 is enhanced by the repetition of **if** with every **any**. The resounding "Indeed there is!" which Paul assumes in response to each "if" sets the stage for the central imperative: Set your minds on the same thing.

Being of the same mind is too weak a translation for the verb Paul uses. It denotes more than mere thinking or feeling in general. It means to center one's thinking on something and to steer one's actions by this mind-set. It is a key word in this passage. Thus Paul says that if the four items of verse 1 are true, the Philippians are to set their minds and to guide their lives by the same thing, to have **the same love**. The opposite of this is stated in verse 3. Verse 4 returns to the norm Paul is developing: concern for one another. The partnership in the gospel (1:5) and in grace (1:7) means partnership not only with Paul but with one another.

Having seen where Paul takes the line of thought we can return to the four axioms of verse 1 and their significance for the whole appeal. Paul's basic question is whether there are any norms or goals in Christ for the daily life of Christians. Hence he mentions first **encouragement in Christ**. The word means both comfort and admonition or exhortation. The accent is not on the psychological state of courage but on the basis of action provided in Christ.

In Christ is to be understood with all four items, not merely with the first. Thus in Christ are found sharing in the **incentive of love**, sharing in the reality of **the Spirit**, and **sympathy**. Paul can then ask that his **joy** be made full by his readers' setting their minds on the same thing.

2:5. *A Mind-Set in Christ.* This single mind-set means, not conformity in thought, but a concentration on the same single norm. That this norm is Christ himself is the point of verses 5-11.

Here, however, we face a lack of clarity in the letter. Because **have this mind** refers to what has already been said (repeating the same "mind-set" verb of verse 2) what follows carries the same theme forward. This is an important thread for the scope of the whole passage. Translators of verse 5*b* must reveal their interpretation, for there is no verb between **which** and **in Christ Jesus** in the Greek text.

The Revised Standard Version supplies **is yours**. The New English Bible sidesteps the question with "Let your bearing towards one another rise out of your life in Christ Jesus," but a footnote has "which was also found in Christ Jesus." The Moffatt translation reads "Treat one another with the same spirit as you experience in Christ Jesus." Beare's commentary suggests "Let this be the disposition that governs in your common life, as is fitting in Christ Jesus." The King James Version has "Let this mind be in you, which was also in Christ Jesus." This is the poorest of all these efforts, for the point is not to have the same mind that Christ had, not to emulate Christ's thinking or to imitate his acts, but to set the common mind of the church ("you" is plural; cf. the Revised Standard Version **yourselves**) on what one thinks in Christ.

Probably Paul means for his main verb to be understood also with "in Christ Jesus." Thus we may paraphrase: Think among yourselves what you think in Christ—that is, think of each other the way you think about Christ: regard each other from the same perspective. This interpretation agrees with II Corinthians 5:16-17: "We regard no one from a human point of view [literally "according to the flesh"]; even though we once regarded Christ from a human point of view, we regard him thus no longer." Whatever the precise nuance, the major point is clear. The readers are to act in the light of what and how they think about Christ. The function of verses 6-11 is to spell out this way of regarding Christ.

2:6-11. *An Early Christian Hymn.* This passage could hardly have been composed by Paul, for some of its terminology is not Pauline and Paul's characteristic ideas are missing. Its phrases fall into verse patterns, and it is doubtless a hymn of the early church. In the nineteenth century some thought that an editor added the hymn. Now scholarly opinion agrees that Paul quoted it and that the hymn is thus older than the letter.

Whether the hymn has two or three parts is not altogether clear. Most prefer to see it in two parts divided by the **therefore** in verse 9. Adapting the Revised Standard Version we get the following structure:

> [Who] though he was in the form of God
> Did not count it robbery
> To be equal with God

> But emptied himself,
> Taking the form of a servant,
> Coming into existence in the likeness of men;

> And being found in human form

He humbled himself
And became obedient to the point of death
   [even death on a cross].

Therefore God has highly exalted him
And bestowed on him the name
Which is above every name,

That at Jesus' name
Every knee should bow—
In heaven and on earth and under the earth—

And every tongue confess
"Jesus Christ is Lord"
To the glory of God the Father.

2:6-8. The first half of the hymn begins with God and descends to the low point, **death**. Each of its three active verbs focuses on a moment in the deathward movement of obedience.

2:6. The "story" begins with **equality with God**, prior to existence in time-space. Existing **in the form of God** means having divine prerogatives, being God's virtual equal. The word translated **to be grasped** is ambiguous. It can mean either "to be held onto" or "to be achieved by grasping." In the latter sense some have seen reference here to Christ's not acting as Adam did, or as the angels who were tempted into insurrection. But the first meaning, that Christ had equality but did not insist on keeping it, seems much more likely. All attention is concentrated on the free surrender of divine authority. Nothing is said about Christ's prior reflecting on this course of action.

2:7. The second verb, **emptied**, is crucial. The two phrases help interpret its meaning. "Empty" here means to take the status of a **servant** (literally "slave") and come into existence as a human. This whole complex of phrases speaks of the incarnation (literally "enfleshment," a word derived from John 1:14 but never actually used in the New Testament). The heart of the matter is the change of roles from divine authority to slave status, from the highest thinkable role to the lowest known.

"Emptied" must be understood metaphorically, not meta-physically. It is a poetic way of celebrating the change of status, not a way of talking about the discarding of divine substances or essences (such ideas may lie *behind* the hymn but are not its concern). The hymn makes precisely the same point as II Corinthians 8:9.

In **servant** some have seen a reference to the suffering servant of Isaiah 53, which Christians early regarded as a description of Jesus' passion. This intepretation is improbable, for the hymn (at least in the first half) uses terms which are generally more at home in Greek than in Old Testament thought.

A better clue to what "servant" means is Galatians 4:3, where human existence is described as slavery to "the elemental spirits of the universe"—the invisible hostile powers which were believed to inhabit planets and to control the destinies of human beings. What the hymn celebrates, therefore, is the movement of Christ from sovereignty over the cosmos to slavery within it.

The next phrase deals with this movement also. **Being born** is an overly free translation. Jesus' birth is not spoken of at all and can be read into the text only by combining it with the Christmas stories. The verb actually means "come to pass" or "happen." The one who pre-existed "came to pass" as a human; he who "is" (as God's equal) "happened"!

The **likeness of men** is a way of saying that this one shared the status of humanity. It falls short of saying he became "just another man," or that "the Word became flesh" (John 1:14; cf. Romans 5:14; 8:3). The point is that he who was equal with God now became equal with humanity. The language is hymnic and should not be pressed to mean that the Son of God did not become a real human but only like a human. Such literalism, advocated by some in the second century, denied the reality of the incarnation and was rejected as heresy, for it turned the intent of the phrase upside down. The point is that God's Son shared the human plight, not that he became a "reasonable facsimile" of a human being.

2:8. The third verb, **humbled**, speaks of self-humbling as the shape of obedience, obedience to the point of **death**. The phrase

350

even death on a cross is apparently Paul's own addition, for it not only disturbs the symmetry of the lines but specifies the particularly degrading character of Christ's death with the typical terminology of Paul. In the self-humbling we should see the sweep of Jesus' life as a whole, not particular incidents in it. It is not clear who is being obeyed here—the cosmic powers or God. Perhaps it is enough to say that he acted as one who was obedient rather than as one who called for obedience to himself, thus taking also this line as an expression of the change of roles.

The first half of the hymn celebrates the movement of the preexistent one (he **was** before he **became**) from the height of authority to the depth of human subjection. "Pre-existence" is a technical category from the ancient philosophical-theological tradition. It was developed in order to be able to speak of a being who "exists" apart from created time-space and prior to entry into it. This conception is assumed by the hymn.

2:9-11. The second half of the hymn begins at this low point of self-humiliation. But instead of reversing the downward movement in stages, it celebrates the one dramatic act of God—the subject of all action in this half. God **highly exalted him** ("raised him to the heights," New English Bible) **and bestowed on him the name** above all names. These two verbs are two aspects of the same act. The self-humbling is answered by the exaltation by God, and the role of slave is answered by the role of master.

The **name** is **Lord** (literally "master"). The point is the same as in I Timothy 3:16 and Hebrews 1:3. "Lord" here means sovereign over the entire cosmos, as the quotations in verses 10 and 11 from Isaiah 45:23 make clear. The entire cosmic power structure under whose authority Christ humbled himself now confesses that he is Lord.

This exaltation is the consequence of the resurrection, though it is not clear whether this means a logical consequence not yet actualized or what has already occurred as a part of the resurrection itself. Paul himself seems to hold the latter view (cf. I Corinthians 15:20-28). But since Paul is quoting a hymn written by someone else, we should be cautious in interpreting this line.

The entire act of God is for God's own glory, for the sake of God's reputation. God's status is vindicated by this act which establishes decisively sovereignty over all cosmic powers. Here there is no cosmic battle, no Armageddon. God's victory over cosmic hostility which tyrannized humanity and taunted God is achieved solely by the resurrection of Jesus, which made him Lord. This triumph is what the hymn celebrates.

Having analyzed the hymn, we may make several overall observations. It has been argued that the hymn comes from the Palestinian church and that its intellectual setting is Jewish. Yet it is increasingly clear that the first stanza at least is really at home in the early Hellenistic church—at Antioch, for example. It draws on the Palestinian, Christian, and Old Testament tradition, of course, but the basic scheme of a divine being who descends to earth and death to save humanity is a Hellenistic pattern. Moreover, the key phrases of the first part of the hymn simply will not translate back into Aramaic.

The purpose of the hymn is not to outline the life of Jesus for Christians to imitate. The movement of the hymn begins with equality with God—where no one else may begin. Paul uses the hymn to remind his readers of the starting point of their own thinking and acting, as verses 12-13 show. With minds set on such an act of God's Son, Paul implies, you are to act out your partnership in relation to one another.

Since this is a hymn, we must not read it as if it were a paragraph in systematic theology. Hymns celebrate emphases; they do not analyze. This one holds before the readers the whole sweep of the Christ event, which begins and ends beyond time-space. Therefore it is clearly as mythological as it is historical, for the historical life of Jesus is only one phase in this total event. Thus the hymn poses more theological questions than it answers. It is not designed to analyze Christ's person but to celebrate and proclaim what God's Son has done.

Because it is a hymn it was sung by congregations before it was used in Paul's exhortation. By singing this hymn Christians celebrated also their involvement in the Christ event, their being grasped by this movement. Therefore the hymn can become the basis of an appeal by Paul. Here worship becomes the basis of action, and praise a motive for ethics. Paul is saying: Act in accord with your praise.

The hymn is nevertheless theological even if it is not a piece of systematic theology. It assumes that salvation depends on this invasion of the world's tyrannies. For the hymn the human situation is not ignorance or transgression but bondage epitomized and climaxed by death. Redemption here requires dealing with these tyrannies, which is precisely what the hymn celebrates as having happened.

2:12-13. *Application of the Hymn.* The immediate, ethical mandate from the hymn is stated dialectically: **Work out your own salvation** because **God is at work in you.** Verse 12*a* picks up the theme of 1:27, showing that 1:27–2:18 must be seen as a whole. The obedience to which Paul refers may be either to himself as founder of the church and pastor in absentia or to the Lord. Actually Paul would not make a sharp distinction, as I Corinthians 11:1 shows. At the same time **fear and trembling** is to characterize their attitudes because this is appropriate to the fact that God is at work. Faith does not exclude such fear but actually causes it. Being obedient to the God whose act is celebrated in the hymn makes it impossible to take God's work for granted.

The mandate to work out one's own salvation must not be understood as meaning: "Devise a way to save yourselves as Christ saved himself," but rather: "Bring to pass your own salvation; make real in your life this lordship of the obedient one." This can be done only because God is at work generating the will and granting the strength to bring it to pass.

This is not an easy cooperation, as if Paul were saying, "God will help you with your problems; do what you can and he will do the rest." Rather God's participation is throughout, from the heart's resolve to the final consummation. Those who know that God is at work in them, bringing to pass in their lives the salvation grounded in the event celebrated in the hymn, know that their very life is a hint, a signpost of salvation to come—as 1:28 has already said.

2:14-18. *Specific Applications.* The above is now applied to the specific situation of the readers and of Paul. To begin with, they are to avoid **grumbling**. They must strive to be **innocent**, persons of integrity in a culture regarded as **crooked and perverse** (phraseology adapted from Deuteronomy 32:5). Paul calls not only for discontinuity with this culture but also for a creative effort to redeem it (verse 16). This is an important reminder that Paul's perspective is the life of the church in the world for the sake of the world. Verse 16*b* shows that Paul has something at stake in the fate of the church at Philippi. If this congregation works out its salvation, his labor will not have been for nothing.

2:17. In turn the Philippians have something at stake in Paul's integrity, even in his death. Without speaking of it explicitly, Paul has returned to the theme of partnership in the gospel. The discussion ends with a note of rejoicing, an attitude possible for those who sing the hymn in the midst of a culture not yet redeemed. With such rejoicing the Philippians will set their minds on the one thing, the event of Christ. This will free them from pettiness. They will be aware that they have been grasped by the grace of God in the world.

D. THE WORK OF TIMOTHY AND EPAPHRODITUS
(2:19-30)

2:19-24. *Paul's Plans for Timothy.* At this point Paul turns to his immediate relations to his readers. He begins with his plan to send Timothy for the express purpose of learning more precisely the state of affairs in the Philippian church. Yet the next verse suggests Paul's real aim: Timothy is to act in Paul's place as pastor and guide. Paul has **no one** else whom he can send who will be as concerned for the church. Note that the **interests** of Jesus Christ and the **welfare** of the church are two ways of saying virtually the same thing—a point more obvious in the Greek.

Verse 22 comments on Timothy's work with Paul. Acts 16:1-3

reports the circumstances in which Timothy joined Paul. Verses 23-24 return to the plan for sending Timothy and reveal that Paul's fate is still undecided, though he fully expects (**trust in the Lord** expresses confidence rather than mere submission to the divine will) to go to Philippi soon. This expectation offers an important clue to where the letter was written (see Introduction).

2:25-30. *Paul's Plans for Epaphroditus.* Paul now turns to Epaphroditus, who apparently is about to set out for Philippi, taking the letter. Sometime earlier he brought money from the Philippian church to Paul (4:18) and remained long enough to become **ill, near to death** (verse 27). The Philippians **heard** of his illness and were disturbed. Epaphroditus in turn learned of their anxiety and was **distressed**, and probably wanted to return as soon as possible. This return is the immediate occasion of the letter.

Timothy is to follow **soon** (verse 19); then Paul himself will come (verse 24). All this communication between Paul and the Philippians indicates that Paul's place of imprisonment was fairly near Philippi (see Introduction). Paul speaks highly of Epaphroditus. He is a **brother and fellow worker and fellow soldier** to Paul and in the church a **minister** and **your messenger.** This last word is literally "apostle"—an indication that for Paul the term was not yet so technical as it became later (cf. Romans 16:7). If we knew the circumstances of Epaphroditus' **risking his life** to carry out his mission, we could doubtless settle many questions concerning Paul's imprisonment. (For the relation of 2:30 to 4:10-20 see comment on 1:3–2:30.)

III. TRUSTING RELIGION OR TRUSTING CHRIST
(3:1–4:1)

Chapter 3 interrupts the flow of thought and changes the mood. All interpreters recognize this, and many are convinced that Philippians incorporates two or more separate letters of Paul (see Introduction). If this is true, Letter B begins with either 3:1*b* or 3:2 (see below on 3:1) and continues at least through 4:1 and probably farther. In this passage Paul's pastoral concern is expressed in a polemic against positions which he considers as alternatives to Christianity—even though they may be put forward in the name of Christ.

Against whom is this polemic addressed? Clearly verses 2-11 are attacking Jews and verses 17-21 oppose libertines. Most commentators, unable to reconcile these descriptions, have assumed there must be two different groups, the second being Gentiles belonging to some sort of religious movement with libertine ethics. Many have taken verse 3 to indicate that the Jews were non-Christian but have judged from Paul's distress in verse 18 that the Gentiles must be Christians.

What is not obvious, however, is which of these two groups Paul has in mind in verses 12-16. More important, nowhere does he give any indication of turning from one group to another. The structure of the passage gives no clear evidence of two groups. It reads more naturally as a unified polemic against a single, though complex, front.

Those who see a single group, however, do not agree on its identity. Some see it as made up of Judaizers—Christian Jews who demanded that all Christians become practicing Jews in order to be the Messiah's people (see Introduction to Galatians and comment on Acts 15). A serious flaw in this theory is that such ardent proponents of the Jewish law could scarcely be described as libertines.

Others maintain that the polemic is aimed throughout at non-Christian Jews and reflects bitter tensions that had already developed between church and synagogue. But the evidence is that there were virtually no Jews in Philippi (see Introduction). Adopting this view would require us to assume that Letter B was addressed to some other city—which is not impossible, for there is no specific reference to the Philippian church or to Paul's imprisonment in chapter 3. It is questionable, however, whether verses 17-21 would describe loyal members of the synagogue.

A third view seems more probable. It is that the opponents

Paul is writing about were gnosticized Jews who had become Christians—part of the same movement that penetrated his churches in Corinth and Asia Minor (see Introductions to Corinthians, Galatians, Colossians). Gnosticism, as known from its serious threat to the church in the second century, was a syncretistic philosophy which viewed all matter as evil. Gnostics thus saw the soul as suffering imprisonment in the body—a plight from which it could be saved only through knowledge (Greek *gnosis*) of the self. The ethics resulting from this view of the body tended either toward ascetic efforts to control the imprisoning body or toward libertine excesses intended to demonstrate that the body was really irrelevant to a saved soul. In this chapter Paul may have in mind both these ethical consequences. He would oppose them both on the basis of God's grace. Every view about Paul's opponents is a guess, of course, since he did not need to describe them to his readers.

The passage consists of the statement of the theme in verses 2-4*a*, its exposition in verses 4*b*-16, and its application in verses 17-21. There is a summary exhortation in 4:1 which also introduces the next paragraph. In the middle of the exposition stands an important autobiographical passage (verses 4*b*-14) in which Paul uses himself as an example to be imitated (verse 17).

3:1. This verse is problematical, for it is not clear whether it goes with chapter 2 or 3—or whether verse 1*a* goes with one and verse 1*b* with the other. No completely satisfactory solution has been proposed. It is probably at least in part an editor's work.

Most of those who defend the unity of Philippians concede that **the same things** cannot refer to anything now in chapters 1–2 and therefore apply it to chapter 3. If we recognize, however, that part of a second letter has been joined on at this point (see Introduction), the phrase can more naturally be understood as referring to what has been lost or omitted from Letter B.

3:2-4*b*. *Warning Against False Teaching.* Three commands are followed by a thematic statement. Paul's warning is put in terms of bitter sarcasm. If we assume a single group of opponents, all three terms refer to the same group. **Dogs** is a

common epithet of contempt as in our use of "bitch."
Evil-workers is so like "deceitful workmen" in II Corinthians
11:13 as to suggest that Paul is attacking the same group who
infiltrated the Corinthian church. This is an important clue for
identifying them as Jewish Christians with gnostic theology.
Paul sees them as undermining the integrity of the gospel as a
whole, not just his own ideas about it, as II Corinthians 11:3-5
shows.

Those who mutilate the flesh paraphrases a Greek word that
puns on "circumcision." Paul uses "circumcision" to speak
metaphorically of the Christian's refusal to live "according to the
flesh" (cf. Romans 8). Therefore he regards those Christians who
require the physical rite as mere mutilators. The readers are to
"look out for the mutilators," Paul says, because **we are the
circumcision** (the Revised Standard Version supplies **true** to
make the point after the paraphrase).

For Paul literal circumcision is only an operation on the body.
Those who insist that it be done are putting **confidence in the
flesh** and in what one does with it. For Paul real circumcision
means repudiating all reliance on the flesh categorically and
serving God by the Spirit (see the Revised Standard Version
footnote) and glorying only in Christ. The opponents required
circumcision as a sign of literal repudiation of the flesh, of fleshly
existence as such. Paul, however, insists that despite their
ideology the fact that they require circumcision at all shows that
they trust in a fleshly rite. If flesh were really repudiated, all
trust in the meaning of fleshly operations would fall away. Paul
centers the issue on where one places trust, not on the problem
of flesh itself.

Paul's Own Life as an Illustration. This is now spelled out.
Verse 4a provides the link by pointing out that Paul himself has
achieved this transition. Verses 4b-6 undergird this by showing
that Paul has a perfect score with regard to everything that
physical circumcision can mean: the rite itself, family background,
participation in the party zealous for the law, zeal in uprooting the
new church which seemed to threaten Judaism, righteousness
insofar as this could be measured by what was required.

These verses have no place for the modern view that before his conversion Paul was a Jew who had an uneasy conscience over the stoning of Stephen and a growing dissatisfaction with his own religion. Rather Paul insists that he was a model Jew. All this, he says, was a putting of his confidence in the flesh, in that which he could measure. Everything that the opponents are requiring of Christians he had achieved already before he became a Christian. He can trump anyone's claim (cf. II Corinthians 11:21b-22).

3:7-11. *Revolution in Values.* Paul now explains what his conversion to Christ meant for this entire way of handling one's relation to God. Verse 7 states the heart of it. The point is that what was **gain** for him suddenly turned into **loss.** Paul does not say that it was lost; he says it was loss. To put it commercially, as Paul does, his profits were discovered to be debts; his money was transformed into IOU's. The long sentence that follows in verses 8-11 amplifies this.

3:8. Twice in this verse Paul uses the verb **count.** This means that both phrases make the same point, counting gain as loss and counting it as trash or garbage (**refuse** is too circumspect). For the sake of Christ all standards have been turned upside down, and all religious effort is utterly useless if one is in Christ. Paul renounces his achievements for the sake of **knowing Christ**—a phrase doubtless designed to take the point away from his opponents, who claim to have true knowledge of what Christ means. Paul claims not only to be the true circumcision precisely by this revaluation of the circumcision rite but also to have the true knowledge as well.

3:9. Likewise, precisely because he has the knowledge and has turned his back on literal circumcision as a significant rite, Paul insists that it is not the opponents but he who is **found in him.** In his explanation of what he means by being in Christ the two modes of Paul's understanding of Christian salvation come together:

(1) the legal (humans are pronounced to be in right relation to God because they trust Christ);

(2) the mystical (the believer is in Christ and Christ is in the believer).

For Paul, being in Christ means two things:

(1) standing before God on the basis, not of the **law**, but of **faith** only, a standing granted by God because of this faith-trust (the legal mode);

(2) knowing Christ, the **power of his resurrection** and partnership in **his sufferings** (the mystical mode, verses 10-11). This is a participative knowing, not simply knowing facts—just as "I know what war is" does not mean, "I have information about war." Likewise, being a partner with Christ's sufferings means having one's existence shaped by Christ's death in order to reach the resurrection life.

Righteousness—a basic theme of Romans 1–8—is a key word in this highly compressed statement. Paul uses it in the sense, not of goodness, but of rectitude. Righteousness is a right relation to God. The issue turns on the basis on which one has such a right relation: doing what is required by the law (Paul's Bible, but in a deeper sense the will of God in it) or having faith in Christ (what Christ means for the way God deals with humanity).

The right relation that depends on faith is a relation that comes from God. Therefore what Paul *does* has really nothing to do with it, for he cannot compel God to consider him "right" nor earn God's verdict in any way (since then God would be reduced to a guarantor of the efficacy of religious practices). Hence no deed, no doing of God's will, is a credit toward this right relation. If this is the case, then the rite of circumcision and the deeds of religious devotion it represents are as worthless as garbage if one trusts only in God on the basis of Christ. What Paul states briefly here he argues at length in Romans 1–3, especially 2:25–3:31.

3:10. This verse deals with the relation to Christ mentioned in verse 9 and explains what faith really means. It is not simply an intellectual position, an idea about Jesus, but trust in him to the point of sharing in him. To have faith in Christ is to **know him**, and this knowledge means entering into his radical transformation by death-resurrection. This in turn means having one's own life conform to Christ's death—in the sense of sharing the meaning of his death as the door to freedom from the tyrannies of this world (see above on 2:6-11).

The opponents doubtless claimed that circumcision marked their repudiation of the flesh and the world too. Paul insists, however, that the real, radical, effectual dealing with the flesh (matter and death) comes, not by rites and religious practices of whatever kind, but only by trusting in the resurrection. Circumcision is a rite of rejecting the flesh. Trusting the resurrection is hoping for transformation of the flesh. Here is a radical repudiation of "religion."

3:11. The **resurrection** here is not yet a possession but a promise. This very **if possible** is crucial to the point Paul makes in verses 12-16. It is essential to the polemic itself, for the opponents were probably claiming that they had attained the resurrection, that they were fully redeemed from time-space. No doubt they practiced circumcision to show their attainment and required it of all who want to claim such perfection too. The same sort of claim to perfection was made in Corinth (I Corinthians 4:8-13).

3:12-16. *Christian Life as Process.* This section develops the tension between having and not having. Paul insists that he has not **obtained this** or appropriated it fully ("got hold of it yet," New English Bible). The most significant phrase is **am already perfect** (literally "have already been perfected") since the opponents probably used "perfection" as a slogan. It was an important word in certain forms of Greco-Roman religion, especially in the gnostic tradition. Paul vigorously insists that perfection is not part of the "already" but belongs to the "not yet."

3:13-14. Paul contends that his life consists of a **straining forward**, that he must **press on** because the **prize** lies ahead. The prize consists, not in a present achievement, but in the **upward call of God in Christ Jesus** ("God's call to the life above," New English Bible). This may refer to God's call to faith as a summons "upward" or, more probably, to the call into eternal life realized at death, as the New English Bible suggests. The opponents claimed already to have heeded the "call" (a favorite gnostic expression). Paul insists that this is an ultimate call toward which he presses.

Again and again Paul uses the slogans of his opponents to deny them their point. Here he denies that the call to perfection can be "answered" now except as a race, a process, a pursuit which demands that he forget the past—that is, the rite of circumcision and all that goes with it.

3:15. The word translated **mature** is the adjective form of the verb "have been perfected" of verse 12 and can mean either "perfect" or "mature." There is a touch of irony here as Paul uses the opponents' self-description to correct their views of perfection: being perfect means struggling throughout life. On this basis **those of us who are mature** (perfect) does not grant that some are in fact already perfected but says in effect, If you want to regard yourselves as perfect you must do so in this way. Therefore verse 15*a* sets a requirement for the whole church, not for its elite.

In verse 15*b* Paul addresses those who disagree. He says that God will reveal to them also the point he has been making. (In Greek the **that** of verse 15*b* repeats the word translated **thus** in verse 15*a*.)

3:16. In the meantime one is to live according to the degree of perfection **attained** in the struggle. This whole paragraph is an eloquent statement of life in Christ as progress toward a goal—a process, not an achievement.

3:17-21. *Application to the Readers' Situation.* Paul intensifies his treatment of the problem of the **brethren** to whom he is writing. He asks that he be imitated (see comment on I Thessalonians 1:6-7). Moreover he appears to ask that the congregation follow those who are already doing this.

3:18-19. Those who live this way are contrasted with the opponents (on the view of many that they are a different group from those attacked thus far see above on 3:1–4:1). Here, as in verse 2, Paul is sarcastic. He characterizes them **as enemies of the cross,** though they doubtless claimed to understand it rightly—probably as the sign that fleshly existence must be destroyed. **Their end is destruction,** though they doubtless believed it to be perfect salvation here and now. **Their god is the belly** (i.e. physical appetites), though they doubtless claimed to worship a purely spiritual God who had no concern for the flesh. Their **glory** is **their shame**, though they doubtless boasted of their "freedom" from all restraint on their fleshly desires as a sign of spirituality. Their **minds** are **set on earthly things**, though they doubtless claimed to be concerned only with abiding spiritual truths. Paul says he weeps as he writes. The **tears** are clearly bitter ones.

3:20-21. Paul now returns to a positive statement that emphasizes the future, "not yet" nature of Christian perfection suggested in verses 12-14. By insisting that **our commonwealth is in heaven** Paul maintains that the goal and guide of Christian life lies beyond time-space. Thereby he excludes again the opponents' claim to have attained it here and now.

When Paul says **we await a Savior** (a word used by Paul only here) he likewise contends that full salvation lies in the future (the New English Bible catches this: "and from heaven we expect our deliverer to come"). Christ will transform us to be as he now is—a theme elaborated in I Corinthians 15:20-57 (presumably this is the "spiritual body"). The transforming **power** here is the power inherent in the lordship of Jesus, a sovereignty conferred by God at the resurrection, according to the hymn of 2:6-11.

The passage reveals that in a sense Paul shares with his opponents the depreciation of the physical body and regards it as the seat (but not the cause) of human problems (cf. Romans 7:7-25; Galatians 5:16-17). However, he is too deeply rooted in the Old Testament conviction that God created the body and matter to regard salvation as sheer release from it.

Paul's opponents agreed with him that "flesh and blood cannot inherit the kingdom of God" (I Corinthians 15:50). But they drew the opposite conclusion: salvation to them was an ultimate release from the body and from all the influence of matter on the soul. Paul insists that Jesus' resurrection means that salvation will bring not destruction but transformation of bodily existence. In his view "the Lord is for the body" (I

363

Corinthians 6:13), and his ethics stand under the mandate "glorify God in your body" (I Corinthians 6:20).

4:1. In conclusion Paul counsels the church to **stand firm . . . in the Lord** (see comment on I Thessalonians 3:8-10).

IV. THE LIFE OF THE CHURCH (4:2-9)

The several brief units of this passage show little connection with each other or with other parts of Philippians. The scholars who have tried to analyze the book as a composite work have varied widely in assigning some or all of them to the respective letters (see Introduction). The chief reason for assuming that all of them probably followed 3:2–4:1 in Letter B is the improbability that any of them immediately preceded verses 10-20 in Letter A (or Letter C; see below on verses 10-20).

4:2-3. Who **Euodia** and **Syntyche** are is not known, nor is the cause of their disagreement. The identity of the **yokefellow** who is to help them resolve their differences has been the subject of various conjectures. For example, it is suggested that the word is a proper name (Syzygus) or that it refers to Lydia (Acts 16:11-15) or to Luke (because in Acts 16:6-10 the author, traditionally assumed to be Luke, shifts to "we" just before Paul's trip to Philippi) or to Epaphroditus (cf. 2:25-30). Some have wanted to identify **Clement** with the author of I Clement, a letter to the church at Corinth written from Rome around A.D. 96 and included in some early manuscripts of the New Testament. But that one of Paul's **fellow workers** should be active so many years later is highly improbable. Moreover, Clement was a common name.

4:4. This exhortation to **rejoice** is one of several references to rejoicing (1:18-19; 2:17-18, 28; 3:1; 4:10) and joy (1:4, 25; 2:2, 29; 4:1) often cited as evidence for the unity of Philippians. Paul frequently uses these words elsewhere, however. The only significant parallelism is the appearance of the phrase **rejoice in the Lord** both here and in 3:1 (see comment).

4:5. The significant note of this verse is that Paul believes **the Lord** is near. By this he means the coming from heaven mentioned in 3:20 and described in I Corinthians 15:51-57 and I

Thessalonians 4:13-18. Paul clearly expected to see this event in his lifetime (see comment on I Thessalonians 4:15-17).

4:6-7. Praying is to be done with **thanksgiving** for what has already been received; this will be an effective antidote to **anxiety.** God's **peace**, which transcends comprehension because it is given in the midst of difficulties—just as salvation is begun here and now—will guard the thinking of the readers in Christ, since such peace is grounded in the meaning of the cross.

4:8. This oft-quoted verse asks the readers to **think about** ("fill all your thoughts with," New English Bible) those things which are worthwhile. The several items were commonplace virtues in Hellenistic morals. Paul takes them up and commends them without explicit Christianization. In this way he shows that Christianity can appropriate sound ethical principles recognized by society in general.

4:9. Paul urges imitation of himself (cf. 3:17). Not the **peace of God** (verse 7) but the **God of peace** is promised as the accompanying presence.

V. CONCLUDING THANKS (4:10-20)

In this passage Paul, without losing his dignity or independence, expresses in detail his thanks for the gift which the Philippians sent by Epaphroditus (cf. 2:25). Among scholars who consider Philippians a composite work (see Introduction) some have argued that this expression of thanks is a third letter written before the other two, immediately after Epaphroditus' arrival. The close connection in both subject and mood, however, suggests strongly that it rather belongs immediately after 2:25-30 as the continuation of Letter A following the interpolated Letter B (3:1–4:9).

4:10-13. Paul speaks of a **revived** support from the Philippians after a period of **no opportunity**. What prevented their steady support is not known, and speculation is futile. Verses 11-12 give an important clue to Paul's attitude. On the experiences mentioned here cf. I Corinthians 4:11-13 and II Corinthians

11:16-29. Paul knows how to live in such a way that his **circumstances** do not control his inner life.

The Greek for **content** (used only here in the New Testament) is a term from Stoic ethics. For the Stoic, however, it meant, not a freedom in the midst of involvement, but an autonomy which permitted neither participation in the lives of others nor compassion for them, and which resulted in a steely serenity in a troubled world. Paul's **secret** is the empowering from God, which does not simply fortify him against difficulty but enables him to live with it creatively. II Corinthians 12:1-10 is an important discussion of this power which comes from allowing Christ's strength to be made visible through the way human weakness is borne.

4:14-16. Beginning a new paragraph with verse 14 (or verse 15 in the New English Bible) is unnecessary. Paul clearly continues to express his appreciation for support, lest his comments about his freedom suggest that he is not grateful. **Share** and **entered into partnership** translate forms of the word emphasized in chapters 1–2 (see above on 1:3-5).

On the help which the Philippians sent see comments on 2:19-30 and I Thessalonians 2:9-12. There is no known reason why only this church supported Paul.

4:17-20. Verses 17-18*a* use commercial terminology and verse 18*b* uses the language of religious ritual; both are metaphors, of course. Verse 19 expresses the same sort of confidence as Jesus expressed in Matthew 6:25-34. By referring to the wealth of God's glory in Christ, Paul speaks of inexhaustible grace through the cross and the resurrection. This proviso keeps Paul's statement from being simply a blank check that will not be honored.

VI. Farewell (4:21-23)

On **saint** see above on 1:1*b*. On **Caesar's household** see Introduction. Here we learn that some imperial servants have been converted—a fact not mentioned in the previous reference to them (1:13).

THE LETTER OF PAUL
TO THE COLOSSIANS

Victor Paul Furnish

INTRODUCTION

Relation to Ephesians

Among the New Testament letters no two exhibit such a
complex tangle of formal, verbal, and theological agreements
and disagreements as Colossians and Ephesians. These writings
deal with many of the same themes, employ a similar theological
vocabulary, and draw on a common fund of Christian hymnody.
In addition, there are numerous and impressive instances in
which, apparently, there is literary dependence of one on the
other. For examples of this, compare the following passages:

Colossians 1:1-2 with Ephesians 1:1-3;
Colossians 1:23b-29 with Ephesians 3:7-9;
Colossians 3:12-15 with Ephesians 4:2-4;
Colossians 3:16-17 with Ephesians 5:19-20;
Colossians 4:7-8 with Ephesians 6:21-22.

On the other hand there are also significant differences. Some
of these involve subtle changes of wording, as a careful study of
the passages listed above will show. It is also noteworthy that,
while Old Testament passages are never cited in Colossians and
there are only a few insignificant allusions to the Old Testament,

important Old Testament allusions abound in Ephesians and Old Testament texts are sometimes specifically invoked.

Moreover, while Ephesians is dominated by the author's concern to define the true nature of the church, Colossians is concerned with an attempt to counteract some false teaching which has sprung up in Colossae. Thus, while Ephesians is a general tractate addressed to the church at large (see Introduction to Ephesians), Colossians deals with a particular problem and is directed to a specific situation.

Many attempts have been made to define the relationship of Colossians and Ephesians, and the variety of current opinions shows that the question has never gained a definitive answer. Most present views may be grouped into the three following:

(1) Colossians and Ephesians are both Paul's own letters, written at the same time, from prison, but for different reasons.

(2) Only Colossians is an authentic Pauline letter. Hence the literary dependence is on the side of Ephesians, written by a follower of Paul who in part understood but in part misunderstood—or intentionally modified and adapted—the teacher's views.

(3) Neither Colossians nor Ephesians was written by Paul himself, though in each some of the authentic Pauline perspectives survive. Ephesians appears to be one step further removed from Paul than Colossians in theology and composition.

In recent years all discussions of this issue have had to reckon with the possibility that many of the parallels formerly seen as instances of literary dependence may in reality reflect a common, independent adaptation of liturgical and ethical materials already formulated and used by the early church. For further comment on this point see the Introduction to Ephesians.

Occasion and Purpose

In contrast to Ephesians, one can speak of a specific occasion for the writing of Colossians. If Paul is the author, at least one reason for his writing the letter was his concern about

Onesimus, the runaway slave on whose behalf he appeals in Philemon. The points of contact between these two letters are impressive (see the Introduction to Philemon). Considerable attention must be paid to those passages in Colossians which may bear on the case of Onesimus (see below on 3:22–4:1; 4:17) and to the fact that Onesimus himself is accompanying the bearer of this letter to Colossae (4:7-9).

Most commentators, however, see Colossians as occasioned primarily by the author's concern about the activity of false teachers among the Colossian Christians. These teachers are never named, nor are their false doctrines ever specifically labeled. But almost from the beginning the letter is directed against the views they are sponsoring. Their teaching is directly attacked in 2:6-23. The author's wish to combat it is also reflected in his constant reference to the tradition which the Colossians have received and to the apostolic authority which stands behind it (1:24–2:5) and in his exhortations to remain faithful to it. The words of 4:12 provide a succinct statement of the author's objective (see comment).

Colossae and the False Teaching. Colossae was a city of Asia Minor situated in the valley of the Lycus River 110 miles east of Ephesus. It had no special prominence in comparison with the neighboring cities of Hierapolis and Laodicea, and the letter indicates that Paul himself had never been there (1:4; 2:1). The Colossian congregation, and probably also those at Hierapolis and Laodicea, had been organized by Epaphras (1:7), himself a native of Colossae (4:12).

It is impossible to reconstruct the details of the false teaching which Colossians opposes. It is likely that the author himself had only general information about its doctrines and sponsors. Certain of its features, however, can be seen. It called itself a "philosophy" (2:8) and appealed to some special tradition in support of its teachings (2:8, 22). Its central doctrine concerned the "elemental spirits of the universe" (2:8), probably to be identified with the "principalities and powers" (or "authorities") mentioned in 1:16; 2:10, 15. These were probably regarded as angelic beings who contributed to the "fullness" of God and exercised demonic control over human lives. To gain freedom from these controlling fates and powers, people probably had to pay them homage (2:18). Perhaps for this reason emphasis was placed on the observance of ritual fast days (2:16).

This teaching stressed not only the importance of mystic visions (2:18) but also, more practically, the necessity of adherence to certain regulations (2:16, 20-23). From the remarks of 2:11-15 one may conclude that the rite of circumcision was urged as prerequisite for salvation. Several other passages suggest that the teachers divided people into classes depending on their level of spiritual attainment (1:28, 3:11).

It is apparent that various religious mythologies and practices converged in this teaching. Its speculation about a hierarchy of cosmic powers and its emphasis on a superior "wisdom," or "philosophy," as well as the stress on a special "tradition," is typical of many religious movements in the Hellenistic world. To these particular movements, influenced by oriental religious speculation and mythology, many scholars have applied the term "Gnosticism." Gnosticism as a specific system was a second century Christian heresy, but gnosticizing tendencies and motifs are identifiable long before. However, one may discern Jewish as well as Gnostic influences—the practice of circumcision, the promotion of dietary laws, and the adherence to statutes and ordinances.

Whether one calls the errant teaching a Jewish Gnosticism or a gnosticizing Judaism, it was basically a syncretistic mixture, typical of its day and not unlike the false teaching propagated among Paul's Galatian churches (see the Introduction to Galatians and comment on Galatians 4:8-10). From the way the argument of Colossians proceeds it is evident that the false teaching was not intended to supplant the Pauline gospel, but to supplement it.

Theological Perspectives

The author's theological position is developed largely in response to this teaching which threatens to unsettle the Colossians. To make his points more effectively he employs some of the very words and concepts used by its teachers, adapting these to his own purposes. But his theological position is also strongly influenced by the traditional language of Christian baptism, for he wishes to recall his readers to a vital memory of their conversion and incorporation into the church.

Because of the nature of the false doctrines the stress is on the role of Christ as sovereign Lord, God's agent in creation and redemption. This view is supported in 1:3-23 chiefly by the quotation of a hymn (1:15-20). As adapted, this hymn speaks of Christ as preexistent ruler of the cosmos who holds all things together, who is head of the body, the church, and through whose death on the cross all things have been reconciled.

Of special importance is the insistence that in Christ alone dwells the fullness of deity (1:19; 2:9; cf. 2:17), that whatever cosmic beings there may be have been disarmed of their power (2:15), and that there is no knowledge or wisdom deeper than that revealed in the "mystery" of the gospel, which is Christ himself (1:26-29; 2:2-3).

The redemptive work of this "cosmic Christ" is interpreted primarily in terms of the forgiveness of sins (1:13-14; 2:13-14) and resurrection to new life in and with Christ (1:21-22; 3:1-4). This is the meaning of Christian baptism, also described as transferral from darkness to light (1:13). The Christian has already been raised to newness of life (see below on 2:12) and "put on the new nature" (3:10).

Believers come to fullest "maturity" in Christ (1:28; 2:10) as they are daily renewed in accord with God's own image (3:10). When one holds fast to Christ (2:19) one is sustained and built up in love, the very stuff and substance of new life (2:2; 3:14). Thereby the Christian walks "worthy of the Lord, fully pleasing to him, bearing fruit in every good work and increasing in the knowledge of God" (1:10). Love expresses itself above all in the common life of Christ's body, the church (1:18, 24; 3:15). There all persons, without respect to class, race, nation, or alleged religious attainment (3:11), are united under the rule of Christ (3:15) for mutual service and love (3:12-14) and for the common praise of God (1:12; 2:7; 3:15*b*-17).

371

Authorship; Date and Place of Writing

Colossians claims to be from Paul (1:1, 23, 24-29; 4:7-18), and the majority of scholars accept the letter as his. The close relationship between Colossians and Philemon—especially the lists of greetings and the references to Onesimus and Archippus—would seem, in view of the now unquestioned authenticity of Philemon, to confirm this judgment. If so, Colossians was evidently written at the same time as Philemon—either from Rome shortly before Paul's death around 59-62 or, as some believe, from an earlier imprisonment at Ephesus around 54-56 (see the Introduction to Philemon).

But the authenticity of Colossians has not gone unchallenged. The technical theological terms it employs, its often liturgical style, and the occurrence of many non-Pauline words support the view that it was written by some later Christian thoroughly at home in Paul's thought. In addition, it has been argued, the Gnostic teaching which the letter combats did not become a problem until the second century, many years after Paul's death.

These arguments, however, are not decisive. While the fully developed systems of Gnosticism date only from the second century, there were Gnostic elements in various Hellenistic religions and in Jewish sectarianism even before the Christian era. Moreover, while Colossians does employ a technically theological, non-Pauline vocabulary, this could be attributed to the specific polemic needs of the moment. And at least some of the stylistic peculiarities of Colossians are due to the use of earlier liturgical materials. This can be seen also in the indisputably authentic letters (cf. Philippians 2:6-11).

Insofar as the authorship of Colossians remains in doubt, it is because of the theological presuppositions on which it rests and the way in which Pauline motifs are handled or omitted. Almost all commentators acknowledge a certain theological distance between Colossians and indisputably authentic letters like Romans and Galatians—though not so great as that between Ephesians and the Pauline letters.

Colossians strongly emphasizes the apostolic tradition and ministry as norms for faith. No longer present is Paul's view of salvation as still moving forward to fulfillment, and his doctrine of justification is altogether lacking. Moreover in numerous smaller ways Pauline ideas as known from the other letters are significantly altered.

To what extent may these points of theological divergence from the incontestably Pauline letters be accounted for by polemic requirements and by a development over the years in Paul's own thinking? The answer is not clear, and it is best to omit Colossians from one's list of primary sources for the study of Paul. The commentary which follows attempts to interpret Colossians in its own terms and context and in the light of the historical circumstances of its writing rather than in the perspective of Pauline theology as a whole.

If Colossians is not authentic, it was probably written by a Christian leader in Asia Minor who was strongly influenced by Paul's thought. It must have been written after Paul's death but before the composition of Ephesians, which seems to be literarily dependent on it. Therefore it can be assigned to a time between 65 and 90, probably closer to the earlier than to the later date.

I. Salutation (1:1-2)

The opening of Colossians is thoroughly Pauline. The letter is addressed to the Christians of Colossae (see Introduction), most of whom were of Gentile background (2:13; cf. 1:21, 27). They are addressed as **saints**, a term which does not imply perfect moral character but designates Christians in general as **faithful brethren in Christ**, consecrated to the service of God.

II. Liturgical and Hortatory Preface (1:3-23)

The Pauline letters regularly open with a section of thanksgiving and prayer. This one, unusually rich in the language of praise, is expanded by a hymn to Christ in verses 15-20 and a concluding exhortation (verses 21-23). In it the readers are reminded of the essential meaning of their conversion and baptism.

A. THANKSGIVING (1:3-8)

1:3-5a. *Faith, Love, and Hope.* God is thanked for the faith and love manifested in the lives of the congregation. Since Paul himself did not found their church (verse 7), the author says that he has only **heard** about the Colossians.

The supposition that **faith** and **love** are integrally related and that neither is authentic without the other is characteristically Pauline (cf. Galatians 5:6). Faith in Christ is never separable from the love of one's family in Christ (**the saints**; see above on verses 1-2). But **hope** here designates that which is hoped for, an inheritance **laid up . . . in heaven**. Thus it does not conform to the general Pauline view of hope as part of the total activity of faith. The author believes that the faith of the Colossians is grounded in their assurance of a heavenly blessing and is expressed in a life of love.

1:5b-7. *The Word of Truth.* The readers are now reminded of their conversion. Colossae was evangelized by **Epaphras**, apparently sent out by Paul from Ephesus as a missionary to the Lycus Valley (4:13). The author is laying the groundwork for his attack against the false teaching which threatens to unsettle his readers. As opposed to that teaching the gospel delivered by Epaphras is the **word of the truth**. It is preached in the **whole world** and therefore not, like the false teaching, a local novelty. It is **bearing fruit and growing**. Foreshadowed here are some of the appeals the later church was to make in its fight against heresy—appeals to tradition, catholicity, and practical results. The **grace of God** stands parallel with the **word of the truth**; both describe the **gospel**.

1:8. *A Good Report.* Once more the author stresses the good report he has had from Epaphras about the Colossians. If there is any reference to God's **Spirit** in Colossians it is here, though some would translate the phrase "in spirit," as in 2:5. In any case the doctrine of the Spirit, so important in Paul's thought as a whole, has no major role in the argument of Colossians.

B. Prayer (1:9-14)

1:9-11. *Petitions.* This prayer includes three main petitions:

(1) that the Colossians understand what God's **will** is;

(2) that they live in a manner befitting their Lord;

(3) that they be **strengthened with** his **power** for joyful **endurance and patience**.

The **knowledge** for which the author pleads is that insight into truth granted by the powerful working of God to those who are open to **spiritual wisdom**. This wisdom expresses itself concretely in the life of the believer who increases in knowledge as their life bears fruit "in active goodness of every kind" (verse 10, New English Bible; cf. 3:10).

In the Greek the phrase used of the gospel in verse 6, "bearing fruit and growing," is exactly repeated with reference to the believer in verse 10. The gospel itself bears fruit and grows when those who have been grasped by it bear fruit in their transformed lives and grow in the knowledge of God. The source of this growth, the strength for endurance and patience in obedience, and the ground for joy is God's own power.

1:12-14. *Thanksgiving.* The petitions of this prayer move without a break into thanksgiving. Three times in Colossians God is called **Father**, each time in connection with the thanks due God for salvation (1:3, 12; 3:17). Here this is specified to be God's call—the essential meaning of **qualified us**—to participate in the whole company of Christians and the **inheritance** which belongs to them. In verses 13-14 the readers are reminded of their baptism, which marked their transferral from **darkness** to **light** (cf. verse 12). The ground for hope is God's own act of deliverance, God's own deed of redemption, viewed as the **forgiveness of sins**.

C. HYMN (1:15-20)

Structural, stylistic, and material analyses of this paragraph have revealed it to be a hymn adopted and adapted by the author. There is no complete agreement as to its origin— whether it is Christian or not, its precise formal structure, or the extent to which it has been modified by the author. Nevertheless two parallel stanzas may be discerned with relative ease:

(1) Verses 15-18*a*, which have undergone extensive modification and expansion in this context, speak of Christ as the agent of **creation**.

(2) Verses 18*b*-20, somewhat less expanded, present the correlative idea of Christ as the agent of redemption. The hymn is adapted in such a way as to underscore the author's main point. Baptism into Christ means deliverance from whatever secondary rulers there may be in the universe and participation in the kingdom of Christ.

1:15-18*a*. *The Agent of Creation.* The first stanza opens with a reference to Christ as the revealer of God. Christ's cosmic role as the agent of creation is even more explicitly noted when it is said that **all things were created . . . in . . . through . . . and for Christ.** A stronger statement of Christ's cosmic sovereignty is hardly possible, especially when it is specified that the existence of every other worldly power is dependent on him. This has particular relevance for the Colossians beset by false teachers insisting on the necessity of paying honor to all the various cosmic powers (see Introduction).

1:17-18*a*. The affirmation that Christ is **before all things** and that **all things hold together** in him further supports the point that his authority is primordial, his reign universal, and his power absolute. This is summarized in verse 18*a*, which in the original hymn probably said only: **He is the head of the body.** This concept held a place in the pre-Christian mythology which spoke of a "primeval man"—sometimes identified as Adam— who was the "head" of the cosmos, his "body." The hymn apparently draws on this idea, declaring that Christ is this primeval man, the cosmic redeemer, in whom the whole universe finds its being and destiny.

In adapting this hymn the author has probably inserted **the church**. In verse 24 he once more identifies "body" with "church" and then presupposes this identification in 3:15. But it is left to the author of Ephesians to develop the concept in his discussion of the nature of the church and its relation to Christ.

1:18b-20. *The Agent of the New Creation.* Verse 18b is parallel with verse 15 and opens the second stanza of the hymn. In verse 15 Christ has been presented as preeminent in creation. Now he is declared to be **preeminent** in the new creation, **first-born from the dead** (cf. I Corinthians 15:20; Revelation 1:5). In Christ these two aspects of God's activity are indissolubly bound together, perhaps in specific opposition to the false teachers in Colossae. Moreover this hymn's emphasis on the absolute sovereignty of Christ would be particularly helpful in combating the teaching that other cosmic powers ought to be worshiped.

1:19-20. The hymn is here further adapted for use in the attack on the errant teachers. **Fulness** was a technical term used by those teachers themselves for the sum of "elemental spirits" which collectively made up the cosmic deity. The author opposes the idea that cosmic rule is distributed among numerous powers. Christ alone is the world ruler; the fullness of divine power belongs exclusively to him (cf. 2:9-10).

Verse 19 is therefore not primarily a declaration about the incarnation but an affirmation of the cosmic sovereignty of Christ, effective in redemption as well as creation. The same Lord who was active in creation is active in renewing that creation and in restoring it to its primeval order and harmony. It is thus **peace** of cosmic dimensions to which the hymn refers. This peace is attained as every power of the universe stands in subjection to Christ.

Though these cosmic proportions of reconciliation and peace are never stressed in the unquestioned Pauline letters, the author makes a typical Pauline addition to the original hymn. This peace is made **by the blood of his cross** (cf. Romans 5:6-11).

The cosmic Lord and Redeemer is identified with the historical crucified Jesus. In a later paragraph (2:13-15) the death itself is viewed as both the moment of cosmic victory and the event through which the believer is given new life.

D. HORTATORY CONCLUSION (1:21-23)

1:21-22. *Reconciliation in Christ*. The readers' pagan past is judged to have been a time of estrangement, hostility, and wickedness. From that moral chaos—analogous to the cosmic chaos which prevails apart from the lordship of Christ—the Christian has been delivered. Being **reconciled** involves a reordering of one's life, a restoration and renewal of it.

Thus again the author corrects the false view that salvation must achieve separation from the created world, either through mystic visions or by adherence to ascetic regulations (see below on 2:16-19). This renewal of life's wholeness enables the Christian to stand before God as one **holy and blameless and irreproachable**. And this renewal has been effected by Christ's incarnation and death.

1:23. *Steadfastness*. Reconciliation requires fidelity to the tradition—**the faith . . . the hope of the gospel**—which has been **preached to every creature under heaven**. This last phrase underscores the cosmic inclusiveness of God's reconciling activity (cf. **all things**, verse 20). The mention of Paul at the end of verse 23 is the transition to what follows.

III. PAUL'S MINISTRY (1:24–2:5)

In the whole liturgical preface, but especially in his quotation of a hymn in verses 15-20, the author has appealed to the Christian tradition into which the Colossians were baptized. Later he will return to this theme as he urges them to resist the dangerous doctrines of false teachers. Meanwhile another basis for the later arguments is established—Paul's apostolic authority. Hence the appeal in Colossians begins to be to two of the bulwarks of faith which the church came increasingly to emphasize in its fight against heresy: the historic tradition and the apostolic office (on the appeal to catholicity and practical results see above on 1:5*b*-7).

1:24-26. *The Apostolic Office.* Joy in the midst of **sufferings** is a characteristically Pauline emphasis, and the remark opening verse 24 agrees with the claim that Colossians is written by Paul from prison (see Introduction).

Precisely what it means to **complete what is lacking in Christ's afflictions** is not clear. It certainly does not mean that Christ's sufferings have in some way been defective in bringing salvation. The general thought is that Paul participates in Christ's sufferings as he endures the trials and afflictions which come to those who preach the gospel. It is not impossible that the author has in mind some "quota" of sufferings which the church must undergo before God's victory is won. But more likely he intends to say only that the sufferings are **for your sake, . . . for the sake of his body**—here, as in verse 18, identified as the **church.** Thus, the preaching of the gospel is attended by **afflictions** not unlike Christ's own.

1:25. This idea is now enforced and the **divine** origin of Paul's **office** is emphasized (cf. Galatians 1:1, 11-12). **For you**, repeated from verse 24, underscores the relationship which exists between apostle and congregation.

1:26. The apostolic office exists to make the word of God **fully known**. That word is a **mystery**, a term which in the New Testament has a consistently different meaning from that in the ancient mystery cults. In the New Testament it is always associated with a message publicly proclaimed (on **saints** see above on verses 1-2), never with a secret reserved for the privileged few (see comment on Ephesians 1:9-10).

1:27-29. *The Mystery of Christ.* The content of the mystery is described as **Christ in you, the hope of glory**. In Colossians hope is something prepared and waiting for the faithful Christian (see above on verses 3-8). It may be used to designate Christian preaching in general (cf. verse 23). The phrase **Christ in you**

must not be read as a mystical formula; it refers to the crucified Christ (verse 22), presented in preaching and received by faith.

1:28-29. The content of preaching is Christ, and the function of the apostolic office is the presentation of **every man mature in Christ**. The word "mature," was a technical term in Hellenistic religion for the fully initiated cult member. It may also have been part of the vocabulary of the Colossian teachers, for whom there were believers of various ranks. But in Christ **every man** may attain fullness and wholeness of life (see above on verses 21-22). In him every religious and social barrier dividing persons is broken through.

2:1-5. *Paul's Relation to the Colossians.* Paul's labor was for his congregations, even those to whom he was related by letter only (see above on 1:3-8). The wealthy city of **Laodicea** lay ten miles northwest of Colossae (cf. 4:13-16).

2:2-3. In view of the immediate context **encouraged** and **knit together** are better translated as "strengthened" and "instructed." The author is concerned to strengthen his readers in their faith by instructing them **in love**—with patience, tact, and goodwill. Thus he will bring them to an authentic insight into the true mystery of God, which is Christ (cf. 1:27). All true **wisdom and knowledge**—no matter what the errant teachers say—are in him alone. They are **hid** there only to those who refuse to receive the proclamation of the gospel (cf. 1:25-29).

2:4-5. The readers are warned about the lure of the "smooth talk" employed by the false teachers. Verse 5*b* suggests that they have as yet made no substantial progress among the Colossians (cf. 1:3-4).

IV. POLEMIC AGAINST THE FALSE TEACHING
(2:6-23)

Earlier paragraphs have attempted to remind the Colossians of the faith into which they were baptized and their commitment to Christ as Lord of all things. Those reminders, as well as the statement about Paul's apostolic authority (1:24–2:5) are in a sense a preface to this section. Here the false teaching being adopted by some of the Colossians is directly under attack. Here one meets the problem which occasioned the writing of this whole letter.

A. FIDELITY TO THE APOSTOLIC TRADITION (2:6-15)

2:6-8. *Authoritative Tradition.* The author's first argument against the false teaching is that it departs from the apostolic tradition. **Received** is a technical term used of that historic, authoritative tradition of formulated doctrines. The whole of this tradition is summarized in the phrase **Christ Jesus the Lord**. The admonition to **live in him** is elaborated in the clauses of verse 7, which stress the need for an unwavering fidelity to Christ and the church's teaching. **Taught** is here virtually synonymous with **received**, indicating the way in which the historic tradition has been delivered to believers. The reference to **thanksgiving** as a continuing dimension of the Christian's life is characteristic of this whole letter (cf. 1:12; 3:15, 17; 4:2).

2-8a. In sharp contrast with the apostolic tradition stands the false teaching which is specifically branded as **human tradition**, a local novelty without historical roots. The only New Testament reference to **philosophy** occurs here, where it is equated with **empty deceit**. The writer is concerned lest his readers be duped into accepting doctrines which have no enduring significance and are not as profound as their exponents pretend.

2:8b. The doctrine of Christ's universal sovereignty is apparently threatened by the emphasis on the **elemental spirits of the universe** (cf. verse 20; Galatians 4:3, 9). They are probably regarded as demonic powers which collectively make up the divine fullness. But for the Christian, Christ alone is cosmic Lord, the mediator of salvation, and the **fulness of God** (1:19; see comment).

2:9-10. *The Fullness of God.* The contrast between the **elemental spirits** and **Christ** in verse 8 leads to a reiteration of Christ as alone God's **fulness** and of his exclusive headship over

all rule and authority. Both ideas were present in the hymn of 1:15-20 (cf. especially verses 18-19). Now it is said that God's fullness lives in Christ **bodily**.

The word here may simply mean "really" or "wholly," in contrast to the dispersal of power and divinity among various elemental spirits. Or it may be intended to stress the bodily incarnation of deity in the historical Jesus. In either sense it would be in opposition to the false teaching. In verse 10 the author applies the idea of fullness to the Christians themselves, who in Christ attain their full maturity (cf. 1:28).

2:11-12. *Baptism.* The contrast between physical and spiritual circumcision is Pauline (cf. Romans 2:25-29. The **circumcision of Christ** is Christian baptism, which is first described as **putting off the body of flesh**, which is the whole realm of demonic powers to which those apart from Christ are enslaved. The act of initiation into Christ and his church frees one from those fateful forces and marks one's transferral into the kingdom of Christ and the forgiveness of sins.

2:12. The interpretation of Christian baptism as burial and resurrection with Christ is again Pauline, but comparing Romans 6:3-11 one notes some difference. In Romans 6:5, 8 resurrection with Christ is still a hope. Here resurrection has already occurred—**you were also raised with him**. This has not been accomplished through the rite of baptism itself. The author does not view baptism as some cultic apparatus for the attainment of salvation. Salvation comes rather through faith in God, who has raised both Christ and the Christian to new life.

2:13-15. *Victory over Cosmic Powers.* The Christian's resurrection is from spiritual and moral death. Baptism marks one's burial and resurrection into new life, and the view that this redemption-resurrection is in its essence forgiveness of sins is now repeated (cf. 1:14).

Reference to the **bond . . . against us with its legal demands** suggests that the false teaching involved some sort of legalistic ordinances, adherence to which was thought to be essential for salvation. Christ in his death has brought freedom from this enslavement to an external code and the attendant moral guilt.

2:15. Christ's death effects forgiveness and ushers in new life because it establishes God's victory over the **principalities and powers** of the cosmos (cf. 1:16; see Introduction). The false teaching is still in the author's mind. Against the doctrine of many cosmic powers he urges once again the absolute supremacy of Christ. **In him,** i.e. Christ, may also be translated "in it," i.e. the cross. But the meaning is not greatly changed, for the idea is that in Christ's triumphant death on the cross God has conquered the lesser lords of the cosmos. Like a victorious general God has disarmed the pretenders to power, parading them about for all to see their disgrace and impotence.

B. WARNING AGAINST FALSE WISDOM
(2:16-23)

2:16-19. *Observances and Regulations.* The false teaching abroad in Colossae apparently stresses the importance of adherence to dietary regulations and a sacred calendar (verse 16). But these have no essential place in true Christianity (verse 17). Christ alone—faith in him as sovereign Lord—is sufficient for salvation.

Verse 18 mentions still other aspects of the Colossian teaching. **Self-abasement** indicates that certain ascetic regulations are proposed (cf. verses 20b-22), and the **angels** are probably to be identified with the elemental spirits of the cosmos (cf. verses 8, 20). The false teachers also stress the importance of **visions** and similar unique religious feats. But again these are criticized as having no importance for the authentic Christian life. Those who insist on them are regarded as "bursting with the futile conceit of worldly minds" (verse 18, New English Bible).

One here gets the picture of a type of false Christianity which seeks to establish—through special rules, rites, and religious experiences—an elite group that thinks to achieve a special status before God and an absolute certainty about salvation. The error in this, the Colossians are told, is the tendency to believe that salvation may be secured by one's own religious works. Preoccupation with these obscures the primacy of God's act in granting salvation through Jesus Christ.

2:19. Christ is once more called the **Head** of the **body** (cf. 1:18*a*). In this instance, however, the author seems to identify the body, not with the church, but with the whole cosmos (see above on 1:17-18*a*). "Body" here is almost parallel with **all rule and authority** in verse 10, and the meaning is that Christ is Lord of all things. In him alone is the source of all life and the strength for all **growth**. The author has already asserted that it is love which makes it possible to **knit together** all people in Christ (verse 2; cf. 3:14).

2:20-23. *Bondage to the World.* For Christians the false doctrines being sponsored in Colossae ought to hold no appeal, for they have **died to the elemental spirits of the universe**. They know that the power to create and redeem resides solely in Christ, the fullness of God's sovereign rule. Thus the cosmic hierarchy of beings which play a central role in the false teaching (see Introduction) is to be disregarded; they have been conquered in Christ. The author's worried question, **Why do you live as if you still belonged to the world?** does not accord with his earlier expression of confidence in the Colossian congregation (verse 5).

2:20*b*-23. Belonging to the world is here understood as bondage to a false religiosity, preoccupation with **regulations** designed to secure some special status (cf. verses 16-19). These allegedly religious exercises are actually only worldly devices of **human** origin. The false doctrines are again attacked as deviating from the authentic apostolic tradition. Both the lure and the perversity of this false teaching reside in its sanctimonious pretensions, in the "air of wisdom" (verse 23*a*, New English Bible) it exudes. Such affected piety is simply a special form of secularism and self-indulgence (verse 23*b*; see the Revised Standard Version footnote).

V. EXHORTATIONS TO LEAD A CHRISTIAN LIFE
(3:1–4:6)

Thus far the readers have been reminded of their baptismal commitment and admonished to stand firm in their faith despite the lure of certain Christian teachers whom the author regards as dangerous deviators. Their doctrine about worshiping elemental spirits and cosmic powers stands in sharp contrast to the Christian doctrine that Christ alone is the cosmic Lord. Now the argument becomes more positive. The readers are exhorted to show in their lives the characteristics appropriate to new life in Christ.

A. THE BASIS OF A CHRISTIAN LIFE
(3:1-4)

These introductory verses reaffirm the theological basis for a transformed life. The Christian has participated in Christ's resurrection and is now free from enslavement to trespasses and the cosmic powers. True life is to be found in the God revealed by Christ. Therefore, Christians are to see that their whole life is reoriented in terms of the "kingdom of [God's] beloved Son" (1:13). The parallel admonitions **Seek the things that are above** and **Set your minds on things that are above** urge in a general way that radically new orientation respecting motives and goals which the following paragraphs more particularly specify.

The description of Christ as **seated at the right hand of God** is frequent in the New Testament. Like the Old Testament verse on which it is based (Psalm 110:1), it stresses the powerful rule of Christ in God's behalf. The reference to the life **hid with Christ in God** corresponds with the author's view of a "hope" (1:5) or "inheritance" (1:12) presently laid up in heaven, which is already accomplished but not yet actualized in its fullest sense for the believer. That actualization will occur **when Christ who is our life appears**.

B. PUTTING OFF THE OLD, PUTTING ON THE NEW
(3:5-17)

3:5-8. *Earthward Inclinations.* The Christian's new life in and with Christ is oriented to **things that are above** (verses 1-2). Therefore one is admonished to **put to death** one's "earthward inclinations" (Weymouth translation). These are enumerated in two groups of five each (verses 5, 8), to which the fivefold enumeration of virtues in verse 12 corresponds. Nothing specific about moral conditions at Colossae should be deduced from these lists, for the particular vices mentioned frequently recur in similar lists contained in Hellenistic moral tractates. The author's intention is only to stress the seriousness of the moral degradation of their former life (verse 7; cf. 2:13). Such immorality in all its various forms stands constantly under God's **wrath**. This is conceived here, not as capricious, vindictive anger, but as God's consistent, aggressive judgment of evil.

3:9-11. *Renewal unto Knowledge.* That the readers have **put off the old nature**, literally "old man," is parallel with the admonitions of verses 5 and 8. Like them this concerns yielding one's life to Christ, by whose death and resurrection the believer is made free from the power of sin. Though in Galatians 3:27 Paul speaks of "putting on Christ" in baptism, there is more stress here on the new life as an already fully accomplished fact (see above on 2:12).

3:10. But the believer's participation in the resurrected life of Christ does not exclude the need for daily obedience. This is the implication of the striking phrase in verse 10 which describes the **new** as always in the process of renewal—"being constantly renewed in the image of its Creator" (New English Bible). God's **image** is an allusion to the creation story (Genesis 1:26-27). The author, in opposition to the Gnostic teachers, affirms the essential integrity of God's creating and redeeming activity.

The goal of this renewal is the **knowledge** of God—"unto knowledge" is a better translation—a concern which has been present in Colossians from the first (cf. 1:9-10). All true knowledge is in Christ (cf. 2:2-3). It consists in a practical commitment to God, expressed in one's life (see above on 1:9-11).

3:11. Where life has been transformed to accord with the creative-redemptive purposes of God, every social, national, racial, and even religious distinction is rendered meaningless—for **Christ is all, and in all.** For the author this occurs in the church, Christ's body. This conviction is true to Paul's own conception of baptism into Christ as an incorporation into a community of believers where all such barriers have been broken (see comments on Galatians 3:27-29 and Philemon 15-19).

Each of the pairs named has contrasting members except **barbarian, Scythian.** The first of these terms would mean to the Colossians "non-Greek," with the slightly derogatory connotation which we usually give to "foreigner." The Scythians were a tribe of Eurasian nomads infamous in antiquity for their allegedly bestial and brutal ways—the most degraded kind of "barbarians." J. B. Phillips' paraphrase "foreigner or savage" is thus true to the author's meaning. The description of Christ as **all, and in all** cannot be too closely analyzed. It is employed only to express Christ's preeminence. Paul also uses the phrase of God (I Corinthians 15:28).

3:12-13. *Qualities of the New Nature.* In verse 10 the author has spoken of the **new nature** which the Christian has **put on.** Now in a typically Pauline way he converts the indicative statement into an imperative: **Put on then.** The list of five characteristics which follows is meant to contrast with the two fivefold lists of vices already presented in verses 5 and 8. They are not proposed as "cardinal virtues" but offered only as typical of the characteristics and attitudes Christianity teaches. While most of the qualities mentioned were widely extolled by non-Christian writers, the word **lowliness** outside of Jewish-Christian circles always conveyed the idea of abject humiliation and was listed among the vices rather than the virtues.

The distinctively Christian element in this passage is not the content of the list but its context. The exhortation has significance because it is addressed to those who have been

raised with Christ (verse 1), and whose lives are already being renewed unto knowledge after the image of their creator (verse 10). Hence the Colossian Christians are **God's chosen ones, holy and beloved**. These descriptions are drawn from the Old Testament, where they are applied to Israel, and found also in Paul's letters. As used here they are virtually synonymous, each referring to the call of God whereby God's people are set aside for obedience to God's will and the praise of God's name.

3:13. All the qualities named in verse 12 have a bearing on one's relationships with others. Here this dimension of the Christian life is further stressed. The author again provides a specifically Christian basis for his exhortation as he appeals to his readers' experience of the forgiving love of God made real at their baptism.

3:14-15a. *The Priority of Love.* Love is **above all** the mark of the new life in Christ. It is the bond wherein life has meaning, vitality, and integrity (cf. 2:2, 19). **Perfect harmony** translates a Greek word which connotes wholeness, completeness, and authenticity. Love establishes wholeness not only within the Christian community but within each participating believer and in the entire cosmos.

3:15a. To **put on** this love (verse 14) means to surrender oneself to Christ's **rule** (cf. 1:15-20). The **peace of Christ** must not be interpreted to mean simply an attitude of inner tranquility. It is a peace which has cosmic dimensions (1:20) and which is a gift to the whole community of believers, not just a feeling of serenity possessed by individuals.

As one is called into the whole **body** of believers one participates in the wonderful reconciliation of all things and all peoples. Therefore **in your hearts** does not describe the place where Christ's peace rules—for that is in the community, where the Christian's obedience to God is concretely evident. It designates rather the depth and sincerity of commitment to Christ's rule which is to characterize one's new life.

3:15b-17. *Thankfulness.* The author insists that the Christian life ought not be regarded as a burden, or its responsibilities grudgingly borne. Christians do not surrender themselves to

God as a conquered enemy capitulates to the victor. Rather their surrender is to take the form of a joyful, grateful presentation of themselves to God. Thanksgiving is thus a further characteristic of the new life (cf. 1:12; 2:7; 4:2). It is to be expressed both in public worship and in one's daily public life.

3:16. Commentators have defined the **word of Christ** as his own preaching, the gospel about Christ, and Christ himself. In any case the idea is that where the church is, God is—working for the mutual upbuilding of all believers. It is not possible to say with certainty whether **psalms and hymns and spiritual songs** represent three distinct types of music in the early church. It is clear, however, that the earliest Christians possessed a rich hymnody. Much of it was drawn from or influenced by Old Testament psalms, but some of it was adapted from nonbiblical sources or newly composed. The New Testament contains many quotations from this hymnody, an especially impressive example being found here in 1:15-20.

3:17. The admonition to give thanks is extended to apply to one's whole life and recalls Paul's exhortation to do everything to the glory of God (I Corinthians 10:31). One must live in accord with the new life to which one has been raised in Christ, thereby **giving thanks** to God in the only way fully appropriate to the magnificence of the gift which has been bestowed.

C. THE CHRISTIAN HOUSEHOLD (3:18–4:1)

This is perhaps the earliest Christian example of what commentators have called a "table of household duties." Other New Testament examples are Ephesians 5:21–6:9; I Peter 2:13–3:12; and Titus 2:1-10. These tables emphasize the need for mutual respect and consideration among the members of a household. Because their specifically Christian content is minimal, many scholars hold that they have been taken from the general ethical teaching of the day and only slightly christianized.

3:18-19. *Wives and Husbands.* Earliest Christianity, in keeping with the prevailing social order, envisioned no role for the woman apart from marriage and homemaking. The feminist movement would have seemed as irrelevant in that day as the abolitionist movement (see Introduction to Philemon). Though the husband's authority in the household is not questioned, the command that he should be loving and considerate of his wife injects at least an element of mutuality into the concept of marriage. Cf. I Corinthians 7:1-40 and Ephesians 5:21-33.

3:20-21. *Children and Parents.* Obedience, not just subjection (cf. verse 18), is expected of the children. The new term connotes an element of instruction and discipline not appropriate in the relationship between husbands and wives. This dimension of the parent-child relationship is emphasized in Ephesians 6:1-4, where this section is significantly expanded.

3:22–4:1. *Slaves and Masters.* The exhortations to slaves and masters dominate this household table—perhaps because of the large number of slaves who were members of the various Christian congregations. Most of the specifically Christian elements in the table are present in these verses—the references to **fearing the Lord**, **serving the Lord Christ**, and the **inheritance** to be received as a **reward**. There is a subtle play running through the whole passage on the word **Lord**, which in Greek is the same as that for a slave's owner.

Slaves, then, are admonished to faithfully serve their **earthly masters** because they can look forward to an inheritance from their heavenly **Master** which will transcend all earthly gains. The masters, on the other hand, are admonished to treat their slaves with justice and equity, knowing that they too have a heavenly Master (see comment on Ephesians 6:5-9). On Christianity's attitude toward the institution of slavery see the Introduction to Philemon.

3:25. Interpretation of this verse depends on one's judgment about the authorship of Colossians. If Paul is the author (see Introduction) the whole table should probably be read in the light of the case of the runaway slave Onesimus mentioned in 4:9 as being from Colossae (see Introduction to Philemon). In that event this verse may be a comment about Onesimus specifically.

He is the **wrongdoer** who must pay for what he has done, and his relationship with Paul provides no special favors. If on the other hand the Pauline authorship of Colossians is questioned, it is likely that the wrongdoer is the master and that slaves are being assured of the impartial administration of justice against all who violate the ordinances of God.

D. CONCLUDING EXHORTATIONS (4:2-6)

4:2-4. *The Importance of Prayer.* Prayer is to be **watchful,** which here may have the double meaning of being expectant about salvation and alert about one's own moral condition. Stress on **thanksgiving** as a vital dimension of prayer accords with the author's earlier remarks on the subject (e.g. 3:15*b*-17). The request that the Colossians pray for the advance of the apostolic ministry accords with the previous emphasis on the bonds uniting Paul to his congregations (1:23–2:5). **Word** and **mystery of Christ** (see above on 1:26 and 2:2-3) are descriptions of the gospel, also called the "word of the truth" (1:5) or the "word of Christ" (3:16).

4:5-6. *Conduct in the World.* The exhortations which conclude this section deal briefly with the relationship of Christians to persons outside the church. On the one hand by wise and discreet conduct Christians are to bear witness to their faith, passing up no opportunity (verse 5; literally "buying up the time"). On the other hand the Christian needs to be prepared to respond to challenge. One's words must be well chosen, temperate yet relevant, and appropriate to each new situation. "Speak pleasantly to them, but never sentimentally, and learn how to give a proper answer to every questioner" (verse 6, Phillips translation).

VI. EPISTOLARY CLOSE (4:7-18)

4:7-9. *Commendation of Tychicus and Onesimus.* Tychicus is named in Acts 20:4 and associated in II Timothy 4:12 with a mission to Ephesus. Here he is represented as the bearer of this letter and is warmly commended. With him goes Onesimus, the slave on whose behalf Philemon was written, and who is here described as himself a Colossian (verse 9). If Colossians is authentically Pauline, presumably part of Tychicus' mission was to return Onesimus to his owner, along with the letter (Philemon) dealing with that problem. It is significant that here Onesimus is assumed to have full status as a **beloved brother** in Christ (cf. Philemon 16).

4:10-14. *Greetings from Paul's Associates.* This list of those who send greetings to the Colossian church is almost identical with that in Philemon 23-24 (see comment). Here there is one additional name, **Jesus . . . Justus,** about whom nothing else is known. He, **Aristarchus,** and **Mark** are described as the only Jewish Christians among Paul's associates. They are **fellow workers** with Paul in obedience to the call and claim of God.

4:12-13. The founder of the Colossian church (cf. 1:7), **Epaphras,** himself a Colossian, labors constantly in prayer on their behalf. The words which identify the object of these prayers summarize the reason for which Colossians was written: "that you may stand up fully grown and fully persuaded in everything that God wills" (verse 12, C. K. Williams translation). On the other hand Colossians admonishes resistance to false teaching, and on the other hand it encourages growth, as individuals and as a community, into the fullness and maturity which is in fact already theirs. Epaphras has also been responsible for the churches in nearby **Laodicea** and **Hierapolis** (see above on 2:1-5).

4:14. Only here in the New Testament is Luke, who is traditionally the author of the third gospel and Acts, called a **physician.** According to II Timothy 4:10 **Demas** later deserted Paul's service.

4:15-17. *Greetings to Paul's Friends.* Now Paul's own greetings are conveyed: to the Laodicean **brethren,** i.e. church, to which this letter is also to be read and to the church meeting in the house of **Nympha.** The instruction that this letter be shared with the Laodicean church and that the letter to that congregation be read also in Colossae shows how the custom of exchanging apostolic letters must have grown up. This led gradually to their collection and joint circulation and ultimately to their finding a place in the New Testament canon. No letter to the Laodiceans survives, though the second century heretic Marcion identified Ephesians as such, and some modern scholars believe it to have been Philemon.

4:17. In Philemon 2 **Archippus** is also named. If Colossians is regarded as Pauline, this verse is impressive evidence in favor of the hypothesis that he rather than Philemon was the owner of Onesimus. Thus the **ministry** which Archippus is to **fulfil** may be the freeing—or at least the kind treatment—of his slave, now returning with Tychicus, the bearer of this letter. Other commentators have conjectured that this ministry might be to continue the work of Epaphras within the congregation or to assist in the collection of Paul's offering for Jerusalem (cf. II Corinthians 9:1).

4:18. *Concluding Apostolic Word.* In conformity with Paul's custom the author concludes with a final apostolic certification of the whole letter (cf. I Corinthians 16:21 and Galatians 6:11). This conclusion was written by himself and not the scribe to whom the rest has been dictated. As always in the apostolic letters, the last word is one of benediction.

THE FIRST LETTER OF PAUL TO THE THESSALONIANS

Leander E. Keck

INTRODUCTION

Date and Occasion

If the books of the New Testament stood in the order in which they were written, I Thessalonians would head the list. Only Galatians might compete for this position (see Introduction to Galatians). I Thessalonians was written by Paul from Corinth around A.D. 51. This simple conclusion results from interpreting both Acts and I Thessalonians.

According to Acts—the only narrative of Paul's work—Paul, Timothy, and Silas came to the Macedonian city of Thessalonica from Philippi. Though the account of their mission there (Acts 17:1-9) speaks of Paul's teaching three sabbaths in the synagogue, the whole period was probably longer. The new church they founded was of mixed membership and included prominent Macedonian women (Act 17:4). Civil disturbances led to a sudden departure by night to nearby Beroea, where their efforts ended when Thessalonian Jews arrived to stir up opposition (Acts 17:10-13). Paul went on to Athens, accompanied by converts, by whom he sent word back to Beroea for Silas and Timothy to join him as soon as possible (Acts 17:14-15). Then he waited for them at Athens (Acts 17:16).

The letter itself enables us to take up the story at this point. From 3:1-3a it is clear that Timothy, at least, met Paul in Athens as instructed and that Paul sent him back from there to Thessalonica to stabilize the young congregation. Later Timothy rejoined Paul, who after hearing his report wrote the letter. This second meeting of Timothy with Paul is evidently to be equated with the arrival of Silas and Timothy from Macedonia after Paul had already moved from Athens to Corinth, which is reported in Acts 18:5. The first meeting in Athens expected in Acts 17:15-16 is missing from the Acts account, as is Timothy's resulting trip to Thessalonica. Therefore we may conclude that the letter was written at Corinth. This is confirmed by the implication in 3:1 that Paul was no longer at Athens.

The date of the writing is determined by the time of Paul's work in Corinth. This is known from an inscription from Delphi which reveals that the proconsul Gallio (Acts 18:12-17) took office in the summer of A.D. 51. The letter, then, was written in 50 or 51.

Structure

The letter is simply but carefully constructed. Its two sections concern the past work of Paul in Thessalonica (chapters 1-3) and the present issues in the church (chapters 4-5). Because Paul had to leave his converts in haste and was not able to return (cf. 2:18) he found it necessary to discuss extensively the nature of his mission among them, lest they conclude that he was simply one more traveling huckster of religion. Paul's paragraphs here provide us with the earliest glimpse into a Christian congregation.

The Eschatological Emphasis

The letter is famous, however, mostly for its remarks on the "second coming" of Christ and for its evidence of the tenor of early Christian eschatology. "Eschatology" (literally doctrine of the end) is a very elastic word that includes all manner of concepts of the future. Eschatology is a built-in aspect of all thinking about the life of humanity and the nature of history. For example, Christian eschatology concerns the kingdom of God, Marxist eschatology concerns the classless society at the end of the historical dialectic, and nihilistic eschatologies speak of the extinction of life on the planet either by uncontrollable technological war or by the disappearance of conditions necessary for life.

In the late literature of the Old Testament, especially Daniel, we find a special type of eschatological thinking—apocalyptic (from a Greek word meaning "unveiling"). Apocalyptic eschatology holds that not only the future is set by God but the schedule as well. Therefore history is not a riddle but the working out of a predetermined plan of God which is revealed to the specially chosen person for the sake of the faithful. A constant ingredient is the view that history is accelerating into insurrection (progress in reverse!) which springs from the disobedience of angels before creation and from human sin since then. History is therefore rushing headlong into a crisis during which God will intervene to set everything right. The Dead Sea Scrolls come from a group that held such views.

Another group holding apocalyptic views was the early church. Early Christians regarded the resurrection of Jesus as the inauguration of the end, and they expected that he would appear soon as final judge and arbiter of history. The two Thessalonian letters, as well as Mark 13 (and its parallels in Matthew and Luke), Revelation, and II Peter, show how widespread and persistent such views were. Moreover the trained eye can detect evidences in the New Testament of the readjustment necessitated by the conversion of Gentiles, who viewed such ideas as strange and peripheral to the meaning of Jesus as they found it, and by the fact that all these hopes were disappointed again and again. The two Thessalonian letters, then, are important documents in the overall story of early Christian apocalyptic eschatology.

A Pastoral Letter

In contrast with Galatians and Colossians this letter does not debate theological alternatives, though it deals with them. In contrast with Romans it is not a theological essay. In contrast with the Corinthian letters it does not deal with a series of crises in the church, though it often seems to touch lightly on some of the same problems. This is a pastoral letter by an apostle who wants to guide the church he has founded but cannot remain with.

I. GREETING (1:1)

Paul's associates share his greeting, which follows the standard pattern of the Pauline letters. For the circumstances in which **Timothy** joined Paul see Acts 16:1-3. On **Silvanus** (doubtless the same as Silas) see Acts 15:22-41.

II. THANKSGIVING FOR THE RECEPTION OF THE GOSPEL (1:2-3:13)

All Paul's letters except Galatians open with paragraphs of thanksgiving. These orient the letter by mentioning the writer and readers in ways which suggest the themes of the letter as a whole. A distinguishing feature of I Thessalonians is the extent of its thanksgiving. 1:6-2:12 is an exposition of the theme of thanks as stated in 1:2-5. Then 2:13 repeats the statement of thanks so as to shift the discussion from Paul's original work in Thessalonica to his subsequent relation to the church. In 3:9-10 Paul returns to the theme of thanks, and 3:11-13 is a prayer for the readers, a standard conclusion to the thanksgivings. Thus giving thanks controls the first three chapters. The remaining two are Paul's exhortation to this church for which he is so deeply grateful.

A. THE THANKSGIVING THEME (1:2-5)

Verses 2-3 say *how* Paul gives thanks, while verses 4-5 say *why*. **Always** ought not to be emphasized because it is a standard item in a thanksgiving paragraph and in prayers as well.

397

1:3. *Faith, Hope, Love.* The famous triad of I Corinthians 13:13 appears here in a different order (cf. 5:8; Colossians 1:3-5). All three phrases must be taken together, and in all three the word **of** is important. Rather than work inspired by faith, etc., Paul speaks of work as a form of faith, labor as the shape of love, steadfastness as the manifestation of hope (cf. the New English Bible: "how your faith has shown itself in action, your love in labor and your hope . . . in fortitude"). When Paul thinks of this quality of life which the gospel has brought about, he gives thanks to God.

1:4. *Election.* Paul believes that his readers are **chosen** by God. This word is a technical term for Paul and the whole Bible. It expresses the belief that in the divine-human relationship the initiative lies with God. Jesus put it tersely: "You did not choose me, but I chose you" (John 15:16). Biblical thought holds in tension God's choice and human choice. Nowhere does God's choosing take responsibility away from persons. Paul's classical treatment of the theme is in Romans 9-11.

1:5. *Paul's Own Gospel.* Paul knows that God has chosen the readers because his message came with **power**, the **Holy Spirit**, and **full conviction**. This theme will be developed in chapter 2. He speaks of **our gospel** because for him the gospel is inseparable from his personal conversion and commission to preach. Though in his summary of his gospel in I Corinthians 15:1-11 he insists that it is not uniquely his, nevertheless he had a distinctive grasp of the meaning of Jesus.

Paul declares that his preaching was not "just talk" but an event marked by power, Spirit, and confidence. It is not clear whether **power** refers to healing power such as Acts reports (Acts 16:16-18; 19:11-20) and as Paul once mentions (II Corinthians 12:12) or whether it refers to the ability of the gospel to elicit faith and reshape life. For Paul the **Holy Spirit** was a basic ingredient of Christian life, the "down payment" of salvation (II Corinthians 1:22; 5:5).

Some take this verse to refer to Paul's own attitude and actions. It is better, however, to take it as referring to the results of his work, for the text speaks of how the gospel **came to you**. What happened when Paul preached confirms for him that God is at work, "choosing" the church. Paul reckons with the possibility that his message might be only words. But because God was at work as he preached, there occurred among the Thessalonians work, labor, and steadfastness. Remembering this he gives thanks.

B. THE RESPONSE TO THE GOSPEL (1:6-10)

Here Paul states the Thessalonian response in more detail. What verses 4-5 said theologically these verses state in terms of specific actions.

1:6-7. *Imitators and Imitated.* The point here is that the readers became first **imitators** and then became an **example** to be imitated by others. Paul did not want to be mistaken as a propagandist of religious ideas; he wanted to be seen as an embodiment of his message of the cross and the resurrection. He demanded that his life be transparent enough that his hearers could glimpse the power of the gospel. This transparency is what Paul wants the believers to imitate. The phrase **and of the Lord** is not a correction, as some suggest, but is another way of saying what is said in I Corinthians 11:1 (cf. the strong language in Galatians 6:17; Colossians 1:24).

What distinguishes Paul from the many hawkers of religion, then and now, is precisely this insistence that his person is inseparable from his message. He did not "sell" the gospel as a commodity external to himself but presented it by word and life (verse 5*b* is important). The Thessalonian response in **affliction** (verse 6) gave Paul evidence that they had indeed imitated him. Because the Corinthians, on the other hand, did not grasp this feature of Paul's gospel, he later fully expounded this point in II Corinthians 10-12, the best commentary on this passage.

1:8-10. *The Spread of the Gospel.* That the Thessalonian response spread **everywhere** is of course an exaggeration. Just as Paul's message united his person and his proclamation, so the Thessalonian response is joined with **the word of the Lord** (i.e. the gospel) as it spreads.

1:9*b*-10. Because this passage seems to fall into rhythmical phrases and uses words not common to Paul, it may be quoted from the common stock of early Christian worship material. If so, we should be cautious in using it as a guide to the way Paul actually preached to the Thessalonians. In any case, however, it is an important clue to the themes of early Christian preaching to Gentiles.

The call to turn from polytheism to the one God was the core of Jewish preaching to Gentiles. It was taken up by Christians, who added the message about Jesus, here stated in three points: the future coming, the identification of the expected one with the resurrected one, and his role as deliverer. This outline assumes more than it says, for it eclipses the whole life of Jesus.

The ideas are put into paradoxical form. The heavenly **Son** of God has a historical earthly name, **Jesus.** The one **from heaven** has already been among **the dead**, presumably under the earth. He will deliver **us** who already believe **from the wrath to come**. The emphasis falls on the future. Early Christianity was much more future-oriented and apocalyptically minded than most Christianity today (see Introduction). The Thessalonians had special problems in this connection (cf. chapters 4-5).

C. PAUL AS PREACHER AND PASTOR (2:1-12)

This passage is an exposition of 1:5*b* and 9*b*. It balances 1:6-10, which has discussed what the Thessalonians became.

2:1-2. *A Thematic Introduction.* Paul's mission was not in vain. Despite maltreatment in Philippi (cf. Acts 16:16-40) he found courage to preach in Thessalonica, again **in the face of great opposition**. The response suggests that God is at work, for the meaning of the resurrection has become real in daily life. Acts 17:1-9 does not suggest the steady hostility implied here.

2:3-8. *Paul's Preaching.* Paul makes his appeal in a way that is appropriate to the fact that God entrusted him with the message. Therefore he seeks to please the God who gave it, not those who hear it (cf. II Corinthians 4:1-6). Paul developed the style of his mission so that the meaning of his commissioning was preserved. This left no room for manipulating his hearers.

2:5-8. This is the most personal part of the letter. The ancient world had an ample supply of traveling preachers and promoters of cults and religions, some of whom took advantage of people. The Christian church did not remain free from such abuse (cf. II John 10-11). In contrast Paul emphasizes his integrity and his involvement with the life of his converts. Precisely what apostolic **demands** he did not make is unclear, though I Corinthians 9 suggests that he means the right to be supported by the church. The entire passage gives us better insight into Paul's mission than anything Acts says.

2:9-12. *Paul's Work as a Pastor.* Paul is proud that he earned his own living (cf. I Corinthians 4:11-12 and II Corinthians 11:27). According to Acts 18:3 he was a tentmaker. Tactfully he ignores the fact that at Thessalonica he received financial help from Philippi more than once (Philippians 4:16); nor does he mention Jason's hospitality (Acts 17:7).

In verses 10-12 he returns to the theme of his solicitous care, now speaking of himself as a **father with his children**—a sterner metaphor than the **nurse** of verse 7. As father Paul refers to his exhortations to live a life appropriate to God's call (another way of referring to God's choosing them; cf. 1:4), which they obeyed. **Kingdom and glory** here mean the complete salvation when the work of God is consummated (cf. Romans 5:2; I Corinthians 15:20-28). Here Christian ethics is not a set of regulations but a mandate to develop a kind of life that is appropriate to the gospel (cf. Philippians 2:1-13).

D. Thanks Restated (2:13)

This gathers up the thrust of the whole discussion so far. Paul calls his message the **word of God.** He recognizes, however, that it is possible to take it simply as the word of a man, as his ideas about Jesus. Yet those who believe it know that Paul's message is the vehicle for God's word. It is the working of this message—its power to elicit the sort of responses Paul has discussed—that convinces the readers that what they have heard and heeded is really God's address to them. Their own changed lives (1:2-10) point to the conclusion that God was at work among them.

E. A POLEMIC AGAINST JEWS (2:14-16)

This passage interrupts the flow of thought between verse 13 and verse 17. It contains a vicious attack on unbelieving Jews from a viewpoint unlike that elsewhere in Paul's writings (cf. especially Romans 9-11). The final sentence traditionally has been taken to be a reference to the Roman destruction of Jerusalem in A.D. 70, and many scholars consider it an interpolation added after that event (see below on verse 16c). Most commentators find various arguments to defend Paul's writing of the passage, with or without verse 16c—for example, a moment of frustration and uncontrolled temper. But these are not persuasive. A number of scholars prefer to regard the whole passage as an interpolation made after the fall of Jerusalem (and after Paul's death).

2:14. *Imitators of Palestinian Christians.* Because the Thessalonians suffered from their fellow citizens just as Jewish Christians endured much from their compatriots, it is said that they are in effect imitators of the Palestinian Christians. While Paul believed strongly in the unity of the whole church—and collected funds from Gentile churches for the needy in Jerusalem to show it—there is no other evidence that he ever regarded Judean Christianity as something to be imitated.

2:15-16. *Attack on the Jews.* That the Jews killed the **prophets** is mentioned also in Matthew 23:34-36, 37 and Luke 11:47-52 and is implied in Matthew 21:33-41. Generally the Old Testament does not say how the prophets died, though intertestamental stories grew up about them, as reflected in Hebrews 11:37. That many of them were persecuted is clear. According to Matthew 5:11-12 and Luke 6:22-23 Jesus himself connected the persecution of his followers with that of the prophets, while according to Matthew 23:37-38 and Luke 13:34-35 he made a similar connection regarding his own fate. This text, however, is the only one that connects all three.

Whether **drove us out** refers to Paul himself, to the apostles, or to Christians in general is uncertain. Also unclear is what they were driven out of—the synagogues? or Palestine? The expulsion of Christians from the Palestinian synagogues did not occur until after A.D. 70. That the Jews **displease God and oppose all men** echoes the anti-Semitic charges of pagans and is difficult to conceive of in the mouth of Paul. That they oppose the spread of the gospel among Gentiles is a possible echo of Acts 13:44-14:20. This opposition is viewed as consummating a sinful history.

2:16c. The phrase translated **at last** can mean either "finally" or "to the end." In either case **wrath** is most naturally understood as an allusion to the destruction of Jerusalem written after the event (see above on verses 14-16). Those who maintain Paul's authorship of the sentence assert either that he foresaw such a catastrophe or that he refers to an apocalyptic day of judgment.

F. TIMOTHY'S VISIT (2:17-3:5)

Following his second note of thanksgiving in 2:13 Paul discusses his relation to the church after he left Thessalonica (cf. Acts 17:1-15). If some are thinking Paul "ran out" on them, he reassures them this is not the case. 2:17-20 states his true attitude and 3:1-5 gives its result: Timothy's trip (see Introduction).

2:17-20. *Paul's Attitude Toward the Thessalonians.* Paul insists that he himself has wanted to return more than once. Of this Acts says nothing. He blames **Satan** for the fact he has not returned. Many interpretations of this have been offered: illness (cf. II Corinthians 12:7); the magistrates at Thessalonica (cf. Acts

17:8-9); the Thessalonian Jews (cf. Acts 17:5-7); problems in Corinth, from where Paul writes (cf. Acts 18:5-17).

In any case Paul sees some historical circumstance as part of a cosmic struggle between God and Satanic opposition (cf. II Corinthians 2:10-11; 11:12-15). In restating his love for his readers (verses 19-20) Paul refers for the first time to the **coming** of the Lord (see below on 4:13-5:11). He assures them that they will be his **glory** (i.e. reward) **and joy** on that day. He has not brought about their conversion with its subsequent difficulties only to abandon them.

3:1-5. *Timothy Sent to Thessalonica.* Paul tells of sending Timothy back from **Athens** to revisit the readers (see Introduction). Why Silvanus (Silas) is not mentioned is unknown. Paul's being **left . . . alone** suggests either that he had stayed on in Beroea (cf. Acts 17:13-15) or that he was sent back with Timothy but to another city in Macedonia (cf. Acts 18:5). The purpose of Timothy's trip was double—to **establish** (strengthen) the church members in their faith and to **exhort** them so that they would not abandon Christianity in difficulty. Timothy went as theologian and as pastor.

3:3*b*-4. Paul reinforces Timothy's work by reminding the readers that he foretold the afflictions they have endured. The first two uses of **we** in verse 4 mean Paul and his associates but the third refers to all Christians. That suffering is an inherent part of Christian life was a characteristic emphasis of Paul. For him suffering was no threat to the truth of the gospel but a potential confirmation of it.

3:5. Even so, those who do not understand this, or agree, might fall away from the faith. Hence Paul sent Timothy to determine whether the Thessalonians were firmly grounded in the gospel, lest **the tempter** (i.e. Satan; **the tempter** is used elsewhere only in Matthew 4:3) seduce them away from Christ and his own work should turn out to have been **in vain**. Paul is a realist. He reckons seriously with the possibility that under pressure Christians might repudiate their faith. He who has been as tender as a nurse (2:7) and as concerned as a father (2:11) is eager to stabilize the church. This is why he sent Timothy.

G. PAUL'S RESPONSE TO TIMOTHY'S REPORT (3:6-10)

Verses 6-8 state the point and verses 9-10 return to the theme of thanks, thereby rounding out the entire thanksgiving section (1:2-3:10).

3:6. *Timothy's Report.* As described here the report was entirely positive, though what follows in chapters 4-5 suggests that Paul's words are too generous. In any case the Thessalonian church is basically firm in its grasp of the Christian faith and in its regard for Paul. **Brought . . . good news** is the normal Greek meaning of a word that in Christian usage came to mean "preach the gospel"—a development which some have traced to Paul himself. Though Timothy spoke favorably about the Thessalonians' **faith** and **love**, nothing is said about their hope (see above on 1:3). Hope is a problem discussed in the next section.

3:7-8. *Paul's Own Involvement.* The news from Thessalonica has comforted Paul in his **distress** in Corinth. Whether this refers to what Acts 18:1-21 tells is unknown. Verse 8 expresses once more Paul's personal involvement in his church (cf. 2:7-8, 17-20), especially his concern for its stability (**stand** is Paul's word for "maintain faith"). Verse 8 should not be taken literally, though II Corinthians 11:28-29 suggests that Paul's involvement in his congregations affected his health (cf. also II Corinthians 1:8; 2:4, 13).

3:9-10. *A Final Thanksgiving.* This concluding mention of **thanksgiving** points up the emphasis throughout chapters 1-3. The closing phrase hints the themes of the next section.

H. A TRANSITIONAL PRAYER (3:11-13)

This prayer takes up the relation of Paul to his readers and places it before the will of God. It gathers up themes already discussed and mentions that of the remaining half of the letter, the **coming of our Lord.** In the petition **may God . . . and our Lord Jesus direct our way** the verb is singular. Paul never says how God and Christ work together. Such statements as this, coupled with references to the work of the Holy Spirit, pose the problems which are not "solved" until the doctrine of the Trinity is worked out. Paul prays that the result of increasing **love** for all people will be increased stability in innocence and in sanctity before God. It is commonly believed that increased **holiness** produces more love; here Paul reverses the process.

III. EXHORTATION:
THE DAILY MEANING OF THE GOSPEL (4:1-5:25)

This section begins and ends with miscellaneous exhortations. In the middle, however, two specific problems are discussed: the impact of death on Christian faith and the proper attitudes toward the time of the end.

A. GENERAL EXHORTATIONS (4:1-12)

4:1-2. *Learning and Instructions.* Paul begins by tactfully building on the present and past. What he calls for is not a new orientation but a continued effort in the same direction. The passage raises an important historical question: To what extent did Paul's gospel preaching include ethical guidance? This text forbids taking literally Paul's saying that he preached only Christ crucified (I Corinthians 2:2). Besides, there is sufficient evidence that Paul did not simply preach the cross and the resurrection. He included the moral meaning of that theme as the indispensable ingredient of Christian faith as such. All of Romans makes this point.

Learned (literally "received") was a technical term for the transmission of tradition. Some think that this passage therefore refers to the transmission of a body of tradition of ethical instruction. For example, the New English Bible translation reads "We passed on to you the tradition of the way we must live." However, this makes Paul's language more technical than it is. Some have even seen here a reference to Paul's

transmitting the teachings of Jesus (the gospels were not yet
written). This is highly dubious. Even if one can find echoes of
Jesus' phrases in the letter, the very fact that they are only
echoes and not references shows that Paul did not emphasize
Jesus' teachings.

4:2. What **instructions** Paul gave the Thessalonians is
unknown. We can be confident they were not mere general
admonitions to "do good" but included specific obligations as
well. When he had no tradition to guide him, he trusted his own
judgment, as I Corinthians 7 shows. In this case, however, he
says the instructions were given **through the Lord Jesus.** Paul's
ethics were shaped by his Christology, his understanding of the
meaning of Jesus in the widest sense, as Philippians 2:1-13
shows. The basis of Christian ethics which he assumes here is
not "the good" or "the useful" but that which pleases God.

This is the fundamental approach of the Bible. What is good
and right is what pleases God. There is no independent good or
right according to which one might assess the deed of even God,
as in Greek thought. What is good and right is what God wills,
not what can be determined rationally or scientifically. Not even
Romans 1-2, which speaks of the innate human ability to
discover what is right, eclipses the will of God as the real arbiter
of the good and the right. There is no understanding of biblical
ethics without seeing this point.

4:3-6. *Sanctification.* Verse 3*a* states the theme: God wills
your sanctification (the translation **the will of God** makes the
point too sweeping). "Sanctification" in Greek means, not the
process of making holy or the ideal of holiness, but the end
product of making holy, the achievement of holiness (cf. Romans
6:19, 22; I Corinthians 1:30). For Paul sanctification is not the
result of ritual or of religious experience as such but a matter of
ethics. Sanctification—making life holy—is living so as to please
God. It is a life-long process, as Romans 6:19-22 recognizes.

4:3*b*-6 spells out what Paul has in mind, focusing on two
problems, sex and greed. Sanctification means abstaining from
sexual immorality—literally "prostitution," but the word had
come to mean a variety of sexual sins. Like our own, the

Hellenistic world was much more tolerant of all manner of sexual practices than were Paul and the biblical tradition.

What Paul demands next is not clear. **A wife for himself** is literally "his vessel." Since early times many have assumed that Paul speaks of marriage—an interpretation said to be supported by I Peter 3:7, where woman is "the weaker vessel" (Revised Standard Version "sex,"). Others believe that Paul speaks rather of self-control—that "his vessel" means "mastery over his body" (New English Bible). That Paul intended the latter sense seems more probable. Verse 5 reveals Paul's contempt for Gentile sexual ethics and traces it, as Jews commonly did, to idolatry and polytheism (discussed in detail in Romans 1:18-32). Here Paul draws on Psalm 79:6 and Jeremiah 10:25.

4:6. In verse 6*a* the Revised Standard Version translators have supplied the word **this** on the assumption that Paul is still speaking of sexual immorality. But in Greek usage **matter** had a commercial sense, and it seems likely that Paul here brings up dishonesty in business (see the Revised Standard Version footnote). Verse 6*b* returns to the basis of Paul's ethics—the judgment of God. He has already implied it in grounding ethics in God's will, since this commits God to carry out the divine will and to respond appropriately to opposition to it. For the Bible as a whole, God's vindicating the divine will corroborates the belief that this will is God's commitment and not merely God's preference. In Romans 12:19-21 Paul insists that the vindication of God's will must be left to God—a point not mentioned in this passage and not followed in I Corinthians 5:3-5.

4:7-8. *God's Call.* These ethical obligations are tied to theological considerations. What Paul has just discussed is consistent with the goal of God's work with the readers—his call (cf. 1:4; 2:12). Verse 8 insists that Paul's counsel is not simply his own notion and explains what it means for God to give the **Holy Spirit** to the Christian. In this passage the Spirit is not an ecstatic power but a presence which sanctifies because it is the *Holy* Spirit. Its work is to elicit the holy life Paul has called for.

4:9-12. *Love and Work.* The phrase **taught by God** may refer to the lesson taught by God's love in the events summed up in the "Christ event," in accord with Romans 5:8. Or it may refer to the consequence of being granted the Spirit, in accord with Romans 5:5. **Love of the brethren** was a characteristic of early Christianity. Perhaps the location of Thessalonica helped this church make contact with other Christians **throughout Macedonia**.

4:11-12. Many commentators have assumed that the Thessalonians were prone to stop **work** because they were excited over the second coming of Christ, which Paul takes up in his next paragraph. But the connection which the text implies in verses 10*b*-12—all one sentence—is a possible abuse of the brotherly love and mutual sharing among Christians. Perhaps some became idlers and busybodies who insisted that their brothers owed them a living.

Paul knows that the character of a Christian's life has an effect on the reputation of the gospel itself (verse 12). He does not want the church to get the reputation of fostering indolence in the name of religion. The word **nobody** probably should be taken as "nothing," so that the second motive Paul suggests for working is not independence of others but to "be in need of nothing." The sharing of goods which early Jerusalem Christians practiced was not transplanted by Paul into his churches.

B. Death and Christian Salvation (4:13-18)

This and the following paragraph constitute the hallmark of I Thessalonians. Paul introduces the topic with the same word, **concerning**, which begins each of his answers to a letter from Corinth (I Corinthians 7:1, 25; 8:1; 12:1; 16:1). This does not necessarily mean that here too Paul is answering a letter brought by Timothy. Knowledge of what needs to be discussed probably depends on Timothy's report (cf. 3:6). Verses 13-14 state the basic point, and 15-17 amplify it. Verse 18 relates the discussion to the present life of the Christian community.

4:13-14. *Hope in the Resurrection of Jesus.* These verses, along with verse 18, are important guides to the problem in the church. The **coming of the Lord** is discussed to deal with certain attitudes toward death and toward Christian faith itself—attitudes characterized as the grief of **others . . . who have no hope**. Who are these? Probably, Paul has in mind pagans in general, whom he has just described as not knowing God (4:5). He is doubtless aware that many Gentiles believed either in the natural immortality of the soul or in immortality conferred by rites of initiation into the many cults. But for Paul such pagan ideas of life after death are **no hope** at all.

4:14. Hope, as Paul sees it, is grounded in the resurrection of Jesus. His purpose in the discussion, then, is not to assuage normal grief caused by death but to deal with despair. This calls, not for comforting sentiments, but for instruction. What was the problem? The common view that the question was whether at the coming of Christ the Christians who had already died would be on the same level as the living is not convincing. The real problem is the fact that Christians have died at all. Some fear that the dead have forfeited their salvation. If this should be true, only those alive at Christ's return would really be saved. Moreover death itself would not really have been dealt with by the resurrection of Jesus, and the Christian message as a whole would be jeopardized. Some may also have thought that baptism into Christ's death and resurrection made them immune to death, immortal, as in the rites of the mystery religions.

The heart of Paul's response is that there is an inseparable relationship between Christ and the Christian (cf. Romans 8:31-39). Hence Paul argues that believing in the resurrection of Jesus means believing also that the believer will participate in Jesus' exaltation to the heavenly realm. Therefore when Jesus "comes," those who died with him will not be left out. Verses 15-17 spell this out in detail.

This is one of the few places where the New Testament says Jesus **rose** (elsewhere only in Mark 8:31; 9:31; 10:34). Usually it says "he was raised"—that is, by God. **Through Jesus** is ambiguous in that it can be taken either with **God will bring**, as in the Revised Standard Version, or with **those who have fallen asleep**, meaning those who "died as Christians" (New English

Bible). However, there is no reference here to martyrs—those who died because of Jesus. **Bring** can mean bring them to earth with Jesus, or bring them to life, or bring them into participation in the consummated salvation, or bring them back into heaven with the triumphant Lord.

4:15-17. *The End.* These verses describe the *eschaton*—the end. Paul's purpose in discussing this must not be forgotten (see above on verses 13-14).

4:15. Paul appeals to the **word of the Lord**. Some think he is referring to a tradition of what Jesus said (the gospels were written twenty to fifty years later). Others think he speaks of a special revelation such as he mentions in II Corinthians 12:1-9 and such as Acts reports (Acts 9:1-9; 18:9-10; 22:17-21; 27:21-26). Probably Paul is appealing to a tradition of Jesus' words—Matthew 24:30 and John 6:40 have often been suggested. It is impossible to reconstruct the saying because the wording is changed—at least **the Lord** and **we** did not belong in Jesus' phrases. This tradition may be otherwise unknown to us. Whether it accurately represented what Jesus said is another matter.

From **we . . . who are left** it is clear that Paul expects to live to see the Lord's coming. Early Christianity generally expected that the Lord would soon consummate his victory over sin and death, which the resurrection had inaugurated.

The technical term for the arrival of the Lord, **coming** (Greek *parousia*), was used in ordinary speech precisely as our English word is used (e.g. Philippians 1:26). It came to be used in a special sense, however, for the state visits of kings and rulers. From this exalted, official meaning it came into Christian usage, the earliest such being in I Thessalonians.

Not until a century later is the expression "second coming" found. For the New Testament period the **coming** was always this imminent, regal arrival of the Lord. The life of Jesus had been far too humble an event to be spoken of as the "first coming." Not until the life of Jesus was glorified, as in John, did one speak of a first and second coming.

Paul insists that those who are alive **shall not precede** the dead. The negative in the Greek is stronger than in this translation. The point is not simply sequence—what would it matter then who came first?—but whether the dead are to be included at all. So strongly does Paul think that the dead will share the event that he says that the living will not even precede them.

4:16. The purpose of this verse is to show why the foregoing is true. The coming is described as a descent, in keeping with the idea that the resurrection took Jesus to heaven (only Luke-Acts separates resurrection from ascent to heaven). The descent will be accompanied by the Lord's **command**, the **archangel's call**, and God's **trumpet**. The entire "power structure" of the heavenly court will be involved. These are traditional symbols of divine authority and sovereignty, and it is pointless to speculate about what the Lord will command, the archangels say, or the trumpet play.

That **the dead in Christ will rise first** is the point Paul has been making throughout the passage. The fate of the non-Christian dead is ignored. Another interpretation, however, puts **in Christ** with **will rise** to make the point that all the dead, Christian or not, "will rise in Christ." This interpretation agrees with I Corinthians 15:22, where clearly all humanity share the benefits of Christ's resurrection.

4:17. Those **who are alive** will join the resurrected ones and will be **caught up together in the clouds** for a rendezvous with the Lord in mid-air. There is no mention of the transformation of the living, emphasized in I Corinthians 15:50-54. Doubtless it is omitted here because this was not a problem in Thessalonica. The goal is **to meet the Lord in the air**—that is, the realm between earth and the sky.

Paul ends the story here, as if to exclude any reference to a continued descent to earth. He may have in mind a triumphal return with all the saints to heaven—a possible meaning of **will bring** in verse 14. There is no word here, or room, for a thousand-year rule of the Messiah on earth as envisaged in Revelation 20:4-6.

4:18. *A Basis for Faith.* Paul reminds the readers that his intent is to provide, not a preview of the future, but a basis for **comfort**. The Greek word means not simply emotional consolation but exhortation, counsel, and admonition. The central concern in the whole discussion is to provide the basis for confident faith in Christ in the face of death.

Some general observations about verses 15-18 are now in order:

(1) This is not a complete statement of Paul's ideas of the end. Even when it is joined with I Corinthians 15 (especially verses 51-56) we do not have a complete picture. Perhaps Paul did not have one either. It is risky, moreover, to fill in the gaps from the rest of the New Testament or from Jewish apocalyptic literature.

(2) The fact that this portrait of the end is not identical with that of Mark 13 or Revelation shows that the early church had a variety of ideas on the subject, just as Judaism did. It is important to let these diversities stand rather than force them into a single, harmonious scheme of the end.

(3) This variety suggests that the real intent of all these views is to announce in dramatic form the consummation of God's saving work in Christ. Where this salvation is understood largely in dynamic terms that deal with release from various tyrannies, the consummation is portrayed as a dramatic victory over opposition to God and as a climactic assertion of God's sovereignty (cf. II Thessalonians 2:1-12).

(4) It is not clear how this apocalyptic line of thought in Paul (including I Corinthians 15) is related to a somewhat different emphasis in II Corinthians 5:1-10 and Philippians 1:21-23. In those passages being **with the Lord** is an immediate alternative to being alive on earth and does not seem to require a resurrection at all. This passage and I Corinthians 15 assume that a resurrection makes being with the Lord possible at the end. Some interpreters have seen in Paul's thinking a later shift away from the Jewish apocalyptic views he held at the time of writing I Thessalonians, but this can scarcely be demonstrated convincingly. Hence it is better to recognize the existence of two lines of thought in Paul and leave open the question of how he related them—if he did.

(5) Whatever one makes of the sequence of events outlined by Paul, it is clear that his scheduling was wrong. The end did not occur during his lifetime. Hence we cannot avoid asking: In view of his miscalculation of the calendar, is there anything of enduring value here, any transcending truth in what Paul has to say?

The answer is that Paul's central point is not when or how the end will come. It is that the prospect of an end to life must not jeopardize one's confidence in Christ, because the relation of the believer to the Lord is indestructible even by death. The real heart of the matter is the confident trust in God stated in Romans 8:31-39, where there is neither schedule nor trumpet. Paul himself, then, shows how to grasp what is at stake without being confused by the details of the timing of it all.

C. Life Today in Light of the End (5:1-11)

The second, related, problem that Paul considers is the uncertain time of the end. This paragraph too begins by stating the theme and ends with an admonition. The passage is not a general treatment of a topic but a theological discussion of a pastoral problem. It makes a single point: the suddenness of the end requires an appropriate moral life now.

5:1-2. *Times and Seasons.* Paul begins his discussion of **the times and the seasons** (an expression taken from the Old Testament; cf. Daniel 2:21) by pointing out that it is not really needed—probably because of previous instruction. Nevertheless he continues in order to anticipate the problems that may arise and to lead to his major concern, the proper quality of life here and now.

5:2. By the **day of the Lord** Paul means the same cluster of events discussed in 4:13-18 as the "coming." As a phrase meaning the end it appeared as early as the eighth century B.C. (Amos 5:18) and became common in apocalyptic literature, though not found in the gospels. Whereas the Old Testament and Jewish literature used "Lord" to speak of God, for Paul it meant Christ, the "Lord Jesus." Elsewhere he speaks of the "day of Christ" (Philippians 1:10; 2:16) and the "day of our Lord Jesus" (I Corinthians 5:5; II Corinthians 1:14). After Christians called Jesus "Lord" it was easy for them to think "Lord Jesus" as they read of "the Lord" in their Greek Old Testament.

Paul's point is that the day **will come like a thief in the night**. Jesus is recorded as using this figure also (Matthew 24:43-44 and Luke 12:39-40, where the one who comes is the Son of man, a phrase Paul does not use). It is uncertain whether Paul had this saying in mind or whether both he and Jesus took it from the common stock of Jewish ideas. At any rate both Jesus and Paul specify precisely how this coming is to be thief-like. The point of comparison is neither stealth nor stealing but surprise. Just as the thief's coming cannot be reckoned in advance, so the time of the day of the Lord cannot be calculated either. It will be here precisely when least expected.

5:3. *Suddenness and Surprise.* The sudden arrival will surprise those who feel secure. This unforeseen reversal of circumstances is a theme that pervades the entire apocalyptic tradition. Its biblical roots go back at least as far as Amos 5, where this same point is made. Similarly, the suddenness will be like the situation of a pregnant **woman** overtaken suddenly by labor pains.

Paul's point must not be confused with the Jewish apocalyptic idea of the "birth pangs of the Messiah"—the conviction that the Messiah would emerge into history only in a time of great distress. Paul is interested here, not in the difficulty that precedes the end (cf. II Thessalonians 2), but only in the surprise.

5:4-5. *Light and Darkness.* Paul next develops his admonition based on the contrast of **night** and **day**. Because Christians **belong to the day** (verse 8), the day that comes will not catch them napping. Paul shifts from simile (the day comes as a thief in the night) to allegory (the night suggests moral darkness). **Darkness** here means not only wickedness but a realm of authority and power to which one may **belong**. Christians (Paul shifts from **you** to **we** in the middle of verse 5) are **sons of**

light—that is, they belong to this field of force, this realm. Therefore the coming of the day (daylight) will not **surprise** them. By implication the coming of the day will not bring a reversal of their relation to God because as sons of light they are already of the day.

How close this passage stands to Jewish apocalyptic has been demonstrated by the Dead Sea Scrolls. Among these is a document that spells out the final battle between the hosts of good and evil—The War of the Sons of Light and the Sons of Darkness. It must not be assumed, of course, that Paul knew or used this document. He simply shared the apocalyptic inheritance from contemporary Judaism.

5:6-7. *Watchfulness.* Paul carries further his allegorical treatment of "night life": Christians are to be alert to the times in which they live and to what these demand. Night and day suggest sleeping and waking; therefore Paul demands wakefulness. Keeping **awake** and going to **sleep** are metaphors of perceptiveness or lack of it. Being **sober** makes the same point. Having added sobriety to wakefulness as appropriate acts of daylight, Paul makes the same point in reverse; people **sleep** and **get drunk . . . at night**.

5:8-11. *The Goal of Salvation.* Paul shifts to military metaphors. Here the triad of **faith . . . love . . . hope** (see above on 1:3) is allegorized as defensive armor (cf. Ephesians 6:10-17). Having mentioned **salvation** Paul goes on to say that this is the whole point of God's work—our salvation, not **wrath** (i.e. destruction). Verse 10, however, turns the **wake or sleep** metaphor in still another direction. Returning to the theme of 4:13-18, Paul uses it to say that we will **live** with Christ whether we are dead or alive at the time of his coming. Verse 11 restates the practical aim of the whole discussion.

The entire paragraph combines rhetorical subtlety with serious pastoral concern. In these eleven verses Paul has insisted that the end cannot be calculated because it will come suddenly and without warning. This should not catch Christians off guard if they are alert to the ethical obligations of the present. A life of faith, hope, and love, with which the letter began, will be the best preparation for a future that cannot be known in advance. In this way Paul uses apocalyptic terminology and themes to turn back a developing curiosity about the time of the end. Though using apocalyptic tradition, Paul refuses to become an apocalyptic predictor. He remains a pastor.

D. COUNSELS FOR THE LIFE OF THE CHURCH (5:12-25)

This series of unconnected admonitions begins with attitudes toward church leaders and ends with a note of prayer.

5:12-14. *Respect for Church Leaders.* Paul speaks of the congregation and its leaders, addressing first the church as a whole, then the leadership. Significantly, he calls both groups **brethren,** the distinction between them being function rather than ordination. There were, strictly speaking, no lay persons in the early church because there were no clergy either. This is why I Thessalonians has no technical terms for the various offices, such as we find in Philippians 1:1 and Ephesians 4:11. The passage is also less specific than I Corinthians 12:4-11. The fact that Paul deals with this matter at all suggests that Timothy reported (3:6) that such guidance was needed.

5:12-13. The leaders exercise three functions: they **labor** (a semi-technical term for spreading the gospel), preside, and **admonish** (discipline). The congregation is to respect these men because of their work, their sole claim to authority. Paul's remarks imply that the church had some who, probably in the name of the Spirit, were unwilling to live with any structured responsibility. Paul recognized the need for order, but like the rest of early Christianity he did not know any priesthood or stratified membership in the church. This is markedly different from the community of the Dead Sea Scrolls, which was highly organized into priestly classes, and whose Manual of Discipline spelled out clearly the rights and privileges of the various ranks to which members were assigned. Such an approach to church order was not found among early Christians.

5:14. Many commentators see here three distinct groups which are causing difficulties:

(1) the **idle** (the word may also mean "disorderly"), explained as excited over the "coming" (see above on 4:11-12);

(2) the **fainthearted,** explained as worried about their dead relatives and their own salvation (thus making 4:13–5:11 addressed especially to them);

(3) the **weak,** explained as the morally unstable.

All this is possible, but it defines the groups much more clearly than the text warrants. These terms probably reflect not three groups, but three kinds of problems, here mentioned to balance rhetorically the three functions of the leaders. (Paul's style here, as elsewhere, reveals his predilection for carefully balanced sentences, a typical rhetorical touch that would make the letter easier to understand when it was read aloud—cf. verse 27.) These problems may have resulted from the pressures which the young church has been facing (cf. 1:6; 3:1-5, 7) and the questions about the validity of the gospel which the deaths have raised. In such circumstances Paul urges the congregation to live peaceably and the leaders to be **patient.** Paul's practical, pastoral concern is clear.

5:15-22. *Bases for Christian Living.* These verses consist of brief admonitions addressed to the whole church. Though Paul does not say so, they show how the church can move forward to actualize the counsels he has just given.

5:15. Paul mentions first the need for a creative response to **evil** deeds. **Seek to do good to one another** is milder than the Greek, which says rather "pursue the good for one another." Paul spells out this same point in Romans 12:17-21. Here he adds **and to all**, lest Christians do good only to one another. Paul compresses what Jesus said more fully in Matthew 5:38-48. Whether he is consciously dependent on Jesus' teaching here is not known.

5:16-18. These three admonitions are characterized by the note of constancy: **rejoice . . . pray . . . give thanks.** The **will of God** refers to all three.

5:19-20. We do not know if Paul is aiming here at particular abuses in the church. Interestingly, he encourages the readers not to **quench the Spirit.** Later he will ask the Corinthians to channel the Spirit without despising the ecstatic manifestations of it (I Corinthians 12–14, especially 14:37-40). Verse 20 makes virtually the same point, since in Paul's view **prophesying** is a work of the Spirit. (Prophesying probably meant articulating in a coherent and rational way the will of God or the "word" of the Lord, as in I Corinthians 14:20-33.

5:21-22. Verse 21 reads like a proverb. In this setting it may mean that prophesying is to be tested to determine **what is good** enough to follow. If so, Paul is making the same prudent point as I John 4:1, though Paul does not supply any criterion for testing the Spirit as does John. He assumes that what is good will be self-evident. The demand that Christians keep from **every form of evil** balances rhetorically the previous demand to hold to the good. These directions are designed to furnish the young church with basic moral standards.

5:23-25. *Injunctions to Pray.* Paul closes this section with a prayerful wish for the readers, balanced by the brief request that they, in turn, pray for him and his associates. Verse 23*a* returns to the theme of sanctification (cf. 4:3), thus setting the whole exhortation section into a framework of sanctification, just as the first three chapters were framed with the emphasis on thanksgiving.

Verse 23*b* not only picks up the theme of the coming again, but is the only place in the New Testament where the triadic nature of human beings is stated as **spirit and soul and body.** This should not be pressed, since it is not really typical of Paul to divide persons into three parts, even though he can use these terms. Here the phrase is a rhetorical expression to interpret **wholly**; more than this should not be made of it. Verse 24 reminds the readers that if the prayer is answered it is because of the faithfulness of God. Paul prays for the end toward which God is working. His prayer makes the same point and serves the same function in the section as the prayer in 3:11-13.

IV. Farewell (5:26-28)

The **holy kiss** apparently was a customary part of early Christian worship, though almost nothing is known of the practice itself. Verse 27 shows two things: (1) the seeds of factionalism may have been germinating to such an extent that Paul emphasizes **all the brethren;** (2) Paul's letters were intended to be read publicly, doubtless as part of worship, right from the start (cf. Colossians 4:16). Verse 28 is one of Paul's briefer benedictions.

THE SECOND LETTER OF PAUL
TO THE THESSALONIANS

Leander E. Keck

INTRODUCTION

Whereas the occasion and purpose of I Thessalonians are relatively simple to discover, the problems of II Thessalonians are so complex that no completely satisfactory solution to them has been found.

The traditional view is that shortly after Paul wrote I Thessalonians, news reached him that the two particular problems to which he had addressed himself—the end of history and the idle Christians—had grown more serious. In response Paul is said to have written II Thessalonians. This traditional view is by far the most widely held. Many see that a strong case cannot be made for it but think that any alternative is even weaker.

The Relationship Between I and II Thessalonians

There are five major issues involved here:

(1) The eschatology, or doctrine of last things, is crucial. The view of the end set forth in chapter 2 does not appear to agree with I Thessalonians 4–5. In the latter Paul argues that there is no warning, no hint of when the end will come. II Thessalonians

2, on the other hand, not only tells what signs to look for but also insists that Paul had already discussed this very point when he was in Thessalonica. Many have tried to show that these chapters can be harmonized. However, the real question is whether each chapter assumes what the other chapters say. This commentary does not make this assumption. In any event the material in II Thessalonians 2 is traditional Jewish apocalyptic, which is slightly Christianized and generally ignored in I Thessalonians (see Introduction to I Thessalonians).

(2) Closely related is a historical issue. 2:3-4 says that the "man of lawlessness" will occupy the temple and claim to be God. This may refer to the emperor Caligula's (A.D. 37-41) attempt to have a statue of himself erected in the Jerusalem temple in A.D. 40. If so, one could argue that Paul, a decade later, is interpreting either that episode or an interpretation of it as a sign of the times. On the other hand, the passage is clearly related to Mark 13:14-27, which was written around A.D. 70 but used older material. Both depend on Daniel (cf. e.g. Daniel 7:25; 8:25; 11:36). Therefore 2:3-4 could simply be using a traditional item in Jewish apocalyptic with no reference to a historical event at all. If so, the reference to the temple does not require a date prior to A.D. 70, when the temple burned.

(3) Some interpreters focus on the literary relation between the two letters. All students are struck by the fact that these two letters are more alike in wording and even in sequence of themes than any two undisputed letters of Paul (Colossians and Ephesians are similar, but Ephesians is disputed). But they differ precisely where one would expect them to be alike: the relation of Paul to the readers. Whereas I Thessalonians is warm and personal, II Thessalonians is distant and formal. Whereas I Thessalonians spends three chapters dealing with Paul's work in Thessalonica, II Thessalonians ignores this completely, except for 2:5, and has no personal touch. Would the same man write a letter such as II Thessalonians to the same church soon after he wrote such a letter as I Thessalonians?

(4) The theological teaching in chapter 1 says Christians will escape the judgment of God while unbelievers will be doomed

to eternal destruction. In Romans 14:10-12 and II Corinthians 5:10, however, Paul speaks of Christians before God's judgment seat. Nowhere else does Paul speak of God's vengeance on unbelievers. This is, however, a basic apocalyptic theme as found in Revelation.

(5) Finally, there is the matter of pseudepigraphy, or writing in someone else's name. This practice was widespread in the ancient world, and the Christian church followed it rather extensively. II Thessalonians itself raises the question twice. In 2:1-2 the author mentions a letter which claims Paul as author and which holds that the day of the Lord has already come. In 3:17, moreover, the author tries to authenticate his letter by appealing to the handwriting. In I Corinthians 16:21 Paul stops dictating and takes up the pen to write a personal greeting. Yet in this letter, which defends his authority, he makes no attempt to authenticate the letter—even though I Corinthians was written after II Thessalonians was (if it is genuinely Pauline) and after it had been circulated. Likewise in Galatians 6:11 Paul calls attention to the size of his handwriting but says nothing about authenticating the letter by this means. Moreover, this criterion is irrelevant anyway, since all letters were penned by scribes. Besides, II Thessalonians assumes that no personal messenger brought the letter but that it arrived impersonally—through the mail so to speak—and had to gain acceptance as best it could.

All these considerations taken together persuade this author that the letter is not from Paul. Those who claim II Thessalonians is genuine must explain why a letter claiming Paul's name would have circulated within weeks after I Thessalonians was written—or else make Paul speak of a hypothetical letter. They must also explain why those who had just read I Thessalonians, and who remembered Paul the way I Thessalonians says, would not know how to tell what was actually written by Paul. The advocates of the traditional view seem to have failed to do this.

These five arguments, then, make a compelling case against the genuineness of II Thessalonians as a Pauline letter. If we had either I or II Thessalonians alone, there would be no problem. It is precisely our having them both that makes the problem acute. And it is precisely the fact that I Thessalonians is genuine that shows that II Thessalonians is not.

Purpose, Place, and Date

Why then was II Thessalonians written? The clue is 2:1-4. A letter had circulated which claimed that Paul taught that the day of the Lord had already come. II Thessalonians opposes that letter by arguing that Paul did not hold this view because the necessary preliminary events of which he spoke had not yet occurred. The author wants to provide a definitive Pauline rebuttal for a misrepresentation of Paul. II Thessalonians reflects the struggle of the later church for a correct understanding of Paul. The author used as a model I Thessalonians, the one letter of Paul's which contained apocalyptic material and which was not as well known as I Corinthians.

II Thessalonians really has nothing to do with the church at Thessalonica—unless it was written there. The exact time and place of writing are unknown; A.D. 75-90 seems adequate. The letter was accepted as genuine from the time it was circulated. No one in the ancient church questioned it. This does not prove it is Pauline, as many think, but only that the author succeeded in what he set out to do.

Arguments for Pauline Authorship

Those who believe the letter to be genuine either take the traditional view (see above) or one of the following variants:

(1) Silas wrote it, having been told generally by Paul what to discuss. This is really a way of saying yes and no at the same time.

(2) Paul wrote II Thessalonians to Jewish Christians in the church but he wrote I Thessalonians to the Gentile wing. This view is discredited because Paul would never have founded a segregated church (cf. Galatians 2).

(3) II Thessalonians was sent to the city of Beroea. This is possible but without any evidence whatever.

424

(4) II Thessalonians was sent to Philippi. Evidence for this is too slight to be persuasive.

(5) II Thessalonians was written first, then I Thessalonians. This fails to account for the fact that I Thessalonians is more personal.

These varying suggestions actually support the view that II Thessalonians is not genuinely Pauline, for they all show that the traditional view cannot account for the phenomena of I and II Thessalonians. The real test of the view advocated here is whether the letter makes sense on the assumption that it was written in the name of Paul but not by him. The value and insight of II Thessalonians of course do not depend on whether or not Paul was the author.

I. GREETING (1:1-2)

This greeting is very similar to that of I Thessalonians, on which it is modeled.

II. THE THANKSGIVING (1:3–2:17)

The author follows Paul's structure of I Thessalonians in which the thanksgiving forms the bulk of the letter (cf. I Thessalonians 1:2–3:13). Just as I Thessalonians 2:13 repeats the thanksgiving formula of 1:2, so II Thessalonians 2:13 restates 1:3. There are two differences however:

(1) The thanksgiving of I Thessalonians moves back and forth between statements about the readers and those about the author. This gives the letter its personal tone. In II Thessalonians, however, the thanksgiving has few personal touches and says nothing which has not already been said of the readers in I Thessalonians.

(2) In contrast with I Thessalonians, the apocalyptic material has been moved from the second section of the letter to the middle of the thanksgiving (2:1-12). No other Pauline thanks-

giving is used as a setting for straightforward theological exposition. Apparently I Thessalonians was the model for II Thessalonians, but the writer abandoned his pattern at just those points where he was out of touch with the living situation of the historical Paul (see Introduction).

The thanksgiving may be divided into three parts:

(1) After a brief reference to the church's founding, attention shifts to the impending punishment for those who are not Christians (1:3-12).

(2) The signs of the times are taken up in 2:1-12.

(3) The section closes with another statement of thanks, followed by a prayer for the readers—standard elements in Pauline thanksgivings (2:13-17).

A. GRATITUDE FOR THE CHURCH'S FIDELITY (1:3-12)

The structure of the thanksgiving is obscured by the Revised Standard Version, which begins a paragraph at verse 5, and by the New English Bible, which begins one at verse 6—perhaps because each phrase of the long sentence (in Greek, verses 3-10 are one sentence) leads into another set of ideas. The whole sentence draws heavily on Old Testament ideas and phrases.

1:3. The formality of the letter can be seen here. Whereas I Thessalonians 1:2 says, "We give thanks to God always," this verse says, **We are bound to give thanks**, and adds, **as is fitting**. Instead of Paul's immediate response of thanks, the author speaks of a judicious, proper act of thanks because **faith** and **love** are growing (cf. I Thessalonians 1:2-3).

1:4. The church is praised for its character in persecution. If II Thessalonians were a genuine letter from Paul, this would be the oldest reference to the persecution of Christians. **Afflictions** and difficulties are mentioned in I Thessalonians 1:6 and 3:3, but not persecution (assuming I Thessalonians 2:14-16 is an interpolation; see comment). II Thessalonians, then, is to be seen as part of early Christian literature of persecution situations. This gives an urgency to the argument. It also points to a date later than A.D. 51, when I Thessalonians was written.

1:5-7a. *The Judgment of God.* This section interprets the persecution situation, while verses 7b-10 describe in detail what has been asserted theologically. The real point of verses 5-7a is that this persecution demonstrates the **righteous judgment of God**. The passage, then, is a kind of theodicy—a rationale for the justice of God. In keeping with the biblical view, the justice of God's ways is vindicated at the end of history rather than by arguing the rightness of things now.

The **evidence** of the righteous judgment of God which the author sees is probably the whole situation, not merely Christian fortitude. Being related to the kingdom brings the **suffering** which in turn makes one **worthy of the kingdom**. This is one side of the situation; verses 6-7a give the other. The righteous judgment of God will afflict the afflicters and relieve the **afflicted**.

Because the judgment of God reverses the present, the future lies with those who are presently persecuted. Hence being made steadfast in persecution is a sign of the righteousness of God, a hint of what God's judgment will do. Such an attitude toward suffering is rooted in the martyr theology of Daniel, reaffirmed by Jesus (Matthew 5:10-12) and ratified by the cross and resurrection.

1:7b-10. *The Revelation of the Lord Jesus.* These verses spell out the time and character of the future judgment in which the roles of the afflicted and the afflicters are reversed. They speak in turn of the time, the event, and the persons involved (both non-Christian and Christian) and their respective destinies. They then return to the theme of the indefinite time when these things will happen.

1:7b. The time will be at the "revelation," or as the Revised Standard Version translates, **when the Lord Jesus is revealed from heaven**, a reference to the "coming" (2:1). Speaking of the end events as the "revelation" implies that matters are decided already. History as we see it contradicts in part the existing lordship of Christ, which will be finally unveiled then. The awesome character of this disclosure, or revelation, of Christ is conveyed by the three phrases that define it: **from heaven,** with **angels,** in **flaming fire** (a standard element for divine judgment in apocalyptic literature).

1:8-10. Whom this act of God will affect and what it will be are dealt with in these verses. The unbelievers are described as those **who do not know God** and **who do not obey the gospel.** The first phrase was a standard Jewish designation for Gentiles. The second is found only in Romans 10:16 and thus is used to defend the Pauline authorship of II Thessalonians.

The two phrases probably do not refer to two groups, Gentiles and unbelievers, but to one group: the non-Christians. Their fate is **eternal destruction.** This destruction is **exclusion from the presence of the Lord.** The author is in the Hebrew tradition (he borrows from Isaiah 2:10), in which being related to God and being in his presence express fulfilled existence. One cannot be cut off from God without being annihilated, for God makes existence possible.

Precisely what the destiny of the believers will be is not stated. By implication theirs is the opposite of destruction—salvation. God will be **glorified in** them and **marveled at** by them. This can only occur if they are in the presence of God, which is the opposite of being cut off. Here it is God who will be glorified, not the believers. The time of this reversal will be **on that day.** The Greek text leaves this phrase dangling at the end to show that the whole complex of events stands in the indefinite future—an important hint of the emphasis of chapter 2.

1:11-12. *Prayer for God's Blessing.* These verses complete the first section of the thanksgiving by picking up the theme of the readers' "worthiness" of God's action toward them (cf. verses 3, 5). The **call** refers to their coming to **faith,** not to death by martyrdom (see comments on I Thessalonians 1:4; 4:7-8). The author asks that God bring to fulfillment their **every good resolve and work of faith** in the midst of persecution, so that Christ and Christians will **be glorified** in one another. The norm of God's activity is the **grace** of Christ, a standard emphasis in the Pauline tradition.

This paragraph uses Jewish apocalyptic tradition to illumine a situation of a persecuted church. It encourages Christians by setting their present moment against the horizon of God's future. This is a stern comfort, for God's vindicating act is said to be vindictive. Nothing is said of the positive, constructive function of God's wrath, nor are Christians summoned to a creative response to suffering.

B. EVENTS OF THE END TIME (2:1-12)

The purpose of the letter is revealed in this passage. It is not an easy passage to understand because its argument is obscure, the terms are vague, and the grammar is not clear. The passage has no evident relation to what precedes or what follows, though it discusses "when he comes" (1:10). Verses 1-2 state the problem. Verses 3-4 make the rebuttal. Verses 5-12 develop the rebuttal.

The entire discussion concentrates on a single point: the time of the end. The passage is not really an apocalypse, however, but uses apocalyptic material to defend orthodox eschatology. Though verse 5—which says Paul had already taught all this—is questionable, it is clear that the author assumes the readers know the apocalyptic tradition.

The passage must be seen as a whole. The author uses apocalyptic ideas to oppose the radical anti-apocalyptic teaching circulating in Paul's name. In a sense the author does not really deal with the problem. He requires the readers to agree with his conception of **the day of the Lord** before they can discuss whether or not it has come. But if a different understanding of the day is itself at issue, then his argument does not touch the matter.

On the other hand, at a deeper level he does deal with the question. He insists (only implicitly, of course) that what the opposing view means by the day of the Lord is not the day of the Lord but only the present Christian anticipation of it. He holds that whatever is the richness of the present life in Christ, one must not restrict the meaning of salvation to believers only or to the present. Such a view of salvation severely limits the lordship of Jesus. This lordship, however, must eliminate all resistance to God or else remain unfulfilled.

This passage has endured much at the hands of interpreters. The ancient church allegorized the **temple** as the church and therefore saw the rebellion as heresy. The Protestant Reformers saw the **lawless one** as the Pope. Premillennialists down through the years have identified the lawless one with the political or religious opponent of the moment.

Historical-critical study of this passage, however, insists that it be read together with all apocalyptic literature. It should be regarded as a distinctive theological interpretation of God, the cosmos, and Christ. This makes it unnecessary to ask whether the author meant the restrainer (verse 7) to be the Roman Empire, as many think—or even Paul's mission to the Gentiles, as a few hold.

This passage is not an apocalyptic allegory of a historical moment in the life of Paul or the early church. Rather it is a theological interpretation of the problem of history seen in the light of Christ's lordship and the oneness of God. This interpretation is made in the apocalyptic mode of thought and is designed to displace an alternative view. Pursuing questions about what historical contemporary figures the text may refer to not only is beside the point but leads away from it.

2:1-2. *Statement of the Problem.* These verses state the problem and set the tone. The author wants to prevent confusion in the church over a point of view. Three things may be noted:

(1) The author states a double problem: the **coming** (cf. I Thessalonians 4:13-18) and **our assembling to meet him**. "Assembling" here is a technical term. In apocalyptic literature it refers to the final gathering together of Israel out of the dispersion. Here it is applied to Christians. This theme can be fitted into I Thessalonians 4:13-18, though Paul neither mentions nor implies a Christian gathering together just prior to

the coming. In any case, having stated these topics, the author ignores them. Instead he deals with what must happen first.

(2) The controversial teaching holds **that the day of the Lord has come**. This must not be weakened to "the day of the Lord is near." Apparently this teaching held the same view combatted in II Timothy 2:18. Early Christianity generally existed in a tension. On one side was the salvation already accessible here and now through Jesus' resurrection and the gift of the Spirit (this is why Paul speaks of the Spirit as a down payment in II Corinthians 5:5). On the other side was the full salvation when all history and all the cosmos would be redeemed and God's kingship fulfilled. This was a tension between the "already" because of Christ's resurrection and the "not yet" until his coming.

The teaching being opposed here apparently dissolved this tension by holding that full salvation was available here and now. The future was dismissed categorically. This view, probably some form of gnosticism, may have emphasized the sacraments as means of grasping complete salvation now. Based partly on ancient Greek philosophy and partly on Near Eastern mythology, gnosticism was a movement whose adherents claimed to have saving *gnosis,* or knowledge, from Christ. It invaded the Christian churches and became a major threat in the second century. Because this was a movement and a mood more than a rival organization or church, it had many forms and interests. Thus it is difficult to trace with certainty today.

The movement opposed by II Thessalonians was a radical transformation of the gospel in which the future redemption of the whole world was given up for the sake of the present salvation of the believers. This new teaching repudiated not merely a future consummation but the redemption of history as a whole and of nature as such. Instead it championed full salvation here and now for those saved individuals who partook of the sacramental means. On this basis Jesus is not the Lord of the cosmos nor of history but only of the saved souls.

(3) How might one come to such a position? Verse 2 mentions three possibilities: **spirit, . . . word,** or **letter.** The Revised

Standard Version and New English Bible assume that **from us** goes only with the letter; it might also go with all three. Here **spirit** does not refer to speaking in tongues (as in I Corinthians 14) but to prophecy (as in I Thessalonians 5:19-20). If Paul's authority stands behind this too, then someone claims that by inspiration Paul said that the day of full salvation is here. But if Paul's authority is claimed only for the letter, then some other teacher claims that the Spirit led him to precisely this point, that the present ecstatic experience makes the future irrelevant. **Word** can mean either a tradition or an argument. For the problem of the **letter** see the Introduction.

2:3-4. *Rebuttal of a False Teaching.* Here is the heart of the rebuttal. The end cannot be here because the two things that must happen first have not happened: the **rebellion** and the rise of the **man of lawlessness**. "Rebellion" became a technical theological term (*the* rebellion) for the consummation of the cosmic opposition to God which began, in apocalyptic thought, with the revolt of the angels before creation. The text thus refers to the general widespread repudiation of religion which the anti-God forces will bring about just before the end. This conception of accelerating opposition to God which results in a cosmic Armageddon was standard in Jewish apocalyptic tradition. The author stands in this tradition. He claims that because the rebellion has not yet occurred the end cannot have come.

He also speaks of the anti-God person, commonly referred to as "antichrist" (named only in I John 2:18, 22; 4:3 and II John 7; cf. Revelation 13, where he is called simply "the beast"). The text gives this person a double name: **man of lawlessness** (some manuscripts read "man of sin") and the **son of perdition**.

2:4. Because the enemy **opposes and exalts himself**, the enemy is the paragon of sin as the Bible understands it. The self-exaltation of the man of lawlessness goes against everything religious. Religion as such is opposed. This is done, however, in the name of religion. The capstone of this work is self-enthronement in the **temple**. Irreligion will take over the worship of God. Here is the utter nadir of God's sovereignty. Not until then can the end come. At the lowest point, however, God will intervene so as to make his triumph clear and complete.

2:5-12. *Development of the Rebuttal.* The exposition of this answer to the false teaching tells of the **coming of the lawless one** and the purpose of his coming.

2:5. This verse is transitional, claiming that Paul had already taught all this (see Introduction).

2:6-7. Verse 6 explains why matters are not yet as bad as they will be. The restrainer is at work too. The way the text shifts from **what is restraining him** to **he who now restrains** is intriguing. The readers are expected to know what and who are being discussed, if indeed it is anyone in particular. The restrainer holds the rebellion in check until the enemy is **revealed in his time**. That forces and persons have their times allotted to them is a fundamental apocalyptic claim. If the enemy is being checkmated, they must **already** be **at work**, as verse 7 actually says in speaking of the **mystery of lawlessness**. Hence the impending revolt will actually bring into full tide the forces already at work but now checked.

2:8-10. These verses deal with the climax of the struggle. Verse 8 picks up the note of the revelation of the antichrist as stated in verse 6 but insists immediately that **the Lord Jesus will slay him**. The **breath of his mouth** probably means that a mere breath will be sufficient. Here is another title for the enemy: **lawless one**, who works by Satan's power (the enemy is not the person **Satan** but Satan's earthly agent). Significantly in verse 9 the lawless one will have its **coming** just as Christ will have his. Satanic power will support the lawless one by spurious miracles and moral **deception** which will lead followers to death. The writer sees that miracles in themselves have nothing to do with the truth. This double stratagem of false **signs** and deceit will work because those who are already under the sway of death will not perceive the deception. They cannot distinguish truth from falsehood because they do not **love the truth**.

2:11-12. Ultimately this failure to understand is traceable to God. Here the relationship between human culpability and the

sovereignty of God is at its sharpest. God causes people to be
misled so that those who are misled **may be condemned**. A
similar relationship is argued by Paul (Romans 9–11; especially
9:6-32, where Pharaoh is as much the instrument of God as is
Moses).

We may shrink from such theology until we see that a strict
monotheistic faith compels such a conclusion. If God alone is
finally responsible for the whole of human history, God cannot
share ultimate responsibility with anyone else, including Satan.
If opposition to God were not traced in some logical way to God,
it would be traced to a counter-god. There is no completely
satisfactory answer to such problems.

The least objectionable view holds that God, the one
ultimately responsible, tolerates evil for the sake of some degree
of human freedom of choice. Since the text speaks of the final
conquest of **Satan**, it must also grant that Satan has no ultimate
independent existence, lest Satan be made into a second god.
Satan actually maintains this revolt only as a parasite whom God
has tolerated for the allotted time. At the Lord's coming the
Lord will annihilate the opposition and thereby consummate
the sovereignty of God.

C. THANKS RESTATED (2:13-17)

2:13. The transition from verse 12 is abrupt. Verse 13 begins
precisely as 1:3—the readers are called **beloved by the Lord**
(cf. I Thessalonians 1:4). The phrase is interpreted immediately: being beloved by God means being chosen by him for
salvation. On the sanctifying work of the **Spirit** see the
comment on I Thessalonians 4:3-6. The **belief in the truth**
apparently intends to be a contrast with the unbelievers in
verse 10.

2:14. This verse restates verse 13*b*, this time speaking of
God's saving work as his calling (see comment on I Thessalonians 2:9-12). Paul never said that God's call is through the
gospel, though he doubtless assumed it. Whereas the goal of

God's choosing in verse 13 is salvation, in verse 14 it is restated as the achievement of the **glory of . . . Christ** (cf. I Thessalonians 4:7-8).

2:15. Here the need to cling to the tradition of what Paul has taught, a basic theme of the letter, is repeated. Once more the author refers to the Pauline authority of **word** or **letter**. Had Paul written this, he probably would have referred more clearly to "my former letter" or some such phrase. The text refers to Paul's letters much more generally, however, and so implies that the readers know of more than one. This was the case in the post-Pauline period in which the letter was written.

2:16-17. These verses end the first section with a prayer, just as I Thessalonians 3:11-13 ends the first section of that letter (see Introduction). Here God, who has already **loved** and given **eternal comfort and good hope**, is also asked to encourage and strengthen in **work and word**.

III. EXHORTATION (3:1-15)

This section reads almost as if it were a farewell. Actually it is a transition to the major problem of the chapter. There is no real unity of thought in these verses but rather a series of ideas.

A. REQUEST FOR PRAYER (3:1-5)

3:1-2. Verses 1-2 begin as I Thessalonians 4:1 begins. But whereas I Thessalonians puts the request for prayer for Paul at the end of the letter (I Thessalonians 5:25), this author moves it forward to this point. He also spells out the aim of the prayer: continued success of the gospel (**the word of the Lord**; cf. I Thessalonians 1:8) and the rescue of Paul **from wicked and evil men**.

What the second point actually means is not clear. Those who assume II Thessalonians was written by Paul think he is speaking of the Jews who opposed him (cf. Acts 18:5-17). Actually the text is much too general to be certain of any identification. If Paul did not write the letter, then the phrases reflect the author's attempt to create the appearance of genuineness, just as verse 17 does. Verse 2*b* reveals this artificiality, since Paul himself would scarcely have based the need for deliverance on such a truism as this.

3:3. Here the author shifts to the readers. He picks up the last word of verse 2 to contrast the faithfulness of God with the lack of faith among humans. The Revised Standard Version is uncertain whether the text speaks of **evil** or of "the evil one" (New Engligh Bible). The latter is preferable. This verse may have in mind the Lord's Prayer (Matthew 6:13). If this is the case, as is probable, we may see here the influence of Christian worship. The author promises no escape from evil but defense against it. It is precisely here that the fidelity of the Lord (presumably Lord Jesus) is actualized.

3:4-5. Verse 4 expresses the author's **confidence** that the readers will respond to what is being written. Verses 14-15, however, reveal a more realistic picture. Verse 5 asks that the Lord guide the readers' wills (**hearts**) to the **love of God and to the steadfastness of Christ**. It is not clear whether in these two phrases **of** refers to God's love or human love for God on the one hand, or to Christ's endurance or the human endurance generated by Christ on the other.

B. The Idle (3:6-15)

This section deals with a problem discussed briefly in I Thessalonians 4:11-12 and 5:14. If II Thessalonians were genuinely from Paul, one would conclude that the problem in Thessalonica grew much worse in a short time. On the other hand, if II Thessalonians is not from Paul but from a follower of his, this section reveals either the persistence of a problem into later decades or the author's efforts to imitate Paul. Probably both are at work here. This section calls for disciplining the idle by ostracism. Verse 6 states the point (restated in verses 14-15). Verses 7-10 deal with Paul's prior work in Thessalonica. Verses 11-13 give positive counsel.

3:6. The author points out that what follows has the authority of Christ behind it. Whereas I Thessalonians 5:14 asked the church to admonish the idlers, here the text calls for dissociation from them. However they are not to be excluded or condemned as the man in Corinth (I Corinthians 5:1-5), for this action is intended as an admonition to a brother (verse 15). The object of this action is **any brother who is living in idleness**. The word literally means "disorderly," but the discussion as a whole shows that the disorderliness consists in refusing to work for a living—with the common result that idle hands make mischief (verse 11). As throughout II Thessalonians, the problem is traced to a disregard for Paul's teaching, here spoken of technically as **the tradition that you received from us**.

3:7-10. The explanation of this tradition begins with the need to imitate Paul. But in contrast with I Thessalonians 1:6 (see comment) what is to be imitated here is Paul's manual **labor**. The author is trying to write like Paul, but he changes Paul's meaning! Verse 8 refers to the labor and independence of Paul while in Thessalonica. Verse 9 says Paul gave up his **right** to be supported by the church (cf. I Corinthians 9) so that he might be independent and set **an example**. The wording of verse 8 depends on I Thessalonians 2:9 (see comment); that of verse 9 is entirely the author's own idea. The **command** of verse 10 sounds like a proverb—its origin is unknown.

3:11-13. These verses address the idlers themselves and ask them to go to work. The author's pun is caught by the Moffatt translation: "Some . . . are loafing, busybodies instead of busy." Verse 13 is general advice whose precise point is not clear in this context.

3:14-15. Cf. Matthew 18:15-17.

IV. FAREWELL (3:16-18)

The final prayer echoes I Thessalonians 5:23. **Peace** is emphasized here because it is the fitting alternative to the disorders which have just been discussed. For verse 17 see the Introduction. The benediction repeats (except for **all**) that of I Thessalonians.

THE FIRST LETTER OF PAUL TO TIMOTHY

Eric Lane Titus

INTRODUCTION

I and II Timothy and Titus have been known as the "Pastoral epistles" since the early part of the eighteenth century. The name is appropriate, for the letters obviously were written by a pastor to pastors. However, they are not pastoral in the sense that they cover the wide range of church affairs. Rather, like all New Testament books, they grow out of the immediate and pressing problems of their time and speak to those problems. This means that the number of "pastoral" problems dealt with is limited. It is determined by the situation confronting the readers for whom they were intended.

Historical Situation and Purpose

A number of problems facing the early church are reflected in the Pastorals. There is some indication of pressure from the state. For example, II Timothy 4:6-8 presents the language of martyrdom: "For I am already on the point of being sacrificed." But the threat of persecution is not a pervasive theme. Rather one has a sense of "the church against the world," the world—or this "present age"—being decidedly hostile. The world is the "enemy" (I Timothy 5:14). Demas has fallen in love with "this present world" (II Timothy 4:10). Christians stand in sharp contrast to the world, since they are God's people (Titus 2:14).

On the other hand, at certain points Christians are to adjust to the world. Slaves are to be submissive and obedient to their masters (Titus 2:9-10). Christians are likewise to be obedient to "rulers and authorities" (Titus 3:1). In both cases obedience is held up as exemplary conduct for a Christian. The Pastorals also reflect problems with respect to the customs of the time—for example, the subordination of women—and with respect to morals.

The major concern of the Pastorals, however, is with certain heretical teachings which have invaded the church. These teachings had their source in the oriental religions which flowed into the Mediterranean world and united with Hellenistic thought to produce a complex movement known as Gnosticism. The movement was at first fluid and unstable. By the middle of the second century A.D. it had become systematized in great Gnostic systems. The Pastorals view this movement as a severe threat to Christianity.

Until recently knowledge of Gnosticism was available solely through Christian sources, especially Irenaeus' great work "Against Heresies" (around 180). But in 1946 there was discovered at Nag Hamadi in Upper Egypt a library of forty-nine Gnostic writings, including the now famous Gospel of Thomas. These documents give firsthand materials on Gnosticism and show more clearly the nature of the movement, which evidently posed a considerable threat to Christianity in the early centuries.

The degree of development represented by the Gnosticism which is reflected in the Pastorals is a good question. Certainly the letters reflect the basic dualism of the Gnostic position, in which matter was considered evil and spirit good. This position led naturally into a view that the material universe, including human beings clothed in flesh, was evil. It led in actual practice in either of two directions—asceticism or libertinism.

Salvation in Gnosticism depended on a special kind of

revealed knowledge. In a sense it was self-knowledge, the knowledge of the spirit as it was before its imprisonment in flesh. Salvation was accomplished through the descent from heaven of a savior or redeemer who brought knowledge of the heavenly or spiritual world and thereby enabled people to escape the prison house of flesh.

Since the major concern of the Gnostics was the problem of evil, they addressed themselves to the question of creation. How could a good God create an evil world? Some held that the universe was created by an inferior deity, the Demiurge, identified by the heretic theologian Marcion as the god of the Old Testament. The Gnostic view of matter as evil also created a problem with respect to Jesus. Since flesh as matter was evil, Jesus, they argued, could not have possessed a material body. Consequently Jesus' body of flesh only *seemed* to exist; it had no concrete reality. Those who held this view were the Docetists.

It would appear that this kind of philosophical-religious viewpoint lies behind the polemic of the Pastorals. By the middle of the second century it had taken specific forms, as in the system of Valentinus. But before that time, undoubtedly, its various elements impinged forcibly on the Christian church. Insistence on one God (I Timothy 2:5), on the goodness of things created by God (I Timothy 4:4), on Christ "manifested in the flesh" (I Timothy 3:16), on the status of the Old Testament as scripture (II Timothy 3:15-17), on opposition to "what is falsely called knowledge" (I Timothy 6:20) points to Gnosticism as the crisis which prompted the writing of the Pastorals. This accounts too for the strong emphasis on true doctrine. This doctrine, and its expression in high moral living, is contrasted with the "godless chatter" (I Timothy 6:20) and moral laxity of the Gnostics.

Authorship

The Pastorals claim Paul as their author. And indeed Pauline authorship has been maintained by the church since the second half of the second century. Before then the evidence is uncertain.

Doubt of Paul's authorship of the Pastorals was first expressed by biblical scholars at the beginning of the nineteenth century. The position that the letters are pseudonymous—that is, written under an assumed name—has become increasingly accepted. Today in scholarly circles Pauline authorship is rarely advanced.

This position grows out of the following considerations:

(1) Relating the historical situation of the Pastorals to the career of Paul as set forth in Acts and in admittedly genuine letters of Paul is difficult.

(2) Church organization seems to be more advanced than that reflected in Paul's letters, especially with respect to church orders.

(3) Gnosticism seems far more in evidence than in Paul's letters.

(4) The great and characteristic Pauline doctrines have little or no place in the thought of the Pastorals.

(5) Differences in style between the Pastorals and Paul's letters are notable. For example, Paul finds difficulty in making the form of his writing conform to the spontaneity of his thought. The sentences of the Pastorals are precise and their thoughts are matter-of-fact.

(6) The vocabulary is not the vocabulary of Paul.

(7) The formality of the letters is inconsistent with the close personal relation between Paul and his two associates.

These points have to be considered in making a judgment on the question of authorship, and the problems involved in defending Pauline authorship in the face of them are very great. Most New Testament scholars today agree that the Pastorals are pseudonymous, that they represent important teachings of a date later than the time of Paul, and that they were written in the name and supposedly the spirit of the great apostle.

Who the author was we cannot now know. What we can know of him must be derived from these three letters. In them he appears as the champion of a practical and well-disciplined religion of "works" which are in harmony with true doctrine. He might be called the champion of orthodoxy, in contrast to the dynamic religion of the Spirit which was characteristic of Paul.

Yet when his orthodoxy is seen against the Gnostic danger which threatened Christianity, we must pay him a tribute for the service he rendered the Christian church. It is possible that the Pastorals, though pseudonymous, contain genuine Pauline fragments—especially II Timothy 4:9-18.

Date of Composition

It is generally admitted that situations mentioned in the letters cannot be fitted into the Acts account of Paul's career. Those who maintain Pauline authorship usually assume that after two years of Roman imprisonment (Acts 28:30) he was released and returned to the East for a further period of ministry there. After this he suffered a second imprisonment and martyrdom at Rome. According to this hypothesis the three letters were written during this post-Acts period and their date would be around 63-67. When the letters are recognized as pseudonymous, their date becomes problematical. Scholars have proposed dates all the way from soon after Paul's death to 180.

Some have argued that the martyr theme (II Timothy 4:6-8) indicates a time relatively late in the second century, in the reign of Antoninus Pius (138-61) or Marcus Aurelius (161-80). But it should be noted that the martyr theme is found as early as the gospels and Acts. Stronger support for a late date might be suggested by the concern with the acute danger from a Gnostic heresy. This has been assumed to be very like the advanced system of Valentinus in the second half of the second century. But the difficulty is that we cannot discern from the letters just how systematized and how advanced the Gnostic heresy they attack actually was. Gnostic elements were present in the environment of the early church long before the emergence of the great Gnostic systems (see comment on Philippians 3:1–4:1).

Some scholars believe that the warning against "contradictions," Greek *antitheseis*, in I Timothy 6:20 refers to Marcion's writing with this title published around 140. If so, a date for the Pastorals about the middle of the second century would seem likely. Aside from this one passage, however, there is little in the Pastorals that appears directed against the distinctive emphases of Marcion.

An important consideration is the similarity of certain phrases in the Pastorals and in the epistle of Polycarp, bishop of Smyrna, to the church at Philippi. This epistle has generally been dated about 115, but a significant study of it has produced evidence that a major part of the content was not composed till about 135. Scholars are not agreed, however, on whether the alleged parallels indicate literary dependence—or, if so, which depends on the other.

Another factor that has been much studied is the status of the office of bishop revealed in the Pastorals. This has been compared with the rather detailed portrait of that office in the seven epistles of Ignatius, bishop of Antioch, written around 115. Since the Pastorals seem to show a more primitive stage of development than appears in Ignatius' letters, some scholars date them a decade or more earlier, around the turn of the first century. But can we assume that the development of church orders was in a straight line from Paul through the Pastorals to Ignatius—or that it went forward at the same pace in the various parts of the Mediterranean world?

It is therefore impossible to pinpoint the date when the Pastorals were written. Among the possibilities a general period within the first half of the second century seems most likely. If it is assumed that Polycarp shows dependence on the Pastorals, the time can perhaps be narrowed to a few years earlier than 135.

Place of Composition

On the assumption that Paul wrote the letters, the place for II Timothy would be a prison in Rome (cf. 1:8, 12; 2:9; 4:6-7). For I Timothy it would probably be Macedonia (cf. 1:3). The locale of Titus is uncertain, but Paul's plan to spend the winter in Nicopolis (3:12) might suggest a place somewhere in Achaia or Macedonia.

Some who consider the Pastorals pseudonymous, especially those who view them as directed against Marcionism, regard

Rome as their place of origin. Syria has been suggested but is only a possibility. The most likely place seems to be Ephesus, where Timothy is represented as being addressed (I Timothy 1:3). Some other place in Asia Minor is a strong possibility, in view of the intense interest in this area shown in the documents themselves. It is probable that the author wrote out of concern for the situation in the churches with which he was personally acquainted. He gave his work a geographical background to appeal to the readers he especially had in mind.

The Question of Sequence

It cannot be assumed that the traditional order of the letters found in the New Testament today reproduces the sequence in which they were written. Naturally the two letters to Timothy are grouped together, leaving Titus to complete the whole. In general scholars have advanced two possibilities as to the original sequence of writing:

I Timothy; Titus; II Timothy
II Timothy; Titus; I Timothy.

The first order is held by those who accept Pauline authorship, and by some who do not. It permits accommodation to the alleged second Roman imprisonment and martyrdom of Paul—note the position in this sequence of II Timothy 4:6-8.

The second position is championed by the majority. They point to such matters as the development of church polity which this arrangement provides, the notable increase in the intensity of opposition to heresy, and a lessening of the personal elements—a feature natural to pseudonymous writings. Some scholars maintain that all the material was composed and published at one time as a single work in the form of three letters. The more common view, however, is that the author wrote three successive letters separated by intervals of time.

Pseudonymity in Antiquity

Ancient pseudonymous writing should not be equated with forgery. The numerous examples of this method in antiquity indicate that it was entirely acceptable and apparently frequently desirable. There are many Jewish examples, and the practice was current among Christians as well. Perhaps the desire for the authority attached to a great name was the main motivation.

But it is also true that the author thought of himself as writing in the spirit of the earlier person. He would not consider his thoughts as a perversion of those of his hero. This is certainly true of the author of the Pastorals. Paul is his idol; Paul's position represents the true doctrine of the church; Paul is the supreme example of heroic living and dying. In the face of dangerous views and practices the church must be confronted with a norm of orthodoxy, and Paul provides the norm.

It has been suggested that the Pastorals were published under the name of Paul because his letters were assailed by Jewish Christians on the one hand and on the other were suspected by some Gentile Christians since they were looked on with favor by the Gnostics. The Pastorals, speaking in Paul's name, become his defense, so that the influence of his writings should not be lost to the orthodox church by default.

It should be kept in mind that in addressing Timothy and Titus the author is writing to church leaders who are his contemporaries. These are not necessarily specific individuals but rather pastors who hold responsible positions in the churches of Asia Minor. The letters were written by a pastor for pastors, and through them to the church.

I. EPISTOLARY INTRODUCTION (1:1-7)

1:1. *Salutation.* The epistle leaves no doubt at the start that it speaks with the authority of an **apostle** and that that apostle is no less than **Paul** himself. Paul's apostleship, it declares, was instituted at the **command of God . . . and of Christ Jesus**. The claims of the historical Paul as to the legitimacy of his apostleship are reflected here (cf. Galatians 1:1, 11-12, 15). Ordinarily the New Testament speaks of Christ as **Savior,** but of course it assumes that God stands behind the saving event of Christ.

Hope was an important concept for Paul. It was basic to his eschatology—his doctrine of last things—in that for him salvation was eschatological. The eschatological element is in the Pastorals also, though it has lost some of the urgency found in Paul's letters. Salvation seems to be both present and future.

1:2a. The letter is directed to **Timothy**, described as Paul's **true child in the faith** (cf. I Corinthians 4:17). Acts 16:1, which refers to Timothy as already a disciple when he met Paul, seems to rule out the idea that he was Paul's "child" in the sense of convert. The general impression in the Pastorals is rather that Paul is an older man talking down to a younger man for whom he nevertheless has great respect. Perhaps this accounts for the "distance" between them. The author finds it a useful teaching device—the venerable Paul writing to the inexperienced Timothy. Yet the element of mere age may be overstressed. Rather Paul speaks out of superiority of office. He is an apostle while Timothy is a subordinate. In any case Timothy is a devoted follower of Paul and in that sense his "child in the faith."

1:2b. The salutation closes with the familiar Pauline triad **grace, mercy, and peace.** In this setting they probably do no more than give the impression of Pauline authenticity. The typical theology of Paul, in which these elements form so important a part, is virtually missing in the Pastorals.

1:3-7. *Charge to Timothy.* The historical note in verse 3 serves two purposes:

(1) to connect the letter with Paul's activities, though in a very general way (see Introduction);

(2) to address it to **Ephesus**, probably the center of intended readership (see Introduction), as instruction against heretical teachings.

These verses set forth the real concern of the Pastorals. The concern is deviations from the normative doctrine of "Paul," which is the doctrine embraced by the author himself. Precise identification of the heretical group or groups is impossible. Judaizing Christianity, Gnosticism, and Marcionism are possibilities. It is probable that elements found in all of these were present in the situation.

Myths and endless genealogies are not precisely explained in these letters. The author may have in mind the complex system of emanation from deity characteristic of Gnosticism (see below on 1:17). But it is notable that myths are closely related to Jewish law (cf. Titus 1:14), and the same may be said for genealogies. The situation here is probably a syncretistic movement in which Gnostic and Jewish elements are intermingled. Over against this **different doctrine** the author urges **sound doctrine** (verse 10) and **love that issues from a pure heart and a good conscience and sincere faith**. It is Timothy's task, then, to guard the true faith in the presence of heretical threats.

II. KNOWLEDGE OF THE TRUTH (1:8–2:15)

1:8-11. *Function of the Law.* The historical Paul's problem with the law is reflected here (cf. Romans 7:12). But a different function for the law is now introduced. It is **not laid down for the just, but for the lawless and disobedient**. These people are then specified in the long list. The thought is that true Christians do not need the law—they stand above it—but the law holds evil persons in check.

1:12-17. *Paul the Great Example.* These verses turn the light on Paul himself as the perfect example of the faithful. He is pictured as the **foremost of sinners**, a reference to his pre-Christian days when he **acted ignorantly in unbelief**. Christ's saving power is fully exemplified in Paul. In Paul's transformed life Jesus Christ displays his **perfect patience for an example to those who were to believe in him for eternal life**.

1:17. This doxology is intended to stress that God alone is supreme. The heretic Marcion held that the god of the Old Testament was not the God of Jesus but an inferior deity. If the Pastorals are in part directed against this teaching, the emphasis on the sole sovereignty of God takes on added meaning. **King of ages** means that God is King both now and in the future. God is the eternal King. This stress on the one high God stands in marked contrast to the complex system of divine beings or emanations from deity advanced by the Gnostics.

1:18-20. *The Prophetic Utterances.* Timothy is charged by Paul to **wage the good warfare, holding faith and a good conscience.** But he does this in accordance with and inspired by the **prophetic utterances,** a reference no doubt to the activity of Christian prophets. Perhaps the author thinks of Timothy's appointment as having taken place in some such manner as described in the "setting apart" of Paul and Barnabas in Acts 13:1-4, where prophets are present.

The Greek word rendered **charge** is intended to stress that Timothy's appointment is not arbitrary but in accordance with God's purposes as made known through the prophetic utterances. Perhaps the meaning is that the prophetic utterances marked out Timothy for the work and that Paul's recognition of him as called of God came at that time. The reference may well be to the occasion of Timothy's ordination.

1:19*b*-20. In contrast to Timothy's steadfastness, **Hymenaeus** (cf. II Timothy 2:17) and **Alexander** (cf. II Timothy 4:14), have fallen away from the faith. The seriousness of their apostasy is evident; Paul has **delivered** them **to Satan** (see comment on I Corinthians 5:5). In this paragraph, then, the author includes an example of heroic and steadfast faith and an example of the failure of faith and its dire consequences.

2:1-7. *Inclusiveness of Christian Prayer.* The position of Christians and the church in the second century was in certain ways precarious. While as yet they were not persecuted simply for being Christians, they were undoubtedly looked on with suspicion by the authorities. Any deviation from established custom might easily lead to serious trouble (cf. Romans 13:1-7 and I Peter 4:14-16). This situation seems to lie behind the author's concern that **prayers . . . be made for . . . kings and all who are in high positions** and his urging that Christians **lead a quiet and peaceable life, godly and respectful in every way.**

But there is another thought here. Kings and lesser government officials are themselves recipients of God's favor (verse 4). **Christ Jesus . . . gave himself as a ransom for all,** including the emperor and his subordinates. It is of interest that at this point the author, in the manner of Paul in Galatians 1:20, feels called on to assert in strong language the reason for his appointment as **preacher and apostle . . ., a teacher of the Gentiles**. As such his concern reaches beyond the masses to those in places of governmental responsibility. It should be added that good and stable government was a condition for the spread of Christianity in the Roman empire.

2:8-15. *Men and Women at Public Worship.* The author continues the subject of prayer. **Lifting up holy hands** is of special interest. It gives the normal posture for prayer common among Christians and Jews at the time. In the art of the Christian catacombs the praying figure always stands with uplifted arms rather than kneels. **Holy hands** might suggest ceremonial washing, but there is here no hint of this. To have holy hands is to be free of **anger or quarreling**; that is, the thought is ethical and not ceremonial.

2:9-15. The rest of the passage deals with the conduct of **women** at public worship. They are to dress **modestly** and **adorn themselves** with **good deeds**. They are to be submissive and never exert **authority over men**; they must be **silent** (cf. his fears for the younger widows in 5:11-15). He supports his position by an appeal to the story of Adam and Eve. Adam was the first to be created, but Eve was the first to sin (cf. Genesis 2:7, 21–3:6). Yet woman will be **saved**, by childbearing and by abiding in **faith and love and holiness, with modesty**—a peculiar approach to salvation.

III. Standards for Christian Officers (3:1-13)

3:1-7. *Qualifications of Bishops.* This passage raises the difficult question of church offices as reflected in the Pastorals. The titles **bishop** (*episkopos,* literally "overseer") and "elder" (*presbyteros*) here seem interchangeable (cf. Titus 1:5-7). It is highly doubtful that they represent two clearly distinct offices such as are evident in the Ignatian letters (see Introduction), where the bishop has monarchical authority. The closest approximation to that here is in the implied offices of Timothy and Titus, who appear to stand apart and above the elders. It has been suggested, therefore, that Timothy and Titus are Ignatian bishops in all but title. According to this view bishop in this passage means the same as elder. Thus apart from the implied offices of Timothy and Titus, the Pastorals deal with two major groups, elders and deacons.

This section describes the personal qualifications of the bishop. The list suggests the importance attached to the ministerial office. In general the thought is clear, though **the husband of one wife** poses a special problem. Since the context does not elaborate, it is possible to see this as forbidding a second marriage after the death of the first wife, the practice of polygamy, concubinage, or remarriage after divorce. It is impossible to be sure which of these is meant. But the import is plain: the bishop must be free of any suspicion of loose sexual relationships. He must be above reproach as the exemplar of family integrity.

Verse 4 makes clear that the author does not advocate celibacy for the clergy. Instead it is taken for granted that the bishop has his own household and that his wise management of it demonstrates his ability to care for God's church. Conversely, inability to do so disqualifies him for the office of bishop.

3:8-13. *Qualifications of Deacons.* The description of a bishop's qualifications is now followed by a similar one for **deacons** (*diakonos*, literally "servant"). Acts 6:1-6 tells of the appointment of seven deacons who would "serve tables" and would care for the needs of widows of the Hellenists who were being "neglected in the daily distribution." Here the close connection of deacons with bishops and the similarity of qualifications suggest the importance of the office. It is probable, though not specified, that their duties included care of the poor.

Qualifications for deacons generally parallel those for bishops. Stress is placed on being **the husband of one wife** and on the good management of **their households**. In both cases, moreover, special mention is made of the temperate use of **wine**. Nowhere, however, does the author advocate total abstinence. Indeed in 5:23 he urges Timothy to "use a little wine" for medicinal purposes. This, together with other emphases, indicates that the author was no advocate of asceticism (see below on 4:1-5).

IV. THE TRUE FAITH (3:14–4:16)

3:14-16. *The Christian Mystery.* The letter is explained as a substitute for a personal visit that may be **delayed**. It now gives **instructions** on how to **behave in the household of God**—that is, the **church of the living God**, described in turn as the **pillar and bulwark of the truth**. In his discussion of bishops and deacons the author has emphasized the importance of their being managers of their own **household** (3:5, 12). This term is now applied to the church, and Timothy is to behave in—not manage—the church in strict accordance with Paul's **instructions**. The church is the custodian of Paul's religion, which is the true religion.

3:16. This **religion** is a **great . . . mystery**. It is set forth in the form of a liturgical confession which undoubtedly the author is quoting from some source. The meaning of the hymn is difficult because it has been removed from its original context. However, it seems to emphasize Christ's incarnation, the vindicating power of his resurrection, his exaltation to heaven, and the spread of his gospel in the world. The simple formula stands in stark contrast to the elaborate system of the Gnostics. Moreover its insistence on the reality of the incarnation refutes the Gnostic view of flesh as evil, which denied the real humanity of Jesus.

4:1-5. *Deviations from the Faith.* The author's concern for sound doctrine in the face of heretical views is seen in his words **Now the Spirit expressly says . . . .** It is unnecessary to ask where it says this. It was generally understood that demonic activity would characterize the **later times** preceding the end of the age. Here the Spirit's role is quite different from that found in the genuine letters of Paul. There the Spirit is a vital, energizing, creative power. Here it is the custodian of the true doctrine, speaking out against departures from the faith (cf. II Timothy 1:14).

This faith includes a positive attitude toward **marriage** and the recognition of **foods** as good because they were **created by God**. The author consequently condemns those who teach celibacy and abstinence. This is undoubtedly a reaction to Gnostic tendencies toward asceticism in the church.

4:6-10. *The Minister and the Faith.* Timothy is told to instruct the church in Paul's teaching on these matters. If he does so, he will be a **good minister of Christ Jesus**. The word translated "minister" is *diakonos* (see above on 3:8-13). If "deacon" in the official sense is intended, this verse places Timothy in that class. As such he becomes representative of the whole group of deacons who are **nourished on the words of faith and of the good doctrine**, and who reject the **godless and silly myths** of the Gnostics. The Christian life, so conceived, calls for discipline in the same way that the athlete disciplines his body (cf. II Timothy 4:7-8). But training in godliness is far more important than **bodily training**. It prepares not only **for the present life** but **also for the life to come**, the goal toward which **we toil and strive**.

4:11-16. *The Example of Timothy.* These verses contain admonitions to Timothy. He is to **teach** the things of which Paul has written. Even though he is young, he is to be an example for believers in **speech . . . conduct . . . love . . . faith . . . purity**. He is to attend to the ministry of the church: **public reading of scripture** (the Old Testament), **preaching**, and **teaching**. The practices of the church in public worship are reflected here.

Timothy is urged to employ the gift given when the **elders laid their hands** on him—that is, at ordination. **Prophetic utterance** was the guide to the selection of Timothy for ordination (see above on 1:18-20). He is to **practice** with diligence the **duties** laid on him at that time and to guard his character and **teaching**. By doing so he will save himself and those under his pastoral care.

V. Conduct of True Christians (5:1–6:10)

5:1-2. *Treatment of Others.* Here we have specific exhortations about the pastor's personal relationships. These are placed between advice about pastoral duties and about the treatment of widows. The addition of **in all purity** with respect to **younger women** betrays an anxiety regarding relations between the sexes in the church. But the author nevertheless refuses to advocate asceticism, as did many second century Christian writers.

5:3-16. *Widows in the Church.* The phrase **real widows** (verses 3, 5, 16) suggests a problem in the qualifications for the "office" of widow. These women so "enrolled" served as Christian workers. What the author has in mind is indicated in verses 11-13, where **younger widows** are described as having a tendency to **grow wanton** and to become **gossips and busybodies**. These women are not to be enrolled as widows. There is a question, moreover, about widows who have **relatives** capable of giving financial support (verses 8, 16). The probability is that verse 5a defines the "real widow." She is one who is **left all alone**, who has no source of financial help outside the church itself. As such she **continues in supplications and prayers night and day**. She devotes herself exclusively to the practice of religion.

5:9-10. Certain qualifications are made quite specific. The real widow must be over **sixty** and married only once. The minimum age limit would limit the number of women qualifying for the office. It would also provide a long period of testing in terms of character and **good deeds**. In general it reinforces the strict qualifications for the office.

Hospitality was important in the spread of the Christian movement. The privilege of staying in Christian homes rather than in the highly undesirable inns made the work of the missionary much easier. There is no reason to think of **washed the feet of the saints** as referring to an established ritual of the church like the Lord's Supper. "Saints" means simply Christians. The expression refers to the task, ordinarily that of a slave, of washing the feet of the traveler—a possible reference to the itinerant missionary. The true widow must not be above the most menial task and must pass the most demanding tests of humility.

5:11-16. The **younger widows** are not real widows; they must not be enrolled. They tend to **desire to marry.** The author has no aversion to marriage, however, for he states his wish that they should marry. The point is that they do not qualify for the order of widows. Apparently there was some justification for this opinion (verse 15).

5:17-22. *Pay and Discipline of Elders.* The author has already dealt with the qualifications for the office of bishop, which apparently he equates with that of **elder** (see above on 3:1-7). He now proceeds to deal with two specific problems of this office: adequate pay and proper disciplinary action for those who have failed its high calling.

5:17-18. Evidently the task of the elder does not include **preaching and teaching.** Those who do preach and teach are **worthy of double honor.** In the light of the context this would be additional pay, perhaps literally double pay. The right of elders to an adequate wage is supported by an appeal to the Old Testament (Deuteronomy 25:4) and to Christian tradition (cf. Matthew 10:10; Luke 10:7; I Corinthians 9:14). It may be that the author thinks of his source for the second saying as **scripture** also. Since the exact words appear in Luke 10:7 some interpreters believe that he knew that gospel as scripture.

5:19-22. Verse 19 introduces the question of proper procedure in dealing with elders against whom some **charge** has been laid. The author seems to apply the general legislation of Deuteronomy 19:15 specifically to the trial of an elder. That matters of discipline earlier began to be hedged about with legal processes is evidenced by Matthew 18:15-17, where the appeal is also to the evidence of **two or three witnesses.** Elders who **persist in sin** are to be publicly rebuked before the whole church—a procedure again reminiscent of Matthew 18:17. The seriousness with which the author views this problem is indicated by his charge to carry out this procedure without **partiality.** Moreover the **laying on of hands,** i.e. the ordination

of new elders—or possibly restoration of elders who have
sinned—is to be conducted only after due deliberation.
Otherwise Timothy will be party to the sin of defective elders.

5:23. *Use of Wine as Medicine.* This oft-quoted verse possibly
should be understood against verse 22*b*—purity does not mean
total abstinence. More especially it should be viewed with
reference to Gnostic asceticism. While the author warns against
drunkenness by bishops (3:3) and instructs deacons not to be
"addicted to much wine" (3:8), he forthrightly proclaims that
"everything created by God is good" (4:4). Since he is no ascetic,
he does not reject the use of wine but recommends it for the
stomach—that is, for medicinal purposes. Here, as elsewhere,
he urges a counsel of moderation.

5:24-25. *Revelation of Character.* The parallelism of these
two verses is striking. Perhaps the author is drawing here from
current moralizing tradition. The connection with the context is
uncertain. Perhaps he is referring to the conduct of elders who
persist in sin (verse 20). The thought seems to be that people will
ultimately be revealed for what they are, good or evil.

6:1-2*b*. *Behavior of Christian Slaves.* Slavery was an
established legal institution in the Roman Empire. When the
slaveholder and/or the slave became Christian, special problems naturally arose in their relationships. This passage urges
that Christian slaves treat their non-Christian **masters** with
complete respect. To do otherwise would defame the **name of
God** and the **teaching**. Similarly they must be respectful toward
Christian masters because they are **brethren** in Christ. Indeed
when the master is a Christian, the slave must render superior
service.

6:2*c*-10. *Failures of False Teachers.* These verses deal with
two issues: heretical teachings and the dangers of riches. It is
probable, however, that the discussion of wealth is not a general
statement on the subject but an outgrowth of problems posed by
heresies. Verse 5*b*, with its reference to **godliness** as **a means of
gain**, leads into the discussion on riches and ties the two sections
together.

6:3-5. The nature of the heresy or heresies against which the author speaks is not specified. But evidently the teaching is at odds with what the author considers normative. **Sound words of our Lord Jesus Christ** does not necessarily indicate that the author had a collection of Jesus' sayings before him. More likely it means that the true **teaching**—that is, Paul's teaching as interpreted by the author—stems ultimately from Jesus. It would be equal, then, to "words of the faith" and "good doctrine" (4:6).

By contrast **morbid craving for controversy and for disputes about words** is the same as the tendency which produces "godless and silly myths" (4:7). This repetition of subject matter betrays the author's major interest. But he goes on to suggest that the evil of departing from true doctrine is evident in the character and conduct of those involved (verses 4c-5). This of course gives the author's estimate of the heresy but does not provide a description of its content.

6:6-10. Seizing the heretics' tendency to exploit people in the name of religion (verse 5b), the author turns to the **craving** for **money** that causes some to leave the **faith**. By contrast the true Christian must realize that **godliness** brings **contentment**, that **food and clothing** are the only essentials of the journey between birth and death. The **desire** for riches causes people to **fall . . . into a snare** and leads in turn to other desires which **plunge** them **into ruin and destruction**.

The emphasis here is on desire for money, rather than money itself, as evil. This may reflect Stoic thought, for Stoicism numbered desire among the four emotions which must be mastered—the other three being pleasure, grief, and fear. In general, however, this passage adds to the long list in early Christian literature which takes a strongly negative view toward wealth.

VI. FINAL CHARGES (6:11-21)

6:11-16. *The Good Fight of the Faith.* In contrast to those who love money Timothy is a **man of God**. This term is apparently used here in a special sense as related to his particular calling and probably to his being set apart by ordination. He is exhorted to **take hold of the eternal life** to which he was called in making the **good confession** before **many witnesses**. The language sounds like that of martyrdom. Indeed verse 13 looks to Jesus himself, who made the good confession **before Pontius Pilate**.

Is this a reflection of the actual martyrdom of Timothy? Tradition has him martyred during the reign of Nerva (96-98). The author's reference may be simply to his ordination or to his baptism. But the similarity to the language of II Timothy 4:6-8, which certainly refers to Paul's martyrdom, reinforces the interpretation that the historical Timothy has already suffered martyrdom and that the author is holding him up as an example to his readers.

6:14-16. Timothy is now charged to **keep the commandments**—the true Pauline doctrine—**unstained**. He must remain faithful to this trust until Christ appears. The sense of urgency characteristic of an earlier period has now grown weak. The church has settled down to the task of finding its place in the world. Nevertheless the idea of the coming last day is maintained. God will usher in that day through the appearance of Christ at the appointed time.

The titles of God in verse 15 are reminiscent of Revelation and may, as in Revelation, be written against the powerful claims of emperors. Verse 16 takes on the lofty language and to some extent the form of a doxology. The idea of the sovereignty of God sounds Jewish, while the language of verse 16 sounds Hellenistic. **Whom no man has ever seen** is reminiscent of John 1:18.

6:17-19. *The True Riches.* The author now returns to the theme of wealth (cf. verses 6-10). The passage assumes that there are wealthy persons in the church. While they are not condemned for their riches, they are not to become **haughty** on account of their wealth. Rather they are to set their hopes on God, the source of all good. They are to engage in sound ethical conduct, which is true riches. Their **good deeds**, done in a liberal and generous spirit, will reap abundance in the **future** in terms of true **life**.

6:20-21. *Warning Against False Knowledge.* These verses have frequently been cited as identifying the heretical group against which the Pastorals were written. The word translated **contradictions** is the title, usually transliterated "Antitheses," of a book by the heretic Marcion (see Introduction). Therefore it is possibly a specific reference to that work. **What is falsely called knowledge** makes the theory more attractive, since Marcion was in some sense a Gnostic in that he claimed revealed knowledge for himself and his followers. But whether or not the reference is to Marcion remains uncertain.

The benediction at the end is extremely simple. It is Pauline in that it employs Paul's great word **grace**, but here it is little more than a convention. The plural form of the personal pronoun **you** is used, whereas in a letter to Timothy we should expect the singular. This is a good indication of the pastoral nature of this letter. It is in fact addressed, not to a certain individual, but through the church leader called Timothy to the church.

THE SECOND LETTER OF PAUL
TO TIMOTHY

Eric Lane Titus

See the Introduction to I Timothy.

I. EPISTOLARY INTRODUCTION (1:1-7)

1:1-2. *Salutation.* The letter is written in the name of **Paul**, whose authority is expressed in the title **apostle of Jesus Christ** but rests ultimately on the authority of God. It is written, then, with full and complete authority, **according to the promise of the life which is in Christ Jesus**. This means that life in Christ provides the norm by which true apostleship must be judged. Life here must be thought of as present as well as future. It is the Christian life in harmony with the true doctrine which the author sets forth. Like I Timothy, the letter is addressed to **Timothy**, characterized as Paul's **beloved child** (see comment on I Timothy 1:2*a*.

1:3-7. *The Faith of Timothy.* All unquestioned letters of Paul, except Galatians, include a thanksgiving. Following that pattern the author introduces a passage of thanksgiving at this point, whereas I Timothy and Titus do not include one. The highly personal character of II Timothy makes its appearance here seem perfectly natural. If, as most scholars believe, II Timothy was written before I Timothy and Titus (see Introduction), the thanksgiving may have been introductory to all three.

1:3-5. The author draws a parallel between the faith of Paul and of Timothy. Paul serves God **with a clear conscience** like his **fathers**. Timothy possesses a **sincere faith** like his **grandmother Lois and his mother Eunice**. It is doubtful that the historical Paul could have made this claim for his fathers. It is more likely the pseudonymous author referring to his own Christian fathers. As for Timothy's forebears, nothing is known of his grandmother Lois apart from this passage. His mother is mentioned, though not by name, in Acts 16:1, where she is described as a "Jewish woman who was a believer" though her husband was a Greek. The impression in verse 5 is that Christianity is now a matter of at least three generations and Timothy is the fine product of a long history of sincere faith.

1:6-7. Timothy's strong Christian background, however, does not guarantee a continuing faith. He must not allow the fire of faith, originally bestowed by the **laying on of my hands,**—the right of ordination—to smolder. Rather he must stir it so that it becomes a blaze. Timothy is twice blessed. He is the product of a Christian home, and he is the recipient of the **gift of God**, officially and supernaturally given by the act of ordination. This divinely touched inner spirit should be characterized, not by **timidity**, but by **power and love and self-control**. Power by itself is not enough. It must be balanced by the warmth of love and by personal discipline.

II. Testifying to the Lord (1:8–2:7)

1:8-14. *Suffering for the Gospel.* Suffering—possibly martyrdom—is part of the Christian's testimony to the Lord. Like Paul, the Lord's **prisoner**, Timothy is not to be **ashamed** to suffer **for the gospel**.

1:9-10. The Christian's **holy calling** is to a consecrated life. This does not depend on **works**, but on the eternal **purpose** of God manifested in the appearance of Christ. The **gospel** is rooted in the **grace** of God.

1:11-12. Paul's suffering is integral to his divine appointment as **preacher and apostle and teacher**. Thus it is not something to be **ashamed** of but an honor and a privilege. His assurance is that God is trustworthy. God will be able to safeguard till **that Day**—that is, the end of the age—the priceless gospel as the author understands it and proclaims it.

1:13-14. Timothy is exhorted to **follow** Paul's example and **guard the truth**, literally "good deposit," by the power of the **Holy Spirit**. This Spirit **dwells within us**. The plural may refer either to Christians generally or to those specially ordained— probably to the former.

1:15-18. *The Household of Onesiphorus.* The first two persons mentioned, **Phygelus and Hermogenes**, are included as a foil for the loyalty and kindness of Onesiphorus. Just as these two **turned away** from Paul, so Onesiphorus turned toward him to refresh him during his imprisonment. None of these persons is known apart from this epistle. It appears that Onesiphorus is dead. The prayer is first for his family (cf. 4:19) and then that he may **find mercy from the Lord on that Day**. If, as some believe, this is a fragment of genuine Pauline correspondence, perhaps it speaks to a recently bereaved family. In any case its inclusion here serves to underscore the preceding injunction for loyalty.

2:1-7. *Unreserved Devotion.* Timothy is now directed to **be strong in the grace that is in Christ Jesus**. The letter has already made clear that he has received a "spirit of power" (1:7). Now it uses three analogies to illustrate the strength of the true Christian:

(1) They must suffer **as a good soldier of Christ Jesus** with single-minded dedication to the Lord.

(2) They must strive in the Christian life as an **athlete** who **competes according to the rules**.

(3) They must be like the **hard-working farmer** who receives the **first share of the crops** as their reward.

Devotion that is unreserved is of course the point in all of this. The admonition in verse 2 culminates the call to loyalty of 1:3-2:2. It seems to refer to a line of teachers and preachers in the tradition of Paul, descending from Paul down through the author, who writes in Paul's name.

III. APPROVED WORKMEN (2:8-26)

2:8-13. *Remembering Jesus Christ.* This section begins with what must be considered an early Christian creed: **Jesus Christ, risen from the dead, descended from David**. This is said to be **preached in my gospel**—that is, it contains basic elements of Paul's gospel. Certainly the doctrine of the Resurrection was central in the historical Paul's thought. But **descended from David** appears only in Romans 1:3 and seems peripheral. Its inclusion here may be for the purpose of refuting the Docetic element in Gnosticism (see Introduction) since it tends to emphasize the humanity of Jesus.

In any case it is for this gospel that Paul was imprisoned **like a criminal**. But unlike Paul, the **word of God**—the gospel which Paul preached—is free. The **elect**, the chosen people of God, is a term now applied to the Christians as it was to Israel in the Old Testament. The suffering of Paul, and by extension the suffering of all Christians, advances the purpose of God with respect to the **salvation . . . in Christ Jesus**.

2:11-13. This relation between endurance in suffering and salvation is reinforced by appeal to a "sure saying." The balanced structure of the lines, together with the introduction, indicates a quotation from a Christian hymn or creed, most likely sung or recited at baptism. The conditional **if we endure** relates it securely to **I endure everything** in verse 10. Endurance in suffering on behalf of the gospel is the main theme of the section.

2:14-19. *God's True Workman.* The author now turns to a familiar theme—the problem of heretical teachers. Their teachings are characterized as **disputing about words** and

godless chatter. Some of them, including **Hymenaeus** (cf. I Timothy 1:20) **and Philetus**, are teaching that the **resurrection** has already taken place. The precise implications of this teaching are not specified. But since the doctrine of the resurrection held so central a place in early Christianity it is natural that groups within the church, both "heretical" and "orthodox," would give a great deal of attention to it. In response to the heresy the author exhorts Timothy to strive to correctly handle the **word of truth**—which is the gospel given to him through Paul. This means in this context that he is to preach and teach it faithfully and exemplify it in his conduct.

2:18b-19. In spite of unorthodox, and therefore untrue, teachings which are **upsetting the faith of some**, the author asserts that **God's firm foundation stands**. He supports this by an appeal to scripture—apparently Numbers 16:5 and Isaiah 26:13.

2:20-26. *Pastor of Good and Bad.* This section is an elaboration of the ideas expressed in verses 14-19. While it is true that men like Hymenaeus and Philetus are in the church, God knows **those who are his** (verse 19). Now the author uses the analogy of a **great house**. He points out that just as there are in the house objects for both **noble** and **ignoble** use, so it is in the church. Timothy is therefore to avoid the ignoble people who deal in **senseless controversies** and **shun youthful passions**. He must correct **his opponents with gentleness**. The hope is that they will turn from their perverse ways. The main thrust of the passage is directed toward the fact that there are good and bad people within the church. Timothy, as a leader, stands in relation to this situation both as ideal ethical example and as teacher.

IV. INSTRUCTIONS FOR THE LAST DAYS (3:1–4:18)

3:1-9. *Signs of the Last Days.* The end of the age was expected to be preceded by terrible conflict, by intense last-ditch efforts of Satan to gain control over the cosmos, and by devastating upheaval in nature (cf. Mark 13; Matthew 24; Luke 21). Here the doctrine of the end of the age—in verse 1 called the **last days**—has lost some of the sense of urgency characteristic of Paul himself. The author uses it to show that the activity of the heretical teachers is not something to cause surprise.

3:2-5. The list of vices set forth in verses 2-4 is undoubtedly a conventional catalog in common usage. It does not necessarily provide a precise description of the heretical teachers. It is likely, however, that verse 5 does characterize them—**holding the form of religion but denying the power of it**. In view of the earlier reference to the resurrection (2:18) it is possible that the author sees the heretics' position as denying the power of the resurrection. Power and resurrection are commonly associated in early Christian writings.

3:6-9. The author feels that **weak women**—literally "little women," an expression of contempt—are especially susceptible to the perverse doctrines of these aggressive heretics. But their **folly** will be made **plain**, like that of **Jannes and Jambres**, who **opposed Moses**. These names, while not mentioned in the Old Testament, appear in nonbiblical early Jewish and Christian literature as Egyptian magicians in the court of Pharaoh.

3:10-17. *Paul the Great Example.* Paul is now held up as the great example of the **life in Christ Jesus**. His life is characterized by **faith . . . patience . . . love . . . steadfastness**. No doubt both the author and his first readers were familiar with the Acts account of his **persecutions . . . at Antioch, at Iconium, and at Lystra**, from which **the Lord rescued** him (cf. Acts 13:14–14:20). Indeed persecution is seen as the lot of true Christians, while **evil men** and those who only pose as Christians will **go on from bad to worse**.

3:14-17. But Timothy is to remain steadfast in the faith. He has been instructed by Paul, and **from childhood** he has been solidly grounded in the scriptures. The **Sacred writings** certainly mean the Old Testament but may also include the letters of Paul. In II Peter 3:15-16 Paul's letters are considered as scripture. It is unlikely that the author of the Pastorals, who was such an ardent admirer of Paul, would consider them less authoritative. In any case **all scripture** would certainly include the Old Testament. If Marcion and his work lie behind the Pastorals (see Introduction) the reference to the function of scripture as **reproof . . . correction, and . . . training in righteousness** would constitute a rebuke to his rejection of the Old Testament.

4:1-5. *Timothy's Responsibility.* Timothy is now charged to **preach the word**—in this context the true doctrine. He is to do this **in season and out of season**—when the times are favorable and when they are adverse. Presumably they were adverse at the time of this letter. The solemnity of the charge is underscored by verse 1. Timothy is ultimately responsible to God, and he must appear before Christ, who will **judge the living and the dead**.

4:3-5. Verses 3-4 refer to the present state of affairs. **The time is coming** is future with reference to the historical Paul but present for the pseudonymous author. Some have turned aside from the **sound teaching** of Paul and **accumulate for themselves teachers** who say what they want to hear. They **wander into myths**—that is, into the extravagant and untrue doctrines of the heretics. In contrast to these fickle people Timothy is to remain **steady** and in all ways to discharge faithfully his responsibility as a minister.

4:6-8. *Imminent Martyrdom of Paul.* Here Paul, the great example of Christian fidelity, is **on the point of being sacrificed**. He compares himself to the disciplined athlete. He has **fought the good fight**; like the contestant in the arena he has done his best. He has **finished the race**—suggesting both the heroic struggle in the race Paul has run and the nearness of its end. He has **kept the faith**—both the athlete's rules of the game and the Pauline religion advocated by the author. Just as the athlete gains a reward by receiving the victor's wreath, so Paul need only await the **crown of righteousness**, to be bestowed by Christ himself at **his appearing**.

4:9-18. *The Loneliness of Paul.* Some scholars believe this section to be a fragment or fragments of genuine correspondence of Paul (see Introduction). The persons mentioned are all friends of Paul except **Demas** and **Alexander the coppersmith** (cf. I Timothy 1:20). Demas was apparently a co-worker (cf. Philemon 24 and Colossians 4:14). For some reason not specifically stated he left Paul, and perhaps Christianity itself, and became enamored with **this present world**—perhaps business pursuits.

The section reflects the mood of loneliness. **Crescens has gone to Galatia**—or, according to some manuscripts, Gaul; Galatia is to be preferred, especially if the historical Paul is the author. **Titus** has gone to **Dalmatia** and **Tychicus** to **Ephesus**. Paul is left alone except for **Luke**. He apparently expects a visit from Timothy in prison, for he instructs him to bring **Mark** also with him. What specifically is meant by **for he is very useful in serving me** is not clear. Perhaps he would act as a secretary or simply lend support to Paul's ministry (cf. Colossians 4:10-11 and Philemon 24). Such added support would strengthen Paul in his hour of extreme loneliness.

This theme of loneliness carries into verse 16 in an allusion to Paul's preliminary hearing before the court. Though forsaken by men and women, he was not forsaken by God, who delivered him from death. Rescue **from the lion's mouth** is probably to be taken figuratively and simply means deliverance from death.

Mention of the **books** and **parchments** suggests a situation quite different from that indicated in verses 6-8, were Paul anticipates imminent martyrdom. Here he looks forward to a future in which the documents would serve a useful function. The same point is suggested by the request to Timothy to bring the **cloak**, a heavy outer garment important for warmth during the coming winter.

This break in thought has seemed to some to support the theory that verses 9-18 are a genuine Pauline fragment which the author has incorporated in his letter. On the other hand the author may have drawn heavily on the genuine Pauline letters for references to persons engaged with Paul in the work of the church.

V. FINAL GREETINGS (4:19-22)

4:19-21. *Personal Greetings.* The final greeting is typical of Paul's letters and is imitated here. On **Prisca and Aquila** cf. Acts 18:2-3, 18-19, 26; I Corinthians 16:19; Romans 16:3. On the **household of Onesiphorus** see above on 1:15-18. On **Erastus** cf. Acts 19:22. On **Trophimus** cf. Acts 20:4; 21:29. Of the others we know nothing. The greeting is an expression of Christian fellowship and solidarity. As used by the author it serves the purpose of giving an authentic Pauline touch to his letter.

4:22. *Benediction.* For the combination of the two elements in the Pauline benediction cf. Galatians 6:18; Philippians 4:23; Philemon 25. For the shortened form cf. I Timothy 6:21; Titus 3:15; Colossians 4:18.

THE LETTER OF PAUL TO TITUS

Eric Lane Titus

INTRODUCTION

See the Introduction to I Timothy.

I. EPISTOLARY INTRODUCTION (1:1-16)

1:1-4. *Salutation.* The characteristic salutation of a Pauline letter is followed here by the author. The statement is carefully worded to stress that Paul's message is not his own but is grounded in:

(1) his **servant** relationship to God;

(2) his office as an **apostle of Jesus Christ**;

(3) the divine promises given **ages ago**;

(4) the commandment of **God our Savior**.

Paul's task as servant and apostle is to **further the faith of God's elect and their knowledge of the truth**.

The author's devotion to Paul's doctrine is thus seen as more than personal admiration. He is convinced that that doctrine represents the manifestation of the promise of the ages. It did not originate with Paul but was mediated through him to the church.

1:4. Whereas the other two Pastoral epistles are addressed to

Timothy, this one is addressed to **Titus**. That Titus should be so honored is understandable in view of the nature of the relationship between him and Paul shown in genuine Pauline letters. It is evident from II Corinthians that Titus brought about a reconciliation between Paul and the Corinthian church after a serious rift had occurred (cf. II Corinthians 7:6-7, 13-14). This historical situation thus provides a fitting background for the choice of Titus, Paul's **true child in a common faith** (see comment on I Timothy 1:2*a*), as the recipient of a letter. For now, in the new church situation, a problem has arisen comparable to that which earlier existed at Corinth. Titus must provide a solution.

1:5-16. *The Task of Titus.* In keeping with his abilty to solve problems in church relations, Titus has been left behind among the difficult Cretans to **amend what was defective** and to **appoint elders** in accordance with Paul's directive. The elders—apparently indistinguishable from the **bishop** (see comment on I Timothy 3:1-7)—must be men of high character. They must be able to **give instruction in sound doctrine**—that is, in Pauline doctrine as understood by the author.

1:10-16. The author has a low view of Cretan society. He quotes the Cretan Epimenides (sixth century B.C.) in characterizing Cretans as **liars, evil beasts, lazy gluttons**. The point, of course, is that false doctrines have grown up in the church in Crete. Certain people are insubordinates, **empty talkers and deceivers**—probably a reference to the **Jewish myths** of verse 14—who are disrupting church family life. Moreover they are utterly immoral. Titus must minister to this difficult situation.

II. Sound Doctrine (2:1-14)

2:1-10. *Titus as Teacher.* In contrast to the perverted ideas of the Cretans with their consequent immorality, Titus is to **teach what befits sound doctrine**. Along with this normative Pauline doctrine he must instruct the church in moral and practical matters. The **older men** must be instructed in sobriety, **in faith, in love, and in steadfastness**. The **women** are to be instructed in **reverent behavior** and to carry on domestic duties faithfully, to be **submissive to their husbands** and to be **chaste**. The **younger men** must be taught to **control themselves**. The **slaves** are to be **submissive to their masters**—a thoroughly typical New Testament teaching. A conscience on slavery had not yet arisen (see Introduction to Philemon). Indeed the slaves' obedient conduct will **adorn the doctrine of God our Savior**.

Titus must himself be a **model of good deeds** and of sound teaching. His very deportment will **put** the enemies of the truth **to shame** and Christianity will be protected from slanderous charges.

2:11-14. *The People of God.* The reason for the radical difference between the opponents of the church and the Christians is that the **grace of God has appeared** and is **training** the Christian in a new way of life which stands in sharp contrast to the way of **irreligion**. It is the Christian's responsibility to live the upright life while awaiting the appearing of Christ. The work of Christ has a twofold meaning: it redeems **from iniquity** and it separates from the world a people who belong to Christ.

A great deal of stress on **good deeds** characterizes the Pastoral letters in general and Titus in particular. This makes it clear that, while the author uses Paul's conventional vocabulary for the **grace of God**, the profound meaning of the term as used by Paul has largely been lost. It is therefore likely that its occurrence in verse 11 means no more than that the true doctrine has been transmitted by Paul, servant and apostle of Jesus Christ.

2:15. *The Authority of Titus.* Here Titus' authority is strongly emphasized. It is grounded in his church office, but it is derived also from his authoritative message. His message, the true doctrine, has been transmitted to him from Paul, and Paul has directed him to carry out certain duties in Crete. In a certain sense, then, the work of Titus is an extension of that of the great apostle himself.

III. Christian Conduct (3:1-11)

3:1-8a. *Contrast with Non-Christians.* Christians are to present themselves blameless before the world. They are to obey the civil **authorities**, engage in **honest work**, be prudent in speech, and display gentleness and **courtesy** in human relations. The conduct of Christians in the days before they experienced the **goodness and loving kindness of God our Savior** was like that of the rest of the world in its sin. Now it is different, and the reason for the difference is God's saving act in Christ. The thought resembles that of the historical Paul. The author throws the weight of the saving act on the fact of God's mercy and **not because of deeds done by us in righteousness**.

3:5b-8a. The conclusion **The saying is sure** suggests that the material preceding it is a quotation, possibly from a Christian baptismal formula. Precisely how much of verses 1-7 should be included in the quotation remains problematical. It may well be that the distinctively Pauline ideas here should be attributed to this source. The phrase **washing of regeneration** does not appear in Paul. However, since the formula was the common property of the church, there is no reason to expect strictly Pauline language to dominate it.

Washing of regeneration refers to baptism, which results in a permanent change in life. The Greek word translated **regeneration** occurs in Matthew 19:28, where it refers to the "new world," the transformed messianic age of the exalted Son of man. The idea here is also transformation, but transformation of the individual through baptism. The radical change produced at baptism is somewhat like the sacramental changes effected in the Hellenistic mystery cults. But it is more nearly paralleled by the historical Paul's view of "newness of life" set forth in Romans 6:4.

3:8b-11. *Insistence on Good Deeds.* The stress on the conduct of Christians as that of good, loyal, law-abiding, industrious citizens seems characteristic of the period. This may be the point of the insistence on good deeds in this section. The status of Christianity with respect to the state was precarious.

Exemplary conduct by Christians was therefore most important. It was quite possible for Christians, with their consciousness of themselves as God's chosen people, to feel themselves above the mundane concerns of citizens of this world. Or it might be that the **factious** and quarrelsome activity of some Christians would throw suspicion on the church generally. The author therefore exhorts Titus to insist that Christians **apply themselves** to **good deeds** and **avoid** conduct that does not befit the new life in Christ. Severe disciplinary measures are to be used when anyone persists in factious ways.

IV. FINAL CHARGES (3:12-15)

3:12-14. *Personal Instructions.* Titus' work in Crete must be nearly complete, for Paul asks him to meet at **Nicopolis**—probably the city of this name on the Adriatic coast of Greece. Nothing is known of **Artemas.** On **Tychicus** see comment on II Timothy 4:12. Nothing further is known of **Zenas** than that he was a **lawyer.** This may mean a lawyer in the sense of a (former?) Jewish scribe, or it may refer to the profession of law in the Greek or Roman sense.

Apollos almost certainly refers to the great Alexandrian Christian mentioned in Acts 18:24–19:1 and I Corinthians 1:12; 3:4-6, 22; 4:6; 16:12. Zenas and Apollos are to be speeded **on their way** by Titus, who is to **see that they lack nothing.** Presumably their mission has to do with the furtherance of the gospel, though this is not said. If Apollos is the eloquent preacher of Acts and I Corinthians, the reference is probably to a preaching mission.

3:14. This seems to follow up the injunction to provide for the physical needs of Zenas and Apollos on their journey. Christians in Crete are to be generous in this respect. One of the **cases of urgent need** would be the support of this mission. But the verse may have a more general application as well.

3:15. *Greetings and Benediction.* The letter ends with greetings from Paul and his companions to Titus and to **those**

who love us in the faith—that is, all loyal Christians. Since the "you" in **Grace be with you all** is plural, the brief benediction means at least that grace is sent to the whole church. Perhaps even the contents of the letter are to be shared by the total church. The benediction may be largely conventional, however, copying general Pauline usage.

THE LETTER OF PAUL TO PHILEMON

Victor Paul Furnish

INTRODUCTION

Character and Purpose

Philemon deals with a single issue. In it Paul is concerned to aid Onesimus, a runaway slave whom he has met while in prison—how is never revealed—and whose master was probably one of Paul's converts (verse 19). Onesimus is returning to his master, evidently bearing Paul's letter. Its appeal is not just that he be treated gently but that he be released into Paul's continuing custody for the service of the gospel. Nowhere in the letter is this latter request explicitly made, but it is implicit throughout.

Even though Philemon was written for a very particular reason, it would be misleading to describe it as a purely private document. While its central appeal is directed to an individual, the opening salutation and concluding benediction presuppose a Christian congregation, a "house church." Moreover Colossians may have been written to this same congregation at the same time, at least in part to bolster the appeal of this letter (see below). Therefore in this as in his other letters Paul speaks as an apostle mindful of a whole community of Christians, and everything he says presupposes that wider context.

The owner of Onesimus is generally assumed to be Philemon, but the theory that the owner is Archippus has been adopted by some scholars (see below on verses 1-3 and on Colossians 4:17). The place of Philemon's residence has usually been regarded as Colossae (see below on verses 1-3). This is based on the close relationship between this letter and Colossians, the remark to the Colossians that Onesimus is "one of yourselves" (Colossians 4:9), and the inclusion of greetings from Epaphras who was evidently the founder of the Colossian church.

Place and Date of Composition

Philemon is one of Paul's prison letters (verses 1, 9, 10, 13, 23), but nothing in the letter indicates the prison's location. Traditionally the place has been assumed to be Rome (cf. Acts 28:16-31), and on this basis the letter is to be dated around 59-62. Caesarea (cf. Acts 23:33–24:27) has also been suggested. This is not generally favored because it seems unlikely that Onesimus would flee to that place.

The hypothesis has been advanced that Paul also suffered imprisonment in Ephesus (see Introduction to Philippians). A number of scholars regard that city's proximity to Colossae as making it a likely spot for Onesimus to meet Paul. If the letter was written from Ephesus, the date would be around 54-56, near the time of the Corinthian correspondence.

Relation to Colossians

Significant relationships between this letter and Colossians are easily recognized. Both are written from prison; Onesimus is mentioned in Colossians 4:9 and described as being from Colossae; Archippus is mentioned in both letters; and in each letter greetings are sent from the same five persons—Epaphras, Mark, Aristarchus, Demas, and Luke. Moreover among the household duties discussed in Colossians 3:18–4:1 the relationships of masters and slaves receive the most attention.

Formerly doubts about Paul's authorship of Colossians

sometimes raised corresponding doubts about this related letter. Today, however, no serious questions about the authenticity of Philemon remain. It is more common to view the close relationship of the two letters as lending support to the authenticity of Colossians.

If Colossians is a genuine letter of Paul, as the majority of scholars hold, then it may be regarded as intended, at least in part, to support and strengthen the appeals Paul makes in Philemon. Further, if the owner of Onesimus is Archippus, as some believe, Paul's urging the Colossians to see that Archippus fulfills his service (Colossians 4:17) is a specific reference to the whole issue discussed in this letter.

Paul and Slavery

Though Paul's objective seems to be the release of Onesimus from his master, one must not regard Philemon as an abolitionist tract. Neither here nor in I Corinthians 7:20-24 does Paul question the rightness or wrongness of slavery as an institution. For Paul, as for early Christianity in general, slavery was regarded as a fixed part of society. There is no New Testament writer who envisions a social order without this institution. On the other hand slavery is never expressly condoned or given theological sanctions. What, then, may one conclude about Paul's view of slavery?

Paul viewed all human institutions as features of a temporary worldly order which was in the process of "passing away" (I Corinthians 7:31). Because he shared the conviction of earliest Christianity that the last days were at hand, the reform of social institutions would have seemed to him irrelevant.

Moreover slave labor was basic to the whole economic structure of the Roman Empire. The abolitionist would have been at the same time an insurrectionist, and the political effects of such a movement would have been unthinkable. The situation of the freedman was often more difficult than that of a slave because the abundance of slave labor made work for others scarce.

Paul was no sponsor of social reform. But his letters do

emphasize those aspects of the Christian gospel which were destined to support and encourage the abolitionist cause. Paul's appeal in Philemon absolutely excludes the idea that Onesimus should be punished, though Roman law allowed the owner of a runaway slave almost unlimited privileges of punishment—on occasion even execution.

In I Corinthians 7:20-24 the point is established that true freedom is achieved as one surrenders one's self to the service of God, and that such freedom is more significant than whether one was born free or a slave. Yet this should not be interpreted as implying that Paul and earliest Christianity regarded only inner freedom as important and had no concern for its outer manifestations. For, perhaps most important of all, the actuality of even the slave's freedom in Christ was made concrete in the life of the Christian community. Paul himself emphatically declared that all people, regardless of their worldly stations, could be baptized into Christ and into the brotherly communion of believers in Christ (Galatians 3:27-28).

Considered in this perspective, Philemon may legitimately be regarded as an eloquent witness to the family status of all persons in Christ. It is a plain testimonial that for the church to be the church—the community of baptized brethren—it must manifest in its life the way in which the social barriers dividing people are not just transcended but actually broken through. Paul therefore bids Philemon receive Onesimus back as "more than a slave, as a beloved brother" (verse 16).

COMMENTARY

Verses 1-3. *Salutation.* Paul writes from prison (see Introduction) and addresses three persons specifically. Of these only **Archippus** is named elsewhere in the New Testament (Colossians 4:17). Most interpreters presume that **Philemon** and **Apphia**, like Archippus, are members of the Christian church at Colossae (see Introduction to Colossians), that Philemon, named first, is probably the one primarily addressed, and that the church which Paul has in mind meets in Philemon's house. It is possible, however, that Archippus is the one to whom the letter is primarily directed, and that the church meets in his house (see comment on Colossians 4:17).

Verses 4-7. *Thanksgiving.* In the Pauline letters a paragraph giving thanks to God for the love and faith of those addressed regularly follows the salutation. Here, and throughout most of the rest of the letter, **you** is singular, indicating that Paul is writing to one person especially, probably Philemon.

It is characteristic that the thanksgiving sections in Paul's letters foreshadow subsequent themes and appeals, and that is true here. He refers to Philemon's **love** and then makes his appeal on that basis (verse 9). He refers to Philemon's **sharing of . . . faith** and later appeals to him as a **partner** (verse 17). He speaks of **the good that is ours in Christ** and then expresses concern that Philemon's **goodness** be of his own **free will** (verse 14). After a reference to the **hearts of the saints** which Philemon has **refreshed** he requests that his own **heart** be refreshed in Christ (verse 20).

Throughout this letter Paul places extraordinary emphasis on the brotherly relationship which exists between himself and Philemon. This is especially seen in this paragraph of thanksgiving. Moreover Philemon is commended as an edifying member of the church (**the saints**), in which he is apparently a leading participant (verses 5, 7).

Verses 8-14. *Appeal on Behalf of Onesimus.* Paul here shows remarkable restraint in exercising his apostolic authority. This is due not so much to the need for tactfulness as it is to his understanding of the nature of ethical decisions. This letter is concerned with a particular ethical question. Onesimus, the slave of a Christian master, has run away, somehow fallen in with Paul, and served him with distinction. Legally Paul should return the slave to his owner and make full restitution. But in this case the owner is one of Paul's Christian brethren, and the runaway slave has been extraordinarily **useful** as an apostolic helper. Here there is a play on words, for the name Onesimus is related to the Greek word "useful."

How does Paul solve the question of right and wrong in this kind of situation?

(1) He is concerned to fulfill his legal obligation; he is returning Onesimus to his owner (verse 12) and offers to reimburse Philemon fully for any financial losses (verse 19).

(2) He lets it be known that, were the final decision his, Onesimus would be retained for the service of the gospel in which he has already been so valuable (verses 11, 13). The affection Paul feels for Philemon is hardly more than that he feels for Philemon's slave (verses 10, 12), and this is said rather explicitly (verses 16, 17).

(3) He makes it clear that, so far as Onesimus is concerned, the responsibility and decision are with Philemon alone (verse 14). Paul does not directly ask Philemon to free Onesimus, nor even to deal gently with him. Rather he praises Philemon for his love, reminds him of his partnership in faith, informs him of Onesimus' usefulness to the gospel, and charges him with making his own decision in the matter.

This whole appeal is made on the basis of love (verse 9). Paul does not spell out in particular what is required of Philemon. His appeal is made with the assurance that those who are partners in one faith and one Spirit also share the common directives of love by which their common life in Christ finds expression. The word **ambassador** in verse 9 is actually "old man." But since the addition of just one letter would form the word "ambassador" and thus conform to the thought of II Corinthians 5:20, many commentators and translators have adopted this conjectural form. Though Paul nowhere in Philemon refers to himself as an "apostle," an appeal to his apostolic authority is nonetheless present.

Verses 15-19. *Christian Family Relations.* Before his escape Onesimus did not measure up to his name—"useful." In fact he was **useless** (verse 11). But since his meeting with Paul that has changed. Perhaps, then, there was a constructive purpose for this whole incident (verses 15-16), and Paul hopes that Philemon will receive Onesimus back as **more than a slave, as a beloved brother, . . . both in the flesh and in the Lord.**

Philemon and Paul are brothers (verses 7, 20). Paul and Onesimus are on the one hand like father and son (verse 10) and on the other also beloved brothers in Christ (verse 16). Therefore in Christ the relationship between Philemon and Onesimus ought now to be transformed.

Paul is not a social reformer (see Introduction), but the seeds of social reform are certainly present here. In Christ people are bound together in ways which transcend and in fact—**in the flesh**—overcome the barriers of race, class, and position. This unity in Christ is constantly stressed in Paul's letters and is summed up in the word *koinonia*, which in its various forms Paul frequently uses. This word is variously translated **sharing** (verse 6; II Corinthians 1:7; Galatians 6:6; Philippians 3:10), **partnership** (verse 17; II Corinthians 6:14; 8:23; Philippians 1:5; 4:15), "participation" (I Corinthians 10:16; Philippians 2:1), and "fellowship" (I Corinthians 1:9; II Corinthians 13:14; Galatians 2:9).

Verses 17-19. Onesimus, then, is to be welcomed back even as Paul himself would be received—a Christian brother free to come and go when the tasks of his ministry may require—in fact a **guest** in Philemon's house! The pledge to make restitution for any losses Philemon may have incurred is certified in Paul's own handwriting. He probably does not expect Philemon to demand payment, for the slave owner's debt to Paul is infinitely greater—a remark which suggests that Philemon was one of Paul's converts. Since Paul himself has never been to Colossae, Philemon's home, their meeting must have occurred elsewhere—perhaps Ephesus.

Verses 20-22. *Onesimus' Future Service.* In verse 20 the term **benefit** is a form of the name Onesimus. Thus with this play on words Paul indicates his actual intent for Onesimus. In the second part of the verse **heart** also has a double significance, recalling the earlier remarks that Philemon has refreshed the **hearts of the saints** (verse 7) and Onesimus himself is Paul's **heart** (verse 12). These expressions show that Paul appeals to Philemon not just to forgive Onesimus but to receive him back as a free man, a Christian brother, an apostolic delegate, and then return him to Paul's service. Paul expresses confidence that Philemon will act with a Christian conscience in this matter, doing **even more** than would be normally required.

These two words constitute a simple yet profound summary of Paul's understanding of the Christian's ethical responsibility. True Christian obedience is not legalistic conformity to prescribed rules. It is the surrender of one's whole life to the unconditional demands of love. Love always asks "even more" than what "normally" would be required or expected.

Verse 22. Though Paul is writing from prison (see Introduction) he anticipates release and the opportunity to visit Philemon in Colossae.

Verses 23-25. *Greetings and Benediction.* The appeal of this letter has been addressed to just one man. Though Paul makes this appeal in the context of an address to the whole Christian community of which Philemon is a part, closing greetings are directed to him alone—**you** in verse 23 is singular. The greetings are from **Epaphras,** who has been an evangelist in Colossae, Laodicea, and Hierapolis (Colossians 1:7; 4:12-13), and from Paul's other **fellow workers.** These include **Mark,** considered the writer of the earliest gospel; Aristarchus (cf. Acts 19:29; 20:4; 27:2); Demas (cf. II Timothy 4:10); and Luke, to whom the third gospel and Acts are ascribed, the "beloved physician" (Colossians 4:14). Greetings from these same men are conveyed in Colossians 4:10-14, though there the name of "Jesus who is called Justus" also occurs. Its absence here is inexplicable.

FOR FURTHER STUDY

THE ACTS OF THE APOSTLES

F. J. Foakes-Jackson and Kirsopp Lake, *The Beginnings of Christianity*, 5 vols., 1920-33. F. J. Foakes-Jackson, *The Acts of the Apostles*, 1931. F. F. Bruce, *Commentary on the Book of Acts*, 1954. G. H. C. Macgregor in *Interpreter's Bible*, 1954. Martin Dibelius, *Studies in the Acts of the Apostles*, 1956. Henry J. Cadbury, *The Making of Luke-Acts*, 1958. C. S. C. Williams, *The Acts of the Apostles*, 1958. J. C. O'Neill, *The Theology of Acts*, 1961. H. J. Cadbury in *Interpreter's Dictionary of the Bible*, 1962, and W. C. Robinson, Jr. in *Interpreter's Dictionary of the Bible, Supplement*, 1976. Floyd V. Filson, *Three Crucial Decades*, 1963.

THE LETTER OF PAUL TO THE ROMANS

C. H. Dodd, *Romans*, 1932. John Knox, in *Interpreter's Bible*, 1954. C. K. Barrett, *Romans*, 1958; an excellent recent exposition. William Sanday and A. C. Headlam, *Romans*, 5th ed., 1962; still the best commentary in English on the Greek text. F. W. Bear in *Interpreter's Dictionary of the Bible*, 1962; G. Klein in *Interpreter's Dictionary of the Bible, Supplement*, 1976.

THE LETTERS OF PAUL TO THE CORINTHIANS

On 1 Corinthians: Commentary by James Moffatt, 1938; C. T. Craig in *Interpreter's Bible*, 1953; S. M. Gilmour in *Interpreter's Dictionary of the Bible*, 1962; D. George in *Interpreter's Dictionary of the Bible, Supplement*, 1976; Commentary by Jean Hering, 1962. On 2 Corinthians: Allan Menzies, 1912; Commentary by R. H. Strachan, 1935; F. V. Filson in *Interpreter's Bible*, 1953; Commentary by R. V. G. Tasker, 1958; S. M. Gilmour in *Interpreter's Dictionary of the Bible*, 1962; D. George in *Interpreter's Dictionary of the Bible, Supplement*, 1976.

THE LETTER OF PAUL TO THE GALATIANS

Commentaries by E. DeW. Burton, 1920; G. S. Duncan, 1934; R. T. Stamm in *Interpreter's Bible*, 1953; Ragnar Bring, 1961. Kirsopp Lake,

The Earlier Epistles of St. Paul, 2nd ed., 1927. J. H. Ropes, *The Singular Problem of the Epistle to the Galatians*, 1929. John Knox, "Galatians," and M. J. Mellink, "Galatia," in *Interpreter's Dictionary of the Bible*, 1962; H. D. Betz in *Interpreter's Dictionary of the Bible Supplement*, 1976.

THE LETTER OF PAUL TO THE EPHESIANS

E. F. Scott, *Colossians, Philemon, Ephesians*, 1930. E. J. Goodspeed, *The Meaning of Ephesians*, 1933; *The Key to Ephesians*, 1956. Stig Hanson, *The Unity of the Church in the New Testament*, 1947. C. L. Mitton, *Ephesians*, 1952. F. W. Beare in *Interpreter's Bible*, 1953. George Johnston in *Interpreter's Dictionary of the Bible*, 1962; N. A. Dahl, in *Interpreter's Dictionary of the Bible, Supplement*, 1976.

THE LETTER OF PAUL TO THE PHILIPPIANS

E. F. Scott, in *Interpreter's Bible*, 1955. F. W. Beare, *Philippians*, 1959. Oscar Cullmann, *The Christology of the New Testament*, tr. S. C. Guthrie and C. A. M. Hall, 1959, pp. 174-81 (on 2:5-11). Karl Barth, *Philippians*, tr. J. W. Leitch, 1962. G. S. Duncan in *Interpreter's Dictionary of the Bible*, 1962. H. Koester in *Interpreter's Dictionary of the Bible, Supplement*, 1976. R. P. Martin, *Carmen Christi*, 1967 (on 2:5-11).

THE LETTER OF PAUL TO THE COLOSSIANS

E. F. Scott, *Colossians, Philemon, and Ephesians*, 1930. F. W. Beare in *Interpreter's Bible*, 1955. C. F. D. Moule, *Colossians and Philemon*, 1957. George Johnston in *Interpreter's Dictionary of the Bible*, 1962; F. O. Francis in *Interpreter's Dictionary of the Bible, Supplement*, 1976.

THE LETTERS OF PAUL TO THE THESSALONIANS

Commentaries by J. E. Frame, 1912; William Neil, 1950; Leon Morris, 1959. J. W. Bailey in *Interpreter's Bible*, 1955. J. W. Bowman,

"Eschatology of the New Testament"; H. K. McArthur, "Parousia"; F. W. Beare, "Thessalonians," in *Interpreter's Dictionary of the Bible*, 1962; J. C. Hurd in *Interpreter's Dictionary of the Bible, Supplement*, 1976.

THE LETTERS OF PAUL TO TIMOTHY

P. N. Harrison, *The Problem of the Pastoral Epistles*, 1921. E. F. Scott, *The Pastoral Epistles*, 1936. B. S. Easton, *The Pastoral Epistles*, 1947. F. D. Gealy in *Interpreter's Bible*, 1955. J. C. Beker in *Interpreter's Dictionary of the Bible*, 1962. C. K. Barrett, *The Pastoral Epistles*, 1963. J. N. D. Kelly, *The Pastoral Epistles*, 1963; maintains Pauline authorship.

THE LETTER OF PAUL TO PHILEMON

M. R. Vincent, *Philippians and Philemon*, 1911. E. F. Scott, *Colossians, Philemon, and Ephesians*, 1930. John Knox in *Interpreter's Bible*, 1955; *Philemon Among the Letters of Paul*, rev. ed., 1959. W. L. Westermann, *The Slave Systems of Greek and Roman Antiquity*, 1955. C. F. D. Moule, *Colossians and Philemon*, 1957. Theo Preiss, *Life in Christ*, 1957. M. E. Lyman in *Interpreter's Dictionary of the Bible*, 1962.

ABBREVIATIONS AND EXPLANATIONS

ABBREVIATIONS

D — Deuteronomic; Deuteronomist source

E — Elohist source
Ecclus. — Ecclesiasticus
ed. — edited by, edition, editor
e.g. — *exempli gratia* (for example)
ERV — English Revised Version
esp. — especially

H — Holiness Code

J — Yahwist source
JPSV — Jewish Publication Society Version

L — Lukan source
LXX — Septuagint, the earliest Greek translation of the Old Testament and Apocrypha (250 B.C. and after)

M — Matthean source
Macc. — Maccabees
MS — manuscript

N — north, northern
NEB — New English Bible

P — Priestly source
p. — page
Pet. — Peter
Phil. — Philippian, Philippians
Philem. — Philemon
Prov. — Proverbs
Pss. Sol. — Psalms of Solomon
pt. — part (of a literary work)

Q — "Sayings" source

rev. — revised
RSV — Revised Standard Version

S — south, southern

trans. — translated by, translation, translator

viz. — *videlicet* (namely)
Vulg. — Vulgate, the accepted Latin version, mostly translated A.D. 383-405 by Jerome

W — west, western
Wisd. Sol. — Wisdom of Solomon

QUOTATIONS AND REFERENCES

In the direct commentary words and phrases quoted from the RSV of the passage under discussion are printed in boldface type, without quotation marks, to facilitate linking the comments to the exact points of the biblical text. If a quotation from the passage under discussion is not in boldface type, it is to be recognized as an alternate translation, either that of another version if so designated (see abbreviations of versions above) or the commentator's own rendering. On the other hand, quotations from other parts of the Bible in direct commentary, as well as all biblical quotations in the introductions, are to be understood as from the RSV unless otherwise identified.

A passage of the biblical text is identified by book, chapter number, and verse number or numbers, the chapter and verse numbers being separated by a colon (cf. Genesis 1:1). Clauses within a verse may be designated by the letters *a, b, c,* etc. following the verse number (e.g. Genesis 1:2*b*). In poetical text each line as printed in the RSV—not counting runovers necessitated by narrow columns—is accorded a letter. If the book is not named, the book under discussion is to be understood; similarly the chapter number appearing in the boldface reference at the beginning of the paragraph, or in a preceding centered head, is to be understood if no chapter is specified.

A suggestion to note another part of the biblical text is usually introduced by the abbreviation "cf." and specifies the exact verses. To be distinguished from this is a suggestion to consult a comment in this volume, which is introduced by "see above on," "see below on," or "see comment on," and which identifies the boldface reference at the head of the paragraph where the comment is to be found or, in the absence of a boldface reference, the reference in a preceding centered head. The suggestion "see Introduction" refers to the introduction of the book under discussion unless another book is named.

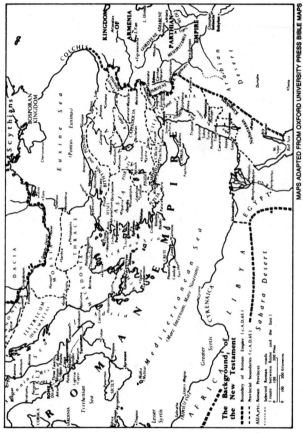

The Background of
the New Testament (c.A.D.65)

▬▬▬ Boundary of Roman Empire (c.A.D.65)
─ ─ ─ Provincial boundaries (c.A.D.65)
ASIA/etc. Roman Provinces
∙∙∙∙∙∙ Selected Roman roads
between Rome and the East

|0   100   200 Miles|
|0 100 200 Kilometers|

MAPS ADAPTED FROM OXFORD UNIVERSITY PRESS BIBLE MAPS